A f-G-II- 1- 65

ARBEITEN AUS DEM INSTITUT FÜR AFRIKA-KUNDE

69

Axel Harneit-Sievers

Namibia: Wahlen zur Verfassunggebenden Versammlung 1989

Analyse und Dokumentation

Inv.-Nr.: A

Geographisches Institut
der Universität Kiel
ausgesonderte Dublette

INSTITUT FÜR AFRIKA-KUNDE

im Verbund der Stiftung Deutsches Übersee-Institut

Geographisches Institut
der Universität Kiel

Harneit-Sievers, Axel:
Namibia : Wahlen zur Verfassunggebenden Versammlung 1989 ;
Analyse und Dokumentation / Axel Harneit-Sievers. -
Hamburg : Institut für Afrika-Kunde ; 1990.
 (Arbeiten aus dem Institut für Afrika-Kunde ; 69)
 ISBN 3-923519-96-6

Alle Rechte vorbehalten
Institut für Afrika-Kunde
im Verbund der Stiftung Deutsches Übersee-Institut
Neuer Jungfernstieg 21, 2000 Hamburg 36

VERBUND STIFTUNG DEUTSCHES ÜBERSEE-INSTITUT

Das Institut für Afrika-Kunde bildet mit anderen, überwiegend
regional ausgerichteten Forschungsinstituten den Verbund der Stiftung Deutsches Übersee-Institut.
Dem Institut für Afrika-Kunde ist die Aufgabe gestellt, die gegen-
wartsbezogene Afrikaforschung zu fördern. Es ist dabei bemüht, in
seinen Publikationen verschiedene Meinungen zu Wort kommen zu
lassen, die jedoch grundsätzlich die Auffassung des jeweiligen
Autors und nicht des Instituts für Afrika-Kunde darstellen.

Hamburg 1990
ISBN 3-923519-96-6

Inhalt

iv

Verzeichnis der Abkürzungen

ACN	Aksie Christelik Nasionaal / Action Christian National
CANU	Caprivi African National Union
CCN	Council of Churches in Namibia
CDA	Christian Democratic Action for Social Justice
CIMS	Churches Information and Monitoring Service
DTA	Democratic Turnhalle Alliance
FCN	Federal Convention of Namibia
NANSO	Namibian National Students' Organisation
NNDP	Namibia National Democratic Party
NNF	Namibia National Front
NPF	National Patriotic Front
NUNW	National Union of Namibian Workers
OPC	Ovamboland People's Congress
OPO	Ovamboland People's Organisation
PLAN	People's Liberation Army of Namibia
RRR	Repatriation, Resettlement, Reconstruction
SADF	South African Defence Force
SWANU	South West Africa National Union
SWAPO	South West Africa People's Organisation
SWAPO-D	SWAPO-Democrats
SWAPOL	South West African Police
SWATF	South West African Territorial Force
UDF	United Democratic Front
UNITA	Uniao Nacional para a Independência Total de Angola
UNTAG	United Nations Transitional Assistance Group

Verzeichnis der Tabellen

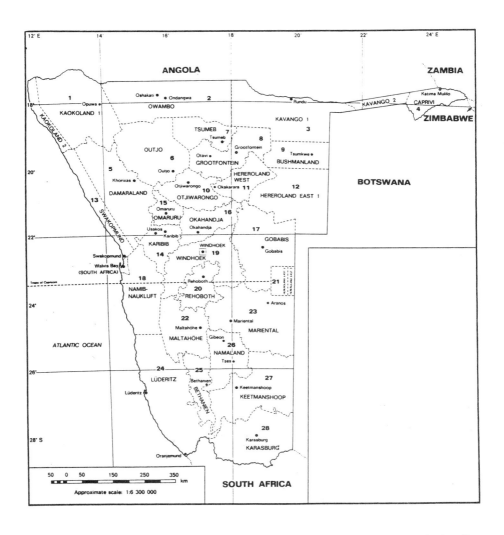

Die regionale Gliederung Namibias in Distrikte, wie sie die Karte wiedergibt, spiegelt noch immer die Aufteilung des Landes in »Homelands« und »weiße« Siedungsgebiete wieder. Die bestehenden Distriktsgrenzen wurden bei der Aufteilung des Landes in Stimmbezirke weitgehend beibehalten. Die Karte wurde dem Band *Namibia. Development and Investment* (zusammengestellt durch die First National Development Corporation), zweite überarbeitete Ausgabe, Windhoek, Oktober 1989, S. 57, entnommen.

Vorbemerkung

Namibia, »Afrikas letzte Kolonie«, hat am 21. März 1990 seine politische Unabhängigkeit erlangt. Damit ist der Namibia-Konflikt nach jahrzehntelangen politischen und militärischen Auseinandersetzungen unter internationaler Kontrolle zu Ende gegangen. Die Wahlen zur Verfassunggebenden Versammlung, die vom 7. bis zum 11. November stattfanden, bildeten das Kernstück eines durch die Vereinten Nationen (UN) überwachten Übergangsprozesses. Durch internationale Verhandlungen seit 1977 vorbereitet, die zwischenzeitlich fast als gescheitert galten, begann dieser Übergangsprozeß am 1. April 1989. Die »South West Africa People's Organisation (SWAPO) of Namibia« gewann die Wahlen im November erwartungsgemäß mit einer deutlichen Mehrheit. Sie verfehlte allerdings ihr erklärtes Wahlziel, eine Zwei-Drittel-Mehrheit, die ihr eine alleinige Entscheidung über die Verfassung eines unabhängigen Namibia ermöglicht hätte. Trotz dieses Wahlergebnisses gestaltete sich die Verfassungsdiskussion zwischen Dezember 1989 und Februar 1990 als geradlinig und - im Kontrast zu vielen Befürchtungen - relativ konfliktfrei, so daß das Unabhängigkeitsdatum im Rahmen des UN-Plans für Namibia eingehalten werden konnte.

Der vorliegende Band will einen Überblick zu Hintergrund und Verlauf der Wahlen, ihren Ergebnissen und zur politischen Entwicklung in Namibia in den Folgemonaten geben. Im einleitenden Artikel werden zunächst der politische Hintergrund des Namibia-Konflikts und die internationalen Verhandlungen im Kontext der Vereinten Nationen (UN) skizziert; es schließen sich eine Analyse des Übergangsprozesses seit April 1989 und der Wahlen selbst sowie eine Skizze der Verfassungsdiskussion an. Die Dokumentation umfaßt die Wahlmanifeste bzw. -programme der wichtigsten Parteien, Materialien zum Wahlkampf und zur eigentlichen Wahl, biographische Skizzen der Mitglieder der Verfassunggebenden Versammlung und schließlich den Text der im Februar 1990 beschlossenen Verfassung für ein unabhängiges Namibia.

Ich hatte Gelegenheit, im Auftrag des Instituts für Afrikakunde, Hamburg, im Oktober/November 1989 für einige Wochen den Wahlprozeß vor Ort zu beobachten. Die dort gewonnenen Eindrücke und die Gespräche und Diskussionen, die ich führen konnte, haben die vorliegende Analyse maßgeblich beeinflußt. Mein Dank geht an viele, die mich mit Material und in der Diskussion unterstützt haben, doch besonders an Na-iem Dollie, Windhoek, der durch eine Kombination von Hilfe und Provokation mein Nachdenken über die Politik im Südlichen Afrika vorangetrieben hat.

Hamburg, im März 1990

1. Der Hintergrund: Politik in Namibia und die Rolle der UN

Auf dem Gebiet des heutigen Namibia entstand ab 1884 die Kolonie Deutsch-Südwestafrika, die im Rahmen des Versailler Vertrags 1919 als Mandatsgebiet des Völkerbunds (und seit 1945 der UN) unter südafrikanische Verwaltung gestellt wurde. Nach dem Zweiten Weltkrieg versuchte Südafrika das Territorium, das de facto bereits als Bestandteil des eigenen Staatsgebiets verwaltet wurde, auch formell zu inkorporieren. Bereits seit Ende der vierziger Jahre protestierten Repräsentanten der afrikanischen Bevölkerung Namibias, besonders die Herero-Chiefs, gegen eine Inkorporation und sandten entsprechende Petitionen nach New York. In den fünfziger Jahren wurden mehrfach Personen entsandt, um als Zeugen vor der UN auftreten zu können. Die Forderung dieser Jahre war die nach einer direkten Übernahme der Verwaltung durch die UN. Nicht zuletzt aufgrund dieser Proteste wurde die Namibia-Frage in den fünfziger Jahren diplomatisch wie völkerrechtlich offengehalten.

Breitere politische Organisationen der afrikanischen Bevölkerung entstanden gegen Ende der fünfziger Jahre mit der »South West African National Union« (SWANU, 1959) und der »South West African People's Organisation« (SWAPO, 1960, bereits 1958 als »Ovamboland People's Congress« gegründet). Nach Protesten gegen Zwangsumsiedlungen in Windhoek im Dezember 1959, die gewaltsam niedergeschlagen wurden, mußten führende Aktivisten das Land verlassen. Sie bildeten den Kern der Befreiungsbewegungen im Exil; manche der damals involvierten Personen nehmen noch heute wichtige Positionen in der namibischen Politik ein.

Seit Beginn der sechziger Jahre bauten SWAPO und (mit abnehmender Bedeutung) SWANU eine Position auf internationaler diplomatischer Ebene - als durch OAU und UN anerkannte Befreiungsbewegungen - auf. In diesem Kontext stand die Aufnahme des bewaffneten Kampfs durch die SWAPO 1966, der sich zunächst allerdings allein auf einige eher symbolische militärische Aktionen beschränkte. Nach weiteren juristischen Auseinandersetzungen beendete die UN-Generalversammlung 1966 formell das Mandat und forderte Südafrika zur Übergabe Namibias an die UN auf, um das Land in die Unabhängigkeit führen zu können. Zu diesem Zweck richtete die UN 1967 einen »Council for Namibia« ein. Der Mandatsentzug wurde 1971 abschließend durch eine »Advisory Opinion« des Internationalen Gerichtshofs bestätigt, die die südafrikanische Präsenz für illegal erklärte.

Südafrika hatte in den sechziger Jahren die Politik der Inkorporation Namibias vorangetrieben - dies wird vor allem durch die Anwendung der südafrikanischen Bantustan-Politik auf Namibia nach dem Odendaal Report von 1964 belegt. Eine offene afrikanische Opposition in Namibia selbst war durch Verhaftung und Verurteilung führender SWAPO-Mitglieder unter dem »Terrorism Act« 1967/68 ausgeschaltet worden.

Ab 1971 kam es zur politischen Dynamisierung in der Namibia-Politik. Ein Streik der Wanderarbeiter in Zentral- und Süd-Namibia zum Jahreswechsel 1971/72 markierte den Beginn verstärkter politischer Mobilisierung im Land; er leitete in eine bäuerliche Rebellion in Ovamboland über und führte zur Erklärung des Ausnahmezustands für Nord-Namibia im Februar 1972. Der internationale Druck auf Südafrika verstärkte sich mit der Stellungnahme des Internationalen Gerichtshofs von 1971 und anschließenden UN-Missionen nach Namibia. 1973 erkannte die UN die SWAPO als »sole and authentic representative of the Namibian people« an. Der Unabhängigkeitsprozeß in Angola ab 1974 schließlich ermöglichte die Flucht tausender politisch engagierter Namibianer und erweiterte die Chancen der SWAPO zum bewaffneten Kampf.

Von Mitte der siebziger Jahre an verfügte die »People's Liberation Army of Namibia« (PLAN, der bewaffnete Arm der SWAPO) über Basen in Süd-Angola, von denen aus eine Guerilla-Kriegsführung nach Namibia hinein möglich wurde, die Anfang der achtziger Jahre ihren Höhepunkt erreichte. Zwar gelang es der PLAN nicht, »befreite Gebiete« in Namibia zu errichten, doch war eine - unbekannte - Anzahl von Guerillas zumindest im Norden des Landes kontinuierlich präsent. Einzelne Angriffe, vor allem aber der Einsatz von Landminen kennzeichneten die Kriegsführung. Darüber hinaus wurden mehrfach Guerilla-Offensiven bis hinein in die nördlichen weißen Farmgebiete um Tsumeb und Grootfontein unternommen. Südafrikanische Truppen intervenierten in Angola, führten mehrere größere Invasionen durch, hielten Gebiete in Süd-Angola besetzt und unterstützten in den achtziger Jahren die Guerilla der UNITA in ihrem Krieg gegen die angolanische Regierung.

Dem wachsenden internationalen Druck zu einer UN-überwachten Unabhängigkeit für Namibia und dem Einfluß der SWAPO setzte Südafrika seit 1975 die Politik der »internen Lösung« entgegen. Hierzu wurde 1975 die »Turnhallen-Konferenz« (so benannt nach ihrem Tagungsgebäude in Windhoek) initiiert, die eine Verfassung entwickeln sollte und in der verschiedene interne politische Parteien repräsentiert waren. Aus diesem Gremium heraus entwickelte sich die »Democratic Turnhalle Alliance« (DTA), eine Dachorganisation bestehend aus etwa einem Dutzend »ethnischer« (nach südafrikanischen Klassifikationskriterien) Parteien. Die DTA basierte vor allem auf einer gemäßigten Fraktion (»verligte«) in der weißen »National Party« sowie afrikanischen Chiefs aus verschiedenen Regionen des Landes und ihrer Gefolgschaft. In den Wahlen zur Verfassunggebenden Versammlung von 1989 sollte die DTA zum wichtigsten Gegner der SWAPO werden.

Die Turnhallen-Konferenz erhielt trotz vielfältiger Public Relations keine internationale Anerkennung. Der UN-Sicherheitsrat bekräftigte 1976 die Forderung nach einem südafrikanischen Rückzug und UN-überwachten Wahlen zur Unabhängigkeit (Resolution 385). Um zu einer international anerkannten Lösung der Namibia-Frage zu gelangen, nahm 1977 die »Kontaktgruppe« (bestehend aus den damaligen Mitgliedern des Sicherheitsrats USA, Großbritannien, Frankreich, BRD und Kanada) Verhandlungen mit SWAPO und Südafrika auf. Das Ergebnis war die Resolution 435 des UN-Sicherheitsrats vom 29. September 1978, die die grundlegenden Strukturen eines international anerkannten Unabhängigkeitsprozesses für Namibia mit einem detaillierten Zeitplan fixierte. Sie bildete die Grundlage für die Wahlen zur Verfassunggebenden Versammlung im November 1989. Die wichtigsten Elemente dieses »UN-Plans« waren:

- die Durchführung freier und fairer Wahlen zu einer Verfassunggebenden Versammlung unter UN-Überwachung als Ziel des gesamten Prozesses,
- die Entsendung einer UN-Überwachungsgruppe (UNTAG, »UN Transitional Assistance Group«) zur Überwachung des Wahlvorgangs und des Unabhängigkeitsprozesses insgesamt,
- die Fixierung der Rahmenbedingungen für einen demokratischen politischen Übergangsprozeß in Namibia: Waffenstillstand, Beschränkung der südafrikanischen Truppen auf ihre Basen und ihr stufenweiser Rückzug, Freilassung aller politischen Gefangenen, Rückkehr der Flüchtlinge, Rücknahme diskriminierender und Notstands-Gesetzgebung usw.

Die SWAPO stimmte diesem Plan nach einigem Zögern Mitte 1978 zu. Südafrika führte nach anfänglicher Zustimmung im Mai 1978 eine spektakuläre Militäraktion gegen das Flüchtlingslager Cassinga in Süd-Angola durch und lehnte nach der Zustimmung durch die SWAPO den Plan de facto ab - wenigstens für den damaligen Zeitpunkt. Maßgeblich für diese Entscheidung war dabei allem Anschein nach die südafrikanische Militärführung, die eine durch Südafrika kontrollierte Namibia-Lösung für durchsetzbar erachtete. In der Folgezeit wurden Schritte einer internen Lösung vorangetrieben, ohne daß es deshalb zu internationalen Sanktionen gekommen wäre.

Im Dezember 1978 fanden in einem Klima von Einschüchterung und Manipulation Wahlen in Namibia statt, die durch SWAPO und einige kleinere Gruppierungen boykottiert wurden. Aus ihnen ging die DTA mit 41 von 50 Sitzen als Sieger hervor. Sie bildete ab 1979 einen Ministerrat, gegenüber dem der Generaladministrator allerdings weiterhin ein Vetorecht besaß. Die DTA dominierte ebenfalls die meisten der durch den Generaladministrator (Verordnung AG 8 von 1980) geschaffenen sogenannten »second tier«-Administrationen. Hierdurch wurden Entscheidungskompetenzen besonders im Erziehungswesen, in der Landwirtschaftspolitik u.a. Bereichen an sekundäre Körperschaften delegiert, die nach ethnischen Kriterien definiert waren. Auf diese Weise wurden einer Umverteilung staatlicher Ressourcen zwischen wohlhabenden und armen Bevölkerungsgruppen und Regionen enge Grenzen gesetzt - auch wenn die DTA für sich in Anspruch nehmen kann, weite Teile der »kleinen Apartheid« in Namibia beseitigt zu haben.

Nach diversen politischen Spaltungsprozessen, Korruptionsskandalen und offenen Konflikten mit der südafrikanischen Verwaltung trat der DTA-dominierte Ministerrat 1983 zurück. Der Generaladministrator übernahm wieder die direkte Kontrolle. Die Politik der internen Lösung war damit vorläufig gescheitert. Neue Versuche in dieser Richtung wurden 1985 mit der Etablierung eines »Transitional Government« auf Basis einer »Multi-Party-Conference« (seit 1983) unternommen; 1986/87 wurde erneut ein Verfassungsentwurf vorgelegt. Die internationale Anerkennung blieb all diesen Gremien letztlich versagt, und mit dem Beginn der Implementation des UN-Plans für Namibia ab April 1989 wurden sie endgültig irrelevant.

Dennoch sollte die Bedeutung all dieser gescheiterten Versuche, eine interne Lösung durchzusetzen, nicht unterschätzt werden, da sie prägend für die politische Dynamik in Namibia war und ist - nicht zuletzt für die Wahlen im November 1989. Neben der SWAPO ist ein internes Parteiensystem entstanden, das vielfältige Brüche und innere Konfliktlinien besitzt, und dessen führende Repräsentanten mittlerweile auf jahrelange politische und (begrenzte) Regierungspraxis zurückblicken können. Zugleich verstärkten die internen Lösungsversuche die politische Polarisierung zwischen ihren Repräsentanten und ihren Gegnern - der »internen« SWAPO, die immer wieder massiver staatlicher Repression ausgesetzt war, aber auch anderen kleineren oppositionellen Gruppen. Andererseits dürften viele ehemalige Repräsentanten der internen Lösung aufgrund ihrer Desillusionierung über die Praxis südafrikanischer Administration in den letzten Jahren inzwischen von der Notwendigkeit einer realen und international anerkannten Unabhängigkeit für Namibia überzeugt sein.

Trotz der durch Südafrika vorangetriebenen Politik der internen Lösung waren die Verhandlungen der Kontaktgruppe mit der SWAPO und Südafrika über den UN-Plan auch nach 1978 fortgesetzt worden. In teilweise langwierigen Auseinandersetzungen kam es zur Klärung von Fragen im Problembereich Demilitarisierung und UN-Überwachung, zu Walvis Bay sowie zu einer Festlegung grundlegender Verfassungsprinzipien für ein unabhängiges Namibia (1982). Damals wurde auch festgelegt, daß eine Verfassung mit einer Zwei-Drittel-Mehrheit angenommen werden müsse - damit war auch das Wahlziel der SWAPO 1989 definiert. Ein erneuter Anlauf zur Realisierung des UN-Plans scheiterte Anfang 1981 auf einem »Pre-Implementation Meeting« in Genf, als sich Südafrika wiederum nicht bereit zeigte, einen Waffenstillstand zu unterzeichnen.

Zu diesem Zeitpunkt führte Südafrika, in dieser Frage gestützt auf die Reagan-Administration in den USA, das als »Junktim« bekannt gewordene Element in die Verhandlungen über Namibia ein: Die Bereitschaft zur Implementation von Resolution 435 wurde von einem Rückzug der kubanischen Truppen aus Angola, die seit 1975 die dortige Regierung stützten, abhängig gemacht. Dies brachte den Verhandlungsprozeß um Namibia zunächst zum Erliegen und führte (mit dem Auszug Frankreichs 1983) de facto zur Auflösung der Kontaktgruppe, während der Krieg in Angola weiter eskalierte, nicht zuletzt durch wachsende Unterstützung der UNITA durch die USA. Ein begrenzter Waffenstillstand und direkte Gespräche zwischen den Konfliktparteien auf den

Kapverdischen Inseln 1984 blieben ergebnislos. Erneute Resolutionen des UN-Sicherheitsrats von 1983 (532 und 539) und 1985 (566), die Südafrika für die Nicht-Einhaltung der Resolution 435 verurteilten und besonders das Junktim kritisierten, blieben ebenfalls ohne Wirkung. Wegen seiner Namibia-Politik wurden jedenfalls nie Sanktionen gegen Südafrika verhängt.

Die Wende kam 1988. Die Serie von Gesprächen zwischen Südafrika, Angola, Kuba und den USA begann im Frühjahr; zu einer umfassenden Einigung kam es bis Dezember. Der Erfolg dieser Verhandlungen wird vor dem Hintergrund einer Kombination von internationaler politischer Situation, von ökonomischen und militärischen Faktoren verständlich.

Im Kontext globaler Entspannungstendenzen zwischen den USA und der UdSSR stand auch das Bemühen um eine Entschärfung von Regionalkonflikten. In den USA verstärkten sich die Sanktionsforderungen gegen Südafrika; schließlich erschien ein Kurswechsel der US-amerikanischen Südafrika-Politik als Folge der Präsidentschaftswahlen möglich. Südafrikanische Politik in Namibia konnte sich weniger als zuvor einer Duldung, wenn nicht Unterstützung durch US-amerikanische Politik sicher sein.

Zur ohnehin vorhandenen finanziellen Dauerbelastung durch permanente Kriegführung in Angola kam die umfassendere ökonomische Krise Südafrikas - der Verfall des Rand, 23 Mrd. Dollar Auslandsverschuldung (1988) und anstehende Umschuldungsverhandlungen. Dies gilt unabhängig von und zusätzlich zu der Tatsache, daß der Staatshaushalt Namibias bereits seit Anfang der achtziger Jahre substantiell durch Südafrika subventioniert wurde (Höhepunkt 1987 mit - offiziell - 469 Mio. Rand).

Schließlich verschob sich das militärische Kräfteverhältnis in Angola zuungunsten Südafrikas, vor allem durch eine gewachsene kubanische Offensivbereitschaft: Indizien dafür waren erfolgreiche kubanische Luftangriffe und die wochenlange Einkesselung einer südafrikanischen Einheit in der Nähe von Cuito Canavale, einer Stadt von strategischer Bedeutung in Süd-Angola, deren Eroberung der südafrikanischen Armee nicht gelang (Mitte 1988). Der Krieg in Angola drohte zwar nicht unmittelbar verloren zu gehen, aber doch vermehrt (weiße) südafrikanische Opfer zu fordern - und dies angesichts einer wachsenden Unruhe gegen diesen Krieg in Teilen der weißen Bevölkerung Südafrikas selbst.

Eine Gewichtung der genannten Faktoren untereinander kann hier nicht im Detail erfolgen. Ob die Verhandlungsbereitschaft Südafrikas tatsächlich eine Umorientierung seiner Regionalpolitik bedeutete oder doch nur wieder Verzögerungstaktik darstellte, war 1988 noch nicht klar erkennbar: Noch im Herbst des Jahres äußerten sich jedenfalls viele Beobachter skeptisch über die Ernsthaftigkeit des südafrikanischen Vorgehens. Tatsächlich waren manche der zur Erklärung der Namibia-Politik Südafrikas im Lauf der Jahre herangezogenen Motive noch immer gültig: Ein unmittelbar ökonomisches Interesse an einer fortdauernden Besetzung Namibias bestand Ende der achtziger Jahre ebensowenig wie an ihrem Beginn, zumal auch ein unabhängiges Namibia sich in starker wirtschaftlicher Abhängigkeit von Südafrika befinden wird; die politisch-psychologischen Auswirkungen einer Unabhängigkeit Namibias in Südafrika selbst (bei der weißen Rechten ebenso wie bei der afrikanischen Bevölkerungsmehrheit) bleiben nach wie vor schwer kalkulierbar. Vor diesem Hintergrund kommt den umrissenen militärischen Faktoren offenbar eine zentrale Bedeutung zu.

Die »Tripartite Agreement«, das - zusammengesetzt aus mehreren Protokollen - bis Ende 1988 zwischen Angola, Kuba und Südafrika zustande kam, umfaßte einen Waffenstillstand in Angola, die Unterlassung aggressiver Akte (d.h. insbesondere ein Ende der südafrikanischen Unterstützung für UNITA und der angolanischen Unterstützung für den ANC) und einen stufenweisen Rückzug der kubanischen Truppen aus Angola bis Mitte 1991 unter internationaler Überwachung (UNAVEM). Das »Agreement« verband dies mit der Implementation des UN-Plans für Namibia nach Resolution 435, deren Beginn für den 1. April 1989 festgelegt wurde. Das Verfahren wurde vom UN-Sicherheitsrat im Januar 1989 gebilligt (Resolutionen 628 und 629).

Die SWAPO war an den Verhandlungen zum »Tripartite Agreement« nicht direkt beteiligt, doch erklärte sie ihre Unterstützung für den Friedensprozeß und beteiligte sich seit Sommer 1988 auch ohne formelles Abkommen am Waffenstillstand. Die Lösung der Namibia-Frage im Kontext der Angola-Abkommen war somit primär Resultat der Verhandlungen von Groß- und Regionalmächten; weder die UN noch die SWAPO spielten eine unmittelbare Rolle. Im Ergebnis setzte Südafrika das Junktim über den kubanischen Rückzug aus Angola durch, wenn auch nicht mehr als Vorbedingung für eine Namibia-Lösung, sondern parallel zu ihr. Dies schuf die Voraussetzungen für die Durchführung des inhaltlich unmodifizierten UN-Plans für Namibia nach insgesamt über zehnjähriger Verzögerung.

2. UN-Plan und Wahlvorbereitungen seit dem 1. April 1989

Zentrales Element des UN-Plans war die Entsendung der UNTAG unter Leitung des UN-Sonderbeauftragten für Namibia, Martti Athisaari. UNTAG umfaßt eine militärische und eine zivile Komponente; sie dient der *Überwachung* von Armee- und Polizeieinheiten ebenso wie der *Beobachtung* des Wahlprozesses. Die *Durchführung* der Wahlen selbst lag bei der namibischen Verwaltung unter dem Generaladministrator Louis Pienaar. Der UN-Plan sah ursprünglich eine Personalstärke der militärischen UNTAG-Komponente von 7.500 vor, doch wurde diese Zahl Anfang 1989 aus finanziellen Erwägungen auf 4.650 gesenkt. Die Stärke der zivilen UNTAG-Komponente erreichte während der Wahlen einen Höhepunkt mit etwa 2.250 Personen. Bei Beginn der Implementation des UN-Plans am 1. April 1989 waren jedoch allenfalls 1.000 UNTAG-Mitglieder im Land.

Die »April-Ereignisse«

Nur wenige Stunden nach dem formellen Inkrafttreten des Waffenstillstands kam es zu schweren Kämpfen zwischen Guerillas der PLAN und südafrikanischen Polizei- und Militäreinheiten in Nord-Namibia. Der Hintergrund dieser Ereignisse läßt sich auch heute noch nicht vollständig aufklären. Südafrika behauptete, Guerillas seien nach Inkrafttreten des Waffenstillstands in großer Zahl (anfangs 1.000, später 2.000) von Angola aus nach Nord-Namibia eingedrungen. Demgegenüber sprach die SWAPO davon, PLAN-Einheiten seien bereits vor dem 1. April im Land gewesen und hätten sich auf UNTAG-Überwachung in Lagern bzw. Entwaffnung vorbereitet; allenfalls nach Ausbruch der Kämpfe seien Verstärkungen aus Angola geholt worden. Nicht nur aus den Erklärungen der SWAPO, sondern auch aus Interviews mit Gefangenen wurde deutlich, daß die Guerillas mit einer UNTAG-Präsenz vor Ort rechneten, denen sie ihre Waffen übergeben wollten. Tatsächlich griffen sie nicht von sich aus an, sondern setzten ihre Waffen erst ein, sobald sie von Polizei oder Armee angegriffen wurden. Dies geschah allerdings mit außerordentlicher Härte und damit zweifellos nicht entsprechend dem Geist des Waffenstillstands: In etwa zehn Tagen Krieg wurden über 300 PLAN-Kämpfer getötet, viele von ihnen in Massengräbern verscharrt, dabei wurden nur etwa 30 Gefangene gemacht. Einem US-amerikanischen Fernsehbericht zufolge wurden gefangene SWAPO-Kämpfer durch die südafrikanischen Sicherheitsorgane geradezu »exekutiert«.

Die südafrikanische Regierung argumentierte, die PLAN-Einheiten hätten sich zum 1. April 1989 auf Basen nördlich des 16. Breitengrads in Angola zurückziehen müssen, um die Vorschriften des »Tripartite Agreement« zu erfüllen. Demgegenüber berief die SWAPO sich darauf, daß sie an diesem »Agreement« nicht unmittelbar beteiligt gewesen sei, und daß entsprechend der Verhandlungen um den UN-Plan schon 1978/79 auch UN-überwachte PLAN-Basen oder »assembly points« in Namibia vorgesehen gewesen seien. Im weiteren Verlauf der damaligen Verhandlungen - es ging um die Schaffung einer »demilitarisierten Zone« im namibisch-angolanischen Grenzgebiet - hatte die SWAPO jedoch, wenn auch widerstrebend, die Forderung nach eigenen Basen in Namibia bereits 1979 wieder fallen lassen. Festzuhalten ist, daß zum 1. April 1989 international niemand mit einer plötzlichen starken militärischen Präsenz der SWAPO in Namibia und daraus möglicherweise resultierenden Kampfhandlungen rechnete - am wenigsten die UNTAG, die sich in dieser Situation als vollkommen handlungsunfähig erwies.

Angesichts des - militärisch gesehen - katastrophalen Ausgangs der Kämpfe mag die Frage gestellt werden, ob die militärische Führung der SWAPO über die fehlende UNTAG-Präsenz nur unzureichend informiert war, als sie ihre Guerillas am 1. April nach Namibia schickte, oder ob sie ein bewußtes Risiko einging, etwa in der Erwartung, Südafrika werde einen Zusammenbruch des Waffenstillstands vermeiden wollen. Angesichts der Erfahrungen mit der Härte südafrikanischer Kriegführung, die die SWAPO seit vielen Jahren besitzt, ist eine solche Erwartung allerdings eher unverständlich.

Das politische Kalkül hingegen ist deutlicher erkennbar: Es ging darum, zum Zeitpunkt des Waffenstillstands eine sichtbare militärische Präsenz der SWAPO in Nord-Namibia herzustellen - um bei Wahlkampfbeginn SWAPO-Stärke zu demonstrieren, vielleicht auch, um den bewaffneten Kampf zum Zeitpunkt seiner Beendigung in seiner Gesamtheit symbolisch zu legitimieren. Für Nord-Namibia ist dieses politische Kalkül aufgegangen, wie nicht nur das Wahlergebnis belegt: Gefangengenommene PLAN-Kämpfer wurden bei ihrer Rückführung nach Angola durch die UNTAG von tausenden von SWAPO-Anhängern geradezu als »Helden« verabschiedet. Aber auch sonst kann der innenpolitische Schaden als eher gering gelten, denn die politischen Gegner in Namibia thematisierten im Wahlkampf die (Mit)Verantwortung der SWAPO am Zusammenbruch des Waffenstillstands im April kaum - wenigstens nicht in der Öffentlichkeit. Für das Image der SWAPO im Ausland hingegen waren die »April-Ereignisse« äußerst negativ. In diplomatischen Kreisen haben sie zu einem Verlust des Vertrauens in die Kalkulierbarkeit und Kontinuität von SWAPO-Politik geführt und zudem die Frage aufgeworfen, inwieweit die politische Führung die Aktivitäten des militärischen Flügels wirklich kontrollieren konnte.

Am 9. April unterzeichneten Angola, Kuba und Südafrika die »Mount Etjo Declaration«. Danach sollten die SWAPO-Kämpfer in Namibia zu UNTAG-kontrollierten Versammlungspunkten kommen und sich von dort aus nach Angola nördlich des 16. Breitengrads zurückziehen. Die SWAPO rief ihre Guerillas dazu auf, direkt nach Angola zurückzukehren. Aufgrund von Sicherheitsbedenken und Unsicherheiten über die Behandlung an den Versammlungspunkten kam es zu Verzögerungen. Nur wenige PLAN-Mitglieder meldeten sich bei der UNTAG; der größte Teil von ihnen verließ Namibia im Verlauf der nächsten Wochen auf direktem Wege nach Angola; noch immer wurde vereinzelt von Kämpfen berichtet. Am 15. Mai schließlich bestätigte die gemeinsame militärische Überwachungskommisson den vollständigen Rückzug der PLAN nach Angola nördlich des 16. Breitengrads. Damit war der Weg für die Fortführung des UN-Plans wieder frei.

Doch auch in den folgenden Monaten waren Nachwirkungen der »April-Ereignisse« spürbar. So nutzte die südafrikanische Administration die Verunsicherung über das politische Verhalten der SWAPO, indem sie mehrfach Meldungen über angebliche PLAN-Präsenz in Namibia oder eine kurz bevorstehende Invasion aus Angola verbreite. All diese Berichte erwiesen sich schließlich als unbegründet. Zur dramatischsten Situation dieser Art kam es am 1. November, als der südafrikanische Außenminister Pik Botha Meldungen über eine unmittelbar bevorstehende SWAPO-Invasion verbreitete, es sich kurz darauf jedoch herausstellte, daß er gefälschten Dokumenten - offenbar aus Teilen des eigenen Militärapparats, der den UN-Plan zu sabotieren suchte - zum Opfer gefallen war.

Die staatlichen Sicherheitsapparate

Die »April-Ereignisse« hatten auch längerfristige Folgen für die Sicherheitssituation im Land. Im April herrschte in Nord-Namibia de facto wieder eine Kriegssituation, und dies erlaubte es den staatlichen Sicherheitsorganen unter südafrikanischer Kontrolle, länger aktiv zu bleiben, als es im UN-Plan vorgesehen war - mit prekären Folgen für die Sicherheitssituation im Land. Der Rückzug der regulären südafrikanischen Armee (SADF) verzögerte sich zunächst, wurde dann aber im Juni entsprechend dem UN-Plan weitgehend abgeschlossen. Es blieb allein ein Kontingent von 1.500 Soldaten, die - auf zwei Militärbasen in Oshivelo und Grootfontein beschränkt - plangemäß bis kurz nach den Wahlen in Namibia blieben. Während der »April-Ereignisse« wurde zeitweise auch die »Territorialarmee« (SWATF), bestehend aus Namibianern, remobilisiert - ursprünglich hatte sie zu diesem Zeitpunkt bereits aufgelöst sein sollen. Die Sicherung von Recht und Ordnung oblag dem UN-Plan gemäß allein der namibischen Polizei (SWAPOL) - Mannschaftssstärke ca. 6.000 - unter Kontrolle des Generaladministrators und überwacht von UNTAG-»police monitors«.

Besonders schwerwiegende Probleme warf »Koevoet« (»Brechstange«) auf, eine 1978 gegründete und für ihre Brutalität gegenüber Guerilla wie Zivilbevölkerung gefürchtete »counterinsurgency«-Sondereinheit. »Koevoet« umfaßte Anfang 1989, südafrikanischen Angaben zufolge, etwa 3.000 Mann und wurde formell - »as a unit« - aufgelöst. Schätzungsweise zwei Drittel ihrer Mitglieder wurden jedoch in SWAPOL integriert, und der ehemalige »Koevoet«-Kommandant Hans Dreyer übernahm die Position als SWAPOL-Kommandant für Nord-Namibia. Nach Ansicht der UNTAG und vieler Beobachter konnten »Koevoet«-Mitglieder jedoch schon allein von ihrer (auf den Anti-Guerilla-Kampf konzentrierten) Ausbildung her gar nicht für reguläre Polizeiaufgaben in Betracht kommen: Als »gelernte Killer« und soziale Außenseiter bildeten sie vor allem ein Unsicherheits- und Gewaltpotential.

Während der »April-Ereignisse« spielten »Koevoet«-Mitglieder eine besonders aggressive Rolle und waren vielfach offenbar diejenigen, die das Feuer auf die PLAN-Einheiten eröffneten. In der Folgezeit waren ehemalige »Koevoet«-Mitglieder in der Polizei bis zu den Wahlen immer wieder verantwortlich für Übergriffe und Einschüchterungsversuche aller Art; besonders betroffen waren Personen in Nord-Namibia, die seit Juni aus dem Exil zurückgekehrt waren. Erst im Oktober wurden nach langem Drängen des UN-Sonderbeauftragten etwa 1.200 »Koevoet«-Mitglieder demobilisiert und erhielten - wie auch ehemalige Angehörige der SWATF - Überbrückungsgehälter; eine unbekannte Anzahl von ihnen befand sich jedoch auch noch während der Wahlen in der SWAPOL.

Doch auch die Demobilisierung löste diese Probleme nicht vollständig, da Überwachungsmöglichkeiten wegfielen. Ehemalige »Koevoet«-Mitglieder sollen bei ihrer Entlassung Gelegenheit erhalten haben, ihre Waffen zu »kaufen«; sie spielten immer wieder eine prominente Rolle als aggressive Aktivisten der

DTA. Kurz nach den Wahlen berichteten Zeitungen, Kommandant Dreyer habe ehemalige »Koevoet«-Mitglieder auf einer Farm versammelt. Meldungen vom Februar 1990 sprachen davon, daß ehemalige »Koevoet«-Mitglieder sich inzwischen an militärischen Aktivitäten der UNITA beteiligten. Die mit »Koevoet« verbundenen Sicherheits- und auch sozialen Probleme sind zum Zeitpunkt der Unabhängigkeit noch nicht endgültig gelöst. Inzwischen ist allerdings begonnen worden, einzelne ehemalige »Koevoet«-Mitglieder - teilweise gemeinsam mit ehemaligen PLAN-Guerillas - für die Polizei des unabhängigen Namibia auszubilden.

»Intimidation« und Gewalt

Der Wahlvorbereitungsprozeß war von Einschüchterungsversuchen, massiven Drohungen und teilweise auch von offenen Gewaltausbrüchen begleitet. »Einschüchterung« (»intimidation«) war der verbreitete Sammelbegriff für ein ganzes Spektrum von Aktivitäten und Verhaltensweisen, die geeignet waren, durch Gewalt oder Drohung mit ihr die freie Wahlentscheidung einer Person zu beeinflussen. Typische, von Wahlbeobachtern immer wieder aufgeführte Beispiele waren Drohungen von »Koevoet«-Mitgliedern gegen SWAPO-Anhänger, darunter besonders gegen Rückkehrer aus dem Exil; das ostentative Auftreten der Sicherheitsorgane mit den gepanzerten Fahrzeugen (Casspirs), die *das* Symbol staatlicher Repression in Südafrika und Namibia darstellen; isolierte Gewaltausbrüche zwischen Anhängern verschiedener Parteien, etwa in Lokalen; schließlich provokative und aggressive Aufmärsche, die verschiedentlich in Ausschreitungen einmündeten. So wurden beispielsweise am 26. September während eines Zuges mehrerer hundert DTA-Anhänger durch Katutura (Windhoek) Steine auf Häuser von SWAPO-Sympathisanten geworfen, 9 Personen verletzt und 34 Häuser beschädigt. Zu Auseinandersetzungen dieser Art kam es vor allem im Norden, und zwar vorrangig zwischen DTA- und SWAPO-Anhängern. In einer deutlichen Mehrheit der von UNTAG registrierten Fälle war es die DTA, von deren Seite das aggressive Verhalten ausging. Viele Beobachter werteten Aspekte der DTA-Wahlkampfführung generell als provokativ, vor allem vor dem Hintergrund der Tatsache, daß diese Partei (ehemalige) Angehörige von Armee und Polizei engagierte. Vereinzelt wurden auch UNTAG-Angehörige sowie Pressevertreter von DTA-Anhängern bedroht und/oder angegriffen.

Das angespannte politische Klima wurde durch Anschläge weißer Rechtsextremisten verschärft. Bei einem Angriff auf eine UNTAG-Station in Outjo wurde am 10. August ein Wachmann getötet. Auch internationales Aufsehen erregte der Mord an dem Windhoeker Rechtsanwalt und prominentesten weißen SWAPO-Mitglied, Anton Lubowski, am 12. September, nur wenige Tage vor der Rückkehr des SWAPO-Präsidenten Sam Nujoma. Teile der weißen »Community« Namibias äußerten offen Genugtuung über diesen Mord.

Der private Besitz von Waffen - teils »Tradition«, teils Kriegsfolge - stellte einen grundlegenden Unsicherheitsfaktor dar. Kurz vor den Wahlen erschienen Zeitungsberichte über die systematische Ausgabe von Waffen an weiße Farmer. Es gab Gerüchte und Vermutungen über Waffenbesitz bei ehemaligen Angehörigen der Sicherheitskräfte, aber auch bei ehemaligen Guerillas, und die Drohung, sie in organisierter Weise zu benutzen, »stand im Raum«.

Während bisweilen »normale« politische Aktivitäten (etwa die Durchführung von Wahlkampfveranstaltungen in Gebieten, die als Hochburgen des Gegners bekannt waren) bereits als »intimidation« mißverstanden wurden, gab es andere, weniger greifbare Aspekte von »intimidation«, deren Auswirkungen nur schwer abschätzbar sind. Es gab Fälle, in denen Arbeitgeber ihren Angestellten, die sich - etwa mit T-Shirts oder Fahnen auf dem Haus - als SWAPO-Anhänger zu erkennen gaben, mit Entlassung drohten. Besonders prekär war in dieser Hinsicht die Lage der afrikanischen Arbeitskräfte auf den etwa 6.000 weißen Farmen, die isoliert und in extremer Abhängigkeit von ihren Arbeitgebern leben, besonders was die Möglichkeit von Kontakten nach außen betrifft. So wurde Mitgliedern von SWAPO-Wahlkampfteams vielfach mit Hinweis auf den privaten Grundbesitz des Farmlands schlicht der Zugang zu den Arbeitern verweigert. Farmarbeiter besaßen nur dann die Chance einer freien Stimmabgabe, wenn sie sich der Geheimhaltung ihrer Stimme vollkommen sicher sein konnten, und eben dies muß angesichts der weitreichenden Kontrolle durch die Arbeitgeber über alle Aspekte ihres täglichen Lebens fraglich bleiben - selbst wenn Geheimhaltung objektiv gegeben war.

Formell war es Aufgabe der Polizei, Vorwürfen von »intimidation« nachzugehen. UNTAG erfüllte auch hier Überwachungsfunktionen und beklagte mehrfach eine ungenügende Ermittlungsarbeit bei der Polizei. Zusätzlich setzte der Generaladministrator im Mai eine Kommission zur Untersuchung von »intimidation«-Vorwürfen unter dem Vorsitz des bekannten liberalen Anwalts Bryan O'Linn ein. Bis Mitte November hatte die Kommission in 128 von insgesamt 215 Fällen, die vorgebracht worden waren, ein Urteil gefällt; nur 10 von ihnen wurden als hinreichend belegt und strafrechtlich relevant genug gewertet, um an die Staatsanwaltschaft weitergeleitet werden zu können.

Repatriierung der Flüchtlinge

Ein wesentlicher Bestandteil des UN-Plans für Namibia war die Rückführung der Flüchtlinge rechtzeitig zur Wahlregistrierung. Insgesamt kehrten zwischen Mitte Juni und September rund 42.000 Namibier zurück. (Frühere Angaben über Flüchtlingszahlen aus Namibia hatten deutlich höher gelegen.) Fast die Hälfte der Rückkehrer waren Kinder und Jugendliche unter 20 Jahren. Mehr als 35.000 von ihnen kamen aus Angola (darunter auch große Teile der ehemaligen PLAN), über 3.000 aus Zambia, kleinere Gruppen schließlich aus verschiedenen europäischen Ländern und den USA.

Das UN-Hochkommissariat für Flüchtlinge übergab die Abwicklung der Repatriierung in Namibia selbst dem namibischen Kirchenrat (CCN), der zu diesem Zweck das sogenannte »RRR«-Komitee (»Repatriation, Resettlement and Reconstruction«) einrichtete. Das RRR schuf »reception centres« zur unmittelbaren Unterbringung der Rückkehrer, betreibt Familienzusammenführung, Arbeitsvermittlung und organisiert die Nahrungsmittelhilfe, die alle Rückkehrer für ein Jahr erhalten. Darüber hinaus ist RRR an längerfristigen Reintegrationsmaßnahmen beteiligt (Ausbau von Schulen, Maßnahmen im Gesundheits- und Wohnungsbereich, therapeutische Projekte, pastorale Betreuung etc.). Trotz einiger Engpässe in der Anfangsphase des Programms und vereinzelter Kritik an der »SWAPO-Lastigkeit« des Kirchenrats (und damit des Programms) wird die Repatriierungsoperation insgesamt allseits als Erfolg gewertet.

Die langfristigen sozialen Probleme der Rückkehrer sind allerdings nicht gelöst. Auch wenn viele von ihnen relativ gut ausgebildet sind, fehlen die adäquaten Arbeitsplätze, so daß manche wohl noch für lange Zeit vor allem auf die Unterstützung durch ihre Familien angewiesen sein werden.

Wählerregistrierung

Die Wählerregistrierung erfolgte vom 3. Juli bis zum 23. September in zentralen Büros und temporären Registrationspunkten überall im Land. Wahlberechtigt waren alle Personen über 18 Jahren, die selbst in Namibia geboren wurden, diejenigen mit mindestens einem im Land geborenen Elternteil und Personen, die seit mindestens vier Jahren kontinuierlich in Namibia lebten. Als Belege waren neben offiziellen Dokumenten, Krankenhausaufzeichnungen u.ä. auch beeidete Aussagen anderer registrierter Wähler oder von Chiefs zulässig. Die Registration erfolgte unabhängig vom Wohnsitz. Der oder die Registrierte erhielt eine Karte, mit Unterschrift oder Fingerabdruck gekennzeichnet, die bei der Wahl selbst erneut vorzulegen war.

In seiner Anfangsphase litt der Prozeß der Wählerregistrierung unter technischen und administrativen Mängeln und Verzögerungen (vor allem in Nord-Namibia), wurde nach seinem Abschluß aber allseits als zufriedenstellend bewertet. Die Zahl der abgelehnten Registrierungen - etwa wegen unzureichender Dokumentation - war gering. In der Schlußphase der Registrierungsperiode - sie wurde über den ursprünglich geplanten Zeitraum hinaus um eine Woche verlängert - bemühten sich Administration und UNTAG offenbar erfolgreich, auch isolierte und bisher vernachlässigte Regionen zu erreichen. Problematische Aspekte der Wählerregistrierung lagen weniger in ihrer praktischen Durchführung als in der Definition namibischer Staatsangehörigkeit, wie sie das Registrierungsgesetz de facto vornahm: Einwohner der umstrittenen südafrikanischen Enklave Walvis Bay waren als solche nicht wahlberechtigt, sondern nur, wenn sie im eigentlichen Namibia geboren waren; im Gegensatz dazu erhielten Südafrikaner das Wahlrecht, die aus Namibia stammten, aber dort - teilweise seit Jahrzehnten - nicht mehr ansässig waren. Schließlich erlaubte die Vier-Jahres-Regelung auch Personen mit begrenzter Aufenthaltsdauer und -perspektive in Namibia (Angehörigen der südafrikanischen Administration ebenso wie Flüchtlingen aus Angola) die Teilnahme an der Wahl.

Tabelle 1
Regionale Daten zur Wählerregistrierung, 3.7.-23.9.1989

Wahlbezirk	Wahlberechtigte: Schätzung vor der Wahl	Registrierung tatsächlich registriert	proz. Anteil zu Schätzwert (Prozent)	an gesamter Wählerschaft
Nord-Namibia				
Ovambo	280.436	248.272	88,5	35,4
Kavango	61.125	64.156	105,0	9,1
Caprivi	21.267	28.096	132,1	4,0
Kaokoland	12.203	13.546	111,0	1,9
Zentral-Namibia				
Windhoek	87.592	105.382	120,3	15,0
Swakopmund	13.996	25.363	181,2	3,6
Grootfontein	17.793	20.510	115,3	2,9
Gobabis	17.485	19.250	110,1	2,7
Hereroland	16.892	16.317	96,6	2,3
Damaraland	15.559	15.127	97,2	2,2
Tsumeb	16.089	14.651	91,1	2,1
Otjiwarongo	12.595	13.287	105,5	1,9
Okahandja	9.973	11.233	112,6	1,6
Outjo	6.249	7.219	115,5	1,0
Omaruru	4.027	6.008	149,2	0,9
Süd-Namibia				
Keetmanshoop	21.042	20.039	95,2	2,9
Karasburg	6.942	18.257	263,0	2,6
Rehoboth	16.873	17.346	102,8	2,5
Mariental	14.212	14.630	102,9	2,1
Lüderitz	13.917	10.740	77,2	1,5
Karibib	5.700	6.955	122,0	1,0
Maltahöhe	3.615	2.635	72,9	0,4
Bethanien	2.074	2.464	118,8	0,4
SUMME:	677.656	701.483	103,5	100,0

Quelle: Generaladministrator

Tabelle 1 gibt einen Überblick zu den Registrationszahlen auf regionaler Basis. Darin sind auch Schätzungen zur Zahl der potentiellen Wähler angegeben, die das Büro des Generaladministrators vor der Registrierung auf Basis der

Bevölkerungszählung von 1981 veröffentlichte. Die erheblichen Größenunterschiede zwischen den Wahlkreisen reflektieren dabei allein die regionalen Unterschiede in der Bevölkerungsdichte Namibias.

Die in dieser Statistik deutlich werdenden Unterschiede zwischen den Schätzungen vor der Wahl und den tatsächlichen Registrationsergebnissen sind erklärbar - auch wenn der besonders ausgeprägte »Rückgang« der Registrations- gegenüber den geschätzten Zahlen im Ovamboland als wichtigstem »SWAPO-Territorium« einen Manipulationsverdacht nahelegte. Andererseits konnte die Zählung in dieser Region im Jahre 1981, d.h. unter Kriegsbedingungen nur von begrenzter Genauigkeit sein; außerdem ist davon auszugehen, daß sich viele Wanderarbeiter aus dem Ovamboland am Ort ihres Arbeitsplatzes registrieren ließen (bei den Wahlen wird dieses Muster noch deutlicher), was zur Erklärung der relativ hohen Registrierungszahlen in Windhoek und Swakopmund beiträgt. Die auffällige Über-Registrierung im Bezirk Karasburg ist eindeutig dem Zustrom von Südafrikanern zuzurechnen, die sich allein für Registrierung und Wahl auf das Nordufer des Oranje begaben. Durch Beamte des Generaladministrators wurde ihre Zahl bereits auf 10.000 bis 12.000 geschätzt (dies offenbar in Anlehnung an die Zahlen für Karasburg). In der Realität lag der südafrikanische Wähleranteil vermutlich noch etwas darüber, weil eine unbekannte Zahl solcher Registrierungen an anderen Orten, vor allem Windhoek, erfolgte.

UNTAG - Beobachtungen bei den Beobachtern

Die »April-Ereignisse« bedeuteten einen denkbar schlechten Start für die Mission der UNTAG: Sie führten die Schwäche internationaler Überwachung und Schadensbegrenzung im militärischen Ernstfall bereits am Beginn ihrer Arbeit in aller Deutlichkeit vor. Dies führte zu einem Verlust des Vertrauensvorschusses, den die UNTAG in breiten Kreisen der Bevölkerung gehabt hatte. Im Verlauf der folgenden Monate gewann UNTAG jedoch deutlich an Profil und konnte sich zum Zeitpunkt der Wahlen als weithin präsente und akzeptierte Kontrollinstanz etablieren.

Wichtige Funktionen der UNTAG lagen im militärischen Bereich: Kontrolle der Truppenreduzierung, Überwachung der angolanischen Grenze etc. Zum vermutlich sensibelsten Punkt im UNTAG-Aufgabenbereich wurde aber die Überwachung der Polizei. Besonders in der Anfangsphase ihrer Tätigkeit besaß UNTAG weder ausreichende technische Möglichkeiten noch Kenntnisse genug, um flächendeckend wirksam zu werden. So gab es beispielsweise viele Berichte über eine unzureichende Ausstattung mit geländegängigen Fahrzeugen, die die Überwachung von Polizeiaktivitäten »im Busch« teilweise unmöglich machte. Unzulängliche Sprachkompetenz - trotz des Einsatzes einer Vielzahl von Übersetzern - erschwerte die adäquate Einschätzung der Situation vor Ort prinzipiell. Die Eingriffsmöglichkeiten der UNTAG waren im Sicherheitsbereich ohnehin beschränkt auf personelle Präsenz, auf Beobachtung und Meldung von Vorfällen und schließlich auf die Ausübung politischen Drucks gegenüber der südafrikanischen Administration. Die Effektivität der UNTAG-Arbeit wuchs jedoch mit zunehmender Erfahrung im Lauf der Zeit - zumindest wurde sie immer weniger kritisiert. Im November galt UNTAG durchweg als akzeptierter Referenzpunkt für Berichte über Vorfälle aller Art und erfüllte nicht zuletzt Schutzfunktionen für Personen, die sich bedroht sahen. Auch wenn ihre Präsenz »intimidation« und Gewalt in der Vorwahlperiode insgesamt nicht verhindern konnte, so darf UNTAG insgesamt sicherlich beanspruchen, Schlimmeres verhütet zu haben.

Die Praxis der UNTAG variierte, abhängig auch von der Initiative der jeweiligen Vertreter vor Ort, zwischen einer rein »beobachtenden« und einer stärker »interventionistischen« Interpretation ihres Auftrags. Dies galt vor allem für die zivile Komponente, die der Überwachung der Wahlvorbereitungen und der Wahl selbst diente. Unterschiedliche Herangehensweisen wurden beispielsweise während der Wählerregistrierung deutlich: Bisweilen beschränkte das UNTAG-Personal sich allein auf Präsenz und vermied jegliche Auseinandersetzungen mit der Administration. An anderen Orten hingegen überprüften UNTAG-Mitglieder die Details des Prozesses, griffen in Befragungen ein und unterstützten die Abwicklung praktisch-organisatorisch bis hin zur Suche nach bisher nicht erfaßten Bevölkerungsgruppen. Verschiedentlich brachte UNTAG auf lokaler Ebene die Vertreter der konkurrierenden Parteien zum Gespräch zusammen. UNTAG unternahm darüber hinaus mit Versammlungen, Plakaten etc. eigene Schritte zur »voters' education«, um auf die Bedeutung der Wahl hinzuweisen, das System zu erklären, Ängste hinsichtlich der Geheimhaltung der Stimmabgabe abzubauen etc. Das Verhältnis zwischen UNTAG und Mitarbeitern der südafrikanischen Administration bei der praktischen Durchführung der Wahlen im November wurde generell als sehr kooperativ bewertet. Vor diesem Hintergrund haben auch Klagen - vor allem von seiten der DTA - über mangelnde Unparteilichkeit der UNTAG an Bedeutung verloren.

Wichtig für das Image der UNTAG in der Öffentlichkeit waren auch die Nebeneffekte ihrer Präsenz. Dank ihrer umfangreichen technischen Möglichkeiten waren UNTAG-Einheiten oft in der Lage, dringend benötigte Dienstleistungen zur Verfügung zu stellen - von der Minenräumung über Krankentransporte bis hin zur Hilfe bei der Abwicklung des Repatriierungsprogramms. Die Zusammensetzung der UNTAG, die Einheiten aus rund 30 verschiedenen Ländern umfaßt, hat Windhoek ein internationales Flair verliehen, und ihre Präsenz führte bisweilen, Geschichten und Anekdoten zufolge, in den konservativen Regionen Namibias zur Auflockerung der noch immer starken sozialen Abgrenzungen einer ehemaligen Apartheid-Gesellschaft. Schließlich sollte die ökonomische Bedeutung der UNTAG nicht unterschätzt werden: Der UN-Etat für die Implementation von Resolution 435 betrug 420 Mio. US-$; ein Gutteil davon - Schätzungen reichen bis zu 500 Mio. Rand - wurden direkt und indirekt in Namibia ausgegeben, das 1988 ein Bruttosozialprodukt von nicht mehr als 3,3 Mrd. Rand aufwies. Die UNTAG-Präsenz schuf Arbeitsplätze (Übersetzer,

Fahrer etc.) und kommerzielle Chancen (Tankstellen, »cuca shops« etc.). Sie kompensierte damit zumindest übergangsweise für die Einkommensverluste, die mit der Demilitarisierung vor allem im Norden einhergehen und deren langfristige Auswirkungen derzeit noch nicht zu überblicken sind.

Andererseits hat die durch UNTAG induzierte Nachfrage zu einem deutlichen Preisschub nicht nur bei Wohnungen und Transport, sondern auch im Grundnahrungsmittelbereich geführt. Kritik daran war unüberhörbar, ebenso auch auch an Lebensstil und Verhaltensweisen einzelner - und nicht notwendigerweise typischer - UNTAG-Mitarbeiter. In der Regel ging dies allerdings nicht über typische Muster der Kritik an ausländischen »Experten« in der Dritten Welt generell hinaus. Insgesamt haben UNTAG-Mitarbeiter sich im Rahmen ihrer begrenzten institutionellen und praktischen Möglichkeiten recht effektiv als - in diesem Sinne - »Experten für Sicherheit und Frieden« erwiesen.

Neben UNTAG hielt sich eine Vielzahl anderer politisch interessierter Personengruppen im Lande auf: Diplomatische Beobachtermissionen, die den Aufbau von Botschaften vorbereiteten; ein großes Aufgebot der internationalen Presse; schließlich Vertreter von Nicht-Regierungs-Organisationen (NGOs) - Kirchen, Entwicklungsagenturen, Anti-Apartheid-Gruppen etc. -, deren Arbeitsergebnisse teilweise durch den »Churches Information and Monitoring Service« (CIMS) gebündelt wurden. Öffentlichkeit war somit hergestellt, wenn auch das internationale Interesse an den Wahlen in Namibia durch die parallel stattfindenen Ereignisse in der DDR deutlich reduziert wurde.

3. Die Parteien und Allianzen

Spaltungen in der nationalistischen Bewegung, vor allem aber die interne politische Dynamik seit der Turnhallen-Konferenz Mitte der siebziger Jahre haben zur Herausbildung eines Parteienspektrums in Namibia geführt, das kaum mehr übersehbar war. Die Wahlen haben hier zum erstenmal Klarheit geschaffen. Insgesamt kandidierten 10 Gruppierungen, 6 davon waren kurz vor den Wahlen gebildete Allianzen, die sich aus insgesamt etwa 40 Einzelparteien zusammensetzten. Zur Wahlzulassung mußte eine Partei/Allianz eine Liste mit 2.000 Unterschriften beibringen sowie eine Kaution von 10.000 Rand hinterlegen. Zwei Parteien (CDA und NNDP) hatten anfänglich Probleme, diese Kriterien zu erfüllen, wurden jedoch später zugelassen.

Im folgenden sollen die zur Wahl zugelassenen Parteien und Allianzen in der Reihenfolge ihres Wahlerfolgs überblicksartig skizziert werden.

SWAPO - »South West Africa People's Organization of Namibia«

Von allen zur Wahl stehenden Parteien konnte allein SWAPO die Tradition, die Hoffnungen und den Mythos einer Befreiungsbewegung und ihres bewaffneten Kampfs für die Unabhängigkeit in Anspruch nehmen. Die Anfänge der

Organisation sind bereits oben dargestellt worden. Auf die Geschichte der Organisation kann hier nicht näher eingegangen werden, es sollen allein die Punkte angesprochen werden, die sich im Lauf des Jahres 1989 - und besonders für die Wahlen - als besonders relevant erwiesen.

SWAPO ist einerseits eine Befreiungsbewegung, die bis 1989 im Guerillakrieg stand und international operierte, andererseits eine in Namibia selbst nie verbotene - wenn auch oft massiver Repression ausgesetzte - politische Partei. Auch wenn es eine klare Aufgabenverteilung zwischen »externem« und »internem« Flügel gab, besaß die Organisation partiell Parallelstrukturen, wobei die politische Führungsrolle der »externen« Partei unbestritten war. Die Rückkehr der »externen« Führung aus dem Exil im Verlauf des Sommers 1989 und ihre Übernahme der Spitzenpositionen in der SWAPO-Hierarchie in Namibia selbst verlief, wenigstens nach außen hin, unproblematisch: Sam Nujomas erster öffentlicher Auftritt in Windhoek im September wurde zum Großereignis mit geschätzten 70.000 Teilnehmern; einige Mitglieder der »internen« Führung wurden 1989 ins Zentralkomitee integriert. Dennoch ist die »interne« Führung - nimmt man die Kandidatenliste der SWAPO für die Wahlen als Indiz - in eine eher nachgeordnete Position gelangt. Ähnliches gilt für verschiedene andere Organisationen, die von der SWAPO unabhängig sind, ihr aber politisch nahestehen. Besonders die Gewerkschaftsbewegung (vor allem die »Mineworkers' Union of Namibia«) und die »Namibian National Students' Organisation« (NANSO) erlebten in den letzten Jahren einen Aufschwung. Befürchtungen über eine Vereinnahmung von Basisbewegungen und ihren Organisationen durch die aus dem Exil zurückgekehrte SWAPO-Führung und - langfristig - durch SWAPO-Politik generell waren weit verbreitet.

Zur schwerwiegendsten Belastung für die SWAPO wurden ihre »detainees«. Das »detainee«-Problem steht im Kontext einer Serie von Krisen in der SWAPO. Die Parteiführung hatte bereits 1976 im Zuge eines internen Machtkonflikts Mitglieder verhaften und internieren lassen, die die Einberufung eines Parteikongresses - der letzte fand 1969 statt - forderten (vgl. Abschnitt zur SWAPO-D). 1980 trennte sich eine seit den sechziger Jahren in die SWAPO integrierte Gruppe von Capriviern unter Führung von Mishake Muyongo von der Partei und reetablierte nach ihrer Rückkehr nach Namibia die »Caprivi African National Union« (CANU, seither mehrfach gespalten). Seit 1983/84 wurden mindestens einige hundert, möglicherweise über tausend Mitglieder in den SWAPO-Camps in Angola durch den Sicherheitsdienst unter - in diesem Umfang - absurden Spionagevorwürfen verhaftet und teilweise jahrelang in Erdlöchern gefangengehalten. Geständnisse wurden teilweise durch Folter erpreßt und auf Videobändern aufgezeichnet. Eine unbekannte Anzahl von Gefangenen kam ums Leben. Die Beschuldigungen richteten sich vornehmlich gegen jüngere SWAPO-Mitglieder, die nicht Ovambo waren und/oder eine höher qualifizierte Ausbildung besaßen. Es waren aber auch höherrangige Personen betroffen, vereinzelt selbst Mitglieder des Zentralkomitees. Die Betroffenen betrachten die Verhaftungen und Mißhandlungen als Versuch einer inkompetenten Parteiführung, sich eines Kritikpotentials zu erwehren; sie seien zum Sündenbock für militärisch-politische Mißerfolge und zu Objekten einer Paranoia gemacht worden.

Ein »Parents' Committee« versuchte bereits seit 1985, Kirchen und Regierungen zur Hilfe für die Gefangenen zu mobilisieren, und bereits 1986 gab die SWAPO zu, 100 »Spione« inhaftiert zu haben. Öffentlich wurden die Menschenrechtsverletzungen der SWAPO in Angola durch Amnesty International, vor allem durch rechtsstehende Kreise in Europa und den USA aufgegriffen. Die politische Bombe platzte in Namibia erst 1989, als im Rahmen des UN-Plans für Namibia die Freilassung aller politischen Gefangenen bevorstand. 200 ehemalige Gefangene kehrten Anfang Juli als Gruppe nach Namibia zurück und berichteten über ihr Schicksal; einige von ihnen gründeten das »Patriotic Unity Movement« (vgl. Abschnitt zur UDF). Anschuldigungen, wonach die SWAPO trotz gegenteiliger Aussagen noch immer Personen gefangen halte, führten im September zur Entsendung einer UN-Mission nach Angola und Zambia. Sie fand alle bekannten Lager aufgelöst vor, doch konnte auch ihr Bericht die Kritiker nicht vollkommen zufriedenstellen.

Die Enthüllungen der Freigelassenen führten zu einer schweren Vertrauenskrise gegenüber der SWAPO, zumindest in Süd-Namibia und bei SWAPO-Sympathisanten im Ausland. Die SWAPO-Führung entschuldigte sich unter Hinweis auf die Kriegssituation, in der man sich in Angola befunden habe, und auf die Vielzahl von Menschenrechtsverletzungen, die durch Südafrika begangen wurden und jetzt nicht in adäquater Weise öffentlich aufgegriffen würden. Eine öffentliche Untersuchung der Vorfälle und Bestrafung der Verantwortlichen lehnte die SWAPO - nach einigen widersprüchlichen Aussagen von Parteiführern - jedoch ab. Viele politische Beobachter werteten das »detainee«-Problem bereits vor den Wahlen als den Faktor, der das Erreichen einer Zwei-Drittel-Mehrheit durch die SWAPO verhindern würde.

Im Gegensatz zu ihrer Selbstdarstellung in der »detainee«-Frage präsentierte sich die SWAPO in der Vorwahlperiode politisch und programmatisch offen und konsistent »gemäßigt«. Fast alle Parteien sprachen sich für eine Politik der »national reconciliation« aus, doch wurde diese durch die SWAPO besonders intensiv propagiert. »Reconciliation« richtete sich bei ihr selbstverständlich besonders an die weiße Bevölkerung Namibias, der versichert wurde, es werde »no wholesale nationalisation« geben. Von symbolischer Bedeutung war die Vergabe von 4 sicheren Listenplätzen für die Wahl an weiße SWAPO-Kandidaten. Die Partei versuchte besonders, mit weißen Farmern ins Gespräch zu kommen, um sie von Flucht- oder auch aggressiven Reaktionen abzuhalten.

Das SWAPO-Wahlmanifest vermeidet Anklänge an den sprachlichen Duktus des »wissenschaftlichen Sozialismus«, den Parteiprogramm und Statut der SWAPO von 1976 enthalten. Verstaatlichung spielt im Manifest von 1989 eine begrenzte Rolle, ein Ein-Parteien-System wird zwar längerfristig nicht ausgeschlossen, doch sollen die Wahlen selbst »the Namibian people's preference of political party system« (Election Manifesto, S. 26) zeigen - dies eine schon traditionelle SWAPO-Formulierung. Was die konkrete Politik betrifft, so entwirft das Manifest unter dem Motto »solidarity, freedom, justice« ein letztlich sozialdemokratisches Gesellschaftsmodell mit Grundrechtskatalog und Gewaltenteilung, einer großen Bandbreite von Eigentumsformen im wirtschaftlichen Bereich und einer Betonung der sozialen Aufgaben des Staats.

DTA - »Democratic Turnhalle Alliance«

Die DTA entstand 1977, wie bereits erwähnt, im Kontext der südafrikanischen Bemühungen um eine »interne« statt einer UN-kontrollierten Unabhängigkeit für Namibia. Die DTA setzt sich aus 12 Parteien mit zumeist einheitlicher ethnischer Basis zusammen. Von größter Bedeutung darunter sind - der Verteilung der DTA-Führungspositionen nach zu urteilen - die »Republican Party« (Weiße, Vorsitz Dirk Mudge), die »National Unity Democratic Organisation« (Herero, Präsident Chief Kuaima Riruako) und »United Democratic Party« (Caprivi, Präsident Mishake Muyongo, der 1980 die SWAPO verließ). Der interne Aufbau der DTA spiegelt damit grundsätzlich die ethnisch organisierten administrativen Strukturen Namibias in den achtziger Jahren wider. Versuche, dieses Prinzip in der DTA zugunsten einer einheitlichen Partei aufzugeben, wurden mehrfach abgeblockt, sind jedoch erneut in der Diskussion. Die Anwendung des ethnischen Prinzips im Regierungssystem eines zukünftigen Namibia lehnt die DTA inzwischen ab und befürwortet - so ihr Wahlprogramm - einen »decentralized unitary state« mit »Regional Councils«, wobei allerdings keine genaueren Angaben zur Aufgaben- und Finanzverteilung gemacht werden.

Die DTA kann für sich in Anspruch nehmen, zu Beginn der achtziger Jahre die Restbestände der »kleinen« Apartheid in Namibia beseitigt zu haben, einige Jahre (wenn auch höchst umstrittener) Regierungserfahrung zu besitzen und - bei aller Abhängigkeit von Südafrika - durchaus nicht ausschließlich als Sachwalterin südafrikanischer Interessen in Namibia aufgetreten zu sein. Tatsächlich scheiterten diverse politische Initiativen der DTA am Widerstand des Generaladministrators und ließen das Bedürfnis nach Selbständigkeit auch bei der DTA wachsen. Die Partei integrierte ein gemäßigtes weißes politisches Spektrum mit etablierten afrikanischen Interessen (Chiefs) aus verschiedenen Regionen des Landes; dabei konnte sie immer auch die Befürchtungen über eine potentielle Ovambo-Dominanz in einem SWAPO-dominierten Namibia aufgreifen. Auf internationaler Ebene konnte die DTA zwar nicht den Status der SWAPO als »sole and authentic representative of the Namibian people« bei der UN beseitigen, doch war sie Zeit ihrer Existenz international als wichtigste der internen Parteien präsent und wurde als Gesprächspartner in westlichen Hauptstädten akzeptiert.

UDF - »United Democratic Front of Namibia«

Die UDF setzt sich aus 8 Parteien zusammen. Ihr Kern ist der »Damara Council« (DC), der bereits in den siebziger Jahren für eine unabhängige anti-südafrikanische Position in Namibia stand, dabei aber auch mit der internen SWAPO in der damaligen »Namibian National Front« zusammenarbeite. Präsident des DC ist Justus Garoeb, Paramount Chief der Damara. Der DC beteiligte sich nicht an den Gremien, die im Kontext der Versuche zur internen Lösung auf zentraler Ebene eingerichtet wurde, besaß aber die Mehrheit in der »second tier«-Administration für Damaraland, die er in unabhängiger Weise nutzte.

Neben zwei Parteien aus Caprivi und der »Labour Party« mit Basis in Rehoboth umfaßt die UDF unter anderem auch die kleine trotzkistische »Workers' Revolutionary Party« (WRP) sowie das »Patriotic Unity Movement« (PUM). Das PUM wurde im Juli 1989 von ehemaligen SWAPO-Gefangenen gegründet, die erst kurz zuvor aus Angola freigekommen waren und, wie sie es ausdrückten, desillusioniert über SWAPO dennoch ihren politischen Zielen treu bleiben wollten. Auch einige Mitglieder der WRP (besonders Erica Beukes) haben sich seit 1984 stark für die Gefangenen der SWAPO engagiert.

ACN - »Aksie Christelik Nasionaal«/»Action Christian National«

ACN wurde durch die »National Party of SWA« (NP) gebildet, um das konservative weiße Stimmenpotential zu bündeln; im August 1989 schloß sich die »Deutsche Aktion/Deutsch-Südwest Komitee« offiziell der ACN an. Ihre führenden Personen sind identisch mit denen der NP, die sich bis 1988 gegen eine Namibia-Lösung nach dem UN-Plan wandte, die Implementation aber als unausweichlich akzeptierte. Zentraler Programmpunkt der ACN ist die Sicherung von »group rights«, d.h. der Fortbestand ethnischer Organisationsprinzipien in der Administration. Wirtschaftspolitisch propagiert die ACN am weitestgehenden von allen Parteien das marktwirtschaftliche Prinzip und die Unterstützung privater Farmwirtschaft.

NPF - »National Patriotic Front of Namibia«

Die NPF ist eine Allianz aus der SWANU-Mehrheitsströmung, dem »Action National Settlement« (ANS) und einer Fraktion der »Caprivi African National Union« (CANU).

Die SWANU, die ihre wichtigste Basis bei den Herero hat, besaß in den frühen sechziger Jahren eine ähnliche Bedeutung als international anerkannte Befreiungsbewegung wie die SWAPO (und war früher als diese explizit sozialistisch orientiert). Sie verlor diese Rolle aber nicht zuletzt deshalb, weil sie den bewaffneten Kampf zwar nicht prinzipiell ablehnte, ihn aber unter den gegebenen Umständen als nicht führbar betrachtete. Viele Führungsmitglieder haben, ähnlich wie bei der SWAPO, lange Jahre des Exils oder Haftstrafen hinter sich.

Die Partei lehnte die internen Lösungsversuche seit der Mitte der siebziger Jahre ab, spaltete sich aber 1983/84 an der Frage einer Beteiligung an der »Multi-Party-Conference«. Der Vorsitzende Moses Katjiuonga hielt eine Ministerposition im »Transitional Government«.

Die ANS, 1987 unter Vorsitz von Eben van Zijl gegründet, umfaßt schwerpunktmäßig ein weißes liberales Spektrum, das vormals der National Party angehörte, sich in den siebziger Jahren aber nicht der DTA anschloß.

FCN - »Federal Convention of Namibia«

Die FCN ist ein Bündnis aus etwa 10 zumeist sehr kleinen Parteien eher konservativen Charakters. Ihr dominanter Bestandteil ist die »Liberation Front/Liberated Democratic Party« aus Rehoboth, die - in den Autonomietraditionen des »Rehoboth Gebied« - dem Schutz von Minoritätenrechten besonderes Gewicht beimißt. Präsident ist Hans Diergaardt, »Kaptein« in Rehoboth und Minister im »Transitional Government«. Beteiligt an der FCN ist außerdem die »NUDO Progressive Party«, deren Präsident Mburumba Kerina eine Zentralfigur im frühen namibischen Nationalismus darstellte.

NNF - »Namibia National Front«

Die NNF umfaßt 5 Parteien, unter ihnen am wichtigsten die Fraktion der SWANU, die sich 1984 als »SWANU-Left« bzw. »-Progressives« konstituierte (vgl. Abschnitt zur NPF). Beteiligt ist außerdem die »Namibia Independence Party« als politische Heimat der »Coloured«-Intelligenz. Die Allianz versteht sich als Nachfolgerin der »alten« NNF der späten siebziger Jahre, die damals die Südafrika-kritischen Kräfte außerhalb der SWAPO zu verbinden suchte. Keine der an der NNF beteiligten Gruppen war am »Transitional Government« beteiligt. Im Wahlkampf legte die NNF besonderes Gewicht auf die Frage der Landreform (»Give the land back to the people«) und betonte die Notwendigkeit des »nation building«.

SWAPO-D - »SWAPO-Democrats«

SWAPO-D entstand als Produkt eines SWAPO-internen Konflikts von 1976. Gründer und Präsident ist Andreas Shipanga, ehemaliger Secretary for Publicity and Information der SWAPO, den die externe SWAPO-Führung zusammen mit einigen Führungsmitgliedern der SWAPO Youth League in Zambia verhaften und bis 1978 in Tanzania gefangen halten ließ; zeitweise waren damals auch Teile der PLAN interniert worden. Shipanga und andere aus seiner Gruppe kehrten über Schweden nach Namibia zurück und gründeten SWAPO-D, die sich als Bewahrerin der traditionellen demokratischen Prinzipien der SWAPO verstand und eine Namibia-Lösung nach Resolution 435 forderte. Die Partei setzte sich für die Aufhebung der nach ethnischen Prinzipien aufgebauten Administration in Namibia ein, beteiligte sich jedoch ab 1985 auch am

»Transitional Government«. Mehrere der zur Wahl im November 1989 aufgestellten Kandidaten waren Mitglieder der Parteiopposition von 1976.

CDA - »Christian Democractic Action for Social Justice«

Die CDA entstand 1982, als Peter T. Kalangula und die Mehrheit seiner »National Democratic Party« (NDP) die DTA, deren Präsident Kalangula gewesen war, verließen, weil diese sich Vorschlägen zur Abschaffung des parteiinternen ethnischen Organisationsprinzips verweigerte. Die CDA besaß seitdem eine Mehrheit in der Ovambo Legislative Assembly. Kalangula, Pfarrer und Gründer einer unabhängigen Kirche, war bereits seit 1973 in verschiedenen Funktionen an der Regierung des Ovambolands beteiligt. Als Vorsitzender der Assembly setzte Kalangula sich für ein Regierungssystem auf Provinz- (statt ethnischer) Ebene und gegen die Übergriffe von Armee und Polizei im Kriegsgebiet ein und erwarb sich dadurch einen Ruf als namibisches Gegenstück zu G. Buthelezi. Die CDA hatte sich nicht am »Transitional Government« beteiligt. Während des Wahlkampfs 1989 war sie nur im Norden präsent.

NNDP - »Namibian National Democratic Party«

Die NNDP wurde Anfang 1989 durch Paul Helmuth und andere ehemalige Mitglieder der NDP (vgl. Abschnitt zur CDA) gegründet. Helmuth gehört zu den frühesten OPO/SWAPO-Aktivisten Ende der fünfziger Jahre, ging 1961 ins Exil, war für die SWAPO in Dar es Salaam und Moskau tätig, trennte sich aber nach 1971 von der Partei und kehrte Ende der siebziger Jahre nach Namibia zurück, um für die DTA zu arbeiten. Im Wahlkampf stellte die NNDP die Kleinbauernförderung in den Vordergrund.

Die Parteien im Wahlkampf

Das Konkurrenzverhältnis unter den 10 zur Wahl angetretenen Parteien und Allianzen besitzt eine starke historische Dimension und ist nicht allein geprägt vom Gegensatz zwischen »interner« und »international überwachter« Namibia-Lösung, sondern auch von Spaltungsprozessen innerhalb der Parteien, regional-ethnischen Besonderheiten und nicht zuletzt persönlichen Konflikten der Parteiführer. Unterschiede in der Programmatik sind nur ein Faktor in diesem Konkurrenzverhältnis - und nicht einmal unbedingt der entscheidende. Der Wahlkampf muß grundsätzlich als Auseinandersetzung zwischen der SWAPO, die auf eine Zwei-Drittel-Mehrheit hinarbeitete, und allen anderen Parteien, die eben diese Mehrheit verhindern wollten, verstanden werden. Andere Faktoren und die Konkurrenz der anderen Parteien untereinander waren demgegenüber von zweitrangiger Bedeutung.

Versucht man dennoch eine grobe politisch-programmatische Einordnung der Parteien, so stehen SWAPO, UDF und NNF eher »links«, die DTA eher »rechts«; ACN und FCN wären als »weit rechts« zu verorten. Ein grundlegender

Konsens bei manchen Themen - über die Unabhängigkeit Namibias von Südafrika, über grundlegende Verfassungsprinzipien, eine »mixed economy« und die Aufhebung des ethnischen Gliederungsprinzips in Politik und Administration - reicht von der DTA bis zur SWAPO. Die Wahlkampfversprechen der Parteien etwa in sozialpolitisch relevanten und mit hohen Erwartungen besetzten Bereichen - Gesundheit, Wohnungsbau etc. - ähnelten sich stark. Die konkrete Ausgestaltung dieser Politikfelder nach der Unabhängigkeit, besonders der Landfrage und der Stärke der zentralen staatlichen Instanzen, bietet für die Zukunft Konfliktstoff genug. Im Wahlkampf jedenfalls spielten Auseinandersetzungen über solche Sachfragen eine relativ geringe Rolle, »Vertrauens- und Imagebildung« waren entscheidender.

Trotz aller Härte in der politischen Auseinandersetzung enthielt der Wahlkampf auch Elemente von Kooperation. Alle wichtigen Parteien unterzeichneten im September einen »Code of Conduct«, der unter Vermittlung von UNTAG entstanden war und Regeln für die Führung der Wahlkampagnen fixierte. Positive Beachtung fand ein informeller Besuch des ACN-Vorsitzenden Johannes de Wet beim Wahlkampfdirektor der SWAPO, Hage G. Geingob. Aufrufe zu Ruhe und Besonnenheit kamen, wenigstens am Vorabend der Wahl, von allen Parteiführern.

Hauptinstrumente des Wahlkampfs waren Großveranstaltungen (»Rallies«), auf denen neben bekannten Politikern auch Musik- oder Tanzgruppen auftraten. Daß die DTA bei solchen Veranstaltungen Freibier und Essen an die Besucher verteilte, wurde von ihren politischen Gegnern süffisant vermerkt; umgekehrt gab es Kritik an der SWAPO, sie kümmere sich nicht ausreichend um die physischen Bedürfnisse ihrer Anhänger (Sonnenschutz, Getränke etc.). Neben den Großereignissen gab es mobile Teams für den Wahlkampf auf dem Land. Verschiedene Parteien organisierten Scheinwahlen im Rahmen ihrer Kampagnen zur »voters' education«, denn eine Mehrheit der Wähler, des Schreibens und Lesens unkundig, war mit den Symbolen der Parteien vertraut zu machen, die neben den Namen auf dem Wahlzettel erscheinen würden. Vor den Wahlen wurde viel über das Verwirrungspotential spekuliert, das diese Symbole besäßen: So verwendete die ACN das christliche Kreuz (das auch auf den Kirchenrat als SWAPO-nahe Institution hätte verweisen können), die SWAPO-D die Fackel (dies war ein traditionelles SWAPO-Symbol), während die SWAPO das Bild eines jungen Mannes mit erhobener Faust (ein vollkommen neues Symbol) einsetzte und die UDF eine Faust alleine.

Vor allem SWAPO und DTA, aber auch mehrere kleine Parteien besaßen hinreichende finanzielle Mittel, um Wahlkampfmaterial - Plakate, T-Shirts, Buttons etc. - in großem Maßstab zu verteilen. Viele Menschen drückten ihre Sympathien dadurch aus, daß sie die Flagge ihrer Partei auf ihrem Haus oder auch auf Bäumen hißten, Kleidungsstücke in Parteifarben trugen etc. Die Handzeichen der Parteien - die erhobene Faust der SWAPO, die zum »V« (= »Victory«) gespreizten Finger der DTA - wurden in den Wochen vor der

Wahl zu gebräuchlichen Erkennungszeichen auf den Straßen Namibias. Neben allen politischen Spannungen waren die letzten Wochen vor der Wahl auch von friedlicher Koexistenz allgegenwärtiger Parteisymbolik gekennzeichnet. Viele der gegen SWAPO angetretenen Parteien erhielten Gelder zur Wahlkampfführung durch die südafrikanisch finanzierte »Namib Stiftung«.

Die Presse war am Wahlkampf intensiv beteiligt, »The Namibian« SWAPO-nah, die »Daily Times« fast ein Parteiblatt der DTA. Mehrere Parteien begannen, eigene Zeitungen herauszugeben (am wichtigsten die »Namibia Today« der SWAPO). Die Berichterstattung in den regierungseigenen Medien Rundfunk und Fernsehen wurde vielfach als unausgewogen kritisiert; immerhin konnten alle Parteien eigene Wahlkampf-Spots senden. Die Public Relations-Kampagne des Generaladministrators für die Wahlen - gehalten im Zeichen des Regenbogens - war neutral. Mit Plakaten, TV-Spots, Broschüren usw. rief sie zur Teilnahme auf (»Vote without fear«, »Our vote brings peace«) und informierte über technische Details von Registrierung und Wahlsystem, analog zur Öffentlichkeitsarbeit der UNTAG.

Auf den Punkt gebracht war es das Wahlkampfziel der SWAPO, eine Zwei-Drittel-Mehrheit zu erreichen, um über die zukünftige Verfassung allein entscheiden zu können; Hauptziel der anderen Parteien war, eben dies zu verhindern. Die Erwartung, die Zwei-Drittel-Mehrheit wirklich zu erreichen, war unmittelbar vor der Wahl bei führenden SWAPO-Vertretern schon nicht mehr ungebrochen vorhanden, auch wenn viele Anhänger entsprechende Hoffnungen noch hegten. Bei der weißen Bevölkerung herrschte - nimmt man das »Wahl-Lotto« einer deutschsprachigen Wochenzeitung zur Basis - sogar die Überzeugung vor, SWAPO werde auch die 50%-Marke verfehlen. Entsprechende Schätzungen für die DTA reichten von 28% bis deutlich über 40%. Ebenso große Unsicherheit bestand hinsichtlich der Wahlchancen der 8 restlichen Parteien.

4. Die Wahlen

Wahlsystem und -organisation

Das Wahlgesetz - »Election (Constituent Assembly) Proclamation, 1989«, AG. 49 - wurde erst am 13. Oktober erlassen. Ein Entwurf vom Juli hatte weithin Bedenken hinsichtlich Geheimhaltung und Zählprozedur hervorgerufen, da er sich in verschiedenen Detailregelungen an den umstrittenen »internen« Wahlen von 1978 orientierte, und der UN-Beauftragte führte intensive Verhandlungen mit dem Generaladministrator um die endgültige Fassung.

Die Wahl erfolgte nach reinem Verhältniswahlrecht mit landesweiten Kandidatenlisten der zugelassenen Parteien. 72 Sitze in der Verfassunggebenden Versammlung waren zu besetzen. Wahltermin war die Periode vom 7.-11. November, von 7.00 bis 19.00 Uhr (verlängerbar im Ermessen der zuständigen Beamten). Die Einteilung in 23 Wahlbezirke hatte organisatorische Bedeutung, aber keine Auswirkung auf das Ergebnis. Die Stimmen von Personen, die nicht in dem Bezirk wählten, in dem sie sich hatten registrieren lassen, wurden zu Verifikationszwecken als »tendered ballots« zentral in Windhoek ausgezählt; die Auszählung der übrigen, lokal verifizierbaren Stimmen erfolgte im Wahlhauptquartier des jeweiligen Bezirks. In den Wahllokalen - sie mußten sich außerhalb von Polizeistationen, Armeebasen etc. befinden - waren neben den Beamten des Generaladministrators und UNTAG-Personal zur Überwachung auch Vertreter der angetretenen Parteien zur Beobachtung zugelassen. Die Wähler hatten die Registrationskarte und einen weiteren Identitätsnachweis (Dokument oder Affidavit nach den für die Registrierung geltenden Regeln) beizubringen. Jeder Person, die wählte, wurde mit einer nur unter UV-Licht sichtbaren und mehrere Tage haftenden Flüssigkeit ein Finger markiert, um die Möglichkeiten für Wahlbetrug weiter zu begrenzen.

Ein Unsicherheitsfaktor, in den Tagen unmittelbar vor der Wahl heftig diskutiert, war der notwendige Zeitaufwand pro Wähler - würden die vorgesehenen 5 Tage reichen angesichts einer mehrheitlich analphabetischen Wählerschaft? Die endgültige Liste der Wahllokale wurde überhaupt erst am ersten Wahltag in der Presse veröffentlicht und umfaßte 219 feste Stationen, in denen fünf Tage lang gewählt werden konnte, sowie weitere 140 mobile Wahllokale, die halb- oder ganztägig an 735 verschiedenen Orten vor allem in Süd- und Zentral-Namibia präsent waren.

Verlauf

Im Kontrast zur Vielzahl von Befürchtungen und Gerüchten, die vorher kursierten, kann der Ablauf der Wahlen selbst insgesamt als sehr gelungen charakterisiert werden.

Am ersten Wahltag bildeten sich bereits nach wenigen Stunden überall im Land lange Schlangen vor den Wahllokalen. Bei (besonders im Norden) sehr hohen Temperaturen und ohne Schatten warteten vielerorts hunderte von Personen den ganzen Tag über auf Einlaß - und manche von ihnen mußten am folgenden Tag noch einmal denselben Gang antreten, weil die Öffnungszeiten am Vortag nicht ausgereicht hatten. Trotz dieser Belastungen verhielten sich die Wartenden außerordentlich diszipliniert. Das große Interesse und Engagement der gesamten Bevölkerung und der Wille, die Wahl mustergültig zu absolvieren, waren für alle Beobachter von Anfang an offensichtlich. Der Ansturm auf die Wahllokale fand vor allem in den ersten beiden Tagen statt, als jeweils rund ein Drittel aller registrierten Wähler ihre Stimme abgaben; insgesamt wurde die beeindruckende Wahlbeteiligung von über 95% erreicht.

Es gab einige technisch-organisatorische Mißstände wie die verspätete Öffnung von Wahllokalen, das Fehlen von Stimmzetteln oder Wahlurnen und ähnliches, doch konnten sie relativ schnell behoben werden. Schwerwiegend waren solche Probleme allenfalls bei den mobilen Wahllokalen, die sich teilweise nur für einen halben Tag an einem Ort aufhielten, doch scheint auch dies nicht dazu geführt zu haben, daß potentielle Wähler am Ende ihre Stimme nicht abgeben konnten - entsprechende Berichte liegen zumindest nicht vor. UNTAG-Mitglieder sprachen von einer generell guten Kooperation mit den Wahlbeamten.

Zu schweren Zwischenfällen mit Gewaltanwendung ist es während der Wahlen nicht gekommen - die Woche war in dieser Hinsicht vermutlich die ruhigste Periode seit geraumer Zeit. Beleg dafür ist nicht zuletzt die Tatsache, daß sich der Löwenanteil der Berichte über Unregelmäßigkeiten und »intimidation« während der Wahl auf eher geringfügige Verstöße gegen die Wahlordnung bezog, etwa das Plakatieren oder andere Formen politischer Agitation in der Nähe von Wahllokalen. Am Wahllokal Windhoek/Flughafen erlebte die Apartheid eine kurze Renaissance, als aus Südafrika eingeflogene weiße Wähler eine Extraschlange beanspruchten, um ihre Rückflüge nicht zu verpassen.

Für Berichte, wonach Angolaner durch UNITA mit Waffengewalt gezwungen worden seien, nach Namibia zu gehen, um dort für die DTA zu stimmen, fehlt die letzte Bestätigung. Welchen Sinn solche Versuche hätten haben sollen, bleibt ohnehin undeutlich, denn im Wahllokal selbst hätte eine solche Stimmabgabe unmittelbar nicht erzwungen werden können. Dies schließt natürlich nicht aus, daß hier eine Strategie der Verunsicherung und Desinformation verfolgt wurde, für die es auch andere Beispiele gab. So wurden während der ersten Wahltage in Nord-Namibia zigtausende Flugblätter von Helikoptern abgeworfen, auf denen angebliche geheime Mitteilungen Sam Nujomas an PLAN-Mitglieder aus seiner Heimatregion zu lesen waren. Die Fälschung war außerordentlich plump und auch für Personen ohne Schulbildung sofort als solche erkennbar, wie auch SWAPO-Anhänger versicherten, die über diese Form von Propaganda sehr verärgert waren. Wenn es wirklich *Strategien* der Verwirrung gab, so blieben sie zumindest in Nord-Namibia (worauf sie vorrangig zielten) ohne Erfolg, wie das Wahlergebnis zeigte.

Fast unmittelbar nach Abschluß der Wahl am Samstagabend - die Stimmenauszählung hatte erst begonnen - gab Mahti Athissari sein Verdikt bekannt: Die Wahlen seien »free and fair« gewesen; nun sei es an den Bürgern und Parteien, die Ergebnisse zu akzeptieren. Widerspruch dagegen gab es nicht.

Die Stimmen wurden nach Bezirken getrennt ausgezählt und unmittelbar nach Auszählung veröffentlicht; erste Ergebnisse - für die kleinen Wahlbezirke in Süd-Namibia - wurden im Verlauf des Montags (13. November) bekannt und weithin mit großer Spannung analysiert und kommentiert. Diese Veröffentlichungspraxis, intendiert als Schutz vor Manipulation, führte allerdings zu einer gewissen Verunsicherung, denn nach den Zahlen, die die Zeitungen am Dienstagmorgen veröffentlichen konnten, führte die DTA mit etwa 43% vor der SWAPO mit 35%. Bis zum Mittag waren jedoch auch die Resultate für die Bezirke Ovambo und Kavango bekannt, die das Bild entscheidend umkehrten. Am Abend des 14. November konnte - nach Auszählung der »tendered ballots«, die immerhin 14% aller Stimmen ausmachten - das Endergebnis veröffentlicht werden.

Danach erhielt SWAPO mit 57,3% der Stimmen eine klare Mehrheit, verfehlte jedoch ebenso deutlich die Zwei-Drittel-Mehrheit; die DTA erhielt 28,6% und lag damit erkennbar unter ihren eigenen Erwartungen. Das Ergebnis und die daraus resultierende Sitzverteilung in der Verfassunggebenden Versammlung gibt die folgende Tabelle wieder.

Tabelle 2
Wahlergebnisse und Sitzverteilung

Partei	Stimmen	Anteil (%)	Zahl der Sitze
SWAPO	384.567	57,3	41
DTA	191.532	28,6	21
UDF	37.874	5,6	4
ACN	23.728	3,5	3
NPF	10.693	1,6	1
FCN	10.452	1,6	1
NNF	5.344	0,8	1
SWAPO-D	3.161	0,5	-
CDA	2.495	0,4	-
NNDP	984	0,1	-
SUMME:	670.830	100,0	72

Zahl der ungültigen Stimmen: 8.532
Wahlbeteiligung: 95,6%

Quelle: The Namibian, 15.11.1989

Ab Dienstagmittag - noch bevor letzte Details des Ergebnisses bekannt waren - versammelten sich SWAPO-Anhänger im Zentrum von Windhoek, um den Wahlsieg mit Tanz und Gesängen auf den Straßen, Hupkonzerten etc. zu feiern. Die »Besetzung« des Schutztruppen-Denkmals, das mit SWAPO-Fahnen geschmückt wurde, markierte symbolisch das Ende des Kolonialismus. Von Aggressivität war in Windhoek nichts spürbar, die Stimmung war gelöst, die Polizei beschränkte sich weitgehend auf Verkehrsregelung auf der, wie manche Beobachter vermerkten, erstmals zu »wirklichem« Leben erwachten Kaiserstraße. Private Parties zogen sich bis spät in die Nacht. Im Norden kam es in den Tagen nach Bekanntgabe der Wahlergebnisse allerdings zu einer Serie gewaltsamer Übergriffe vor allem auf SWAPO-Mitglieder, vereinzelt auch auf Anhänger der DTA.

Athisaari bezeichnete die Wahlen als »shining lesson in democracy«, und alle Parteien erklärten, das Resultat zu akzeptieren. Auch wenn vereinzelt Vorbehalte geltend gemacht wurden, ging keiner der politischen Führer so weit, das Ergebnis insgesamt öffentlich infrage zu stellen; vielmehr sagten alle Parteien ihre konstruktive Mitarbeit bei der Verfassungsentwicklung für ein unabhängiges Namibia zu. Es gebe »keine Verlierer«, erklärte Sam Nujoma auf seiner ersten Pressekonferenz nach der Wahl.

Es gibt keinen Zweifel daran, daß die Wahlen »free and fair« im formalen, juristischen Sinn waren - die freie und geheime individuelle Entscheidung war möglich, es wurde kein unmittelbarer Druck ausgeübt, es gibt keine Anzeichen für eine Manipulation an den Ergebnissen. Der Kernpunkt des UN-Plans war somit - juristisch und politisch bindend - absolviert. Für die weite Akzeptanz des Wahlergebnisses - in Namibia wie international - war vermutlich ebenso hilfreich, daß keine relevante Interessengruppe in den Wahlen eine Total-niederlage erlitt: Das Wahlergebnis begrenzte die Ängste vor einer überwältigenden SWAPO-Dominanz, ohne das Selbstverständnis der SWAPO als entscheidende politische Gruppierung in Namibia so weit zu erschüttern, daß Panikreaktionen zu befürchten wären. Die Sitzverteilung in der Verfassunggebenden Versammlung verhindert außerdem, daß SWAPO und DTA als Blöcke aufeinanderprallen; vielmehr erlaubt die Präsenz mehrerer kleiner Parteien eine Vielzahl von Konstellationen, Kooperation ist gefordert. Aus diesen Gründen werteten vor allem liberale Beobachter das Wahlergebnis denn auch als geradezu ideales Resultat.

Andere, eher linksorientierte Beobachter hingegen hielten Zweifel daran aufrecht, ob die Wahl in einem umfassenderen Sinne wirklich das Verdikt »free and fair« verdienten. Dabei lenkten sie den Blick über den Wahlprozeß selbst hinaus auf die Vorgeschichte: die »intimidation« in der Vorwahlperiode, die während des Kriegs und erneut bei den »April-Ereignissen« vorgeführte Schlagkraft der südafrikanischen Staatsmacht, die Rolle der politisch-administrativ geförderten Ethnizität etc. Eine Beobachtergruppe des »Canadian Council for International Co-operation« faßte diese Einschätzung so zusammen: »[...] at least some of the black anti-SWAPO vote was a reflection of the pervasive influence of the white power structure and the economic dependence of black Namibians on that structure.« All die - für sich genommen geringfügigen - Vorfälle, Einflußmöglichkeiten und anderen Vorteile, die die Administration und die ihr nahestehenden Parteien gegen die SWAPO nutzen konnten, mögen sich durchaus zu merklichen Stimmenverlusten der SWAPO aufaddiert und einen deutlicheren Wahlsieg verhindert haben. Deshalb sollten diese Faktoren bei jeder Erklärung des Wahlergebnisses im Blick bleiben. Für eine umfassende Interpretation sind sie jedoch gewiß nicht hinreichend.

Tabelle 3: Die Wahlergebnisse in regionaler Aufgliederung: Anzahl der Stimmen

Bezirk	ACN	CDA	DTA	FCN	NNDP	NNF	NPF	SWAPO-D	SWAPO	UDF	gesamt
Nord-Namibia											
Ovambo	247	449	9.200	107	186	73	428	1172	197.100	4.674	213.636
Kavango	407	413	22.046	356	156	134	455	284	27.256	1.202	52.709
Caprivi	86	154	12.782	411	40	38	649	80	9.350	514	24.104
Kaokoland	33	71	6.699	83	51	31	2.152	20	1.025	41	10.206
Zentral-Namibia											
Windhoek	4.153	194	30.475	1.208	65	1.574	1.554	287	39.060	6.147	84.717
Swakopmund	1.020	24	4.998	318	4	207	119	49	11.479	1.400	19.618
Grootfontein	1.418	93	7.226	198	22	45	323	41	5.336	1.094	15.796
Gobabis	1.801	151	10.539	137	41	289	320	52	2.119	374	15.823
Hereroland	44	74	8.440	147	23	486	1.573	26	1.835	58	12.706
Damaraland	140	23	2.040	26	4	73	39	19	3.407	6.944	12.715
Tsumeb	848	32	3.452	78	7	41	45	44	6.476	1.085	12.108
Otjiwarongo	626	38	4.274	56	10	99	79	16	3.194	1.540	9.932
Okahandja	611	41	3.672	30	8	45	283	20	3.256	993	8.959
Outjo	719	32	2.658	73	2	21	39	9	984	1.186	5.723
Omaruru	198	38	2.538	30	3	152	280	18	1.022	499	4.778
Süd-Namibia											
Keetmanshoop	1.312	92	8.229	284	44	404	192	103	4.778	1.314	16.752
Karasburg	3.588	39	7.727	323	26	26	111	35	1.830	651	14.356
Rehoboth	96	58	6.590	4.499	68	252	196	38	2.460	326	14.583
Mariental	1.319	72	6.584	307	18	59	78	24	2.411	878	11.750
Lüderitz	453	15	1.890	56	7	204	56	21	5.422	342	8.466
Karibib	344	20	1.637	47	2	45	139	12	1.932	1.289	5.467
Maltahöhe	355	13	579	128	12	8	10	7	758	334	2.204
Bethanien	258	30	1.153	51	2	6	8	15	398	69	1.990
Zwischensumme:	20.076	2.166	165.428	8.953	801	4.312	9.128	2.392	332.888	32.954	579.098
»tendered votes«	3.652	329	26.104	1.499	183	1.032	1.565	769	51.679	4.920	91.732
SUMME:	23.728	2.495	191.532	10.452	984	5.344	10.693	3.161	384.567	37.874	670.830

Quelle: The Namibian, 15.11.1989, Angaben über »tendered votes« korrigiert.

Tabelle 4: Die Wahlergebnisse in regionaler Aufgliederung: Prozentuale Anteile

Bezirk	ACN	CDA	DTA	FCN	NNDP	NNF	NPF	SWAPO-D	SWAPO	UDF
Nord-Namibia										
Ovambo	0,1	0,2	4,3	0,1	0,1	0,0	0,2	0,5	92,3	2,2
Kavango	0,8	0,8	41,8	0,7	0,3	0,3	0,9	0,5	51,7	2,3
Caprivi	0,4	0,6	53,0	1,7	0,2	0,2	2,7	0,3	38,8	2,1
Kaokoland	0,3	0,7	65,6	0,8	0,5	0,3	21,1	0,2	10,0	0,4
Zentral-Namibia										
Windhoek	4,9	0,2	36,0	1,4	0,1	1,9	1,8	0,3	46,1	7,3
Swakopmund	5,2	0,1	25,5	1,6	0,0	1,1	0,6	0,2	58,5	7,1
Grootfontein	9,0	0,6	45,7	1,3	0,1	0,3	2,0	0,3	33,8	6,9
Gobabis	11,4	1,0	66,6	0,9	0,3	1,8	2,0	0,3	13,4	2,4
Hereroland	0,3	0,6	66,4	1,2	0,2	3,8	12,4	0,2	14,4	0,5
Damaraland	1,1	0,2	16,0	0,2	0,0	0,6	0,3	0,1	26,8	54,6
Tsumeb	7,0	0,3	28,5	0,6	0,1	0,3	0,4	0,4	53,5	9,0
Otjiwarongo	6,3	0,4	43,0	0,6	0,1	1,0	0,8	0,2	32,2	15,5
Okahandja	6,8	0,5	41,0	0,3	0,1	0,5	3,2	0,2	36,3	11,1
Outjo	12,6	0,6	46,4	1,3	0,0	0,4	0,7	0,2	17,2	20,7
Omaruru	4,1	0,8	53,1	0,6	0,1	3,2	5,9	0,4	21,4	10,4
Süd-Namibia										
Keetmanshoop	7,8	0,5	49,1	1,7	0,3	2,4	1,1	0,6	28,5	7,8
Karasburg	25,0	0,3	53,8	2,2	0,2	0,2	0,8	0,2	12,7	4,5
Rehoboth	0,7	0,4	45,2	30,9	0,5	1,7	1,3	0,3	16,9	2,2
Mariental	11,2	0,6	56,0	2,6	0,2	0,5	0,7	0,2	20,5	7,5
Lüderitz	5,4	0,2	22,3	0,7	0,1	2,4	0,7	0,2	64,0	4,0
Karibib	6,3	0,4	29,9	0,9	0,0	0,8	2,5	0,2	35,3	23,6
Maltahöhe	16,1	0,6	26,3	5,8	0,5	0,4	0,5	0,3	34,4	15,2
Bethanien	13,0	1,5	57,9	2,6	0,1	0,3	0,4	0,8	20,0	3,5
Zwischensumme:	3,5	0,4	28,6	1,5	0,1	0,7	1,6	0,4	57,5	5,7
»tendered votes«	4,0	0,4	28,5	1,6	0,2	1,1	1,7	0,8	56,3	5,4
SUMME:	3,5	0,4	28,6	1,6	0,1	0,8	1,6	0,5	57,3	5,6

Quelle: The Namibian, 15.11.1989, Angaben über »tendered votes« korrigiert.

Zur Analyse des Wahlergebnisses

Im Folgenden sollen die Wahlergebnisse etwas eingehender erläutert und Erklärungsansätze gegeben werden. Einen Überblick zur Verteilung der Stimmen in den Bezirken geben die Tabellen 3 und 4. (Die in Windhoek zentral ausgezählten »tendered votes« können aus prinzipiellen Gründen regional nicht eindeutig zugeordnet werden.)

Auch ein nur flüchtiger Blick auf die regionale Stimmenverteilung macht dramatische regionale Unterschiede und insbesondere die starke ethnische Komponente im Wahlergebnis deutlich, wie namibische und ausländische Beobachter sogleich vermerkten. Die SWAPO erhielt mehr als 92% der Stimmen im Ovamboland, und dieses Ergebnis war schon aufgrund der Größe des Bezirks - er umfaßte mehr als ein Drittel aller Wähler - in hohem Maße wahlentscheidend. Dieser Wahlerfolg übertraf die ohnehin schon hohen Erwartungen, und bei der DTA war man sichtlich schockiert über den eigenen Anteil von nur 4% der Stimmen.

Die Wahlen im Ovamboland folgten, so waren die meisten Beobachter sich einig, dem Muster der Unabhängigkeitswahlen in Zimbabwe im Jahre 1980. Zumindest in dieser Region Namibias entsprach die SWAPO dem Selbstbild einer Befreiungsbewegung als »authentische Vertretung« der gesamten Bevölkerung. Im Ovamboland hat die SWAPO nicht nur ihre historischen Wurzeln, sondern gewann im Verlauf des langwierigen Krieges offensichtlich auch eine Massenbasis, die unterschiedliche soziale Gruppen und Interessen - vom Kleinbauern über den Lehrer und den Pfarrer bis zum Geschäftsmann - integriert. Soweit erkennbar, bestand diese Massenbasis kaum in einer organisierten Form, denn unter Kriegsbedingungen war die SWAPO vermutlich kaum dazu in der Lage gewesen, permanente Untergrundstrukturen auszubilden, und der Wahlkampf, in dessen Verlauf sie - im Norden wie im restlichen Namibia - ein Netz von Regionalbüros aufbaute, war nur kurz. Der Wahlerfolg der SWAPO im Ovamboland beruhte somit wesentlich auf der Legitimation, die sich die Organisation durch den bewaffneten Kampf gegen Südafrika erworben hatte. Ein Wahlsieg der SWAPO würde darüber hinaus - dies war allseits erkennbar - das Ende des Kriegs und den endgültigen Abzug der südafrikanischen Armee bedeuten. In diesem Sinne gab es im Ovamboland wenig Alternativen zu einer Stimmabgabe für die SWAPO. Festzuhalten bleibt aber auch, daß der relativ hohe Grad von Gewalt und »intimidation«, der vor den Wahlen im Ovamboland stärker als irgendwo sonst in Namibia präsent war, keinerlei negative Auswirkungen auf den Wahlerfolg der SWAPO hatte. Im Endergebnis könnten sich diese Faktoren sogar als kontraproduktiv erwiesen haben, indem sie unbeabsichtigt Solidarisierungseffekte innerhalb der afrikanischen Gesellschaft gegenüber allen Einflüssen hervorriefen, die als südafrikanisch gesteuert verstanden wurden.

Die SWAPO konnte Wahlergebnisse, die ihrem Erfolg im Ovamboland vergleichbar wären, nirgendwo sonst in Namibia erzielen. Absolute Mehrheiten erreichte die Partei vor allem in Wahlbezirken mit einem hohen Anteil von Wanderarbeitern aus dem Ovamboland (Lüderitz, Swakopmund, Tsumeb) sowie im Bezirk Kavango. In Windhoek, dem zweitgrößten Wahlbezirk und politischen Zentrum des Landes, wurde die SWAPO zwar stärkste Partei, doch nur mit einem enttäuschenden Anteil von 46% der Stimmen. Im Rest des Landes, in dem andere ethnische Gruppen als die Ovambo dominieren, erzielte die SWAPO fast überall (Ausnahmen waren Karibib und Maltahöhe) drastisch geringere Stimmenanteile und wurde allenfalls zweitstärkste Partei, in der Regel nach der DTA.

Eine »ethnische Interpretation« des Wahlergebnisses liegt somit auf der Hand. Tatsächlich machten führende Politiker der anderen Parteien (besonders DTA und NPF) denn auch unmittelbar nach Bekanntwerden der Wahlergebnisse deutlich, daß die SWAPO sich mit diesem Ergebnis ihrer Auffassung nach endgültig als »Ovambo-Partei« erwiesen habe - wie ihre Gegner es schon immer behauptet hatten. Freilich gilt der ethnische Faktor nicht allein für das Wahlergebnis der SWAPO, sondern betrifft auch die meisten anderen Parteien Namibias.

Klare ethnische Schwerpunkte zeigten sich bei der FCN (Rehoboth), der NPF (Herero), der UDF (Damara) und der ACN (Weiße). Die ersten drei der genannten Gruppierungen waren dabei mit dem Anspruch angetreten, überethnische Allianzen zu sein, doch erwies sich bei allen von ihnen jeweils eine Partei als dominant. Die ACN war von vornherein allein als Partei der Weißen konzipiert. Die NNF, die nur äußerst knapp einen Sitz in der Verfassunggebenden Versammlung erreichte, besaß ebenfalls - wenn auch schwächer ausgeprägt - einen ethnischen Schwerpunkt (bei der Bevölkerungsgruppe der Herero, Folge der Einbeziehung der SWANU-»Progressives«), auch wenn sie stärker als die anderen Parteien die programmatisch-ideologische Orientierung in den Vordergrund ihres Wahlkampfs gerückt hatte und ihre Stimmen in Windhoek und im Süden aus diesem Grund erhielt.

Eine relativ »ausgeglichene ethnische Bilanz« kann allein die DTA für sich in Anspruch nehmen - und dies gilt auch nur dann, wenn die Bevölkerungsgruppen Ovambo und Damara von der Betrachtung ebenso ausgeklammert werden wie die »Überrepräsentation« der Herero. Das Wahlresultat der DTA trägt deutlich den Charakter einer Koalition der nicht-Ovambo-Gruppen in Namibia, zentriert um die Herero-Politik, und ist damit selbst Ausdruck einer ethnisch orientierten Politik. Die DTA hat diese Politik seit ihrer Gründung verfolgt und sie sogar in ihrer Parteiverfassung formell fixiert. Man mag die Bedeutung von Ethnizität als organisierendem Faktor der Politik in Namibia beklagen, doch haben manche derjenigen, die dies jetzt tun, Ethnizität lange genug in »homelands« und »second tier«-Verwaltungen kultiviert. Eine Kritik an der starken Ovambo-Basis der SWAPO fällt nach dem Wahlergebnis vom November 1989 leicht, doch sollte dabei nicht übersehen werden, daß der ethnische Faktor in der namibischen Politik in Namibia jahrzehntelang durch die südafrikanische Apartheid-Politik zugespitzt wurde und ihr historisches Erbe darstellt.

Einige weitere Anmerkungen sind angebracht, um die allzu gradlinige ethnische Interpretation des Wahlergebnisses, wie sie vor allem in der Berichterstattung der internationalen Presse erfolgte, zumindest zu relativieren. Das Wahlergebnis läßt sich durchaus etwas differenzierter betrachten - sowohl im Hinblick auf die ethnische Interpretation als auch durch Berücksichtigung anderer Faktoren.

Zunächst einmal ist zu betonen, daß bei den Wahlen unterschiedliche Muster der politischen Affiliierung bei den verschiedenen ethnischen Gruppen deutlich wurden. Einen ähnlich weitreichenden und eindeutigen ethnischen Integrationserfolg wie die SWAPO im Ovamboland erzielte keine andere Partei bei irgendeiner anderen Bevölkerungsgruppe. Das Ovamboland stimmte als ethnischer Block für die SWAPO, und die beiden Parteien, deren wichtigstes Wählerpotential man in dieser Region vermutet hatte - SWAPO-D und CDA - erlitten eine vernichtende Wahlniederlage. Für diese beiden Gruppierungen gilt gleichermaßen, daß ihre führenden Politiker bei aller Kritik an Südafrika vermutlich durch ihre Mitarbeit in »Übergangs-« bzw. »second tier«-Regierungen diskreditiert worden waren. Bei allen anderen Bevölkerungsgruppen verteilten sich die Stimmen auf mehrere Parteien, in manchen Fällen kam es sogar zu einer ausgesprochen starken Parteienkonkurrenz. So teilten SWAPO und DTA die Stimmen in Caprivi und Kavango untereinander auf, DTA und FCN die in Rehoboth, DTA und ACN die Stimmen der Weißen und DTA, NPF und - in begrenztem Maße - NNF die der Herero. Trotz aller Erfolge der DTA gibt es keinen geschlossenen gegen die SWAPO gerichteten ethnischen Block.

Zweitens wird bei einer rein ethnischen Interpretation des Wahlergebnisses leicht übersehen, daß die SWAPO auch außerhalb des Ovambolands bei fast allen Bevölkerungsgruppen des Landes substantielle Stimmenanteile erhielt, auch wenn sie dort keine Mehrheiten gewann. Die Gesamtzahl der Stimmen, die die SWAPO außerhalb des Wahlbezirks Ovambo erreichte, betrug immerhin mehr als 80% dessen, was die DTA in ganz Namibia erzielte. Klammert man die SWAPO-Hochburgen (im Norden und in den Zentren der Wanderarbeit) aus, so erzielte die SWAPO durchschnittlich noch immer einen Stimmenanteil von 20% (bzw. 34%, wenn Windhoek in die Berechnung mit einbezogen wird). Für das Erreichen der absoluten Mehrheit war es unumgänglich, daß die SWAPO neben dem fast vollständigen Ovambo-Wählerpotential diese Wähler in anderen Landesteilen für sich zu mobilisieren vermochte.

Ihre stärksten Einbrüche erlitt die SWAPO im Kaokoland, das einen starken Herero-Bevölkerungsanteil aufweist, und wo zudem viele Jahre lang Teile der Bevölkerung durch die südafrikanische Armee direkt in den Krieg gegen die Guerillas der PLAN mit einbezogen worden waren, in Rehoboth, das seine spezifischen Traditionen regionaler Autonomie besitzt, und in allen Bezirken Zentral-Namibias mit einem hohen Anteil von Herero-Bevölkerung. Hier kam der langjährige politische Konflikt zwischen SWAPO einerseits und den Herero-Chiefs und der SWANU andererseits (bei allen Konflikten der beiden letztgenannten Gruppen untereinander) zur Geltung. In Teilen Süd-Namibias (»Namaland«) dagegen konnte die SWAPO ein deutlich besseres Resultat erzielen und in zwei Bezirken sogar stärkste Partei werden, auch wenn dies angesichts der geringen Bevölkerungsdichte dieser Regionen von geringer Bedeutung für das nationale Wahlergebnis blieb. Wichtig waren hierfür die Verbindungen zwischen Nama-Organisationen und der SWAPO, die bereits seit Mitte der siebziger Jahre bestehen und im SWAPO-Vizepräsidenten Hendrik Witbooi personifiziert sind.

Der SWAPO-Stimmenanteil in Zentral- und Süd-Namibia fällt aus dem ethnischen Interpretationsmuster heraus, doch ist ohne genauere Wahl- und Sozialforschung schwer zu ermitteln, wer eigentlich die typischen SWAPO-Wähler in diesen Gebieten waren. Dennoch lassen sich zumindest vorläufige Schlüsse aus einzelnen Beobachtungen und Berichten ziehen. Manches weist darauf hin, daß in Zentral- und Süd-Namibia vor allem diejenigen Gruppen der Bevölkerung die SWAPO unterstützten, die eine bessere Schulausbildung und einen (relativ) höheren materiellen Standard besitzen. Demgegenüber tendierten die armen Bevölkerungsgruppen eher zu einer Stimmabgabe für die DTA. Nicht zuletzt die Tatsache, daß die DTA auf ihren Wahlkampfveranstaltungen häufig Nahrungsmittel umsonst verteilte, mag als Indiz dafür gewertet werden, auf welche Gruppen ihre Kampagne besonders abzielte. Das unter SWAPO-Aktivisten in Windhoek kursierende Motto »We eat at DTA, but we vote for SWAPO« besaß jedenfalls, wie das Wahlergebnis zeigte, nicht unbedingt im ganzen Land Gültigkeit. Die Abhängigkeit armer Bevölkerungsgruppen von sozialer und materieller Patronage hat auf diese Weise sicherlich das Wahlergebnis geprägt, auch wenn die Stimmabgabe selbst geheim war.

Es ist viel darüber spekuliert und diskutiert worden, inwieweit die beiden schwerwiegendsten politischen Fehlleistungen der SWAPO - ihre Rolle in den »April-Ereignissen« und die Behandlung ihrer Gefangenen in Angola - das Wahlergebnis entscheidend zu ihren Ungunsten geprägt haben. Auch hier sind definitive Aussagen schwer zu treffen, da nicht auf Meinungsumfragen o.ä. zurückgegriffen werden kann. Die Kämpfe im April 1989 führten zweifellos zu einer Vertrauenskrise gegenüber der SWAPO, vorrangig allerdings in der internationalen Politik, weniger in Namibia selbst, wo sie, wie bereits erwähnt, während der Wahlen kein Thema mehr waren. Innenpolitisch weitaus brisanter hingegen waren die Enthüllungen im Zusammenhang mit den »detainees«, wenn auch nicht in Nord-Namibia, wo die von der Partei gegebenen Erklärungen - die immer präsente Gefahr der Spionage, der Hinweis auf die Kriegssituation - generell akzeptiert wurden. Im Süden dagegen ist der Vertrauensverlust am Wahlergebnis direkt ablesbar, insbesondere im Wahlbezirk Keetmannshoop, in dem SWAPO-Vizepräsident Hendrik Witbooi lebt (Personen aus Witboois Familienkreis waren von den Verhaftungen und Folterungen betroffen). Die

SWAPO wurde hier nur zweitstärkste Partei mit deutlichem Abstand nach der DTA. Die UDF, in der sich ehemalige Gefangene organisiert hatten, erreichte in Keetmanshoop (und ähnlich im Nachbarbezirk Mariental) einen Anteil von knapp 8% der Stimmen, im Bezirk Maltahöhe, der direkt an Witboois Heimatort Gibeon angrenzt, sogar 15%. Daß die UDF darüber hinaus 2,2% der Stimmen im Ovamboland erhielt - es überraschte sie selbst, da sie dort gar keinen Wahlkampf betrieben hatte - mag ebenfalls auf das »detainee«-Problem zurückzuführen sein; SWAPO-Anhänger sind allerdings eher der Meinung, daß manche Wähler hier die Symbole von SWAPO und UDF auf dem Stimmzettel verwechselten. Insgesamt gesehen ist aber unzweifelhaft, daß die UDF nicht mit den Damara-Stimmen allein zur drittstärksten Partei in Namibia wurde, sondern auch als Ergebnis des »detainee«-Problems der SWAPO.

Die DTA erhielt deutlich weniger Stimmen, als man im Parteihauptquartier vor den Wahlen erwartet hatte. Unerklärlich blieb für sie vor allem der dramatische Einbruch im Bezirk Ovambo: Die Bevölkerungsgruppe, die besonders als DTA-Klientel infragegekommen wäre - Angehörige der süd(west)afrikanischen Verwaltungen und des Sicherheitsapparats - war größer als die Anzahl von 9200 Stimmen, die die DTA am Ende erhielt. Enttäuscht war man bei der DTA auch über den Erfolg der ACN bei den weißen Wählern, da mit einer Verstärkung liberaler Positionen in dieser Wählergruppe gerechnet worden war. Die auffällige Konzentration von ACN-Stimmen im Bezirk Karasburg (25%) ist allerdings vor allem auf Wähler aus Südafrika zurückzuführen, die sich hier konzentrierten. Inwieweit die ACN auch Stimmen aus der schwarzen Wählerschaft erhielt, ist nicht zu ermitteln.

Ihre größten Erfolge erzielte die DTA in Wahlbezirken mit einem hohen Anteil von Herero-Bevölkerung - dies, wie bereits erwähnt, ein traditionelles Muster ethnischer Polarisierung. Für das DTA-Gesamtergebnis wichtig waren auch ihre Erfolge in Kavango und Caprivi. In beiden Fällen wurde das Wahlresultat durch sub-ethnische Gegensätze beeinflußt. In Caprivi erwies sich der DTA-Spitzenkandidat Mishake Muyongo trotz - oder gerade wegen - seiner bewegten politischen Vergangenheit (als ehemaliger SWAPO-Vizepräsident) als Integrationsfigur. Vielleicht hat auch der föderative Charakter der DTA dem Bedürfnis nach einer gewissen Eigenständigkeit einer Region wie Caprivi eher entsprochen, die sich soziokulturell in mancher Hinsicht stärker nach Zimbabwe oder Zambia orientiert als nach Windhoek.

Die DTA hat bei den Wahlen vermutlich vom »bandwagon effect« profitiert: Potentielle Wähler kleinerer Parteien sahen sie zusehends als einzig »sichere«, weil ausreichend starke Alternative in Opposition zu einer als dominant wahrgenommenen SWAPO. Die unübersehbare Polarisierung zwischen SWAPO und DTA im Wahlkampf hat diesen Prozeß gefördert, der auf Kosten vor allem von NPF und FCN, vielleicht auch der CDA, ging. Alle kleinen Parteien betrachteten darüber hinaus ihre organisatorischen und finanziellen Schwierigkeiten als wichtige Gründe für ihr schlechtes Abschneiden bei der Wahl. Die NNF litt hierunter sicher am stärksten, weil sie - nach eigenen Aussagen - keine Finanzierung von außen erhielt.

Zusammenfassend gesprochen hatte der ethnische Faktor in der Politik Namibias unbestreitbar ein entscheidendes Gewicht für den Ausgang der Wahlen zur Verfassunggebenden Versammlung im November 1989, doch er war nicht der einzige relevante Faktor. Im Gegensatz von SWAPO und DTA drückte sich eine ethnische Polarisierung zwischen der Bevölkerungsgruppe der Ovambo und den anderen Gruppen des Landes (zentriert um Herero und Weiße) aus. Er hat auch Elemente eines Nord-Süd-Gegensatzes. Einige Gruppen fallen aus diesem Muster jedoch heraus, speziell die Damara um die UDF, aber auch die Bevölkerung in Kavango und Caprivi, deren politische Affiliierung zwischen SWAPO und DTA gespalten ist. Zugleich steht diese ethnische Polarisierung aber auch für den jahrzehntelang gewachsenen und erbittert umkämpften Gegensatz zwischen einer stringent anti-südafrikanischen Politik einerseits und einer von Südafrika angeleiteten und unterstützten Politik andererseits. Dieser Gegensatz hat das ethnische Moment in den Wahlen bei weitem nicht auslöschen können, doch er hat es zumindest an einigen Stellen aufgebrochen. Dies ist ein wesentlicher, wenn auch begrenzter Erfolg eines namibischen Nationalismus, wie ihn die SWAPO repräsentiert.

Für Prognosen über zukünftige Entwicklungen im Parteiensystem Namibias ist es noch sehr früh; dennoch scheint zumindest eine Spekulation sinnvoll. Die Option eines Ein-Parteien-Systems, die sich die SWAPO in ihrem Wahlprogramm vorbehalten hatte, ist durch das Wahlergebnis in weite Ferne gerückt und auf absehbare Zeit nicht ohne massive innenpolitische Konflikte (und letztlich Verfassungsbruch) durchsetzbar. Sieben Parteien sind im Parlament nach der Unabhängigkeit vertreten. Dennoch kann die Polarisierung zwischen SWAPO und DTA als Ausgangspunkt für die faktische Herausbildung eines Zwei-Parteien-Systems verstanden werden, in das die kleinen Parteien sich mehr und mehr werden einfügen müssen. Ob diese Zuordnung vor allem nach ethnischen oder nach anderen politischen Prinzipien erfolgt, ist eine entscheidende Frage für die politische Kultur in Namibia nach der Unabhängigkeit. Die Antwort ist offen; das vorhandene interethnische Mißtrauen, das die Wahlen zur Verfassunggebenden Versammlung so prägte, wird eine behutsame Politik erfordern.

5. Verfassungsdiskussion und Entwicklungen nach der Wahl

Die Sitzverteilung in der Verfassunggebenden Versammlung ließ vielfältige Spekulationen über mögliche Konstellationen und Koalitionen oder auch über potentielle Blockade-Strategien einzelner Parteien zu. Andererseits erklärten alle Parteien, am Verfassungsprozeß konstruktiv mitwirken zu wollen; an einer Verzögerung und damit Gefährdung des Unabhängigkeitsprozesses habe niemand Interesse, alle Parteien erklärten Kompromißbereitschaft. Entsprechende Gespräche zwischen den Parteien setzten unmittelbar nach der Wahl ein.

Am 21. November - nur eine Woche nach Bekanntgabe der Wahlergebnisse - wurde die Verfassunggebende Versammlung in Windhoeks Tintenpalast feierlich eröffnet. SWAPO-Wahlkampfdirektor Hage G. Geingob wurde mit 47 Stimmen (d.h. nicht nur von den SWAPO-Vertretern) zum Vorsitzenden gewählt. Den politischen Höhepunkt der ersten Sitzung bildete die überraschende formelle Anerkennung der »Prinzipien von 1982« durch die SWAPO. Dieser Katalog rechtsstaatlich-demokratischer Verfassungsprinzipien war im Kontext der Verhandlungen der Kontaktgruppe entstanden, und die SWAPO hatte ihn bereits damals akzeptiert. In der Schlußphase des Wahlkampfs waren die »Prinzipien« jedoch erneut in die Diskussion gekommen. Die SWAPO hatte erklärt, sie inhaltlich nach wie vor zu unterstützen, doch wolle sie sich nicht durch Südafrika oder die UN formell darauf festschreiben lassen. Die Erklärung Geingobs vom 21. November, die SWAPO betrachte die »Prinzipien« als Arbeitsgrundlage der Versammlung, löste eine breite Zustimmung quer durch die Parteienlandschaft aus und diente zugleich als Signal für Kooperations- und Kompromißbereitschaft.

Die Arbeit an der Formulierung der Verfassung konnte unter diesen Bedingungen zügig voranschreiten. Hält man sich die nicht unproblematische Sitzverteilung in der Versammlung vor Augen, verlief dieser Prozeß sogar ausgesprochen kooperativ und relativ konfliktarm, wie viele Beobachter überrascht vermerkten. Bereits nach vier Wochen hieß es, in fast allen grundsätzlichen Fragen sei Einigkeit erzielt worden, und obwohl es im Januar 1990 schließlich doch noch zu Auseinandersetzungen um einige Fragen kam, vermochte dies den Gesamteindruck der Kooperation aller Parteien kaum zu schmälern. Am 9. Februar 1990 - nach nicht einmal drei Monaten Beratungszeit - wurde die Verfassung verabschiedet, und sämtliche in der Versammlung vertretenen Parteien stimmten ihr zu. Als Unabhängigkeitsdatum wurde der 21. März 1990 festgesetzt. Eine tiefergehende Analyse der Diskussionen um die Verfassung kann hier nicht erfolgen, doch soll zumindest ein Überblick zu den wichtigsten Entwicklungen gegeben werden.

Die Formulierung des Verfassungstexts erfolgte weitgehend unter Ausschluß der Öffentlichkeit. Keine der Parteien hatte bis zur Eröffnung der Verfassunggebenden Versammlung einen ausformulierten eigenen Entwurf der Öffentlichkeit präsentiert - bei der SWAPO arbeitete man offenbar noch daran, für mehrere der anderen Parteien dienten überarbeitete Versionen eines 1986/87 im Rahmen der »Multi-Party-Conference« erarbeiteten Verfassungsentwurfs als Ausgangs- und Bezugspunkt der weiteren Diskussion. Die Beratungen wurden nach wenigen Sitzungen der Verfassunggebenden Versammlung in ein »Standing Committee« (mit Repräsentanten aus allen in der Versammlung vertretenen Parteien) verlagert und auf diese Weise effektiv dem Blick - und der Einflußnahme und Kritik - der Öffentlichkeit entzogen. Zentrale Funktionen als juristische Experten besaßen die Rechtsanwälte Hartmut Ruppel (SWAPO) und Vekuii Rukoro (NNF), beide Vertreter ihrer jeweiligen Parteien in der Versammlung. Am 20. Dezember legte das Komitee einen Bericht vor, wonach über alle wichtigen Punkte Einigkeit erzielt worden sei. Daraufhin wurde die Ausarbeitung des eigentlichen Verfassungstexts einer Gruppe von drei südfrikanischen Juristen übertragen, die in einem Vertrauensverhältnis zu verschiedenen namibischen Parteien standen. Sie legten dem Komitee am 9. Januar 1990 einen ausformulierten Entwurf vor, der im Verlauf der Diskussionen in den folgenden Wochen in mehreren Punkten modifiziert wurde. Dieser Entwurf wurde nicht publiziert, doch gelangten Exemplare in die Öffentlichkeit, und die lokale Presse berichtete ausführlich über ihn. Der Gewerkschaftsbund NUNW forderte sogleich eine offizielle Publikation des Entwurfs, um allen interessierten Gruppen und Personen Gelegenheit zur Stellungsnahme zu geben. Dies geschah jedoch nicht, und südafrikanischen Zeitungsberichten zufolge soll dies zu einem ernsthaften Konflikt zwischen NUNW und SWAPO geführt haben, was der Gewerkschaftsbund allerdings dementierte. Zur ersten öffentlichen Diskussion des Entwurfs in der Verfassunggebenden Versammlung kam es erst am 29. Januar - elf Tage vor der endgültigen Verabschiedung. Kritik an unzureichender öffentlicher Diskussion und an einer allzu schnellen Verabschiedung der Verfassung wurde weiterhin vereinzelt geübt, etwa durch die »Interessengemeinschaft deutschsprachiger Südwester«.

Die Verfassung des unabhängigen Namibia etabliert ein Modell westlichparlamentarischer Demokratie mit einer starken Position des Staatspräsidenten nach US-amerikanischem Vorbild, das von allen Seiten als vorbildhaft gewertet wurde. Der Verfassungstext ist im Dokumentationsteil im Wortlaut wiedergegeben, deshalb werden an dieser Stelle nur Grundelemente und einige Spezifika, die ihre Ursachen in der besonderen Situation und historischen Erfahrung Namibias haben, aufgeführt.

- Die Republik Namibia wird als »sovereign, secular, democratic and unitary State« mit klassischer Gewaltenteilung beschrieben; ihr Territorium umfaßt Walvis Bay und einige Inseln, die derzeit von Südafrika beansprucht werden.
- Ein Grundrechtskatalog definiert Persönlichkeits- und Freiheitsrechte, wie sie in einer demokratischen Gesellschaft üblich sind. Besonders betont werden u.a. das Verbot von Zwangsarbeit, spezielle Rechte für Kinder (Begrenzung der Kinderarbeit auf Farmen) sowie ein Recht auf Ausbildung (Schulpflicht bis ins Alter von 16 Jahren). Die Todesstrafe wird abgeschafft - eine Ausnahme in Afrika. Das Recht auf Eigentum und - im Enteignungsfall - auf »gerechte« Entschädigung wird garantiert. Ein Ombudsman soll nach skandinavischem Vorbild die Durchsetzung der Persönlichkeitsrechte gegenüber Politik und Verwaltung erleichtern.
- Ein Staatspräsident wird direkt durch das Volk für einen Zeitraum von fünf Jahren mit absoluter Mehrheit gewählt; er kann nur einmal wiedergewählt werden. Der Präsident besitzt weitreichende Vollmachten bei der Formulie-

rung seiner Politik, bei der Ernennung des Kabinetts, bei der Besetzung von Spitzenpositionen im Öffentlichen Dienst und letztlich auch im Prozeß der Gesetzgebung, denn er kann im Konfliktfall nur nach einem komplizierten Verfahren und mit einer Zwei-Drittel-Mehrheit des Parlaments zur Zustimmung zu Gesetzen gezwungen werden. Umgekehrt kann der Präsident bei verfassungsändernden Gesetzen ein Referendum abhalten lassen, wenn die Zwei-Drittel-Mehrheit im Parlament dafür fehlt. Der Staatspräsident kann bei schweren Gesetzesverstößen durch »impeachment« (dazu ist eine Zwei-Drittel-Mehrheit in beiden Kammern des Parlaments notwendig) abgesetzt werden.

- Allgemeine Wahlen zum Parlament (»National Assembly«) werden ebenfalls im Fünf-Jahres-Turnus abgehalten (Verhältniswahlrecht). Eine zweite Kammer, der »National Council«, wird durch die »Regional Councils« gewählt und besitzt Einspruchsmöglichkeiten im Gesetzgebungsprozeß, soweit es nicht Steuer- und Finanzfragen betrifft, bei denen sie nur konsultativ tätig wird. Die Regional Councils wiederum werden direkt gewählt (Mehrheitswahlrecht) und besitzen Kompetenzen im lokalen und regionalen Bereich. Die regionale Gliederung Namibias erfolgt nach der Unabhängigkeit durch eine speziell dafür eingesetzte Kommission. Das Ziel ist, regionale Belange politisch zur Geltung zu bringen und ein Gegengewicht zum Zentralstaat zu schaffen, ohne dabei die Strukturen der Apartheid-Gesellschaft zu reproduzieren.

- Die Unabhängigkeit der Gerichte wird garantiert, u.a. durch die Ernennung von Richtern auf Lebenszeit. Ein »Supreme Court« stellt die Einklagbarkeit von Grundrechten sicher.

- Das in der Verfassung enthaltene Notstandsrecht erlaubt die Suspendierung von Grundrechten. Ein Notstand kann vom Staatspräsidenten ausgerufen und muß durch die Nationalversammlung innerhalb eines Monats bestätigt werden.

- Englisch wird Amtssprache, alle anderen in Namibia gesprochenen Sprachen werden in Schulen und - nach entsprechender Gesetzgebung - auch in Verwaltung und Justiz zugelassen. Damit ist die Bedeutung von Afrikaans de jure entscheidend zurückgedrängt. Privatschulen werden - dies war besonders der deutschen Minderheit wichtig - aber in allen relevanten Sprachen zugelassen, soweit sie bei der Aufnahme von Schülern nicht ethnisch diskriminieren.

- Die Verfassung enthält eine Liste von »politischen Prinzipien« (»Principles of State Policy«), die als solche allerdings nicht einklagbar sind. Sie umfaßt insbesondere soziale Rechte (Gleichberechtigung von Frauen, Rechte von Arbeitern und alten Menschen u.a.), ökologische Prinzipien, Grundregeln der Außenpolitik (insbesondere die Blockfreiheit) sowie die Grundprinzipien der Eigentumsordnung im Sinne einer »mixed economy«. Das Parlament soll einen »Investment Code« für Auslandsinvestitionen beschließen. Was an spezifischer SWAPO-Programmatik in die Verfassung des unabhängigen Namibia eingegangen ist, findet sich (neben der Präambel) vor allem in diesen Artikeln.

- Als Übergangsregelung werden die zum Zeitpunkt der Unabhängigkeit bestehende Verfassunggebende Versammlung ohne Neuwahlen in die erste »National Assembly« überführt und der erste Staatspräsident durch sie (und nicht direkt vom Volk) gewählt.

In mehreren Punkten weicht die gültige Verfassung signifikant von der Version ab, die zum Jahreswechsel 1989/90 durch die südafrikanische Expertengruppe erarbeitet worden war. Auf diese Weise lassen sich einige Bereiche identifizieren, in denen es Dissens gab, allerdings ohne daß dabei in allen Fällen ermittelt werden kann, welche Partei welche Position vertrat. Der ursprüngliche Entwurf hatte eine Wahl des Staatspräsidenten durch die »National Assembly« vorgesehen, aber auch mehr parlamentarische Kontrollen über ihn (besonders bei Personal- und Besetzungsfragen), als dies in der endgültigen Fassung zu finden ist. Insgesamt war eine Tendenz zur Stärkung der Exekutive gegenüber dem Parlament unverkennbar; damit setzten sich allem Anschein nach vor allem die Vorstellungen der SWAPO in diesem Bereich durch. Im Gegenzug wurden die Bestimmungen für die zweite parlamentarische Kammer konkretisiert und die Kompetenzen dieses Gremiums erheblich ausgeweitet. Hier wurde den Forderungen der kleineren Parteien nach Elementen regionaler Repräsentation Rechnung getragen, ohne daß dies Föderalisierung oder gar eine erneute ethnische Gliederung des Landes bedeutet. Es ist bemerkenswert, daß in dieser aufgrund der Apartheid-Erfahrungen außerordentlich sensiblen Frage ohne von außen erkennbare Konflikte zwischen den Parteien eine Übereinkunft erzielt werden konnte.

Manche Formulierungen in den »politischen Prinzipien« (ebenso in der Präambel) wurden überarbeitet, und auch wenn es sich dabei nur um Nuancen handelt, bedeutete dies doch eine Tendenz zur Ersetzung programmatischer Prinzipien der SWAPO durch »neutralere« Formulierungen im Verfassungstext. So hatte der Entwurf noch von »social, economic and political justice« gesprochen, dagegen heißt es in der Endfassung nur mehr »justice for all«. Öffentlich kaum registriert wurde die Verlagerung des Asylrechts vom Grundrechtskatalog in die geringerwertigen »politischen Prinzipien« - der biographischen Erfahrung vieler SWAPO-Mitglieder und auch manch führendem Politiker in anderen Parteien wird dies sicher nicht gerecht. Öffentliche Auseinandersetzungen gab es hingegen Anfang Februar 1990 um die Frage, ob Namibia überhaupt eine Armee bekommen (und dies in der Verfassung fixiert werden) sollte. Die »Association for the Handicapped« führte eine Kampagne für Demilitarisierung durch, die viele Politiker und Kommentatoren mit Wohlwollen betrachteten, aber am Ende erfolglos blieb.

Das auch in der Öffentlichkeit am stärksten umstrittene Element der Verfassung waren die Regelungen zur »preventive detention«, die der Entwurf vom

Januar vorgesehen hatte. Danach wäre Vorbeugehaft (d.h. Haft ohne richterliche Überprüfung innerhalb der üblichen 48 Stunden) bei »clear and present danger to the security of the State« für einen Zeitraum von 30 Tagen zugelassen und bei Zustimmung durch einen »Advisory Board« im individuellen Fall bis auf ein Jahr verlängerbar gewesen. Vorbeugehaft gehört zum üblichen staatlichen Instrumentarium im ganzen Südlichen Afrika und hätte insofern kaum eine staatrechtliche Besonderheit dargestellt. Andererseits war sie in Namibia unter südafrikanischer Kontrolle oft eingesetzt worden, auch und gerade gegen SWAPO-Mitglieder; vor allem aber weckte sie Mißtrauen angesichts der Erfahrungen der SWAPO-»detainees«. In der Verfassunggebenden Versammlung kam es in dieser Frage zu einer Koalition der Staatsraison aus SWAPO und DTA, die sich beide für die Beibehaltung der Vorbeugehaft aussprachen, während die kleinen Parteien (vor allem UDF, NNF und NPF) erbittert dagegen argumentierten. Auch die SWAPO-nahe Presse stand der Vorbeugehaft kritisch gegenüber. Nach langer Diskussion in der Versammlung und erneuten parteiinternen Beratungen wurde die Vorbeugehaft am 31. Januar 1990 schließlich aus dem Entwurf gestrichen, was nicht nur in Namibia Erleichterung auslöste. Als Bestandteil des Notstandsrechts freilich bleibt Vorbeugehaft weiterhin möglich.

Die Verfassung Namibias gilt, nachdem mit der Vorbeugehaft der »black spot on an otherwise impeccable document« (Vekuii Rukoro, NNF) gestrichen wurde, als Musterbeispiel demokratischer Ordnung und wurde von allen Parteien als solches anerkannt, auch wenn einzelne Vorbehalte formuliert wurden. So verwahrte sich die ACN gegen die radikale Verurteilung der Apartheid in der Präambel und kritisierte eine mangelnde Berücksichtigung von »group rights« und kulturellen Besonderheiten. Die FCN protestierte sogar mit einer spektakukären, aber friedlich verlaufenden Besetzung der Regierungsgebäude in Rehoboth am 4. Februar 1990 gegen eine als unzureichend empfundene regionale und lokale Selbständigkeit. Beide Parteien erklärten zunächst, sie wollten sich bei der Abstimmung über die Verfassung der Stimme enthalten oder - im Falle der FCN - sogar gegen sie votieren. Die Annahme am 9. Februar erfolgte jedoch ohne Gegenstimme. Die Wahl Sam Nujomas zum ersten Staatspräsidenten des unabhängigen Namibia genau eine Woche später erfolgte, ohne daß überhaupt ein Gegenkandidat aufgestellt wurde.

Die schnellen Fortschritte in der Arbeit der Verfassunggebenden Versammlung führten zu einem generellen Optimismus über die politische Entwicklung im Land. Bereits am 21. Dezember 1989 hatte Sam Nujoma eine (an einzelnen Punkten noch unvollständige) Kabinettsliste vorgestellt und damit die Grundzüge zukünftiger SWAPO-Regierungspolitik deutlich gemacht (vgl. Anhang). Premierminister wurde der aufgrund seiner Tätigkeit als Vorsitzender der Verfassunggebenden Versammlung allseits anerkannte Hage G. Geingob. Viele wichtige Ministerpositionen gingen an bekannte SWAPO-Politiker, die teilweise bereits analoge Funktionen für die Partei im Exil ausgeübt hatten. Die erste SWAPO-Regierung des unabhängigen Namibia ist keine breite

Koalitionsregierung, doch wurden UDF und NNF durch Vergabe von stellvertretenden Ministerpositionen (an Reggie Diergaardt und Vekuii Rukoro) in die Regierung eingebunden. Mehrere Schlüsselfunktionen im wirtschaftlichen Bereich (Finanzen, Landwirtschaft, Planungskommission, Rechnungsprüfung) wurden von parteipolitisch ungebundenen Experten aus der europäischen Bevölkerungsgruppe übernommen. Gerade diese Ernennungen sind als Signale der Vertrauensbildung an die weiße Bevölkerung und an die in Namibia engagierten internationalen Firmen zu verstehen. Über mehrere Wochen hielten sich sogar Spekulationen, ein führender ACN-Politiker könnte Landwirtschaftsminister werden, was schließlich an ACN-internen Konflikten gescheitert sein soll. Eine Mitte Februar gehaltene Rede des designierten Finanzministers, Otto Herrigel, zur zukünftigen Wirtschaftspolitik traf auf breite Zustimmung bei den anderen Parteien und - vor allem - in Geschäftskreisen. Dazu gehörten insbesondere der vorläufige Verbleib Namibias in der südafrikanischen Zollunion (an deren Einnahmen das Land besser beteiligt werden soll) und auch der vorläufige Verzicht auf eine eigene Währung und Zentralbank (auf einen Zeitpunkt von zwei Jahren nach der Unabhängigkeit verschoben). Die Politik der »national reconciliation« und der Versuch, Kapitalflucht zu verhindern, sind in zukünftiger SWAPO-Regierungspolitik eng miteinander verbunden.

Schluß

Die SWAPO hat im Verlauf der Wahlen und der Verfassungsdiskussion ein hohes Maß an Pragmatismus, Kooperations- und Kompromißbereitschaft gezeigt, um sich als maßgebliche Kraft für politische und wirtschaftliche Stabilität in Namibia zu präsentieren. Die kleineren Parteien haben dieses Bemühen aufgegriffen. In dieser Hinsicht gibt der Verlauf der letzten Monate des Unabhängigkeitsprozesses grundsätzlich Anlaß zu positiven Erwartungen für die weitere politische Entwicklung des Landes.

Probleme und Konflikte können jedoch nicht ausbleiben. An der wirtschaftlichen Abhängigkeit Namibias von Südafrika und von den Konjunkturbewegungen auf den Rohstoffmärkten wird sich zunächst grundsätzlich wenig ändern, auch wenn internationale Entwicklungshilfe Diversifizierung im kleinindustriellen Bereich und Importsubstitution im Nahrungsmittelsektor anstrebt. Um die Mittel für Entwicklungsprojekte, für soziale Aufgaben, den Ausbildungssektor usw. aufzubringen bzw. zu erhalten, muß die SWAPO-Regierung auf gesamtwirtschaftliche Stabilität hinarbeiten: Dies beinhaltet die Beibehaltung vieler Elemente des sozio-ökonomischen Status Quo. Andererseits steht die Regierung unter einem hohen Erwartungsdruck nach unmittelbarer Verbesserung der Lebenssituation für die (arme) Mehrheit der Bevölkerung, was nach deutlicher Umschichtung von Ressourcen verlangt. Langfristig gesehen - und bei positiver gesamtwirtschaftlicher Entwicklung - mögen beide Ziele sich gegenseitig unterstützen; kurzfristig stehen sie jedenfalls in Konflikt zueinander. Bislang hat die SWAPO unter dem Motto der »national reconciliation« einen offenen Konflikt zwischen beiden Zielen verhindern können und sich auf die erste der beiden politischen Optionen - Stabilität und Kontinuität - konzentriert. Welche weitergehenden politischen Kompromisse - etwa in der Landfrage, bei Arbeitnehmerrechten usw. - zwischen den Parteien bereits im Zuge der Verfassungsdiskussion ausgehandelt wurden, ist derzeit noch nicht in vollem Ausmaß erkennbar. Berichte über Konflikte zwischen SWAPO/Regierung und den Gewerkschaften geben schon jetzt einen Eindruck von den Konfliktkonstellationen, die in Namibia nach der Euphorie von »national reconciliation« und Unabhängigkeitprozeß auf die politische Tagesordnung kommen können.

Auf der Ebene nationaler Politik hat die SWAPO ihre Bereitschaft zur Kooperation mit allen demokratischen Kräften und ihren Willen zur »national reconciliation« deutlich gemacht. Sie hat damit bereits vor dem Zeitpunkt der Unabhängigkeit manche Ängste über eine SWAPO-Regierungsübernahme gedämpft. Unsicherheit bleibt vor allem im Hinblick auf ihre innerparteiliche Demokratie bestehen. Die Partei ist nach wie vor durch das »detainee«-Problem belastet: Die Erklärung Sam Nujomas unmittelbar nach der Wahl, die ehemaligen SWAPO-Gefangenen stünden unter demselben Schutz des Gesetzes wie alle anderen Bürgerinnen und Bürger Namibias auch, enttäuschte viele Beobachter, die auf eine klare Stellungnahmen nach einer gewonnenen Wahl (und auf eventuelle personelle Konsequenzen) gehofft hatten. Die Haltung der SWAPO zu den Verfassungsbestimmungen zur Vorbeugehaft hat Ängsten in diesem Bereich erneut Vorschub geleistet. Auch ein Parteikongreß - längst überfällig - läßt noch immer auf sich warten. In der Partei sind allerdings Diskussionsprozesse hierüber in Gang gekommen, und es besteht die Hoffnung, daß die SWAPO sich nach der Regierungsübernahme stark genug auch zur Bewältigung ihrer innerparteilichen Probleme fühlt. Dies wäre nicht mehr als ein konsequenter Abschluß des Übergangsprozesses vom kolonialen zum unabhängigen Namibia.

Literatur

Anglin, Douglas G. [CIMS]: National Reconciliation. The Response of the Political Parties; Windhoek, August 1989
- : Post-Mortem on the Namibian Independence Election: Party Perspectives [Windhoek, November 1989]
Ansprenger, Franz: Die SWAPO. Profil einer afrikanischen Befreiungsbewegung; Mainz / München 1984
- : Die SWAPO als Regierungspartei; in: Aus Politik und Zeitgeschichte, 16.2.1990, S. 14-23
Basson, Nico / Motinga, Ben: Call Them Spies. The Namibian Spy Drama; Windhoek / Johannesburg, October 1989
Constitution of the Republic of Namibia
Draft Constitution of Namibia [ca. 9. Januar 1990]
Die Grünen im Bundestag (Hg.): Unabhängigkeit für Namibia. Symposium der Grünen im Bundestag aus Anlaß des 10. Jahrestages der Verabschiedung der Resolution 435 des UN-Sicherheitsrats [19. September 1989]. Dokumentation [Bonn 1989]
Dugard, John (Hg.): The South West Africa / Namibia Dispute; Berkeley 1973
[Evangelisches Missionswerk:] Namibia auf dem Weg in die Freiheit. Dokumente und Texte April bis November 1989; Hamburg, Dezember 1989 (= EMW-Informationen Nr. 86)
Harneit-Sievers, Axel: SWAPO of Namibia. Entwicklung, Programmatik und Politik seit 1959; Hamburg 1985
Katjavivi, Peter H.: A History of Resistance in Namibia; London / Addis Abeba / Paris 1988
Kühne, Winrich: Frieden in Namibia und Angola?; in: Institut für Afrika-Kunde (Hg.): Afrika Jahrbuch 1988; Opladen 1989, S. 34-41
- : Südafrika nach der Unabhängigkeit Namibias: Durchbruch zu Verhandlungen?; in: Aus Politik und Zeitgeschichte, 16.2.1990, S. 33-46
Namibia Communications Centre: Press Information Pack [Windhoek / London 1989]
NPP 435 / Die Grünen im Bundestag (Hg.): Die Wahl! Namibia Friedensplan 435 oder Gesellschaft im Belagerungszustand!; Bonn 1988
Press Statement by Sam Nujoma, President of SWAPO, Windhoek, 21 December 1989
Pütz, Joe / Egidi, Heidi von / Caplan, Perri: Namibia Handbook and Political Who's Who; 2nd revised and expanded version, Windhoek, October 1989
[South Africa] Dept. of Foreign Affairs: Namibian Independence and Cuban Troop Withdrawal; Pretoria, May 1989
Tötemeyer, Gerhard: The Prospects for Democracy and Development in an Independent Namibia; Windhoek, October 1989 (= Namibia Institute for Social and Economic Research. Discussion Paper No. 1)

[UNTAG:] Report of the United Nations Mission on Detainees, 11 October 1989 [Windhoek]

Weiland, Heribert: Namibia auf dem Weg zur Unabhängigkeit. Perspektiven des Entkolonisierungsprozesses; in: Europa-Archiv 44(10.12.1989)23, S. 711-718

- : Namibia - wohin? Perspektiven des Entkolonisierungsprozesses; Bonn, Februar 1990 (= Justitia und Pax Arbeitspapier 51)

Zeitungen und Zeitungsdokumentationen

Aktueller Informationsdienst Afrika (Hamburg)
die tageszeitung (Berlin)
Frankfurter Allgemeine Zeitung (Frankfurt/Main)
Namibia Nachrichten (Windhoek)
The Namibian (Windhoek)
Times of Namibia (Windhoek)
Windhoek Observer (Windhoek)

Beobachterberichte

Leif Herman, »Action of West European Parliamentarians Against Apartheid (AWEPAA) Monitoring Team«: Report on the Actual Situation in Namibia, Windhoek, 4th October 1989

Churches Information and Monitoring Services (CIMS), Windhoek / Katutura: CIMS Update, 6 October 1989 und ff. [etwa 14-tägig]

The Commission on Independence for Namibia (Lawyers' Committee for Civil Rights Under Law, Washington): Report of the First Observer Mission (...), July 1989

- : Report of the Second Observer Mission (...), August 1989

[Commonwealth Secretariat, London:] Preparing for a Free Namibia: Elections Transition and Independence. The Report of the Commonwealth Observer Group on Namibia, Windhoek 10/10/1989

Statement by the International Oxfams' Delegation to Observe Voting in the Namibian Elections, Windhoek 10th November 1989; 15th November 1989

Statement by the C.C.I.C. [Canadian Council for International Co-operation] Mission to the Namibian Elections, November 16, 1989

Anhang I: Mitglieder der Verfassunggebenden Versammlung - Biographische Angaben

Dieser Anhang enthält eine Liste der im November 1989 in die Verfassungsgebende Versammlung gewählten Personen, die auch die Parlamentarier und Parlamentarierinnen in den ersten Jahren des unabhängigen Namibia sein werden. Die biographischen Kurzprofile, geordnet nach der Position der betreffenden Person auf der Kandidatenliste der jeweiligen Partei, umfassen (in dieser Reihenfolge)
- gegenwärtige Funktion in der jeweiligen Partei,
- Geburtsdatum und -ort (mit Angabe des Distrikts, falls nicht identisch),
- Ausbildung (in der Regel nur letzter Abschluß bzw. Studium) und berufliche Position (de facto oft »Politiker«, dennoch wurde, wo eine andere Berufsbezeichnung auffindbar war, diese genannt),
- andere Angaben zur politischen Karriere (Exil, schon gehaltene Ministerpositionen u.ä.).

Hauptquelle für biographische Angaben in der namibischen Politik ist das »Namibia Handbook and Political Who's Who« (verfaßt von Joe Pütz, Heidi von Egidy und Perri Caplan, 2. Auflage, Windhoek, Oktober 1989). Es ist extensiv, erschien jedoch noch vor Bekanntwerden der Kandidatenlisten und besonders für die hinteren Listenplätze der SWAPO noch lückenhaft. Ergänzende Angaben wurden der Übersicht in den »Namibia Nachrichten«, 26./27. November 1989 entnommen. Weitere Angaben beruhen auf Auskünften der Pressestellen von SWAPO und DTA sowie auf Interviews des Verfassers in Namibia, doch konnte nicht in allen Fällen Vollständigkeit erreicht werden.

A. SWAPO

(PB/CC: Mitglied des »Politbureau«/»Central Committee«)

1. Nujoma, Sam:
President (seit 1960), PB; geb. 12.5.1929 in Okahao (Ovamboland); Ausbildung: 1937-48 Finnish Mission Primary School Okahao, 1949-54 Abendschule in Windhoek, 1977 Ehrendoktorwürde der Universität Kaduna (Nigeria); Beruf: Politiker. Arbeitete in den fünfziger Jahren als Steward bei der Eisenbahn und städtischer Angestellter in Windhoek, wurde 1959 Präsident der »Ovamboland People's Organisation« und mußte Namibia 1960 verlassen (Rückkehr 1989). 1969 als Präsident bestätigt und seither u.a. Verhandlungsführer der SWAPO in der internationalen Diplomatie.

2. Witbooi, Chief Hendrik:
Vice-President (seit 1984), PB; geb. 7.1.1934 in Gibeon (Namaland); Ausbildung: 1954-55 Lehrerzertifikat, Augustineum, Okahandja; Beruf: vormals

Lehrer, Schuldirektor (AME School, Gibeon) und Pastor (AME Church, Gibeon); Chief der Witbooi Nama, ein Urenkel des Hendrik Witbooi, der im Kampf gegen die deutsche Kolonialmacht 1905 getötet wurde. Witbooi trat als Führer von 5 Nama-Clans 1976 der SWAPO bei und wurde zur Symbol- und Integrationsfigur der Partei in Süd-Namibia.

3. Meroro, David:

National Chairman (seit 1964), PB; geb. September 1917 in Keetmanshoop; Ausbildung: Missionsschule Keetmanshoop, später Abendschule in Windhoek; Beruf: Politiker. Vormals städtischer Angestellter und Ladenbesitzer in Windhoek, trat Meroro 1960 zunächst der SWANU, 1962 der SWAPO bei. Als führender Aktivist der Partei in Namibia Anfang der siebziger Jahre wurde er 1975 zeitweise verhaftet und verließ das Land (Rückkehr 1989).

4. Toivo ja Toivo, Andimba:

General Secretary (seit 1986), PB; geb. 22.8.1924 in Umungundu (Ovamboland); Ausbildung: Missionsschulen in Ongwediva und Odibo, Lehrerzertifikat; Beruf: Politiker. Ja Toivo leistete während des Zweiten Weltkriegs Militärdienst in der südafrikanischen Armee und arbeitete später als Lehrer und Eisenbahnpolizist, war 1957 in Cape Town einer der Mitbegründer des »Ovamboland People's Congress«, der Vorläuferorganisation der SWAPO. 1958 nach Ovamboland verbannt, wo er als führender Parteiaktivist tätig war, wurde er 1966 verhaftet und 1967 in einem aufsehenerregenden Prozeß unter dem »Terrorism Act« zu 20 Jahren Haft in Robben Island verurteilt. 1984 wurde er aus der Haft entlassen und verließ Namibia bald darauf, um zur Exilführung zu stoßen (Rückkehr 1989).

5. Garoeb, Moses:

Administrative Secretary (seit 1969), PB. Er verließ Namibia in den frühen sechziger Jahren; verwandt mit Justus Garoeb (UDF); Rückkehr 1989.

6. Mweshihange, Peter:

Secretary for Defence (seit 1986), PB. Er war in den fünfziger Jahren einer der Mitbegründer des OPC und verließ Namibia in den frühen sechziger Jahren; 1969 zum Secretary for Foreign Affairs gewählt, nach Peter Nanyembas Tod 1983 Acting Secretary for Defence; Rückkehr 1989.

7. Geingob, Hage Gottfried:

Director of Election Directorate (1989), PB; geb. 3.8.1941 in Otjiwarongo; Ausbildung: Standard 8 in Otavi, 1958-61 Lehrerdiplom am Augustineum in Okahandja, Studium in den USA (1972 M.A. International Relations) Beruf: vormals Lehrer, jetzt Politiker. 1960 aus politischen Gründen vom Augustineum relegiert, trat er 1962 der SWAPO bei und verließ das Land; 1964-72 de facto Vertreter der SWAPO in New York, seit 1969 Organizing Secretary der SWAPO, 1972-75 Assistant Political Officer am UN Council for Namibia, seit 1975 Direktor des UN Institute for Namibia (UNIN) in Lusaka; 1989 Rückkehr nach Namibia als Wahlkampfleiter der SWAPO.

8. Pohamba, Hifikepunje Lukas:

Treasurer, PB; geb. 8.8.1935 in Okanghudi (Ovamboland); Ausbildung: Anglikanische Missionsschule. Er arbeitete Ende der fünfziger Jahre als Angestellter in Tsumeb, war während der frühen sechziger Jahre SWAPO-Aktivist, verließ das Land 1964 und baute das SWAPO-Büro in Lusaka auf. Anschließend verschiedene Tätigkeiten für die Partei; Rückkehr 1989 als Finanz- und Verwaltungschef der SWAPO-Wahlkampfleitung.

9. Gurirab, Theo-Ben:

Secretary for Foreign Affairs (seit 1986), PB; geb. 23.1.1938 in Usakos (Karibib); Ausbildung: 1960 Lehrerdiplom am Augustineum in Okahandja, Studium in den USA (1971 M.A. International Relations); Beruf: vormals Lehrer, jetzt Politiker. War bis 1972 SWAPO-Vertreter für Nord-Amerika, seitdem Leiter der SWAPO-Mission bei der UN und spielte eine wichtige Rolle in den internationalen Verhandlungen um Namibia (Rückkehr 1989).

10. Amathila, Dr. Libertine:

Deputy Secretary for Health and Welfare, Director of Womens' Council (seit 1969), CC; geb. Appolus am 10.12.1940 in Fransfontein (Outjo); Ausbildung: Medizinstudium in Polen, Großbritannien und Schweden; Beruf: Ärztin. Sie verließ Namibia 1962 und war ab 1975 für die Gesundheitsversorgung in den SWAPO-Flüchtlingslagern in Angola zuständig; Rückkehr 1989.

11. Hamutenya, Hidipo:

Secretary for Information and Publicity (seit 1981), PB; geb. 17.6.1939; Ausbildung: St. Mary's Mission School, Odibo; Augustineum; Studium in den USA und Canada; Beruf: Politiker. Verließ Namibia Anfang der sechziger Jahre; Gründungsmitglied und Assistant Director des UNIN; Rückkehr 1989; zuständig für »Mobilization and Publicity« in der SWAPO-Wahlkampfleitung.

12. Bessinger, Nico:

CC (seit 1989); geb. 12.6.1948 in Walvis Bay; Ausbildung: Sekundarschule und Studium in Cape Town, 1978-81 Studium in USA; Beruf: Architekt. Seit 1981 Secretary for Foreign Affairs der internen SWAPO und einer ihrer bekanntesten Sprecher.

13. Kameeta, Dr. Zephania:

SWAPO-Mitglied; geb. 7.8.1945 in Otjimbingwe; Ausbildung: Paulineum, Otjimbingwe, und Ökumenisches Institut des Weltkirchenrats, Bossey (Schweiz); Beruf: Pfarrer, Stellvertretender Bischof der »Evangelical Lutheran Church« (ELC). Gründungsvorsitzender der »Namibia National Convention« (NNC) 1975 und Secretary for Health and Welfare der internen SWAPO.

14. Tjiriange, Dr. Ernest:

Secretary for Legal Affairs (seit 1976, stellvertretend seit 1969), CC; geb. 12.7.1943 in Windhoek; Ausbildung: 1964-73 Jura-Studium in der UdSSR; Beruf: Dozent für Rechtswissenschaften am UNIN, Lusaka. 1963-64 Sekretär

Geographisches Institut
der Universität Kiel
Neue Universität

der SWAPO-Sektion in Windhoek, danach ins Exil; vertrat SWAPO als Rechtsexperte auf internationalen Konferenzen; Rückkehr 1989.

15. Ithana, Pendukeni:
Secretary, Women's Council (seit 1980), CC; geb. 11.10.1952 in Okaho (Ovamboland); Ausbildung: Oshivambo High School und Studium »Public Administration and Management«, UNIN, Jura-Fernstudium. Führungsmitglied der SWAPO Youth League in den frühen siebziger Jahren, verließ das Land 1974; sie gehörte zu den ersten weiblichen Mitgliedern der PLAN; Rückkehr 1989 als Deputy Head, Legal Services, in der Wahlkampfleitung.

16. Iyambo, Dr. Nicky:
1969 zum Secretary for Education and Culture der externen SWAPO gewählt.

17. Tjitendero, Dr. Mose:
CC; geb. 25.12.1943 in Otjiwarongo; Ausbildung: Augustineum, Studium (Sozialwissenschaften u.a.) in Tanzania und USA; Beruf: Leitende Funktionen in diversen pädagogischen Projekten der SWAPO. Er verließ Namibia nach Relegation vom Augustineum 1964, anschließend Student Representative in Tanzania; Gründungsmitglied des UNIN; Direktor des UN Vocational Training Centre in Angola; Rückkehr 1989 als Leiter des SWAPO-Regionalbüros Otjiwarongo.

18. Mbuende, Dr. Kaire:
Leiter des Regionalbüros Gobabis; geb. 28.11.1953 in Windhoek; Ausbildung: Augustineum (1971 relegiert), anschließend Paulineum und Martin Luther High School, Studium (Wirtschaftsgeschichte, Soziologie) in Tanzania (1975-78) und Schweden (1979-86), dort anschließend Forschungsarbeiten. Beruf: Soziologe, Politiker. Er ging 1974 ins Exil und kehrte 1989 zurück.

19. Angula, Nahas:
Secretary for Education (seit 1981), PB; geb. 22.8.1943 in Onyaanya (Ovamboland); Ausbildung: Studium (Pädagogik) in Zambia (1969-72) und den USA (1976-78); Beruf: Lehrer. SWAPO Youth League-Mitglied in den frühen sechziger Jahren, verließ er Namibia 1965; ab 1981 Betreuung der SWAPO-Ausbildungsmaßnahmen im Ausland; Rückkehr 1989, in der SWAPO-Wahlkampfleitung zuständig für die Wählerregistrierung.

20. Hausiku, Markus Mokoso:
Langjähriger SWAPO-Vorsitzender für den Bereich Windhoek, 1989 Leiter des Regionalbüros Rundu; geb. 25.11.1953 in Kapako (Kavango); Beruf: Lehrer. Hausiku ist Präsident der Lehrergewerkschaft NANTU.

21. Wohler, Siegfried Paul:
SWAPO-Vorsitzender in Rehoboth; geb. 2.10.1945 in Windhoek; Beruf: Geschäftsmann.

22. Ruppel, Hartmut:

Geb. 4.5.1954 in Hannover (BRD); Ausbildung: Jura-Studium in Stellenbosch; Beruf: Rechtsanwalt; war als Verteidiger in Prozessen gegen Mitglieder von SWAPO/PLAN tätig; deutschsprachig.

23. Wietersheim, Anton von:

Geb. 20.6.1951 in Windhoek; Beruf: Farmer (Kalkrand); deutschsprachig.

24. Katjavivi, Dr. Peter:

Leiter der Forschungsabteilung im SWAPO-Hauptquartier; geb. 12.5.1941 in Okahandja; Beruf: Historiker. Er verließ Namibia 1962, war seit 1969 SWAPO-Vertreter für Großbritannien und West-Europa, von 1976 bis 1979 Secretary for Information and Publicity; anschließend Rückzug aus der SWAPO-Führung und Dissertation in Oxford; Rückkehr 1989.

25. Wentworth, "Buddy" J.W.:

Lehrer in Swakopmund, langjähriges Mitglied der internen SWAPO.

26. Botha, Daniel Petrus:

Geb. am 25.5.1954 in Cape Town (RSA); Ausbildung: Studium der Religionswissenschaften in Stellenbosch; Beruf: Dozent für "Biblical Studies". Er stammt aus einer (nach eigener Darstellung) "conservative Afrikaner nationalist family" und kam 1984 an die »Academy« (jetzt "University of Namibia") nach Windhoek.

27. Amadhila, Matti:

Pastor der Lutherischen Kirche, Exekutivmitglied des namibischen Kirchenrats CCN.

28. Hishongwa, Hadino T.:

Youth League Secretary (seit 1987), CC; geb. 10.4.1943 in Odibo (Ovamboland); Ausbildung: Augustineum (1962-64); Studium (Wirtschaftswissenschaften, Journalismus, Sprachen) in Tanzania, der Tschechoslowakei, der DDR, im Senegal und in Schweden; Beruf: Politiker. Verließ Namibia 1964 und war als SWAPO-Vertreter in Dar es Salaam (1971), Dakar (1973), Stockholm (1976-83) tätig, anschließend im Department of Foreign Affairs. Rückkehr 1989 als Leiter des Regionalbüros Oshakati.

29. Amathila, Ben:

Secretary for Economic Affairs (seit 1976), CC; geb. 1.10.1939 in Walvis Bay; Ausbildung: Augustineum (ohne Abschluß); Beruf: Politiker. Mitglied der OPO 1958, in der ersten Hälfte der sechziger Jahre SWAPO-Vorsitzender in Walvis Bay, 1966 ins Exil, 1971 SWAPO-Vertreter in Stockholm. Rückkehr 1989 als Leiter des Regionalbüros Swakopmund.

30. Ya Otto, John:

Secretary for Labour (seit 1976), PB; geb. Februar 1938 in Ovamboland; Ausbildung: Augustineum, Hochschulreife im Abendkurs, Studium (Labour Administration) in Bulgarien (1981-82); Beruf: Lehrer. 1961 Stellvertreter

Generalsekretär der SWAPO; 1966 unter dem »Terrorism Act« verhaftet, 1968 freigelassen; führender SWAPO-Aktivist in den frühen siebziger Jahren, 1974 ins Exil. Rückkehr 1989 als Leiter des Regionalbüros Windhoek und Wahl zum Generalsekretär des Gewerkschaftsbundes NUNW.

31. Kapelwa, Richard:
1969 Acting Secretary for Defence and Transport; später Führungsposition in PLAN. Rückkehr 1989 als Leiter des Regionalbüros Katima Mulilo.

32. Nathaniel, Immanuel Gottlieb Maxuilili:
Acting President (seit 1960), CC; geb. 10.10.1927 in Tsumeb; Ausbildung: Standard 6, St. Mary's Mission School, Odibo; Beruf: Angestellter, Politiker. Ehemals Eisenbahnpolizist, kam er 1959 zur OPO; führender Aktivist in der ersten Hälfte der sechziger Jahre, 1966 verhaftet, 1968 freigelassen, aber bis 1985 unter Bann in Walvis Bay.

33. Hübschle, Michaela:
Geb. 21.9.1950 in Otjiwarongo; Ausbildung: Studium (B.A. Kunstgeschichte, Theaterwissenschaften) in Südafrika; Beruf: Übersetzerin/Studentin; deutschsprachig.

34. Ulenga, Ben:
Geb. 22.6.1952 in Otanga (Ovamboland); Ausbildung: Studium (B.A. Geschichte, Englisch, Philosophie); Beruf: Gewerkschaftsführer. Ehemaliger Guerilla der PLAN; verbüßte in den siebziger Jahren eine Haftstrafe (Robben Island, dort auch Ausbildung); spielte eine maßgebliche Rolle in der Entwicklung der namibischen Gewerkschaftsbewegung in den achtziger Jahren; Generalsekretär der »Mineworkers' Union of Namibia« (MUN).

35. Ekandjo, Jerry:
Geb. am 17.3.1947 in Okahandja; Ausbildung: Standard 9; Beruf: Lehrer; führendes Mitglied der internen SWAPO Youth League in der ersten Hälfte der siebziger Jahre.

36. Hoebeb, Joshua:
Secretary for Education der internen SWAPO, PB; geb. 14.8.1935 in Rooikraal (Gobabis); Ausbildung: Lehrerausbildung. Direktor des "Namibian Literacy Programme".

37. Biwa, Willem:
SWAPO-Aktivist und Branch Chairman in Mariental (?).

38. Hausiku, Heiki:
(keine Angaben)

39. Nauyala, Kapuka Nickey:
SWAPO-Vertreter in Zimbabwe, PB; Rückkehr 1989; verstarb im Dezember 1989.

40. Shoombe, Pashukeni:

Vice-Secretary, Women's Council, CC; geb. 12.12.1938 in Okadiwa (Ovamboland); Ausbildung: Studium (Politische Wissenschaften, Verwaltung) am UNIN; Beruf: Lehrerin. Rückkehr 1989; ihr Ehemann war in den achtziger Jahren SWAPO-Vertreter in Bonn.

41. Konjore, Willem:

Geb. 30.7.1945 in Warmbad; Beruf: Lehrer, Pastor. Langjähriger Aktivist der internen SWAPO.

(42.) Tsheehama, Peter:

Ehemaliger SWAPO-Vertreter in Kuba, hoher Kommandeur der PLAN; Rückkehr 1989 als Leiter des Regionalbüros Tsumeb. Mitglied der Verfassunggebenden Versammlung seit Mitte Dezember 1989 als Nachfolger für K.N. Nauyala (39).[1]

B. DTA

(EC/HC: Mitglied des »Executive«/»Head Committee«)

1. Muyongo, Mishake:

DTA Senior Vice-President (seit 1987), EC, HC; President, »United Democratic Party« (UDP, Caprivi); geb. 28.4.1940 in Linyanti (Caprivi), Mitglied des Mafwe Royal House; Ausbildung: Lehrerdiplom, Mafeking (RSA) (1963); Beruf: Politiker. Gemeinsam mit Brendan Simbwaye gründete er 1963 die »Caprivi African National Union« (CANU), ging 1964 nach Zambia und vereinigte dort die CANU mit der SWAPO; 1969 zum Vizepräsidenten der SWAPO gewählt; in den siebziger Jahren an den Verhandlungen mit der Kontaktgruppe beteiligt; trennte sich 1980 von der SWAPO und reetablierte CANU als eigenständige Partei; Rückkehr nach Namibia 1985, anschließend Abspaltung von der CANU und Gründung der UDP, mit der er sich der DTA anschloß.

2. Mudge, Dirk Frederick:

DTA Chairman (seit 1977), EC, HC; Leader, »Republican Party« (RP, Weiße); geb. 16.1.1928 in Otjiwarongo; Ausbildung: B.Comm. (Stellenbosch, RSA) (1947); Beruf: Farmer, Politiker. Ab 1961 Mitglied der SWA Legislative Assembly, 1970-77 Stellvertretender Vorsitzender der »National Party« (NP/SWA); 1975-77 Vorsitzender der Turnhallen-Konferenz; trennte sich 1977 von der NP und gründete die RP; 1985 Finanzminister im Transitional Government.

---

[1]   Tsheehama war ursprünglich nicht auf der Kandidatenliste der SWAPO zur Wahl, sondern wurde nach §4 der Constituent Assembly Proclamation, 1989, (AG. 62, Official Gazette, 6.11.1989) durch die Partei als Vertreter ernannt.

3. Kozonguizi, Fanuel Jariretundu:

DTA EC, HC; »Legal Advisor« der »National Unity Democratic Organization« (NUDO, Herero); geb. 26.1.1932 in Windhoek; Ausbildung: Studium (Erziehungswissenschaften) in Fort Hare (RSA), Jura-Studium in London; Beruf: Rechtsanwalt. 1952 Gründungsmitglied des »SWA Student Body« in Fort Hare, der einen Kern des frühen namibischen Nationalismus bildete; Kontakte mit Ja Toivo und anderen Gründern der OPO; ab 1958 für die Herero-Chiefs mit der Übermittlung von Petitionen an die UN beauftragt; 1959 in Abwesenheit zum Präsidenten der SWANU gewählt, die er bis Ende der sechziger Jahre international repräsentierte; 1976 Rückkehr nach Namibia als Rechtsberater des Herero-Chiefs Clemens Kapuuo bei der Turnhallen-Konferenz; seitdem verschiedene offizielle Positionen und Ministerposten im Transitional Government ab 1985.

4. Luipert, Daniel

DTA Vice-President, EC, HC; Leader, »Democratic Turnhalle Party of Namibia« (DTPN, Nama); geb. 7.2.1937 in Fransfontein (Outjo); Ausbildung: Augustineum (1961), Studium (Erziehungswissenschaften, abgebrochen) an der University of the North (Transvaal, RSA); Beruf: vormals Lehrer, Schulinspektor von 1968-74. Gewählter Führer der Nama-Delegation zur Turnhallen-Konferenz 1975, 1977 Gründungsmitglied der DTA; 1985-89 Vorsitzender der Nama Second Tier Representative Authority; 1986 Kaptein der Swaartbooi.

5. Haraseb, Joseph Max:

DTA Vice-President, EC, HC; President, »SWA People's Democratic United Front« (SWAPDUF, Damaraland); geb. 13.6.1942 in Windhoek; Ausbildung: Augustineum Training College; Beruf: Lehrer. Chief Secretary der »SWA Teachers' Association«; 1980-82 Erziehungsminister der Damara-Administration.

6. Dan, Gottlieb:

DTA HC; Chairman, »National Democratic Party« (NDP, Ovambo); geb. 6.4.1924 in Ohalushu (Ovamboland); Ausbildung: Standard 6 (Olupando); Beruf: »Headman« und Politiker.

7. Junius, Piet Matheus:

DTA HC; Leader »Christian Democratic Party« (CDP, Rehoboth); geb. 20.9.1941 in Rehoboth; Ausbildung: Lehrerdiplom, Johannesburg; Beruf: Lehrer, Farmer, Politiker. Gründungsmitglied der »Rehoboth Baster Association« (RBA) 1971; 1975 Mitglied der Baster-Delegation zur Turnhallen-Konferenz; 1977 Gründungsmitglied der DTA; 1986 Ausschluß aus der RBA, der schließlich (1989) zur Gründung der CDP führte; 1985 Stellvertretender Erziehungsminister im Transitional Government.

8. Africa, Dr. Ben Jakobus:

DTA Vice-President, EC, HC; Leader, »Rehoboth DTA Party« (RDTAP, Rehoboth); geb. 13.10.1938 in Rehoboth; Ausbildung: Medizinstudium, Cape Town (Abschluß 1964); Beruf: Arzt. Gründungsmitglied der RBA 1971 (1986 umbenannt in RDTAP) und - hierdurch - der DTA 1977; Kaptein von Rehoboth 1975-77; 1980-83 Mitglied des Ministerrats.

9. Barnes, Barney Leonard Joseph:

DTA HC; President, »United Party of Namibia« (UPN, Coloureds); geb. 6.3.1933 in Salt River, Cape Town (RSA); Ausbildung: Athlone High School (Abschluß 1952), Ausbildung als Seemann; Beruf: Geschäftsmann (Beerdigungsunternehmen) und Politiker. Kam in den frühen sechziger Jahren als Seemann nach Walvis Bay; ab 1969 Führungsmitglied der »Coloured People's Organization«; 1980-83 Vorsitzender des Exekutivkomitees der Coloured Second Tier Legislative Assembly; gründete die UPN 1986 und trat mit ihr 1989 der DTA bei.

10. Kgosimang, Constance:

DTA HC; Leader, »Seoposengwe Party« (Tswana); geb. 5.8.1946 in Aminuis Reserve (Hereroland); Ausbildung: Döbra Training College, Windhoek; Beruf: Kaptein der Tswana seit 1979. Vormals Angestellter in Walvis Bay, gründete er 1980 die Seoposengwe, die die Tswana Second Tier Representative Authority beherrschte.

11. Majavero, Alfons:

DTA HC; President, »National Democratic Unity Party« (NDUP, Kavango); geb. 15.5.1934 in Mukwe (Mbukushu, Kavango); Ausbildung: Lehrerzertifikat, Döbra Training College; Beruf: Politiker, Farmer; (Hompa) Chief der Mbukushu. Justizminister in der ersten Kavango Legislative Assembly 1970, Chief Minister 1974-80, Mitglied der DTA seit 1977 und der Kavango Second Tier Legislative Assembly 1980-89.

12. Kashe, Geelbooi:

DTA HC; Leader »Bushman Alliance« (BA); geb. 15.9.1931 oder 11.3.1931 in D/Gam (Bushmanland); Ausbildung: keine formale Schulbildung; Beruf: bis 1972 Übersetzer, später Arbeiter und Polizist, jetzt Politiker, Farmer. Die BA wurde 1978 durch die DTA gegründet; Kashe war 1980-83 Minister für Wasserfragen.

13. Kaura, N. Katuutire:

DTA Vice-President, EC, HC; National Chairman, NUDO; geb. 3.2.1941 in Ombujondjumba/Okakarara (Hereroland); Ausbildung: Augustineum, Studium in den USA (M.Sc. 1973, M.Ed. 1976); Beruf: Lehrer und Dozent in den USA, Farmer. Mitglied der SWANU seit 1959, SWANU-Vertreter bei der UN 1961-71, 1964 ins Exil nach Tanzania; trat 1975 NUDO bei und kehrte 1978 nach Namibia zurück; DTA-Sprecher bei den Namibia-Verhandlungen in Genf 1981; stellvertretende Ministerpositionen im Transitional Government.

14. Barnes, Margaret:

President, DTA Woman's League; Mitglied der UPN; geb. 25.10.1953 in Keetmanshoop; Ausbildung: 1973-77 Studium (B.A. Honours), University of the Western Cape; Beruf: Lehrerin.

15. Matjila, Andrew Nick:

DTA EC, HC; Mitglied der Seoposongwe; geb. am 15.6.1932 in Pretoria (RSA); Ausbildung: Grundschullehrerausbildung, PAX Training Institution, Pietersburg (RSA); Beruf: Lehrer (1964-71), Schulinspektor (1971-75), Übersetzer. Arbeitete seit 1976 in verschiedenen Positionen bei der Administration für Caprivi, seit 1981 Arbeit für die DTA, Vorstandsmitglied der Akademie und der »First National Development Corporation« (FNDC); 1985-89 Erziehungsminister im Transitional Government.

16. Staby, Hans-Eric:

DTA HC; Chairman, RP; geb. 8.9.1935 in Otjimbingwe; Ausbildung:· Studium (Architektur) in Cape Town und West-Berlin; Beruf: Architekt. 1977 Gründungsmitglied der »Interessengemeinschaft Deutschsprachiger Südwester« (IG); 1978 zur RP; DTA-Vertreter in der White Second Tier Legislative Assembly 1980-88 und der National Assembly 1985-89.

17. Gende, Aloys:

DTA Secretary General, Regionen Kavango und Caprivi; geb. 12.3.1952 in Sampiu (Kavango); Ausbildung: Rundu Senior Secondary School (Matrik); Beruf: 1974-88 Berufssoldat (Major). DTA-Mitglied seit 1977.

18. Jagger, Jeremiah Wilfriedt:

DTA HC; Additional Executive Member, DTPN; geb. 29.9.1933 in Rehoboth; Ausbildung: Lehrerdiplom, Stofberg Memorial College (RSA); Beruf: Lehrer, Politiker. 1959 SWANU Assistant Secretary for Information, 1966 SWANU Acting President; verließ die SWANU 1967 und gründete »Voice of the People«; 1975 Teilnahme an der Nama-Delegation zur Turnhallen-Konferenz, anschließend verschiedene Positionen in der Nama Second Tier-Gremien; 1985 zur DTPN.

19. Gaseb, Johannes:

DTA HC; Chairman, SWAPDUF; geb. 19.3.1946 in Usakos (Karibib); Ausbildung: Lehrerzertifikat; Beruf: vormals Lehrer, jetzt Politiker, Farmer. Vertreter in der Damara Second Tier Representative Authority.

20. Nuule, Abner:

DTA HC; Vice-President, NDP; geb. 12.2.1935 in Otuuala (Ovamboland); Ausbildung: Standard 5; Beruf: Senior Headman. Bis 1989 Vertreter in der Ovambo Second Tier Representative Authority.

21. Van Wyk, Charles:

DTA HC; First Deputy Leader, CDP; geb. 2.1.1922 in Upington (RSA); Ausbildung: Lehrerdiplom, Uitenhage Teachers' Training College (RSA);

Beruf: Lehrer, Bauunternehmer. 1959 National Secretary der »SWA Coloured Organization«, in der Folgezeit an mehreren Parteigründungen beteiligt; 1985-89 Vertreter in der National Assembly.

C. UDF

1. Garoeb, Justus:
UDF President; President, »Damara Council« (DC); geb. 16.12.1942 in Omaruru; Ausbildung: Augustineum, abgebrochenes Medizinstudium; Beruf: Paramount Chief der Damara, Politiker. Führungspositionen in der Damara-Politik seit den frühen siebziger Jahren, phasenweise Zusammenarbeit mit SWAPO.

2. Diergaardt, »Reggie« R.:
UDF National Chairman; Leader, »Labour Party« (LP); geb. 9.8.1957 in Kalkveld; Ausbildung: Lehrerdiplom, Dower Training College, Port Elizabeth (RSA); Beruf: vormals Lehrer, Politiker. Seit 1978 bei der LP (Herkunft aus der »SWA Coloured Organization« von 1959), die phasenweise in der DTA arbeitete. Diergaardt war 1985-87 Mitglied des Constitutional Council.

3. Soroseb, Theophilus:
UDF Deputy National Chairman; Leader, »Original People's Party of Namibia« (OPPN, eine Partei der Khoi-San, »Bushmen«); geb. 11.5.1952 in Otjiwarongo District; Ausbildung: Form 2, Khorikas, und Ausbildung als Maurer; Beruf: Maurer und Bauunternehmer. Gründer der OPPN, die 1981 die DTA verließ; arbeitete bei der privaten »Bushman Foundation«.

4. Siseho, Gabriel:
UDF Vice-President; President, »Caprivi Alliance Party« (CAP); geb. 11.7.1937 in Lusese Village (Caprivi); Ausbildung: Matrik; Beruf: 1957-67 Polizist in Zambia. Politische Betätigung unter Einfluß der SWAPO seit Beginn der siebziger Jahre; Teilnahme an der Turnhallen-Konferenz für die spätere CAP, die sich nach der Rückkehr Mishake Muyongos (vgl. DTA, Nr. 1) 1985 spaltete.

(5) Biwa, Eric
President, »Patriotic Unity Movement« (PUM); geb. 8.5.1953; Ausbildung: Studium in Südafrika, Kenya, Sowjetunion und Cuba; Beruf: Politiker. Wurde 1973 Mitglied der SWAPO Youth League, 1976 SWAPO Secretary for Information and Publicity in Süd-Namibia; ging 1978 ins Exil; wurde 1984 durch die SWAPO in Angola in Haft gehalten; Rückkehr 1989 und Gründungsmitglied der PUM; rückte 1990 anstelle eines anderen UDF-Mitglieds in die Verfassunggebende Versammlung nach.

D. ACN

1. De Wet, Johannes »Jannie« M.:

ACN Chairman; Vice-Chairman, »National Party« (NP); geb. 10.11.1927 in Rouxville (RSA); Ausbildung: Studium (B.Sc. Agriculture 1951) in Stellenbosch (RSA); Beruf: Farmer. De Wet war seit 1964 Mitglied der SWA Legislative Assembly und hielt diverse weitere politische Ämter; er war Minister für Landwirtschaft, Wasserwesen und Fischerei im Transitional Government 1987-88.

2. Pretorius, Jacobus »Kosie« W.M.:

ACN Head Committee-Mitglied; Leader, NP; geboren 5.9.1935 in Swakopmund; Ausbildung: Studium (M.A. Political Science 1959), University of the Orange Free State (RSA); Beruf: Farmer und Geschäftsmann (Suidwes Drukkery). Mitglied der Legislative Assembly für Gobabis seit 1961, seitdem führende Positionen in der NP; Minister für Wasserwesen, Post und Telekommunikation im Transitional Government 1985-89.

3. Aston, Walter O.:

NP-Mitglied; geb. 29.12.1926 in Okahandja; Ausbildung: Matrik, Diplom des Institute of Secretaries (1948); Beruf: Geschäftsmann. 1985-89 Mitglied der National Assembly des Transitional Government; deutschsprachig.

E. NPF

1. Katjiuongua, Moses:

NPF Chairman; President, SWANU (NPF) (seit 1982); geb. 24.4.1942 in Windhoek; Ausbildung: Studium in der DDR, in Schweden und in Canada; Beruf: Journalist und Politiker. Verließ Namibia 1959 und repräsentierte in der ersten Hälfte der sechziger Jahre die SWANU international; kehrte 1982 nach Namibia zurück (zeitweise Deputy Public Relations Manager bei Rössing Uranium); nach der SWANU-Spaltung 1984 (um die Frage der Teilnahme an der Multi-Party-Conference) als Präsident wiedergewählt; 1985-89 Minister of Manpower, National Health and Welfare im Transitional Government.

F. FCN

1. Diergaardt, Hans:

FCN President; President, »Liberation Front/Liberated Democratic Party« (LF/LDP); geb. 16.9.1927 in Rehoboth; Ausbildung: 1938-43 Methodist School, Rehoboth, Ausbildung als KFZ-Mechaniker; Beruf: Geschäftsmann und Farmer. Seit 1947 in der Rehobother Politik, 1979 zum Kaptein von Rehoboth gewählt; Ministerpositionen im Transitional Government; Rücktritt von seinem

Sitz in der Verfassunggebenden Versammlung aus Altersgründen im Dezember 1989.

(2) Kerina, Dr. Mburumba:

FCN First Vice-President for Constitutional and Legal Affairs; President, NUDO-PP; geb. etwa 1928 als Eric William Getzen in Tsumeb; Ausbildung: Medizinstudium (nicht abgeschlossen) in den USA, andere Details nicht bekannt; Beruf: Universitätsdozent, Consultant, Politiker. Kerina gehört zu den frühesten namibischen Nationalisten, die Namen »OPO«, »SWAPO« und »Namibia« gehen auf ihn zurück. Er agierte in den fünfziger Jahren während seines Medizinstudiums in den USA als Übermittler für Petitionen der Herero-Chiefs an die UN; erster SWAPO Chairman 1960-63, danach Trennung von der Partei; Gründung der NUDO 1964, jedoch 1966 Trennung von den Herero-Chiefs; anschließend eigene erfolglose Parteigründung; 1976 zurück nach Namibia; beteiligt an diversen erfolglosen geschäftlichen Unternehmungen; rückte im Dezember 1989 für Hans Diergaardt in die Verfassunggebende Versammlung nach.

G. NNF

1. Rukoro, Vekuii Reinhard:

NNF President; President, SWANU (NNF) (seit 1988); geb. 11.11.1954 in Otjiwarongo; Ausbildung: Jura-Studium in Großbritannien (1980-84); Beruf: Rechtsanwalt. Trat 1975 der SWANU bei; 1976-80 General Secretary der SWANU, erneut ab 1984 nach der Spaltung der SWANU. Arbeitete in diversen Projekten zum Schutz der Menschenrechte.

Anhang II: Das Kabinett

Am 21. Dezember 1989 stellte Sam Nujoma ein »Schattenkabinett« vor (vgl. Press Statement by Sam Nujoma, President of SWAPO, Windhoek, 21 December 1989), die hier aufgeführt wird. Einige Benennungen wurden erst Anfang 1990 ergänzt. In der folgenden Liste bedeuten:

(a) Minister;
(b) Stellvertreter;
(c) weiterer Stellvertreter)
(*) Mitglied der Verfassunggebenden Versammlung und damit der »National Assembly« nach der Unabhängigkeit (biographische Angaben in Anhang I)

Staatspräsident: Sam Nujoma (*)

1. Premierminister:
(a) Hage Geingob (*)
(b) Nangolo Mbumba

2. Inneres:
(a) Hifikepunye Pohamba (*)
(b) Nangolo Ithete
(c) Ndali Kamati

3. Äußeres:
(a) Theo-Ben Gurirab (*)
(b) Netumbo Ndaitwah
(c) Andreas Guibeb

4. Verteidigung:
(a) Peter Mueshihange (*)
(b) Philemon Malima
(c) Frans Kapofi

5. Finanzen:
(a) Otto Herrigel[1]
(b) Godfrey Gaoseb

6. Bildung, Kultur und Sport:
(a) Nahas Angula (*)
(b) Buddy Wentworth (*)
(c) Vitalis Ankama

---

[1] Deutschsprachiger Finanzfachmann.

7. Information und Rundfunk:
(a) Hidipo Hamutenya (*)
(b) Daniel Tjongarero[1]
(c) Vezera Kandetu

8. Gesundheit und Soziales:
(a) Dr. Nicky Iyambo (*)
(b) Dr. Solomon Amadhila

9. Arbeit, Öffentlicher Dienst und »Manpower Development«:
(a) Hendrik Witbooi (*)
(b) Hadino Hishongwa (*)
(c) Tuli Hiveluah

10. Bergwerke und Energie:
(a) Andimba Toivo ja Toivo (*)
(b) Helmut Angula
(c) Dr. Leake Hangala

11. Justiz:
(a) Ngarikutuke Tjiriange (*)
(b) Vekuii Rukoro (NNF) (*)
(c) Dr. Albert Kawana

12. »Local Government and Housing«:
(a) Dr. Libertine Amathila (*)
(b) Jerry Ekandjo (*)
(c) Nghidimondjila Shoombe

13. Landwirtschaft, Fischerei, Wasser und ländliche Entwicklung:
(a) Gert Hanekom[2]
(b) Dr. Kaire Mbuende (*)
(c) Calle Schlettwein, Vilho Hipondoka

14. Handel und Industrie:
(a) Ben Amathila (*)
(b) Reggie Diergaardt (UDF) (*)

15. Naturschutz und Tourismus:
(a) Nico Bessinger (*)
(b) Pendukeni Ithana (*)
(c) Hanno Rumpf[3]

---

[1] Führendes Mitglied der internen SWAPO in den siebziger Jahren.
[2] Geschäftsmann und Farmer, geboren in Südafrika, seit 1957 in Namibia.
[3] Vormals Mitarbeiter im SWAPO-Büro, Bonn.

16. Öffentliche Arbeiten, Transport und Kommunikation:
(a) Richard Kapelwa (*)
(b) Klaus Dierks[1]
(c) Peingeondjabi Shipoh

17. »Land, Resettlement and Rehabilitation«:
(a) Marco Hausiku (*)
(b) Dr. Marcus Shivute
(c) Ulitala Hiveluah

Neben der Besetzung der Ministerposten stellte Nujoma ebenfalls noch im Dezember auch Kandidaten für einige andere Schlüsselfunktionen vor. Benannt wurden als
- Generaldirektor der Nationalen Planungskommission: Dr. Zedekia Ngavirue
- Staatsminister für Sicherheitsfragen beim Büro des Präsidenten: Peter Tsheehama (*)
- Generalstaatsanwalt: Hartmut Ruppel (*)
- Chef des Rechnungshofs: zunächst war Gert Hanekom vorgesehen, der später jedoch als Landwirtschaftsminister designiert wurde.

---

[1] Deutschsprachiger Bauingenieur.

Vorbemerkung zur Dokumentation

Die im Dokumentationsteil wiedergegebenen Materialien sollen ein Bild des politischen Klimas in Namibia vor und während der Wahlen zur Verfassunggebenden Versammlung ermöglichen und zugleich die wichtigsten politischen Parteien vorstellen - letzteres vor allem anhand ihrer programmatischen Aussagen und ihres Wahlkampfstils. Die Darstellung und Analyse der Wahlen im ersten Teil des vorliegenden Bandes hat auf die hier wiedergegebenen Dokumente an vielen Stellen zurückgegriffen. Eine thematisch und zeitlich umfassende Darstellung der Wahlen in Form der Dokumentation wird allerdings nicht angestrebt. Vielmehr konzentriert sich die Materialauswahl zeitlich auf die Wochen unmittelbar vor und während der Wahl und inhaltlich auf die Vorgänge in Namibia selbst (im Gegensatz zum internationalen politischen Umfeld, das die Durchführung der Wahlen erst möglich machte). Neben Zeitungsberichten bilden Dokumente der Parteien und andere Materialien wie Beobachterberichte einen Schwerpunkt dieser Dokumentation. Dies dient nicht zuletzt der Materialsicherung bei Dokumenten, die nicht über die üblichen Wege veröffentlicht wurden und die erst auf diese Weise einer breiteren interessierten Öffentlichkeit zugänglich gemacht werden können.

In der Gruppe A der Dokumentation werden die Wahlmanifeste der wichtigsten Parteien (bzw. eine ähnlich gelagerte Selbstdarstellung im Fall der NNF, deren Wahlprogramm für die vorliegende Dokumentation zu umfangreich war) wiedergegeben. Mit Ausnahme der FCN (dem Autoren gelang es nicht, eines Programms dieser Partei, deren Organisation kaum über Rehoboth hinausreichte, habhaft zu werden) sind dabei alle Parteien vertreten, die einen Sitz in der Verfassunggebenden Versammlung erhielten (A.1 bis A.6). Besonders die umfänglichen Dokumente der Hauptkontrahenten SWAPO und DTA machen die gegensätzlichen historischen und politischen Erfahrungen und Perspektiven, die hinter den beiden Parteien stehen, deutlich. Ebenso wird aber auch erkennbar, daß sie in vielen »Sachfragen« - etwa bei der Sozial- und Entwicklungspolitik - einander näher standen, als es die politische Polarisierung in Namibia vor den Wahlen zunächst vermuten ließe. Dies gilt partiell auch für die kleineren Parteien, die zumeist allerdings weniger weit ausgearbeitete - und weniger umfangreiche - Wahlprogramme vorlegten.

Bei SWAPO und DTA werden die programmatischen Aussagen der Parteien ergänzt durch eine Reihe anderer Materialien, die den Wahlkampfstil illustrieren (A.1 und A.2). Ausschnitte aus zwei Wahlkampfzeitungen der SWAPO, ein Flugblatt der DTA und ein vergleichender Bericht über Wahlkampfveranstaltungen in einer DTA-nahen Zeitung geben Muster der Argumentation und Selbstdarstellung wieder, wie sie typisch für die Vorwahlperiode waren. Bemerkenswert sind dabei die Unterschiede zwischen »staatsmännischer« und auf »national reconciliation« zielender Argumentation hoher Parteiführer und härteren Formen der Auseinandersetzung mit dem politischen Gegner beim Wahlkampf niedrigerer Parteifunktionäre außerhalb von Windhoek. Abgedruckt sind außerdem zwei unsignierte, aller Wahrscheinlichkeit nach von der DTA stammende Flugblätter, die während der ersten Wahltage in großem Maßstab von Hubschraubern über Ondangwa und Oshakati (Ovamboland) abgeworfen wurden und offenbar darauf abzielten, die Bevölkerung zu verwirren. Sie illustrieren die »schmutzige Seite« des Wahlkampfs, dem die UNTAG mit ihrem »Code of Conduct« zu begegnen suchte (A.7). Wiedergegeben ist auch der zur Wahl verwendete Stimmzettel (A.8); die auf ihm verwendeten Symbole der politischen Parteien lieferten vor der Wahl reichlich Diskussionsstoff.

Gruppe B der Dokumentation enthält eine Auswahl von Berichten, die durch internationale Beobachtermissionen erstellt wurden. In zwei Fällen konnten aus Platzgründen nur die Zusammenfassungen abgedruckt werden; die Berichte sind in der zeitlichen Reihenfolge ihrer Entstehung angeordnet. Die Beobachterberichte haben im allgemeinen versucht, umfassende Einschätzungen der Situation und der Atmosphäre im Land wiederzugeben. Dabei zeigten sie insbesondere die Befürchtungen, Ängste und Unsicherheiten auf, die in der Vorwahlperiode bestanden. Die meisten Beobachtermissionen erhielten ihre Informationen auf Rundreisen durch das Land vor allem durch Gespräche mit Politikern, Administratoren, Kirchenvertretern, UNTAG-Personal usw., so daß ihre Berichte den jeweiligen Diskussionsstand in diesen Kreisen reflektierten. Nicht zuletzt bildeten Beobachterberichte, wie sie hier dokumentiert sind, eine wichtige Quelle für die Wahlberichterstattung der internationalen Presse.

Eine besondere Rolle spielten die etwa 14-tägig erschienenen »Updates« des kirchlich organisierten »Churches Information and Monitoring Service« (CIMS) in Katutura, die auf einem über mehrere Monate bestehenden Netz von Beobachtern in allen Distriktzentren beruhten und deshalb eine besondere Nähe zur lokalen Situation aufweisen. Exemplarisch wird eines dieser »Updates« ungekürzt wiedergegeben.

Neben halb- oder inoffiziellen Beobachtermissionen, deren Berichte hier teilweise dokumentiert sind, waren während der Wahlen »diplomatische Beobachtermissionen« präsent, die den Aufbau von Botschaften ihrer jeweiligen Staaten vorbereiteten. Ihre Berichte waren allerdings nicht für die Öffentlichkeit bestimmt.

Gruppe C der Dokumentation umfaßt eine Reihe von Zeitungsberichten aus der namibischen Presse, die den Wahlverlauf selbst und die Tage unmittelbar danach darstellen (Bekanntgabe der Wahlergebnisse und Reaktionen darauf sowie Berichte über das erste Zusammentreten der Verfassunggebenden Versammlung). Abgesehen von ihrer unmittelbar illustrativen und Informationsfunktion schließen sie die Berichte der Beobachtermissionen in Gruppe B, die vornehmlich die unmittelbare Vorwahlperiode abdecken, zeitlich ab.

Ergänzt und abgeschlossen wird die Sammlung von Dokumenten zu Wahlvorbereitung und -verlauf durch einen Abdruck des Verfassungstexts, wie er am 9. Februar 1990 verabschiedet wurde (D). Über den Zweck der aktuellen Information hinaus ermöglicht er einen Vergleich zwischen dem politischen Kompromiß, den die Verfassung in manchen Punkten darstellt, und den programmatischen Aussagen der Parteien vor der Wahl, wie sie im Teil A der Dokumentation dargestellt sind. Ein Versuch, den »Weg dorthin« - die Verfassungsdiskussion selbst - in Dokumenten festzuhalten, wird hier allerdings nicht unternommen, weil dies neben einer Dokumentation der Berichterstattung in den Zeitungen auch den Abdruck umfangreicher Entwurfs- und Diskussionsversionen erfordern würde, die zur Zeit teilweise noch gar nicht zugänglich sind. Für die öffentlichen Diskussionen im Zusammenhang mit der Formulierung der Verfassung sei deshalb allein auf die zusammenfassende Darstellung im ersten Teil dieses Bandes verwiesen.

SWAPO ELECTION MANIFESTO

Towards an independent and democratic Namibia: SWAPO's policy positions

TOWARDS AN INDEPENDENT AND DEMOCRATIC NAMIBIA: SWAPO'S POLICY POSITIONS

Introduction

Today Namibia is at the crossroads of its independence. The agony of death and destruction that the Namibians have endured for the past 105 years of colonial oppression is about to come to an end and freedom is in sight.

The process of transition to independence has already started. On 1 November 1989, the Namibian people will exercise their long-denied right to self-determination by electing their own leaders who, by virtue of being elected by the masses will have the sovereign right to draft the constitution of independent Namibia. This will bring about a new political and socio-economic order.

The task before the Namibian people is to seize this historic opportunity and ensure that they join hands to safeguard the revolutionary gains we have made in bringing our country to the threshold of independence. Seizing this opportunity means, first, to register as a voter, and second, to vote and send to the Constituent Assembly men, and women with a revolutionary will, honourable record, vision for a better future, integrity, experience and proven ability to fight for the interests of the broad masses of the Namibian people.

Such men and women are to be found in SWAPO. SWAPO has stood tall in the face of formidable odds over the last twenty-nine years of its struggle to free Namibia. Because of this fact, SWAPO had participated in the formulation of Resolution 435 and fought bravely for the last 11 years for its implementation. The motivating force behind this struggle has always been to guarantee that power is given to the Namibian people to decide the future of our country through free and fair elections.

Now that Resolution 435 is being implemented, the Central Committee of SWAPO has the honour to place before the people of Namibia its concrete programme of action in the form of SWAPO's policy positions on a broad spectrum of political, economic, social and cultural issues. Together, these policy positions form SWAPO's Election Manifesto.

1. SWAPO'S ELECTION MANIFESTO

Philosophy of Government

For SWAPO, the ideals of **solidarity, freedom** and **justice** constitute the political guide to action. They are the basis of the brotherhood of mankind. The perspective of life flowing from our commitment to these ideals is that individuals should subordinate their own personal interests to the greater good of all.

We in SWAPO have fought for decades, and been imprisoned for the noble cause of putting an end to the denial of our people's democratic rights. Thousands of SWAPO members have laid down their lives so that the oppressed majority of our society can have freedom. Such supreme sacrifice for the welfare of others is the highest expression of **solidarity.** SWAPO wants to see all sections of our people working in solidarity to attain objectives that are common to the whole society. Our struggle has not only been to liberate the black majority from colonial domination, but also to emancipate the whites from the narrow and dehumanizing confines of class and race privileges. A SWAPO-led government of independent Namibia will thus take concrete actions to promote fraternal and humane social relations in our country. The ideal of solidarity obliges our movement to address the essential needs of all our people who find themselves in difficult social and economic plight.

SWAPO recognises the fact that it was international solidarity that enabled our people to endure the long years of war, imprisonment, detention, torture and exile, and to arrive at the present stage of our liberation struggle. In this connection, Namibia under a SWAPO government will affirm the inadmissibility of any oppression of one nation or people by another and will extend solidarity to all peoples fighting for freedom and social justice.

The ideal or principle of **freedom** embodies for us a wide range of democratic rights and freedoms, the most basic of which is the right of all nations to determine their own destiny and to exercise sovereignty over their lands and resources.

Freedom includes the rights to life and personal liberty; rights to freedom of movement, expression, conscience, worship, speech, press, assembly and association; right to the due process and equality before the law; right to protection from arbitrary deprivation of personal and private property; and the right to freedom from racial, ethnic, religious or gender discrimination.

Most of these democratic rights have been denied the majority of the Namibian people for over one century by both German and South African colonialists. Therefore, the primary objective of a SWAPO government will be to restore and defend these rights. Their restoration requires the final and definitive end to foreign rule. In a liberated Namibia under a SWAPO-led government, freedom will also mean an opportunity for all the people to realise their potentials and to participate in decision-making and in directing the development of our society in a way that creates the necessary material requirements and achieves higher forms of social consciousness. The creation of a viable, participatory and genuinely representative political system in our country is central to the realisation of such freedom. A SWAPO-led government will thus work to establish this form of political system.

Justice means fairness to all people. In Namibia, gross injustices have been the hallmark of colonial rule. Policies and social practices by the colonial ruling class have been grossly unjust to the dignity, rights, and socio-economic requirements of the majority of the Namibians. These unjust policies and practices are responsible for the present division of our society into two distinct social groups: the landless and propertyless black majority, on the one hand, and the propertied and privileged white minority, on the other. The deprivation of the indigenous Namibian people of their liberty, land and other means of livelihood has inflicted deep wounds on our society. The black majority has not only been robbed of its land, but also of its fair share of the wealth it produces.

A SWAPO-led government will ensure that in independent Namibia social justice and equality for all is the fundamental principle governing the decision-making process. In order to bring about social justice and to heal the wounds of colonial oppression, a SWAPO-led government will not only restore the Namibian people's lost political and legal rights, but will also effect a fundamental social, industrial and economic change.

In short, the ideals of solidarity, freedom and justice are the beacon of light which guides our Movement towards the future. They constitute SWAPO's philosophy of government. They are principles that must underlie the actions and behaviour of people in control of state power.

2. The Namibian State

SWAPO will establish an independent, unitary, secular and democratic state whose territory includes the 1,124 square kilometre area of Walvis Bay and all the offshore islands (the Penguin Islands) between the Orange River and Walvis Bay.

The constitution to be written by the Constituent Assembly will be the fundamental law of the land. It will be a product of the Namibian people's democratic choice in the sense that its basic principles will be discussed and approved by the vast majority of our people during this election campaign. SWAPO has fought for the implementation of Resolution 435 because it wants the Namibian people to have the freedom to discuss, throughout the country, such principles on which the Namibian state will be founded.

Namibia's independence constitution must, among other things, provide for a genuine bill of fundamental rights, a bill that is radically different from all the bogus ones previously produced by the appointees of the colonial power in our country. The organisation, aims and functions of the Namibian state will express the interests and will of the people. Its basic features will be: the participation of the people in determining the government's policy; social changes; and consistent struggle for economic independence and against neo-colonialism.

Unlike in the colonial era, when the state power was used as an instrument of a small colonial ruling class to defend its accumulated privileges and to suppress the colonised majority, in a SWAPO-led independent Namibia the state will operate in the interest of the people as a whole.

The key organs of the Namibian state will be the executive, the legislature, and the judiciary.

(a) The Executive

The executive will be made up of the Head of State, in whom the executive power of the state will be vested, and a Cabinet. The power and authority of the Head of State will emanate from democratic elections. The Head of State will appoint ministers who may or may not be members of the National Assembly or Parliament.

The Cabinet will have the collective responsibility regarding decision-making. Ministers, who are members of the Cabinet, will also have their own individual ministerial duties and will be accountable to the Head of State and, where appropriate, to the Parliament.

The Cabinet will be assisted in the execution of its duties by a Public Service which will be responsible for the implementation of government policy-decisions and the management of public enterprises. Recruitment into the public service will be on the basis of proven skill, experience and accountability. Racial, sex, and ethnic discrimination will be strictly prohibited as a basis for the recruitment of personnel into the public service.

(b) The Legislature

The legislature will be the law-making organ of the state. Its members will be elected through universal adult suffrage to represent the various constituencies. Thus, the Parliament will be the focal point of popular representation and articulation of the just interests of the constituent provinces or regions of the state. The Parliament will consist of a single chamber. Its immediate tasks will be the repeal of all discriminatory legislation.

(c) The Judiciary

Under colonialism, the judges and other judicial officials have upheld repressive laws and excused murders, atrocities and other forms of abuses which the colonial state power committed against the Namibian people. Their actions often negated the principles of due process of the law.

In a democratic Namibia, under the leadership of SWAPO, the primary function of the judiciary will be to establish a new legal system with an independent judiciary that can provide speedy and efficient provision of justice. The judiciary will be staffed with men and women of integrity whose legal philosophy and ideological disposition will ensure that our people's long cry for justice is answered. The new judicial structure will be unified and will consist of the supreme court, a high court, and various district and community courts.

3. Foreign Policy

The vast majority of Namibians, like the millions of other citizens of the developing world, live in abject poverty. Their very survival is at the mercy of a group of small but powerful nations and the privileged few in the society. Independent Namibia, under a SWAPO government will join the other developing countries in their common struggle against this condemnable injustice.

The commitment of a SWAPO government to democracy and social justice at home would be equal only to its commitment to the imperative need for the democratization of international political and economic relations.

Guided by the noble ideals of a just international order, a SWAPO government will seek to join SADCC, thereby strengthening this vital community of neighbouring states for greater regional unity, integration and development. SWAPO believes that liberated Namibia together with its neghbours can build a future that is prosperous, more just and more secure.

A SWAPO government will also seek to join the Organisation of African Unity and help make its mission for unity, liberation, peace and prosperity possible for all the peoples of our continent. In this connection, SWAPO upholds the special role the Frontline States have played in support of and in solidarity with the struggling peoples in the region. Independent Namibia will join these states in their demand for the eradication of the evil system of apartheid. The state of Namibia will render moral, political and material assistance through the OAU to the heroic people of South Africa and their national liberation movement to enable them to win their victory and replace apartheid with justice and democracy.

The United Nations is an indispensable world forum. In pledging to uphold the United Nations Charter, upon joining the organisation, Namibia will seek to make its contribution to the efforts that are already afoot for the reform of its charter, institutions and procedures.

SWAPO considers itself a founding member of the Non-Aligned Movement. The state of Namibia will, therefore, promptly formalise its membership in this movement. The principles and objectives of the movement will be at the core of Namibia's foreign policy, which will seek to promote friendship, co-operation, solidarity, non-interference in other countries' internal affairs, mutual respect, and the establishment of diplomatic and commercial relations with other states.

As a non-aligned and a developing country, Namibia will strive to promote South-South co-operation for the adoption of common strategies and policies in trade, commodity prices, science and technology.

The state of Namibia will seek to pursue policies that support all efforts aimed at striking a balance between the often conflicting priorities of liberation, disarmament, peace, security, environmental protection and socio-economic development.

4. Citizenship

Upon accession to statehood, Namibia will have its own citizenship law, defining the relationship between each individual living in the country and the state. This law will be enshrined in the constitution of the country.

Namibian citizenship will be acquired on the basis of the following criteria: birth in Namibia, descent from a Namibian parentage, marriage to a Namibian citizen, and naturalisation.

Citizenship by birth will mean that any person born in Namibia will, regardless of the origins of the parents, have the right to the country's citizenship. A person who acquired citizenship by birth cannot be deprived of it. Citizenship by birth will be automatic, except for the children of diplomatic representatives of other countries.

A person will have the right to become à citizen on the ground that either one of his or her parents or grandparents was born in Namibia. Also, a person one of whose grandparents was a Namibian or belonged to a community indigenous to Namibia may qualify for Namibian citizenship.

A person may acquire Namibian citizenship through marriage to a Namibian citizen.

An alien or foreigner may become a Namibian citizen by naturalisation, that is, by adopting, as a matter of personal choice, Namibia as his or her homeland. He or she must show sufficient evidence of commitment or attachment to Namibia and declare his or her intention to renounce any other previous citizenship. A period of at least 10 years of permanent residence in Namibia and proof that the applicant is of good character and has no record of fascist crimes against humanity will be required for a person to qualify for citizenship.

A Namibian citizen will be prohibited from keeping the citizenship of another country. In this context, SWAPO demands that those charged with the implementation of the UN Plan for the Independence of Namibia must ensure that non-Namibian nationals are not permitted to vote in the election for the Constituent Assembly. Specifically, SWAPO demands that appropriate provisions be made to control effectively the determination of eligibility of voters in the forthcoming UN supervised and controlled elections.

5. Language Policy

The Namibian nation is made up of cultural and linguistic heritage of its various groups. Democratic Namibia will be enriched by all which is healthy in this heritage. A SWAPO government will therefore pursue a language policy that accords equal status and respect to all locally spoken languages. The new policy will redress the present injustice whereby the German and South African colonial states have placed emphasis on the teaching, development and use of German and Afrikaans at the expense of all other local languages, such as, Damara/Nama, Kuangari, Otjiherero, Oshiwambo, Silozi, etc., will be improved to a satisfactory standard.

Mother language will be used as the medium of instruction at the lower primary school level. The concern here is not with so-called group identity or ethnic consciousness and exclusivity, as has been the case with the apartheid colonial regime, but with the fulfillment of cognitive and communicative functions. Since it is through the mother languages that infants first acquire social habits, manners, feelings, tastes, skills and other cultural norms, it is important that their formal schooling starts with those languages of everyday life at home.

At the higher primary school level, English, which SWAPO proposes to make the official language for independent Namibia, will be introduced as a compulsory subject. English will then be used through the secondary level to higher education as the medium of instruction. This policy objective is based on the realisation that none of the locally spoken languages, Afrikaans included, is a medium of international communication; and that in this day and age of increased interdependence among nations, parochial outlook does not serve the interests of any nation. Also, to improve Namibian people's quality of life requires that our country adopts, as a practical sovereign right, a language that will help our people to speedily acquire the vital scientific knowledge and technological know-how. English is one such language.

6. State and Religion

Freedom of conscience and religious worship will be enshrined in the constitution. Every person will be entitled to propagate or preach his or her religious belief.

All denominations will be free to provide religious instruction to their members, pupils and students attending educational institutions which belong to church communities. Church schools will be fully recognised by the state as long as such institutions include in their syllabuses subjects stipulated in the curricula of the national education system. This is essential to achieve uniformity regarding standards of examination and certification.

Other religious institutions, such as, hospitals, printing houses, etc., will also enjoy the protection of the state.

On the other hand, since the political objective of SWAPO is to create a democratic society and to defend the democratic rights of everybody, no person shall be required to undergo religious instruction or to take part in or attend religious observance if such observance or instruction is in conflict with that person's own beliefs.

7. Economic Policies

The Namibian economy under South African colonial rule has been characterized by total lack of coordination. There are minimal linkages within the various sectors of the economy. Each of the three groups that have dominated the Namibian economy, namely, foreign mining companies, white commercial farmers, and South African fishing companies, have only sought to maximise profits by concentrating on the production of primary products for export at the expense of domestic consumption. The benefits accruing from the production processes are distributed on unequal and unjust racial lines in favour of the ruling white group. Exchange of what is produced brings profits only for the owners of the mines, the white farmers, and the fishing companies. In spite of their vital labour input, the black workers get only meagre or starvation wages. For example, in urban areas the whites' per capita income is on average 12 times more than that of the blacks. In the rural areas, this gap is even wider - there, on average a white person's income is 25 times more than that of a black person.

The goal of SWAPO's policy on economic reconstruction and development will, therefore, be to bring change in ownership relations, bring about equitable distribution of national income, create rational linkages of sectors and diversify the economy.

The mining sector that accounts for a third of the Gross Domestic Product (GDP) and 85 per cent or more of all the goods exported from the country, could have been the pillar of a strong and self-sustaining economy in our country. The tax receipts from this source make up about half of the estimated government revenue in spite of the fact that some of the mining companies have been allowed to operate without paying taxes for years and others provide false information about their true incomes in order to avoid paying full taxes.

Of course, there is not a single mining company operating in Namibia that is wholly or partially owned by Namibians. This has meant that Namibia's minerals are effectively monopolised by Western and South African corporations; and with such a stranglehold on the country's key economic sector, these corporations have oriented our economy towards exports of unprocessed raw materials. Thus, much of the wealth from the mining industry - up to 35 per cent of the country's Gross National Product (GNP) - flows to foreign bank accounts of the transnational and South African corporations in the form of profits, dividends, remittances and capital transfers; this has been extreme poverty for the black workers and peasants.

As a movement committed to the values of social justice, solidarity and public interest, SWAPO does not conceal its belief in the moral superiority of socialism over capitalism. Egalitarianism forms the basis of its vision of a just social order.

Under a SWAPO government, Namibia will not allow the *status quo* to continue whereby the structure of the economy is tailored to the needs and demands of foreign and local private capital. Change will have to be brought about. The present unjust state of affairs characterised by the supremacy of foreign capital, on one hand,

and the total subordination of national capital formation, on the other, will have to go.

SWAPO's economic policy on ownership relations is that there will be state, cooperative, joint venture and private participation in the economy. The state will have ownership of a significant part of the country's economic resources. No wholesale nationalization of the mines, land and other productive sectors is, however, envisaged in the foreseeable future.

The independent state of Namibia will stand ready to negotiate new and appropriate agreements with both the existing foreign companies and new investors interested in participating in the development of Namibia's resources for mutual benefit. The central plank of SWAPO's policy on economic restructuring and development is to achieve a measure of national control over the country's resources and to bring about a balance between just economic returns for the Namibian people and reasonable profits for foreign and local private investors.

(a) The Mining Industry

The revenue and foreign exchange earnings from Namibia's mining industry will become the most important element in restructuring and developing the country's national economy. To this end, investors will be required to reinvest into the country's economy a significant part of their profits. Areas of the economy where such financial "plough back" will be necessary include agriculture, manufacturing and mineral exploration and development.

SWAPO's mineral development strategy will also aim at the integration of this key sector with the rest of the economy. This will include the development of mineral-based processing industries such as the manufacture of fertilizers, production of agricultural implements, manufacture of construction materials, metal refining, and fabricating, diamond sorting, valuation and cutting.

SWAPO government will also pursue a tight fiscal policy in respect of the country's mineral industry. This will include the curbing of corrupt practice of transfer pricing and the introduction of state lease and other taxes by the mining companies operating in the country. At present, the transnational corporations are taxed considerably less than in other African countries. For example, CDM pays higher taxes in Botswana than it does in colonial Namibia. In the future, all the corporations will be required to pay tax rates that are commensurate with their actual earnings.

(b) Land Reform and Agricultural Policy

SWAPO is committed to land reform in order to redress the imbalance created by the colonial policies of land allocation on racial basis. The objective of the new policy will be to transfer some of the land from the few with too much of it to the landless majority.

At present, some 65 per cent of the land is owned by the whites. There are about 6,000 cattle and karakul ranches owned by some 5,000 white commercial farmers. According to official figures, as many as 48 per cent of all these farms are owned by foreign absentee landlords. There are also certain whites who own several large farms. The land occupied by absentee landlords, and some of the land of the farmers with many farms will be redistributed to the landless.

But, as in the case of mining, there will be no full-scale nationalisation of the land. Instead, state farms, cooperatives, peasant family farming units, and private commercial farms will be promoted. This strategy of mixed ownership or use of land will seek to promote broad participation of the Namibian people in the country's agricultural production and in the sharing of its surplus value. The second objective of this policy is to increase agricultural production and achieve appropriate product mix.

SWAPO's agricultural policy aims to minimise dependence on imports of foodstuffs. To this end, areas, such as, the north-eastern, northern and north-central Namibia — covering what are presently known as the Ovambo, Kavango and Caprivi regions as well as the Tsumeb/Grootfontein/Otavi triangle - will be designated high priority zones for crop production and intensive irrigation projects. A SWAPO government will strive to provide the necessary support services to the agricultural sector in these and other zones in the form of credit, marketing, extension services for peasant farmers, infrastructure, and adequate producer prices.

To realise these policy goals, it will be necessary to transfer a considerable part of the state revenues from the mining sector to the development of agriculture.

As part of its policy to achieve agricultural self-sufficiency and rural economic development, a SWAPO government will promote the establishment of agro-industries such as grain mills, fertiliser plants, timber mills, edible oil refineries, bag making, food processing, packing and canning factories, as well as the production of simple agricultural implements.

Also a SWAPO government will seek to put an end to the export of unprocessed karakul pelts that are now auctioned in London and processed for wholesalers in Europe and North America. A SWAPO government will seek joint ventures with interested investors to establish a local processing and manufacturing industry in order to export the pelts as finished products.

(c) Policy on Fisheries

Fisheries is a massive resource whose benefits have long been denied to the Namibian people and has instead been over-exploited mainly by South African fishing companies. Allocation of high catching quotas to the South African fishing fleet and lax controls over fishing fleets have greatly contributed to the devastation of Namibia's fish resource. A SWAPO-led government of independent Namibia will take immediate corrective actions to rehabilitate the fishing industry.

A SWAPO government would declare a 200 nautical mile Exclusive Economic Zone off its coast and assume the responsibility for the management and control of fishing in that zone. The government will introduce appropriate levies for all fishing rights to foreign fleets fishing in its territorial waters. Licensing will be linked to adequate policing procedures and reporting. State allocation of quotas and controls over all the catching operations will be aimed at allowing the fish stock to recover after a decade of ruthless over-exploitation and to ensure that the fishing industry will, once again, become an important revenue generating and export-earning sector that it used to be.

SWAPO's ownership policy on fishery envisages the creation of a state fishery sector, in the form of a national company; joint venture operations with experienced and technologically better equipped foreign enterprises; local private ownership as well as workers' co-operatives.

(d) Wildlife and Tourism

Protection of Namibia's unique wildlife resource, historical sites, vegetation, wild landscape,etc, will be among the top priorities of a SWAPO government. Wildlife is a major resource base for Namibia's tourist industry. The present colonial misuse of the country's wildlife and the destructive over-use of its plant reserves will be stopped. Legislation will be passed by the Namibian Parliament to prohibit all forms of encroachment on the country's national parks and nature reserves.

The legislation will also provide for both state patrol of game parks and education about the importance of environmental proctection. National recreation areas and other types of tourist attraction, such as, historical architecture, rock art, sceneries etc.will receive greater state attention than has been the case in the past. This will include better management and conservation strategy. To this end, a SWAPO government will establish a wildlife and nature conservation authority whose main function will be to monitor the well-being and progress of wildlife populations against all destructive and destabilizing forces, such as, drought, the movement and settlement of people, poaching, etc.

(e) Economic independence

There is a simplistic view that Namibia's economy is tied to that of South Africa and that whatever the political and ideological colour of the government that emerges from the UN-supervised elections in Namibia, that government will have to toe the Pretoria line if Namibia is to survive economically. This is a false argument.

Although presently more than two-thirds of all the investment in the Namibian mining industry is owned by South African-based transnational corporations, these corporations are themselves haunted by the spectre of sanctions against South Africa and have, therefore, already embarked on their own investment risk-spreading policies. They are in fact busy establishing separate and locally incorporated companies outside South Africa in pursuit of their own corporate interests. This means that unlike other countries which export capital, the South African white minority state will not have the kind of economic leverage that it would wish to have in Namibia.

Regarding the supply of mining equipment, Namibia can readily find suppliers in Europe, North America and the Pacific - it does not need to import such equipment from South Africa.

Furthermore, unlike some of the south-central African countries,. Namibia does not need access to South African rail routes or ports to transport its goods to the international markets, the claim for sovereignty over Walvis Bay by South Africa notwithstanding. The present use of South African routes and ports is contrived. It is not dictated by any natural necessity. Rather, it came about as a result of colonial connection and is in fact unnecessarily expensive and counterproductive for Namibia.

Since much of Namibia's output of fishmeal and oil, some tinned fish and just about all beef cattle are sent to South Africa to satisfy that country's own demand at prices usually far lower than those obtainable at the world market, Namibian food producers are quite often denied higher earnings from their export.

Further, instead of benefitting from this imperial/client relationship with South Africa, Namibia has had to forego the development of its own slaughtering, cold storage and processing industry and is denied direct access to the lucrative

European, Middle Eastern, Asian and other world markets for its products. Independence will end this unjust relationship.

As mentioned earlier, Namibia also has enough arable land to produce the crops but the colonial rule has deliberately discouraged Namibian farmers from going into commercial production of cereals, fruits and vegetables in order to keep the country a captive market for South Africa's own food surplus

Thus, contrary to the repeated claim that Namibia is heavily dependent of South Africa, the country is in a position to establish its own independent national economy, with its own trade routes to the world markets.

A SWAPO government will thus ensure that Namibian producers will be freed from imperial control. They will be able to diversify their trade and establish alternative markets where their products could obtain better trade terms. They would, for example, be able to benefit from EEC preferential beef quotas under the Lome IV Convention. Independent Namibia will also stand to benefit economically from other multilateral economic associations like the Southern African Development Coordinating Conference (SADCC), the Preferential Trade Area (PTA), the Council for Mutual Economic Assistance (CMEA), the General Agreement on Trade and Tariff (GATT), the Generalised system of Preferences, etc. The country will also, for the first time, have the freedom to produce for domestic and regional markets, instead of remaining a perpetual dumping ground for South African goods.

The current situation regarding Namibia's presence in the Southern African Custom Union (SACU) is not one of equality. Allocation of customs revenues to Namibia are at the discretion of South Africa. It permits free flow of South African agricultural and manufactured products to Namibia, thereby undermining the development and growth of local agricultural output and manufacturing firms. Under SACU, Namibia in fact pays indirect tax to South Africa. This horse and rider economic relationship cannot continue.

Nevertheless, independent Namibia may consider the possibility of staying in the SACU if there are genuine prospects for a non-racial and democratic change in South Africa; and if Pretoria is willing to accept the principle of equality of nations and non-interference in other countries' internal affairs.

It is common knowledge that since 1915 Namibia's Balance of Payments (BOP) has been significantly favourable. South Africa has all the statistics. SWAPO would, therefore, insist on the repatriation to Namibia of the country's share of foreign exchange reserves accumulated and invested in South Africa and elsewhere in the world by the Reserve Bank of South Africa. '

SWAPO does not underestimate the enormity of the task of economic restructuring and development ahead and the considerable magnitude of the financial, technological and managerial requirements for which provisions must be made. A SWAPO government will, therefore, make concerted efforts to obtain the necessary capital assistance, and technological, training and managerial support from friendly countries and international organisations in order to implement its policy of restructuring and developing Namibia's national economy to achieve growth with equity and economic independence.

8. Science and Technology

The acquisition, adaptation and development of science and technology are crucial for any society that wishes to meet the basic needs of its people. Under colonialism, black Namibians have been excluded from the execution of technical tasks and duties. This practice has inhibited the evolution and development of a technological culture among our people.

Under a SWAPO government, independent Namibia will emphasise a scientific-technological culture. It will follow a policy of acquiring, adapting and using science and technology to meet the people's basic human needs and to improve the quality of life of all Namibian citizens.

The acquisition and adaptation of science and technology will entail measures to train cadres at all levels in technical and professional fields. Technical training institutions will be established to build up technical skills.

A SWAPO government will, furthermore, embark upon programmes for the popularisation of science and technology through the dissemination of technical information that is relevant to the day to day activities of the masses. Science and mathematics will be a strong element in our school curricula; and the school syllabuses will strive to ensure an organic link between scientific/technological theory and application.

Independent Namibia will also seek to enter into multilateral and bilateral agreements in co-operation with other countries regarding science and technology exchanges.

9 Policy on Health

Health services is one of the areas where colonialism has found its most cruel expression in Namibia. Disproportionately large sums of money are spent on luxurious hospitals and clinics for the white minority, while health facilities for the black majority are underfinanced, poorly staffed and equipped.

Curative, preventive and promotion medical services for the black majority of the population are hopelessly inadequate. As a consequence, infant mortality rate amongst the blacks is high and life expectancy, low.

The provision of public preventive and curative health care services for all Namibians will be a high priority for a SWAPO government. The government will also strive to introduce primary health care services throughout the country.

To carry out this task of providing a comprehensive health service to all Namibians, SWAPO government will establish a nationwide network of public health centres, clinics and hospitals.

It will also improve the training of health personnel. To this end, medical, and nursing schools will be established to train doctors, dentists, nurses, clinical officers, laboratory technicians, radiographers, psychiatrists, public health inspectors to man the health institutions adequately.

Traditional medical practice will be accommodated to enhance research and utilisation of an important local medical resource.

A Namibian National Red Cross will be established and the government will support and work towards the WHO goal of health for all by the year 2000. Thus, a healthy nation will be the primary goal of a SWAPO-led government in independent Namibia.

10. Education and Culture

One of the most glaring inequalities perpetrated in Namibia by the colonialists has been the gross neglect of the education of the indigenous Namibian population as a deliberate policy designed to subjugate the masses of our people through the perpetuation of ignorance and illiteracy. The colonialists understood that knowledge is power, and they were not prepared to share power with the black majority. The objective of the system of Bantu education imposed in Namibia was simply to provide an inferior education to produce barely literate Namibians who would then be useful tools for the colonial administration in carrying out its dictates. A sanitised curriculum which denied the scholars a broader and open education emphasised their contrived racial inferiority. Scholars were imbued with the virtues of their colonial masters' history at the expense of their own. They were also denied a proper foundation in the sciences, since they were expected to know only enough to service the colonial *status quo.*

Advancement of Namibians to higher learning was greatly circumscribed. Only a handful of Namibians could matriculate. For any furhter studies, the high school graduates had to compete for the few places available at South African Bantu colleges. Namibia can hardly boast of any institutions of higher learning. Adult education has largely been ignored. The colonialists have ensured that Namibians remain a semi-educated people. This has been an inexcusable denial of the basic human rights of our people.

SWAPO views education and training as the right of every Namibian and not a privilege. Against this background, a SWAPO government would work to correct this wrong. SWAPO's basic policy is **education for all.** Education will be at the centre of the transformation of the Namibian society. There will be universal and compulsory education for all Namibians of school-going age. A SWAPO government will encourage and subsidise nursery schools to better prepare Namibian children for their long and important educational journey to adulthood. The government will provide seven years of basic education at the primary level, three years junior secondary level. Education will be compulsory up to the important part of the senior secondary school curriculum to prepare students for further technical, vocational and professional training.

Priority will be given to the expansion of schools, teacher training, and production of appropriate educational materials.

Students unable to proceed beyond junior secondary school level would be encouraged to continue their schooling at junior polytechnics to develop skills in fields such as metal-work, carpentry, bricklaying, motor mechanics, plumbing, catering, tailoring, etc.

Senior secondary school graduates will be given opportunity to advance to universities for degree studies or progress to specialised institutions, such as, institutes of technology; agricultural schools; fishery institutions; commercial, secretarial and accountancy schools; journalism; teacher training colleges; and public administration institutions, etc. At present, these opportunities and institutions exist only for the education and training of the privileged white minority. A SWAPO government will make it a priority to establish such facilities for all Namibians.

A mass literacy campaign will be carried out to eradicate the colonial humiliation of being denied the opportunity to learn, read, and write. Provision will be made for adult education through on-the-job training, and extension, continuing education, non-formal education as well as other skills development programmes.

Provision will also be made to cater for the special educational need of the disabled and handicapped members of our society, such as, war victims, the blind, the deaf and dumb, the emotionally disturbed, and the physically disabled.

Education in rural and urban areas will be equalised. All districts will have government secondary schools and all regions will have specialised state institutions of tertiary or higher education which will be affiliated to the national university.

A SWAPO government will thus invest adequate resources in education in order to uplift and improve the quality of life of all the Namibian people.

Culture is a product of history. In a situation where a nation is dominated by another, the culture of the dominated nation will always carry the mark of domination and oppression. The Namibian people's cultural development was suppressed and retarded for over a century.

At the spiritual level of culture, our people's songs, dances, poetry, arts, languages, traditions, values and beliefs were ruthlessly denigrated by the dominant ruling ideology of racism. At the material level, our indigenous technology collapsed in the face of western manufactured goods. Our artisans and craftsmen were forced out of the productive processes. As a result, the indigenous industry lost the opportunity of further innovation and production because the invading western traders would brook no local competition.

Our architectual designs and building expertise gave way to the dominant alien skills and techniques. National independence should bring with it the liberation of our people's culture from the fetters of colonial domination.

An independent Namibia under a SWAPO government will promote the revival and development of our people's cultural expression and creativity. It will launch a comprehensive cultural programme entailing the establishment of national museums and monuments, theatres for arts and drama, literacy associations, a foundation for arts and crafts, as well as institutes of music and dance, films and languages.

The rekindling of the cultural pride among Namibians is of vital importance because it will serve as a vehicle of their creative reflection upon their past and present realities as well as an expression of their aspirations for a better future.

11. Policy on Rural Development

In the interest of equality and social justice, a SWAPO government will endeavour to eliminate the wide differences between the urban and rural standards of living by initiating development programmes designed to bring about improvements in the income earning activities of the rural communities.

It will do this through equitable allocation of investment funds. Investment funds will be allocated for the development of rural physical infrastructure, such as, hospitals and clinics, schools, water wells, dams and irrigation facilities, etc.

Since there will be limits to the availability of investment funds, independent Namibia will emphasise the use of labour-intensive methods.

The people's government will work to help improve the organisation of rural production and distribution of goods through the provision of extension services and promotion of grassroots voluntary organisations, especially women associations, whose aim will be production co-operation among the peasants. Such organisations will include peasant co-operative movements, self-help housing committees, small-scale industrial development associations, etc.

Rural development will be an integral part of the national development plan; and the government, as the common agent of all the Namibian people, will have the responsibility to provide the necessary support for rural development in the form of funds, leadership, and technical expertise.

12. Local Government and Housing

(a) Local Government

In colonial Namibia, authority at local levels of government has been divided along racial and ethnic lines. Much of the regional government responsibility has been delegated to the so-called second tier authorities.

In the rest of the country, local government responsibility has largely been delegated to a number of white magistrates. White municipal authorities for cities and towns have powers to raise revenue from taxes and provide services; peri-urban boards are also run by whites. In this same urban setting, there are separate councils for whites and blacks. The councils for blacks are mere advisory boards with no power to raise taxes or to make decisions of any consequence.

The black majority have, therefore, been left out of the decision making process at the local government levels, as is the case at the central level.

Democratization of the Namibian society would require the eradication of all the apartheid local government structures. Under a SWAPO government, independent Namibia will have democratically elected local authorities, both in rural and urban areas, in order to give power to the people at the grassroots level to make decisions on matters affecting their lives.

For administrative convenience and development requirements, a SWAPO-led government will restructure and divide the country into regional, district, municipal and village units of local government. This division will not be based on tribal and racial lines, as has been the case. The present tribal "homelands" will be done away with. But local government will be organized in such a way as to protect local cultural traditions and institutions.

Local government structures will be organised in such a way that they can directly influence policy decisions at the central government level.

Chiefs and other traditional leaders of the Namibian communities of our society will have a significant role to play in the local government.

(b) Housing

Housing is one of the forms in which racial stratification of our society has found its most appalling expression. Discriminatory and racist practices remain firmly entrenched. Black workers in urban areas live in squalid conditions of labour compounds, single quarter housing, and in segregated ghettos.

The housing conditions of the overwhelming majority of rural blacks are equally appalling. The often corrupt administrations of the so-called second tier authorities did nothing to improve the housing conditions for the masses.

A SWAPO government will therefore make the provision of adequate housing as one of its top priorities. It will set up a public housing sector to help provide appropriate and affordable shelters for all sections of the Namibian population. Such a public housing sector will be charged with the responsibility for a rapid expansion of housing construction activities in the country.

Housing construction for the lower income groups will receive state subsidies. State support will also be given in the form of appropriate housing legislation, giving access to various forms of credit to enable individuals and groups to build and improve their own houses. There will also be provision for building material loans and crash training programmes for construction workers and artisans in order to ensure the successful implementation of the government's housing policy and programmes.

Local government at regional, district, municipality and village levels will be called upon to support self-help housing projects and technical services in the form of land survey, water supply, electricity and sanitation. The central government will make provision for the upgrading of the administrative, managerial and technical capacity of the local government authorities to enable them carry out this task.

The government will also mobilise and encourage privately-owned construction companies to contribute to the housing programme through an incentive package.

13. Policy on Women

The socio-economic position of women in colonial Namibia has been characterised by brutal oppression. Black women have been oppressed on the basis of race, sex and class. A SWAPO-led government will bring about social justice by bringing women in the mainstream of national life.

Namibian women are actively involved in the creation of our society's material requirements. In the rural areas, they constitute well over 60 per cent of the subsistence agricultural work force. But, the extent of their participation in the production process is by and large invisible. Many of their economic and home activities often go unrecorded and undercompensated. Namibian women face greater discrimination than men in achieving full recognition for their role in the economy.

In the urban areas, where women participate in the wage paying sector of the economy, there is a clear division of labour. Women are concentrated in the low-paying, unskilled, domestic and casual jobs.

Black women, are the most hard-hit by the present high rate of unemployment. The few employers in this country, who provide some kind of training for their workers, tend to discriminate against their female workers, arguing that women stop working when they give birth to children; and, as such, money spent on training them is a "waiste."

SWAPO fully recognises the specific oppression which Namibian women have suffered under colonialism. Its government will therefore, accord full and equal rights to women in all aspects of our future democratic society. Their full and unfettered admission to all levels of government responsibility, and to the industrial, commercial, agricultural, scientific, academic and professional life will be defended. Women will have the right to paid maternity leave and job security. Linked to this right will be state provision for free child care facilities to enable the women to return to their jobs after maternity leave.

The campaign to root out discrimination against women will involve not only provisions for equal education, better training and job security for women, but also minimum quotas for their participation in decision-making bodies at all levels of the government, trade unions, political parties, etc. There will be a national women organisation to promote the interests of the Namibian women. Gender-neutral criteria, based on skills, training, responsibility and working conditions, will be used to ensure equal pay for equal work. Sexual harassment in the workplace will be a legal offense.

14. Youth and Students

Youth account for 55 per cent of Namibia's total population. As a group, it has borne the brunt of the liberation war. Many young Namibians have been in the firing line and have made enormous sacrifices. They have demonstrated an impressive will to work in various fronts of our people's bitter and bloody anti-colonial resistance.The majority of the black Namibian youth have also suffered from the inequality inherent in Bantu education which is restrictive both in terms of coverage and content.

A SWAPO government will, as pointed out in the education section of this manifesto, pursue a policy of comprehensive programmes of education and training to better prepare the Namibian youth for a productive and fulfilling role in adulthood.

It will also guarantee the right and freedom to the Namibian youth and students to mobilize and organize themselves into independent organizations. Such organizations will be free to establish fraternal relations with other youth and students' organizations regionally and internationally.

There will be a Ministry of Youth Affairs. Youth representation in decision-making structures of government at all levels will be guaranteed to ensure their active participation in the national reconstruction, development and defence. The Ministry of Youth Affairs will have specific budget for the promotion of cultural activity among the youth through the establishment of multi-purpose art and craft centres throughout the country. Such centres will have training programmes in music, dance, drama, painting, drawing, etc for the youth. The aim of such activities will be to project among the young people Namibia's cultural identity, values and aspirations. Youth sports' clubs also will be established in urban and rural areas.

On the economic front, the government will pursue a policy of job creating projects for the young people through the provision of rural and urban youth co-operatives and vocational training centres for school leavers.

Since the Namibian youth has been on the front ranks of the armed liberation struggle, quite a number of them are victims of war for whom a SWAPO government will establish a comprehensive programme of rehabilitation, involving skills and training.

15. Labour in Independent Namibia

In line with our movement's policy of economic reconstruction, a SWAPO government will bring about fundamental changes in the country's labour system. There will be a new labour legislation whose major purpose would be to protect the workers' economic interests and rights.

Racist practices whereby black workers are treated as an expendable commodity, that is useful only for its contribution to output, will be done away with. The new labour legislation will include, among other things, provision for a minimum or living wage which each employer will be required to pay his workers.

All the remnants of the oppressive contract labour system will be abolished. Restrictions on population movements will be ended. Migrant workers or contract labourers from the so-called homelands will be fully integrated into the areas of the country in which they work, and will have freedom to live with their families or dependents. Equality of opportunity and treatment in workplace will be strictly demanded of all employers. To redress the effect of past racial and gender discrimination , the government will immediately take measures to eliminate all forms of injustice in recruitment, promotion, wages and training .

The Namibian workers will enjoy the full democratic right to organize themselves into trade unions, and to enable them to participate in economic unit management. The right to trade union activities will be extended to all categories of workers, including farm and domestic workers.

A SWAPO government's labour policy will call for the introduction of workers' education programmes aimed at skill development and raising the workers' level of general education. These will include on-the-job training, adult literacy and continuing education so as to enable the workers to advance through ranks, to managerial, administrative, professional and technical levels of employment.

Employers will be required to provide their employees with housing subsidies, life and health insurance, annual and maternity leave and other necessary fringe benefits. The observance of health and safety standards will be required of every enterprise in the country.

16. Armed Forces

Independent Namibia under a SWAPO government will pursue a policy of peaceful co-existence with its neighbours. However, for the purpose of national defence, the country will establish a national army. The army will recruit all loyal and able-bodied Namibians of the age between 17 and 45 years. All male youth of 17 years will undergo military training and perform at least two years of military duty or national service.

Soldiers of the People's Liberation Army of Namibia (PLAN), who have fought for the independence of the country, will form the core of national army; and those soldiers of liberation who sacrificed their lives in the course of the struggle for independence will be recognised and honoured as national heroes and heroines. Their families and dependents will be looked after by the state.

The Namibian national army will be constituted so as to be of a defensive character. The army will take part in agricultural production, construction and other civil duties.

17. The Mass Media

In colonised Namibia, mass media, i.e., press, radio and television, has been part and parcel of the occupation regime's propaganda machinery. In this, it has been reinforced by a host of publications owned or sponsored by political groupings or business interests that thave been in alliance with the occupation regime against the independence movement.

The South West African Broadcasting Corporation (SWABC), for example, has functioned as an integral section of the South African Broadcasting Corporation (SABC), controlled from Johannesburg with policy decided there and the key personnel appointed or seconded by the parent. Similarly, progressive journalists and publications that emerged in recent years from independent and church sources, were ruthlessly suppressed.

A galaxy of draconian laws, such as, the Prohibition of Information Act, Riotous Assembly Act, the Terrorism Act and martial laws imposed in the war zones of northern Namibia, restricted not only the freedom of movement, assembly, expression, association, etc.; they have also been utilised to gag the mass media.

SWAPO believes that freedom of expression is a basic human right. As such, journalists will have an important role to play in promoting democracy and people's power in an independent Namibia. *Bona fide* journalists, both local and foreign, will be accredited to perform their duties. Newspapers, magazines, periodicals, newsletters and other news and information publications will be certified and registered by the appropriate government agency.

Under a SWAPO government, there will be state-owned media which will serve as a vehicle to promote national unity, reconciliation, reconstruction, development and international solidarity. Media functionaries will be encouraged to disseminate information and ideas.

The mass media in Namibia will subscribe to the United Nations' New International Information Order in providing an accurate and balanced account of information and events on and about Namibia and the world at large.

In order to settle complaints and conflicts between the mass media and the general public, the government will set up a Mass Media Council or (Press Council) composed of leading citizens and representatives of mass media workers (unions or associations) and mass media owners (proprietors/management), headed by a prominent judge to arbitrate on such cases. The normal courts of law will settle with libel, defamation and slander cases according to the law.

18. Corruption in Public Life

In colonial Namibia, as the South African appointed Thirion Commission revealed, widespread graft, malpractices, maladministration, abuse of power and public office and squandering of public funds by holders of public office in some of the "ethnic" governments have been widespread.

A SWAPO-led government will put a definitive stop to this cancerous rot in public life by introducing stringent measures to curb corrupt practices. Corruption in all its manifestations will be regarded as a serious crime.

A SWAPO government will require persons entrusted with public positions to declare their business interests to avoid conflict of interest. It will also set up adequate machinery to ensure that public funds are properly utilised and accounted for.

In addition, an Office of the Ombudsman will be created as a watchdog against the misuse of public office. This office will operate independent of the government to ensure non-interference in its investigations, and fairness in handling complaints. It will have investigative powers to look into cases and complaints brought before it by the general public about unfair practices, such as, bribery, fraud, favouritism, tribalism, racism, victimisation, undue influences, etc. Complainants and witnesses will be protected and the confidentiality of evidence will be guaranteed. Public servants accused of wrong-doing will have the right to defend themselves against such charges and be cleared of any wrong-doing, if found innocent of the allegations. On the other hand, the government will take appropriate action against offending public officials upon the recommendation of the Office of the Ombudsman, should they be found guilty of corrupt practices.

The government will, furthermore, establish an Anti-Corruption Commission to investigate all serious cases of corruption in national life. The citizenry will be free to report genuine cases of corruption and corrupt practices to the Commission, which will have investigatory and prosecution powers.

19. Policy on Public Finance

A SWAPO-led governmment will adopt procedures of strict financial management and overall budget balancing. The specific objectives of such public finance policy will be :

(a)   to secure the necessary funds through appropriate and efficient mobilization of public revenue for implementing the government's various social service and developmental programmes;

(b)   to maintain a proper balance between productive investment and consumption;

(c)   to minimize budget deficit and avoid excessive external borrowing, through concerted efforts to mobilize internal financial resources;

(d)   to encourage and promote domestic investment, through state, private and joint ventures;

(e)   to effect substantial cuts in the public expenditure through a reduction in the present huge state bureaucracy resulting from the existence of eleven so-called second-tier authorities; and

(f)   to adopt more efficient methods of tax collection to increase tax revenue from corporate profits, individual income tax, non-resident shareholders tax, import and excise duties, sales tax, transfer and stamp duties etc.

Independent Namibia under a SWAPO government will also strive to correct imbalances in supply and demand of certain commodities and reduce the inequalities of income distribution.

20. Electoral Process

SWAPO played an important role in the formulation of the United Nations Security Council Resolution 385 of January 1976 and 435 of September 1978. Both resolutions called for free and fair elections in Namibia under the supervision and control of the UN, as a key step towards independence.

Therefore, while deeply deploring and condemning the event of April 1, SWAPO reaffirms its commitment to Resolution 435 and support for its implementation. At the same time, it demands and expects UNTAG to exert the necessary pressure on the South African administration to withdraw all Koevoet paramilitary elements from the police and to put an immediate stop to the on-going acts of intimidation and terrorism by these elements.

As to the future, independent Namibia under a SWAPO government will respect the democratic principle of periodic elections on the basis of universal adult suffrage. All racial and ethnic obstacles to the exercise of such democratic right will be done away with. The only restrictions on the exercise of this democratic right will be age, citizenship, mental deficiency and records of serious criminal offences.

The scheduled independence election will be a multi-party contest which will hopefully provide indication of the Namibian people's preference of political party system.

In line with our commitment to democracy, a SWAPO government will establish an electoral commission to look into issues of national census, demarcation of constituencies, voters' qualifications etc. in preparation for future elections.

-end-

Quelle: SWAPO-Wahlkampfbüro, Windhoek

NAMIBIA TODAY

SOLIDARITY ★ FREEDOM ★ JUSTICE

Vol. 1 No. 3   Saturday 16 September 1989   40c (GST Included)

HOME AT LAST!

by Mocks Shivute

The President of SWAPO, Comrade Sam Nujoma returned on Thursday to his native country after years in exile to a hero's welcome by more than 30,000 people from all over the country. Cde Nujoma, accompanied by the organization's Administrative Secretary, Cde Moses Garoeb, arrived on board an Ethiopian airliner, Boeing 767, piloted by Ethiopian-trained Namibian pilots, which landed for the first time on Namibian soil.

When Cde Nujoma touched the ground from the aircraft steps he first dropped to his knees and kissed the tarmac of the soil he left in 1960. Though he returned in 1966 he was sent back from the airport. After kissing the tarmac Cde Nujoma then hugged his 89 year-old mother, Helvi Kondombolo, who was also at the airport to meet her son.

The SWAPO President then proceeded to greet the few leaders of his organization who were allowed onto the tarmac, before meeting other SWAPO officials in the airport terminal as well as members of foreign observer missions in Namibia and hundreds of media personnel. His only comment to journalists at the airport was "I am happy to be home."

After leaving the airport President Nujoma was whisked away to the African township of Katutura where he addressed a press conference. Cde Nujoma told journalists that if apartheid and white domination were eradicated, then independent Namibia under SWAPO would not have any problem in establishing diplomatic relations with a non-racial South Africa.

He said: "Our policy will be to support fully our brothers and sisters in South Africa who are fighting for the genuine establishment of a non-racial society."

Cde Nujoma invited those who claimed that their families have been killed by SWAPO to come forward and discuss the matter in order to find a way of working together as Namibians. SWAPO did confine certain elements who were sent as enemy agents, who were responsible for the deaths of many Namibians by passing information on to South Africa.

President Nujoma said his organization's task ahead is one of national reconciliation and nation-building.

"If we continue digging the old wounds of the sad history of colonialism, we are not going to achieve anything."

The SWAPO leader described the tragic assassination of a leading SWAPO member, Cde Anton Lubowski, as a very sad affair. He further said that there was a deliberate negligence of the security situation in this country.

President Sam Nujoma's press conference

"Exercise restraint and rally behind SWAPO"

I have had occasion over the years to meet some of you in exile but there never can be any substitute for meeting people in your own land. I am back to be reunited with my people.

Since the formation of SWAPO on the 19th April 1960, our Organization was fully committed to the peaceful campaign to achieve peace and independence. Unfortunately, the colonial system could not allow us to undertake a peaceful campaign for the liberation of our country. As a result, we were faced with only two options, namely to remain passive and be in perpetual slavery and oppression or to resist through the armed struggle. The Namibian people chose patriotic armed resistance with a view to ending the abominable colonial system.

The three decades of bitter struggle for national independence and twenty three years of a bloody war have inflicted deep wounds on our society. Tens of thousands of Namibians have died in the course of the struggle. Thousands of others have been maimed. It is a well-known fact that during the course of the armed struggle, it is only SWAPO which has borne the brunt of the war and suffering. Thousands of our members have suffered imprisonment, torture and mental derailments.

It is as a result of the armed struggle that the South African Government was forced to implement the United Nations Security Council Resolution 435. Therefore, the armed struggle waged by SWAPO brought about Resolution 435. This state of affairs is reinforced by the fact that among the political organizations which are to take part in the forthcoming elections, SWAPO is the only political organization which actively participated in the process which brought about the UN Plan. Furthermore, SWAPO was ready and willing to implement the said Resolution as far back as 1978 when others were dragging their feet.

It would be recalled that subsequent to its adoption, Resolution 435 was not immediately implemented. It became the subject of attempts to revise and rewrite some of its essential provisions. A barrage of criticisms have been levelled at Resolution 435 in terms which suggest either a misunderstanding of what was agreed or a deliberate attempt to misread and insist on inclusion of afterthoughts. Yet those, who a few years ago regarded the prospect of implementing Resolution 435 as wishful thinking are now purporting to be the champions of the said Resolution.

Regarding constitutional principles, several proposals were put forward to be embodied in the future constitution in order to ensure more confidence in the future.

SWAPO took part in the discussion of these proposals and expressed its agreement that the principles were not objectionable to us. SWAPO is committed to these principles, and any suggestion to the contrary, or that we are less than committed to these principles is simply unfounded.

Resolution 435 calls for the signing of a cease-fire agreement between the two warring parties, namely SWAPO and South Africa as the first step towards the implementation of the independence plan. After a painful delay of 10 years, this was done in March this year and came into effect on April 1. Our signing of the cease-fire agreement paved the way for the present political process to take effect, thus providing a unique opportunity to the people of Namibia with the help of the international community to elect their representative to the Constituent Assembly which will draw up a constitution for an independent Namibia.

We have signed that cease-fire agreement in order to close the dark chapter of war and to embark on a peaceful democratic process of decolonizing our country. To this end, the Central Committee of SWAPO instructed the SWAPO Election Directorate to extend a hand of peace, friendship and to strive for reconciliation. My arrival in this beloved country is to reinforce and enhance this objective.

SWAPO considers the healing of the wounds of the armed liberation struggle its top priority. We are committed to turn a new leaf in our history by working to overcome the divisions and conflicts which have characterized the Namibian society. We seek understanding, tolerance, cooperation and unity with all sections of our society. On behalf of SWAPO leadership, I pledge before the Namibian people to conduct a genuinely clean and fair election campaign.

A clean campaign means the absence of intrigues as well as absence of violence, so that all can accept the result of the elections. Intrigues only mar the fairness of the electoral process.

After many years of war, our country badly needs peace and mutual tolerance of each other's respective political messages and promises. It stands to reason therefore, that all parties should refrain from using violence and other forms of intimidation as a means of getting voters to support their programmes. In this regard, the commitment made by a number of parties participating in the coming elections a few days ago,

also check behaviour unbecoming of participating in this important process, is to be welcomed.

On the issue of reconciliation, I must note with appreciation and gratitude that even the business community, which has in the past taken a rather skeptical view of SWAPO's intentions, has reacted with an impressive degree of understanding concerning our agenda for the future of our country, particularly our economic policy to urge everybody to remain in this country and contribute to its future development. Whites have nothing to fear and I call upon those who contemplate leaving the country to remain and take part in Namibia's future development. This is a big country, it is capable of accommodating every Namibian both black and white.

I should also point out that reconciliation is a two way process. It is a fact of life that the Namibian society is divided into two, namely, the haves and the have nots. Therefore, it is also imperative to accommodate the have nots in the

reconciliation process. It is my humble opinion that reconciliation should not only be a political gesture but should also extend to all spheres of life including the economic sphere. Our focus, as shown in the SWAPO Election Manifesto, will concentrate on the burning issues affecting the welfare of the Namibian people as a whole.

I call upon the people of Namibia to exercise restraint and rally behind SWAPO to bring an early end to violence and march towards Namibia's independence in peace. It is extremely unfortunate, and indeed deeply regrettable to learn that the nation is mourning the untimely death of a beloved Namibian son Comrade Anton Lubowski a hero who was dedicated to the peace and justice in our country. He was a bridge between our divided society and he tirelessly worked for the independence of this country. What is even more shocking is the fact that his untimely came barely four hours after the signing of the Code of Conduct For Political Parties

During Present Election Campaign.

On behalf of my organization, I strongly appeal to all political groupings and individuals in this country, and particularly those organizations which will participate in the forthcoming elections to show a spirit of political maturity, reconciliation and commitment to the democratic process. Furthermore, I appeal to those in position of authority to work tirelessly in order to ensure that acts of political violence are severely dealt with. It is my sincere hope that no efforts will be spared in apprehending those responsible for the untimely death of our hero.

Finally, we wish to express our gratitude to men and women of the United Nations, currently serving in our country, far away from their countries. We call upon them to remain vigilant and work within the letter and spirit of Resolution 435 so as to ascertain an outcome which will guarantee Namibia's genuine independence.

Quelle: Namibia Today, 16.9.1989

An hour of history for the Namibian nation

by Mocks Shivute

It took only an hour for SWAPO's President, Comrade Sam Nujoma, to deliver his first public address to the Namibian nation. But it was hour that had been long and keenly awaited.

For the more than 70,000 people who crowded the Windhoek Athletics Stadium on Sunday, this was the first opportunity they had to see in person the living legend who had fathered the liberation struggle, who had endured nearly three decades of exile fighting for the Namibian people's cause.

Some had travelled overnight from the far corners of the land. The long wait at the gates may have been patience-sapping for the many in SWAPO's colours of blue, red and green. From early in morning they streamed to the stadium in order to secure a good position from where they could at least catch a glimpse of the man of whom their parents and grandparents had told them – a man who launched the national liberation struggle before many of them had born. For the older members of the vast crowd, this was a moment for which they had been waiting 30 years.

As Cde Nujoma went to the microphone to express his pleasure to be addressing the Namibian people after the long exile, the packed stadium broke into cheers

and ululation. The vast audience welcomed him back with all their heart and soul.

President Nujoma's message to the people indicated that a future independent Namibia under SWAPO did not intend to rule the country alone, but would seek the participation of others in formulation and implementation of policies. He said: "SWAPO will strive to achieve popular support in making policy decisions."

Cde Nujoma explained that SWAPO would not impose a one-party political system on the Namibian people against their will. He added that SWAPO was committed to a policy of mixed economy and land reform.

He urged the white community not to sit on the fence, but to participate actively in the country's independence process in order to exercise their democratic rights.

The SWAPO leader said that the principle of national reconciliation and the guaranteeing of the democratic rights of the Namibian people could not be realized without a corresponding change in the social and economic sphere.

He said that a SWAPO government would do everything possible to provide incentives to national and international business concerns to generate sufficient employment opportunities, and to contribute to the objectives of economic reconstruction and

prosperity for all.

He continued that SWAPO would strive to bring about a revolutionary change in the dispensation of the country's social services. He cited equitable distribution in the education, health and housing services to the population with development priorities to the hitherto neglected black population in the rural areas, urban squatters and ghettoes.

SWAPO commits itself to job creation through encouragement of the rural economy, and plans subsidies to the producers of maize, millet and rice in the agricultural areas, which are presently marginalized with the South African government policy to maintain Namibia's dependence on the South African market.

The SWAPO leader called on the international community to follow closely and monitor the process of the implementation of UNSC Resolution 435, in order to ensure that Namibia's independence election will indeed be free and fair.

President Nujoma reiterated SWAPO's wish to contribute to the achievement of peace and security in Southern Africa. He added: "SWAPO believes, however, that the achievement of this noble goal in this region will remain elusive as long as the problem of apartheid remained unresolved."

Cde Nujoma vehemently

condemned the participation of foreign voters in Namibia's independence process, which he described as an obvious example of unfairness. "There is no justification for foreign spoilers to come in order to influence the outcome of the elections in favour of pro-South African political groups in this country," he said.

Cde Nujoma gave as an example: that he has been living in Tanzania for ten years, another ten in Angola and eight in Zambia, but he has never voted in those countries, why should white South Africans be allowed to vote in Namibia, whereas they were denying their own African citizens the right to vote?

He said the application of the AG-23 proclamation requiring prior authorization for the holding of political rallies was hindering rather than enhancing the freedom and fairness of the campaign process.

"We are receiving reports of our campaigns and meetings being broken up or prevented to take place by police on account of enforcing that particular proclamation."

He urged the UN Secretary General, Javier Perez de Cuellar, to give urgent consideration to the problems caused by the passing and application of AG-23 in the midst of the election campaign.

Quelle:
Namibia Today, 27.9.1989

Vol.5 No.5 Monday 9 October 1989

SWAPO
ELECTION NEWS LETTER

Published by SWAPO Directorate of Elections

P.O. Box 72
KATIMA MULILO
Namibia

VOTE
SWAPO

HAMUTENYA ADDRESSSES CAPRIVI

The Monday October 2, 1989 mammoth meeting with estimated attendance of over a thousand people was a huge success. The Katima Mulilo Community hall, the venue of the meeting, was over-filled with peopel that hundreds of them could not even manage to enter the premises. The guest of honor and main speaker was Comrade Hidipo Hamutenya, Politburo member of the Central Committee of SWAPO, Secretary of Information and publicity and Head of Mobilization at SWAPO Election headquarters.

Comrade Hamutenya opened the meeting by conveying revolutionary greetings from SWAPO President Sam Nujoma and the leadership from the Directorate of election Headquarters in Windhoek. As he put it "the leadership of SWAPO is following very closely events happening in this region and I and my colleagues are extremely very happy to be in this region because this region has for a very long time sustained the war for Liberation started by PLAN on 26 August 1966".

He broached a couple of issues of national concern. Firstly, he stated that SWAPO wants PEACE as the war is over. Thus, "SWAPO is capable of fighting DTA, Koevoet elements, etc. but SWAPO wants PEACE, UNITY AND RECONCILIATION because these will win the elections" he pointed out. There is no doubt that divisive elements want to delay the independence process, he continued. SWAPO, however, must refuse to play in their hands, he cautioned. He further observed:

"Let us proceed with the mobilization of voters, voters education, etc. Teach people how to vote, where to vote in order to have an overwhelming majority victory during the coming November election.

We are a mature political organization. We are certain of victory. As a people who will govern this nation in eleven months, we have the responsibility to UNIFY the masses for the difficult task ahead of us of developing this wonderful country".

Secondly, Comrade Hamutenya pointed out in response to allegations by right wing mass media here and abroad that SWAPO was "Communist" that all that was required of a member of SWAPO was OPPOSITION TO ALL FORMS OF FOREIGN DOMINATION, A READINESS TO FIGHT FOR, AND IF NECESSARY DIE FOR, THE FREEDOM AND INDEPENDENCE AND A COMMITMENT TO UNITY. as he pointed out, SWAPO was opposed to exploitation of man by man and believed in social justice and we:

"We believe after independence Namibia must have the power to check the excesses of capitalist greed. This is not the same as Communism".

He further stated that a SWAPO led government will be a people's government which will be run by Namibians and for Namibians regardless of colour, creed or national origin. Thus SWAPO's philosophy of government centre upon these three (3) principles:

(a) JUSTICE denotes equity equality etc of classes within the social order as Comrade Hamutenya put it", it is not justice to have two (2) hospitals -one of whites- with the most up to date equipment and facilities and one for blacks with sub-standard resources, the same goes for education, recreational facilities, unjustice of the landless, lack of housing, lack of education, etc". Thus, when we call for the end of injustice, we are labelled Communists, he retorted.

(b) FREEDOM which entails LIBERTY- basic rights of all nations to determine their own destiny in their own sovereignty state. Thus, denotes the opportunity of all the people to realize their potentialities and needs.

(c) SOLIDARITY is an effort to strive to achieve noble goals. SWAPO will have a programme to give solidarity to workers as well as help workers with their needs.

Thirdly, Comrade Hamutenya elaborated upon HEALING THE WOUNDS OF WAR by bringing messages from SWAPO President Sam Nujoma and top SWAPO leadership which are (i) that war is over and peace is here because of SWAPO, (ii) that unity is paramount and that the policy of SWAPO is UNITY TOGETHERNESS and (iiI) national reconciliation. This policy involves among others, a general pardon for all those Namibians who were MILED and MISUSED by the colonial power to prevent the achievement of Namibia's Independence. As Cde Hamutenya put it:

"SWAPO extend a hand of reconciliation to those Namibians who were in the service of the colonial power, including those who were in its armed forces, security and intelligence network".

In an emotionally raised voice, Comrade Hamutenya strongly denounced surrogates of colonial South Africa, such as DTA, so called Parents Committee, etc who due to lack of issues on which to attack SWAPO, have raised the issue of the so called SWAPO DETAINEES still in Angola and Zambia when in fact there are none in these countries. He further commented, "They make a lot of noise about SWAPO Detainees but we never hear them ask for the whereabouts of SWAPO Vice-President Brendan Simbwaye, Lyamboloma, Maswahu, Masinda or Kulibalika. Mishake Muyongo's boss, Dirk Mudge was one of the senior government officials who knew (and still knows) the whereabouts of Comrade Simbwaye and why doesn't Muyongo ask Mudge?.

Finally, in his concluding remarks Comrade Hamutenya called on all Caprivian to accord a decisive victory to SWAPO in the region. As he pointed out.

"Go and work very hard for the remaining five (5) weeks Make Katima shine with an overwhelming victory to SWAPO in this region. Let's make sure that we teach people how to vote so that they can vote correctly using sample ballot papers".

Before concluding his historic and inspiring speech, he told a jubilant cheering mammoth crowd that Cde President Sam Nujoma, the undisputed leader and father of the subjugated but struggling Namibian masses will be touring this region soon. He is scheduled to hold a gigantic mammoth rally on SATURDAY OCTOBER 28, 1989.

SWAPO MEETING AT IMPALILA ISLAND

The SWAPO meeting which took place on Sunday October 1, 1989 at Impalila Island was a gigantic success. It had an estimated attendance of about 200 people comprising of teachers, students and villagers. Cde Shadrick Mwilima, Head of Impalila sub-centre, chaired the meeting and introduced the member of the delegation who included Cde George Bupilo, Member of the Central Committee of SWAPO Youth league and Deputy Director of Elections in the region, Cde George Liswaniso , Deputy head of the Dept of Mobilization and Voters Registration in the region, Cde Josephat Inambao Sinvula of the Dept of Mobilization and Voters Registration , Cde Gullen Kolokwe, Deputy Head of legal Affairs Dept in the region and George Shingisa of the Dept of technical and repairs Services in the region.

The meeting began with a word of prayer by Cde Charles Sampati, Deputy Head of Impalila sub-Centre. Consequently, Cde Mwilima introduced the main speaker, Cde George Bupilo. Cde Bupilo started addressing the meeting by tracing and or outlining the historical background of SWAPO, elaborating on the present and future chain of events in the region. He began the meeting by reminding the audience that SWAPO which was formed in 1960 first used the NON VIOLENT

STRATEGY to redress the inequity and oppression perpetrated by first the German Colonial Empire and later by racist fascist South Africa. It was only after this peaceful strategy failed that SWAPO resorted to the ARMED STRUGGLE on August 26, 1966. It so happens,therefore, that the subsequent arrival of returnees as well as UNTAG in Namibia drives from the relentless and uncompromising struggle waged by SWAPO in the past years. The perception of 'PEACE" in Namibia was brought by SWAPO.

This is why, emphasized, the cease-fire had not been between any one other than SWAPO and South Africa which were the two parties to the conflict in Namibia. Cde Bupilo told his audience that now the war over, SWAPO had come with a message of UNITY, RECONCILIATION and PEACE and appealed to all Namibians to ensure a SWAPO victory in the coming November elections. Thus, as far as he was concerned, he still regarded the DTA, CANU, NPF, UDF and NPP members in this region as his "lost brothers and sisters with lost souls" and appealed to them to join SWAPO before it is too late.

On the former detainees, Cde Bupilo pointed out that unlike political prisoners, "they were just South African spies and traitors who led to the demise of your young brothers and sisters in exile" He said innocent Namibia lives were lost at Oshatotwa, Cassinga and other place as a result of information supplied to the attacking forces by South African agents. He also questioned why surrogate Mishake Muyongo and his henchmen in the DTA did not question the whereabouts of SWAPO Vice President Brendan Simbwaye, Lyamboloma, Maswahu, Masinda or Kulibalika.

In his concluding remarks, Cde Bupilo explained that the people of Impalila Island and all Namibians should vote for SWAPO in coming November elections for three major reasons: Firstly,SWAPO fought for your right to be respected as human beings.Thirdly, SWAPO negotiated for UNSC Resolution 435 and campaigned relentlessly for its implementation. To quote Cde Bupilo "the choice of the people must be the choice between FREEDOM and oppression, in-human policy and JUST POLICY, JUSTICE and injustice, inequality and EQUALITY".

As Cde Bupilo put it, "Namibians do not want colonialism, they do not want it now neither will they want it in the future" (BATU BA NAMIBIA NEBA SA TOKWI BUKOBA, ABA BU TOKWI KACENU, MANE ABA NA KUBU LATA KAMUSO)

Quelle: SWAPO Election Newsletter, Katima Mulilo, 9.10.1989

How to Vote

1

GIVE THE ELECTION OFFICER YOUR REGISTRATION CARD. HE WILL TAKE THE CARD AND KEEP IT.

2

THE ELECTION OFFICER WILL LOOK AT YOUR FINGERS UNDER A SPECIAL LIGHT TO SEE IF YOU HAVE VOTED BEFORE.

3

YOU MUST SIGN THE REGISTRATION CARD OR MAKE A FINGERPRINT ON IT, JUST AS YOU DID WHEN YOU REGISTERED.

4

THE ELECTION OFFICER WILL PUT A SPECIAL KIND OF INK ON YOUR FINGER TO SHOW THAT YOU HAVE VOTED. NO ONE CAN SEE THIS INK EXCEPT UNDER THE SPECIAL LIGHT.

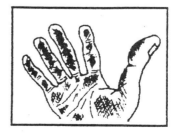

5

YOU WILL BE GIVEN A
BALLOT PAPER WITH THE
NAMES AND SYMBOLS OF
ALL THE POLITICAL
PARTIES.
SWAPO IS SECOND FROM
THE BOTTOM.

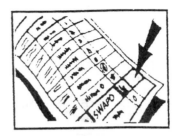

6

TAKE THE BALLOT PAPER
INTO THE VOTING
COMPARTMENT–A
PRIVATE PLACE WHERE
NO ONE CAN SEE WHO
YOU VOTE FOR. PUT YOUR
X NEXT TO THE SWAPO
SYMBOL.

7

FOLD THE BALLOT PAPER
IN HALF AND THEN FOLD
IT AGAIN.

8

PLACE THE PAPER IN THE
BALLOT BOX.
YOU HAVE NOW VOTED.

98

Quelle: Namibia Today, 28.10.1989

DTA: Wahlmanifest

NAMIBIA ON THE ROAD TO TRUE FREEDOM AND MEANINGFUL INDEPENDENCE

1. THE DTA OF NAMIBIA'S ROLE IN THE STRUGGLE FOR FREEDOM

The freedom struggle of the people of Namibia has been a long and bitter struggle which has continued for a century and has been waged by different groups and intstances against two success..e colonial powers.

It started with the Herero war of 1904 - 1906. After the Second World War it was continued by Hosea Kutako and the Chiefs Council which presented regular petitions to the United Nations after the inception of that world body.

This was followed up ten years later by the establishment of various political organisations who strived for the independence of Namibia, but without the intended success.

During November 1977, the DTA (Democratic Turnhalle Alliance), which included eleven political parties,was established. Some had been in existence for years and were represented by leaders who were already involved in the freedom struggle.

The DTA of Namibia came into existence as a result of two major considerations.

First, because a few months previously, the Western nations had come to the fore with a settlement plan which would later become known as Resolution 435. This provided for election for an Assembly to draft a constitution.

The leaders of the parties in the future DTA awarded their full support to this independence plan as an alternative for the senseless war which had at that stage already claimed many lives without independence being anywhere in sight.

It became clear that it would be meaningless for individual ethnic parties to take part separately in the envisioned elections.

The second consideration taken into account during the formation of the DTA, was the increasing desire for greater national unity, for the termination of institutionalised ethnicity and for the total abolition of apartheid and discrimination on the grounds of race and colour.

The DTA used peaceful methods to achieve its aims. The DTA for instance, participated in two interim governments during the following two decades and despite limited powers succeeded in bringing about vast changes to the system and the attitude of people.

This caused many clashes with the government of the RSA and in 1983 even led to the disbandment of the first interim government.

During this government's term the following milestones, amongst others, were reached.

* For the first time a Namibian government was in power, one which represented all the inhabitants of the country. For the first time black Namibians participated in both the legislative as well as the executive authority of their country.

* A Namibian government service was established in the country by this DTA government. Once again, for the first time, black Namibians occupied prominent posts in the government service. Despite the great handicap experienced by black inhabitants of the country until this stage, new doors were now open to them.

After the Pass Laws, the Law on Mixed Marriages and the Immorality Act had been abolished at the request of the DTA, in 1979 the DTA piloted a measure through the National Assembly which would abolish separate residential areas and open facilities. This legislation provoked violent reaction and even protest in certain circles.

Inhabitants could now purchase land anywhere and live where they wished. This provided them with investment opportunities for the first time.

Attempts were made by the DTA government to limit the powers of the ethnic authorities, which they possessed in terms of AG 8. This led to the dissolution of the DTA government by the government of the RSA, because South Africa would only support an ethnically constituted party.

Despite the confrontation with the RSA government, the DTA decided to make a second attempt in expectation of the implementation of Resolution 435, by taking part, with various other political parties, in a government of National Unity, with the principal aim of making a new constitutional dispensation operational during the interim period.

The colonial governor in the person of the Administrator General, Mr Louis Pienaar however, stubbornly refused to accept any dispensation which did not guarantee minority rights.

The DTA however persevered with their standpoint that a multiparty democracy with a Bill of Fundamental Rights was the best guarantee for a protection of minority groups.

The second interim government will be remembered especially for what it did for the economy and the workers. During this period the economy flourished and many employment opportunities were created principally in the construction industry.

Labour legislation was also passed during this period, to give the worker more bargaining power in the settlement of disputes.

At last the end of the struggle came into view when an agreement was reached to implement Resolution 435 on April 1 ,1989.

A new day was to break for Namibia. A day for which people of the country had longed for for nearly a hundred years, had now become reality. That which lay behind us, was now only a bad memory. The challenge which we now have to accept is to make a success of the country's independence.

We will not permit the process to be delayed again as happened in 1979. We also may not allow what has happened in many African countries to happen in our's.

The DTA of Namibia is proud that it took the initiative for a peaceful independence. With courage and honesty we prepared the people of the country for what was to come - True Freedom and Independence.

2. **THE CONCEPT OF TRUE FREEDOM**

There are many different opinions about the concept of "True Freedom" in this country. This is probably the most important point of difference between the DTA and its principal opponents.

History has shown that independence alone is not enough to ensure true freedom. Today still, there are many independent countries whose citizens possess very little, if any, freedom.

Independence does free a country from colonial control. It frees it from laws and decisions which are forced upon it from outside, but there it ends. A Bill of Fundamental Rights has become an essential part of every constitution in this day and age, to protect the rights and freedom of the individual within his own country - it could even be the guarantee that the government does not exceed its authority over the citizens of that country.

The DTA guarantees true freedom for the inhabitants of a future independent Namibia, which will include

* political freedom
* social freedom
* economic freedom.

In an independent Namibia, the inhabitants must be entitled to choose their own government on a regular basis and in a democratic fashion. Each citizen of the country must be allowed to belong to the party of his choice, which party must have the right to be elected in the government of the country.

In this way each citizen of our country will have the right to influence the formation of laws and the taking of decisions which he himself will be subjected to. The highest form of freedom is to be found in obedience to self-made laws.

Someone who does not have these rights, cannot be truly free. Therefore the DTA chooses a multiparty democracy, and rejects a one-party state.

3. THE REPUBLIC OF NAMIBIA

A. BILL OF FUNDAMENTAL RIGHTS

A Bill of Fundamental Rights will be entrenched in the Constitution. This Bill will include, amongst others, the following fundamental rights and liberties:

* The right to live

* The right to freedom, personal safety and privacy

* The right to equality before the law

* The right to a fair trial

* The right to free expression, conscience and belief

* The right to gather

* The right to free association

* The right to enjoy, preserve, practice, protect and promote culture, language, tradition and religion

* The right to free movement and choice of place of residence

* The right to own property

* The right to education

* The right to take part in politics and in the government.

B. THE CONSTITUTION

The DTA promises the people of this country a constitution as the highest authority in which is entrenched a Bill of Fundamental Rights, which is binding on the government and all its instances and which can be enforced by independent courts of law.

The constitution will embody the following:

1. this country will be re-created as an independent and sovereign state - The Republic of Namibia -

(a) in which, first of all, the supremacy of God is acknowledged.

(b) in which the people of Namibia, free of domination from outside, will be able to bring their chosen government to power,

(c) which will be based on the principles of democracy, fundamental freedom and the responsibilities and authority of the law,

(d) which guarantees an economy based on private, public and cooperative property rights and initiative, social justice and equal opportunities for all, and

(e) which will be in possession of its own national flag, anthem, emblem, seal, citizenship, monetary unit and official language.

2. Equality is guaranteed for all

(a) through which all people in Namibia are awarded equal rights so that they cannot be oppressed either by the government or any other instance,

(b) through which everyone will be equal before the law, and

(c) through which no-one can be disadvantaged or advantaged by the government or any public institution or any group or other people on the grounds of ethnic or social origin, sex, race, language, colour, religious belief or persuasions.

3.   Freedom for all the people of Namibia is guaranteed.

This entails

(a)   the right to freedom of speech (including the freedom to communicate information and ideas through the media),

(b)   liberty of conscience of religious beliefs,

(c)   freedom of movement and choice of domicile, and

(d)   freedom to enter and leave the country.

4.   Peace as ultimate goal will be sought amongst

(a)   au the people of Namibia,

(b)   all the political, religious, cultural, language and ethnic groups in Namibia,

(c)   Namibia and other states in that the territory of Namibia will not be utilised by any person, group or government to launch attacks on other countries, their governments or people.

5.   Progress and prosperity are made possible to all the people of Namibia in that,

(a)   the state will develop its human resources to their full potential by giving each person in Namibia the opportunity of acquiring knowledge, education, know-how and expertise,

(b)   an economic policy be followed that will ensure substantial growth and guarantee job opportunities,

(c)   each person's right to acquire property, possess or sell it, is guaranteed,

(d)   each person may associate freely with any other person or group of people and initiate, maintain or join associations or partnerships, including trade associations for the protection of workers' interests,

(e)   a system of communal property ownership by tribes or communities is recognised and provision is made by the state for the intensive development through financing, technology, counselling, research, training, planning, etc, which will ensure that a subsistence economy is transformed to a market economy,

6.   Security will be maintained so that

(a)   no-one need feel threatened or insecure,

(b)   no-one is martyred or punished in an inhumane or humiliating manner or is detained or taken into custody in conflict with the law,

(c)   each individual's personal freedom, right to live and right of privacy is recognised.

7.   Justice is guaranteed for all

(a)   which is enforced by an independent judiciary consisting of judges who are subject to the law alone (and not to the government or any other instance).

(b)   which guarantees each person a fair and impartial trial and decides his rights or responsibilities in civil cases or decides his guilt of a crime in criminal cases,

(c)   which grants each person accused of a crime the right

i)   to be considered innocent until proved guilty,

ii)   to bear witness or call witnesses should he so desire,

iii)   to be allowed sufficient time and reasonable facilities for the preparation and presentation of his defence and to acquire legal representation

C. THE GOVERNMENT STRUCTURE

The Cor- titution will provide for a structure of government consisting of the following.

1. The Central Government

A democratic orderly and effective government, elected on the principle of proportional representation and which is constituted as follows:

(a) A President, elected for a term of six (6) years by both Houses of Parliament as Head of State, who has certain ceremonial and executive powers which he will exercise in the best interest of the country and its inhabitants in accordance with the Constitution and other laws of the country;

(b) A Cabinet, which consists of the Prime Minister, elected by the National Assembly and Ministers who are appointed by the Prime Minister from the members of the National Assembly, and who will be responsible for the execution of the laws of the country;

(c) A Parliament, consisting of the National Assembly and a Senate, elected by the enfranchised voters of Namibia for a period of five (5) years, with the power to pass laws for Namibia which are not contrary to the Constitution and the Bill of Fundamental Rights.

2. Regional Authorities

The DTA rejects the system of second tier authorities based on ethnic groups as this system has proved impractical and discriminating in practice. It has had the added result of creating tension and suspicion between the different population groups.

The DTA proposes a decentralised unitary state which makes provision for Regional Councils which will not only bring the government to the inhabitants and thus serve local interests, but will also allow the people of the region to participate in the Central Government. Thus the DTA proposes that Regional Councils be represented in the Central Government.

Furthermore, the DTA undertakes that traditional leaders and traditional authority will play a very important role in the future government, especially as regards communal matters.

3. Municipal Authorities

The DTA stresses the importance of efficient government on municipal management level, as this level of government is responsible for the welfare of large population concentrations. It is here that social and economic evils exist, especially in unproclaimed towns in the north.

The DTA rejects the existing system, which has until now excluded certain communities in our urban areas from direct participation in local management. The DTA has available comprehensive proposals for a system of municipal management in terms of which only one municipal council with only one management committee in each urban area will be established. This municipal council will be elected in a democratic fashion.

This municipal authority will be responsible for urban development, the availability of erven, building of streets and the provision of services e.g. water, electricity, sanitation, public transport and recreational facilities. The DTA however, believes that the provision of low-cost housing should not be the responsibility of the municipal authorities owing to the limited financial capabilities of this authority. The responsibility of low-cost housing and rented houses belongs with other institutions such as building societies.

4. The Peri-urban Board

The Peri-urban Board consists of people appointed by the Cabinet, to deal with the affairs of communities outside the areas under municipal jurisdiction.

5. The Ombudsman

An independent ombudsman, appointed by the legislative authority who will freely be able to investigate all complaints of one-sidedness, inefficiency or inefficient administration and report to Parliament on those matters.

The Constitution will contain the principles whereby a future civil service will be operated.

4. GOVERNMENT SERVICE

The DTA will implement a sovereign and multi-party democratic system of government with a constitution and a legislative, executive and an independent judicial branch of power. The government will be supported by a politically neutral and dynamic civil service.

For the purpose of sufficient administration of the country, the principles of merit and efficiency in personnel administration as embodied by means of an independent Public Service Commission as an objective and impartial personnel authority, are emphasised to promote acceptable personnel practices.

Persistent and deliberate training and development of manpower to improve their knowledge, disposition and skills will be dealt with in an organised manner. Formal training will be undertaken on a sentralised basis through the Institute for Public Service Training, while in-service training will take place at the point where a service is rendered. Particular emphasis is placed on this last mentioned aspect of training.

With reference to the Bill of Fundamental Rights the following normative code of conduct will be prescribed to officials for the benefit of efficient public administration:

* the honouring of the supreme political authority,

* public accountability,

* the principles of fairness and reasonableness, balance, thoroughness, unassailibility and legality. On these grounds it will be precisely monitored that the civil service is on all levels representative of the population of the country.

The present Government Service will be extended to become a model civil service. Existing expertise in the Government Service will be utilised for this purpose.

5. CITIZENSHIP

Citizenship in an independent Namibia can be acquired in the following way:

a) Birth.

b) Children or grandchildren of a person born in Namibia, on condition that that person meets all other requirements, with the exception of the minimum period of residence which is applicable in other cases.

c) A person entering a marriage contract with a citizen of this country.

d) A person resident in the country for at least four uninterrupted years and who meets all the requirements of neutralization.

6. ECONOMY

To live up to the expectations of our population in the economic field, a sensible economic policy will have to be followed after independence. There is a tremendous economic and social imbalance among the people of Namibia.

To talk about a redistribution of wealth would be senseless if there is no wealth to distribute. The DTA will therefore follow a policy which will lead to economic growth, because this is a prerequisite for the creation of prosperity.

However, the DTA also regards it as essential that that section of the population which in the past did not fully have the opportunity to become involved in the economy of the country, must now have the opportunity.

The DTA is responsible for the fact that everybody can now, without restriction, own fixed property, but it should not end here. Affirmative action will be necessary to wipe out backlogs and to bring about the ideal circumstances to provide equal economic opportunities, so that a decent standard of living is attainable by everyone.

It must, however, be pointed out once again that this will only be possible if Namibia has the necessary means at its disposal. In the past, when reference was made to the redistribution of wealth, mistakes were made by assuming that wealth was a static unit that should be divided, instead of emphasising that everyone should be entitled to an equal share of the prosperity of the country. Too often in the past reference was made only to the natural resources of our country, such as minerals, fish and agricultural land, while the other factors of economic growth, such as capital, knowledge and expertise, which includes entrepreneurs, were not accounted for. So as to broaden the basis of our economy and achieve socio-economic development we are very dependent on investors from abroad for technology and capital.

The question that must therefore be answered is which economic policy should be followed to attract capital, technology and entrepreneurs to our country. Socialism as an economic system has failed all over the world. There is currently a movement away from socialism throughout the world. As a result of the wrong way in which the redistribution of land was handled the central control of the economic social ownership has been responsible for many of the failures in Africa. Interference by the state, over-taxation and nationalisation has been responsible for the fact that many African countries have received no investment from abroad.

Foreign investors will be influenced by the way a future government treats existing investors. One cannot expect to gain new investors if one treats existing investors unjustly.

For economic growth to be achieved attention should especially be given to favourable financing for the small entrepreneur to start his own business.

Participation in larger industries, by means of shares in for instance fish factories and workers' participation according to which workers can share in the profits of large companies, will be provided for. A person who cannot become involved in the economy in his own right is not really free.

Any system in terms of which everything belongs to the state or is controlled by the state, turns people into slaves who must be given everything as handouts from the state.

The DTA recognises the fact that a sound economy is primarily founded on the meaningful utilisation of human resources. This implies that investment in the development of Namibia's human resources is of prime importance.

7. MONETARY POLICY

It is the aim of the DTA to implement a monetary policy which will underwrite the total independence of Namibia in the long run. It will be achieved by instituting the following measures:

* Pass legislation for a central bank, a new currency and financial institutions.

* Establish an own central bank and approach international institutions such as the IMF or World Bank for technical assistance.

* Establish our own gold reserves from gold produced in Namibia.

* Calculate the precise extent of imports into Namibia and implement measures which will enable local entrepreneurs to fulfil these demands in the consumer market.

* Appoint a monetary policy commission to look after the interests of Namibia in terms of monetary development. The commission's activities should primarily address issues like exchange controls, balance of payments, RMA, SACV, exchange rate, etc.

8. FISCAL POLICY

Namibia has a narrow and inelastic tax base, therefore extreme care must be exercised not to raise taxes drastically as this will result in evasion. The outcome would be erratic economic behaviour. Economic competition and economic attractiveness will be greatly reduced.

The DTA will aim to introduce tax reform by broadening the tax base and simplifying tax administration. Tax reform will depend on economic reform as spelled out in the economic policy of the DTA.

In Namibia's case it would be wise to consider taxing consumption as this would generate taxes from the spectrum of the population Apart from basic necessary spending, this furnishes the taxpayer with a rudimentary instrument to control individual taxation.

Taxation of consumption can be done through sales tax (VAT- value added tax) or trade measures.

The DTA will consider the following measures:

* Strengthening of the tax administration.

* Introduction of a new tax system, for example taxes on agricultural land on a progressive scale according to the size of the land and average rainfall.

* Amendments to existing legislation for example luxury articles write off only up to a certain value.

* Differentiation in sales tax to distinguish between luxury goods and basic consumer goods

The DTA will not introduce tax on capital gains as this would seriously discourage both foreign and local investors.

Fiscal Reforms

The DTA accepts the fact that major fiscal reform needs to be implemented. This reform will take place along the following guidelines:

* Creation of our own capital market. Deficits on the budget will be funded by issuing government bonds rather than by loans. The DTA will implement its economic policy in such a manner that the deficit on the budget should not exceed 4 % of the gross domestic product.

* Broadening of the tax base.

* Improvement of tax administration.

* Charging for public services.

* Development assistance on condition of a rate of return.

An investment code has been prepared by the DTA and it will be published on the date of independence in order to state clearly what the DTA will expect from foreign investors and what their expected return would be.

The harmonization of taxes with the tax levels of neighbouring countries will be pursued with the specific aim to provide the most favourable conditions to investors.

9. COMMERCE AND INDUSTRY

Because of historical reasons, a large section of the population has not been sufficiently actively involved in the economy of the country, except for offering their labour. There has, however, been active participation in the retail trade, especially in certain areas.

The DTA consequently has set itself as a goal involving by means of special schemes, those Namibians who in this respect are behind so that they can enjoy economic freedom. It is not acceptable that the inhabitants of the country will be dependent on a government that controls all production sources centrally.

Participation in the small industries and small business undertakings must be encouraged by training and financing, while markets must be created for products. Shareholding in larger industries and worker participation in larger undertakings must also be introduced. Although shareholding and worker participation are still foreign concepts to the inhabitants of the country, as they probably prefer a system of sole ownership, they will have to be enlightened and encouraged on this respect. Participation in the mining and fishing industries and larger business undertakings should especially be promoted.

Although attention will have to be paid throughout to affirmative action, normal economic principles must apply throughout.

It is so that a large part of our population will remain dependent on the labour market.

Work opportunities for a living remuneration are still a high priority. This is possible only in a growing economy.

Work Opportunities

It is a fact that most of our country's population are dependent on work opportunities. The DTA intends to govern the country in such a way that many new work opportunities are created, amongst others in the building industry.

10. LAND DIVISION AND AGRICULTURE

The DTA accepts and regrets the fact that in terms of the policy of separate development and a discriminatory policy in respect of agricultural financing, many inhabitants of our country have not been able to own land in the past. The DTA takes pride for having had this policy changed so that today everybody can own land, but the backlog has not yet been eliminated.

The DTA therefore will ensure that in future agricultural land will be owned and utilised on a fair basis. Farmers without land who already have assets and capital at their disposal, must be assisted financially under very favourable conditions to purchase farms, provided that a high rate of production is maintained and that the standard of living of other dependents on the farm, such as labourers, will not be affected negatively, but will rather improve. The principle of affirmative action must apply throughout.

All unutilised and under-utilised land must be put into full production as soon as possible. The state must accept responsibility to provide water to such land and to settle beginner farmers on the land in terms of a settlement scheme, whether on an individual or co-operative basis. Rules must be formulated to ensure that all land privately owned is utilised optimally.

It is accepted that the system of communal land cannot be totally abolished. The cooperation of the inhabitants of communal areas must be gained by means of their traditional authorities for the transformation from the subsistence economy to a market economy. For this information, training, financing and the creation of marketing opportunities are prerequisites.

The ultimate aim however, must be to promote economic growth in general and to render our country self-sufficient as far as the production of food is concerned by means of scientific and economic farming methods, while at the same time an increase in the quality of life of everyone dependent on agriculture must be ensured.

In an independent Namibia the DTA will pay special attention to the following:

* Local processing and refinement of agricultural products by the creation and stimulation of secondary industries.

* Import replacement.

* Creation of work opportunities.

* Agricultural financing and the gaining of development assistance from abroad for the creation of an agricultural infrastructure and agricultural training.

Entering into treaties and agreements with organistions such as the EEC, Lome Convention and the SADCC.

11. MINING

The DTA accepts the following basic premises:

* The mining industry, as earner of foreign currency, as contributor to the gross domestic product and as work provider, represents a very important subsection of the Namibian economy.

* In Namibia the mineral rights reside with the state. This has distinct advantages compared to the system where the mineral rights are owned privately.

* The state must deal with the mineral rights for the direct and indirect benefit of all the inhabitants of Namibia.

* As an integral part of Africa, cooperation with neighbouring countries will necessarily be directed towards the accomplishment of optimal development and utilisation of our mineral resources.

* Namibia is one of the large number of developing countries in the world and will therefore out of necessity have to compete on the international capital markets for investment.

* Industrial development and environmental conservation are essential antipodes and can only be sensibly integrated by judicious management.

The DTA of Namibia undertakes to establish a healthy mining industry by means of:

* Intensive prospecting of minerals by encouraging experts in the field by inter alia arranging for the fair granting of mineral rights to members of the private sector, and by guaranteeing the certainty of the possession of mineral rights as long as the holders of these

rights maintain meaningful and active exploration programmes.

* To see that, taking into consideration the trade cycles of the economy, mineral deposits can be mined optimally so that these sources will last as long as possible.

* To ensure that the extraction and processing of minerals is done optimally and that processing and value enhancement is done locally as far as is practically feasible, with the current creation of world opportunities to the benefit of the inhabitants of Namibia.

* To give preference to companies which are prepared to accomplish maximum local participation and investment in the mining industry and other industries and which declare themselves willing to re-invest.

* Timously pay attention to infrastructure development in under-developed areas where new discoveries of economic mineral deposits justify it.

* To create mechanisms for ensuring the safety and reasonable treatment of the workers in the mining industry at all times, and to apply the principle of workers participation.

* To create a small but effective mining department in the government service which will be instructed to execute the mining policy as laid down.

12. SEA FISHERIES

Background

Without any doubt the marine resources of Namibia have the potential to be one of the most important national assets of the inhabitants of Namibia. The objectives of the DTA's policy and strategy directed towards the recovery and maintenance of the optimal utilisation levels to the best possible advantage of all the inhabitants of the country, is based inter alia on an evaluation of the current state of our fish resources.

(a) White Fish Resources

It appears that the white fish resources of Namibia are in a very bad way because of excessive over-exploitation by member countries of ICSEAF; These semi-pelagic (mid-water species) and bottom trawl-fish resources will not reach their optimal utilisation level until provision has been made for a recovery phase to accomplish the renewable potential of these resources to the desired level. Every careful utilisation policy with moderate exploitation is indicated for the foreseeable future. Especially the much sought after Hake resources of Namibia have been seriously impaired and it also seems that a total withdrawal of the current extractors is indicated.

(b) Other Marine Resources

The closed ICSEAF zone which extends 13,5 nautical miles from the coast has to some extent made provision for the conservation of our pelagic fish and allowed for the catches of member countries of this organisation to be inspected by Namibia's patrol service. In contrast to the white fish resources, there are currently promising trends in the general condition and tendencies of Namibia's pelagic fish stocks, due to corrective conservation practices and exploitation levels followed and with which the DTA has been continually involved, with the renewal of these resources as objective.

The rock lobster resources of Namibia have been properly conserved and the stringent maintenance of their utilisation levels has ensured that the commercially exploitable concentrations that occur on the coast in the vicinity of Lüderitz are utilised on a reasonably optimal exploitation level that should ensure the economically viable survival of the resource. The only fluctuation is currently caused by climatic conditions. Namibia's rock lobster resource is currently its most important marine resource as far as the earning of foreign currency is concerned.

The other resources within this 13,5 nautical mile zone, such as seals, crabs, sea farming activities, guano and kelp utilisation, are also subject to adequate conservation practices and the DTA strives for their continuation.

Objectives of the DTA's Marine Resource Utilisation Policy

(a) The DTA aims firstly to apply its marine resource utilisation policy in such a way that the national interests of all our inhabitants are served as highest priority. In the execution of this policy there will inter alia be strived for:

* The creation of opportunities for the greatest possible involvement and participation of Namibians in marine resource utilisation activities.

* The provision and creation of benefit drawing investment opportunities that also in this way will make participation possible under favourable conditions for as many of the citizens of Namibia as possible in the utilisation of our living marine resources - which in turn will stimulate the tendency of our people to save, will cultivate an investment awareness and counteract capital outflow.

* The promotion of orderly participation and acknowledgement of the involvement of trade unions in this industry.

* The stimulation of workers participation schemes for the workers of the fishing industry.

* The requirements of concession conditions that will ensure that as many as possible local supportive products are used in the fishing industry for example tomatoes, salt, pepper, wrapping and packaging.

* The promotion of the re-investment of profits into other branches of industry in Namibia by the creation of a favourable and attractive climate for all investors in the fishing industry with a view to stimulation of growth and development which must take care of further work creating investments for our population increase.

* The education and training of our own people in the fishing industry with a view to promotion to the highest positions and the creation of a self pride towards involvement in what belongs to Namibia.

* The stringent protection, maintenance and broadening of the taxation basis so as to enable the state to be able to fulfil on a continuous basis the responsibilities that the state must of necessity take on itself on behalf of the inhabitants.

* To make provision for more concessionaires so as to promote competition with a view to stimulating effectiveness, productivity, competitive prices and the exclusion of monopolistic conditions in the fishing industry.

* The assurance of stable long-term optimal utilisation levels of Namibia's marine resources relative to the strength of these resources.

* The maintenance of disciplined and orderly utilisation and processing activities and practices that will honour the prescribed resource conservation regulations of a DTA government.

* To limit to the minimum state interference in the industry.

(b) The DTA will supervise the establishment, proclamation and protection of Namibia's territorial waters inclusive of the marine resources.

The DTA will endeavour to get international recognition of Namibia's own territorial sea and fishing zone (and EEZ) so as to establish Namibia's correct claims

(c) The entering into of a fair agreement with the Republic of South Africa in order to establish Namibia's fishing industry at Walvis Bay as the centre of our fishing industry with a view to the prevention of a disruption of our utilisation and processing activities. The DTA has full confidence that it will be able to negotiate favourable conditions for Namibia.

(d) Decentralisation and the extension of centres for the fishing industry possibly to a different site in the north of Namibia.

13. INTERNATIONAL RELATIONS

The foreign policy of the Namibian state will be directed to the maintenance of the sovereign independence of a united Namibia and the advancement of international peace and understanding.

Sound and mutually beneficial relations will be developed with foreign countries in accordance with the principle of sovereign equality, and diplomatic and consular representation will be established as appropriate on a reciprocal basis.

Namibia shall enter into such alliances and international treaties as are necessary and appropriate for the protection and advancement of its national interests, but shall not formally align itself with any major power bloc.

Namibia will strive to promote a continuing reduction of regional tensions and the development of a climate of co-operation and understanding between the states of the Southern African region, thereby laying the groundwork for increased prosperity. It will play its full role in programmes designed to develop the physical, economic and social infrastructure of the region, protect and restore the environment, and encourage a pooling of scarce regional resources to the overall benefit of all the states of Southern Africa.

Namibia will be an active member of the United Nations and its specialised agencies, the Organisation of African Unity and the Southern African Development Coordination Conference. Application will be made for accession to the General Agreement on Tariffs and Trade and the Lome IV Agreement between the European Communities and the ACP Countries. The value of membership of the Commonwealth and continued membership of the Southern African and (Rand) Common Monetary Area will be evaluated by the appropriate governmental agencies after independence.

Investment by foreign nationals will be encouraged in accordance with an investment code, to ensure that such investments contribute to the country's development and advance the interests of the Namibian people.

14. DEFENCE AND NATIONAL SERVICE

The task of the armed forces is to protect the sovereignty and territorial integrity of Namibia. Whereas we desire to live in peace with all nations, it would be irresponsible not to ensure that we have the capacity to defend the country's borders in the event of an unprovoked attack.

The armed forces will comprise the Namibian Army, with a fast reaction capability, a Navy with responsibility for coastal defence and maritime patrol for the protection of Namibia's Exclusive Economic Zone, and a small Air Force to be deployed in support of the Ground Forces and the Navy.

National Service in Namibia has historically meant service in the Armed Forces. Whereas we believe that every citizen has the duty to contribute to the defence of his country, we do not see his responsibilities as ending with military service.

National Service is an all-embracing concept. It expresses the duty of each citizen to serve his community and the nation. Such service should be appropriate to the real needs of the nation at any time. In other times of threat, this service will probably be military. At other times other needs will be paramount.

15. JUSTICE AND POLICE

The law, in any society, is the codification of the particular set of norms and taboos which that society has concluded are necessary in order to maintain its preferred social, economic and political order. In those societies with a legal tradition based on the cultural history of their citizens, and with political institutions which respond effectively to shifts of democratic option, harmonising of the law with justice is relatively easy.

In Namibia, where we face the challenge of reconciling a variety of social and political cultures in our efforts to build a nation, we need to understand the importance, and the difficulty, of defining legal norms deriving from these various cultures which will be respected by the whole community.

After independence, we can afford neither merely to cling to the legal system inherited from our colonial past, nor simply to reject it in the name of liberation. Much of enduring value has been institutionalised in the legal systems deriving from the Roman-Dutch and English traditions, but our present laws and the procedures which have grown up around them, do not meet the needs of our society in all respects.

The DTA intends to appoint a Law Review Commission to consider critically the Statutes and the procedural systems we inherit at independence, so as to ensure that they meet the demands or justice applicable to the post-colonial period. The aim will be to adapt our legal system and statute law to the degree necessary to make them intelligible to, and responsive to the needs of, all members of our society. A Bill of Fundamental Rights, based on universal legal values, will lie at the heart of our legal system.

The Police Force is charged with the task of maintaining law and order in a society characterised by a range of divergent and often competing demands made by different members of the community. The Police are thus required to maintain a delicate balance of society, upholding and enforcing the law, while keeping the peace.

As we have already seen from the discussion of our policy on Justice, this requires a considerable degree of tolerance and cultural sensitivity, in addition to a knowledge of the law and the courage to act in enforcing it. The selection and training of the men and women who serve in our Police Force is therefore of the greatest importance.

Continuing education and the upgrading of relevant skills must be undertaken to ensure that all members of the Police Force are able to shoulder effectively the great demands which our society makes of them.

We recognise that the years of conflict which have preceded our independence, have resulted in the SWA Police being identified with one side in the struggle. Neither they, nor those who opposed them, can afford to allow this conflict to characterise their relations in the future. The time has come to put the past behind us and to unite to build a stable, law-abiding and prosperous Namibian nation.

16. LANGUAGE

For practical reasons and in consideration of the overwhelming option of the population, the DTA proposes a gradual change-over to only one official language for Namibia, namely English, but without this affecting the continued existence of other languages used in the country.

The DTA pleads for realism, common sense, tolerance, patience and great diffidence in deciding on the status of languages. There may be no insensitivity when dealing with so important an aspect of cultural communities, as language.

It is however realities which should be taken into consideration and the language policy of a country should be worked out and implemented with these in mind.

The facts which the DTA have taken into consideration are the following:

* As soon as more than one official language is accepted, the immediate question becomes: Which other language or languages? If the precedent of more official languages than English is set, there are no grounds to limit the number of official languages implemented. This country simply cannot afford to have an indeterminate number of official languages;

* The majority of the population prefers English as the official language of Namibia;

* The overwhelming majority of the population also prefers English as the official education medium.

However, the establishment of English as official language should not be seen as the suppressing of other languages.

There must be a differentiation between the two categories of languages in the country. The one category is the official language, English, which will gradually be established as the only official language. The other category is the mother tongues or community languages.

Each of these categories has its own value and status.

The Bill of Fundamental Rights as advocated by the DTA specifically accentuates the rights of the individual.

The individual is regarded as the most basic group. This forms the basis of all relevant rights such as property rights and so forth.

The Bill stipulates that the individual has a right to speak, promote and develop his own language.

Where English will be the only official language on the one hand, the state will have to afford individuals and communities space and opportunities to exercise their particular rights on the other.

The practising of these rights may, however, never result in discrimination.

If a specific community decides on a specific language for use in its schools, the official language may in no way be excluded or degraded in status by this. The change-over in education from a mother tongue to the official language may not occur arbitrarily, but in deliberation with the authorities or as decreed by the government of the day. The presupposition is that these arrangements will occur after due consolidation.

The same applies to, for instance, private schools. Communities will be free to provide for specific requirements through private initiative but would have to abide with the general laws of the state.

Where fairness and wisdom underlie decisions, satisfaction will be achieved in all ways.

As regards the implementation of the language policy of a future Namibia, the DTA must point out that there are certain factors to be taken into consideration.

* The Government Service is presently not equipped to serve the public in only one

language, namely English.

* In addition, the general public in turn, is not capable of being served in just English.

The same applies to education. During the past few years, the DTA was instrumental in working out a sensible educational policy and as far as possible to begin with its application.

Through this sensible action there was no disruption. In contrast, there was very purposeful movement of great benefit to education.

With the institution of English as official language the same deliberation should be applied. An interim period would be a necessity. The duration of such a period cannot be determined beforehand.

17. EDUCATION

The DTA of Namibia supports the principle that education is a basic human right and not a privilege available to a few individuals.

We further believe that true freedom can only be achieved when built on a firm foundation of free and equal education of a high standard, which provides an opportunity for all people to develop their abilities as best as possible, to fully realise their potential and to improve their standard of living. In this way, they will be capable of offering a positive contribution to the general social and economic well-being and progress of Namibia as a prosperous country with a proud nation.

The DTA of Namibia thus binds itself to bringing equal education of a high standard within the reach of all Namibians in order to

* contribute to the formation of people with inquiring minds and the ability to analyse things in a rational fashion to express options, while each one is also able to hold his own in the labour market,

* ensure that Namibians possess the necessary knowledge and ability to maintain an independent lifestyle and are capable of coping with the challenges of a fast changing world,

* ensure that they can use both language and figures efficiently,

* promote respect for religious and moral values, as well as tolerance of others, their religion and culture,

* contribute to insight into the world in which we live, the interdependence of individuals, groups and nations,

* promote appreciation for human endeavour and aspirations.

In an independent Namibia, the DTA government will thus make provision for:

* a standard of education which will enable all Namibians of present and future generations to compete successfully with the rest of the world,

* the opportunity for parents and communities to share in the education of their children,

* religious education as part of the schools curriculum in line with the values of our people and in recognition of the principles of religious freedom,

* equal education on primary, secondary and tertiary levels, regardless of colour, race or creed, in order to promote national unity and the building of a nation with mutual respect, social pride and loyalty to our motherland and its people,

* the necessary systems to facilitate the smooth transition from home to school and from formal education to the professional world,

* compulsory education, provided free of charge, for all children up to the age of sixteen years,

* education and syllabi based on the abilities, requirements and interests of students, in other words, a variety of courses with increasing emphasis on career orientated education,

* qualified teachers to provide for the requirements of the students of Namibia,

* educational opportunities for less qualified teachers so that they are able to develop their full potential, thus increasing their level of competence.

* comprehensive, informal education to provide for the requirements of illiterate adults who have not had the educational opportunities to qualify for a specific profession,

* sufficient educational facilities and aids to ensure that education will take place under the best possible circumstances,

* state aid to private, church and other schools which meet special requirements, on the condition that such schools do not discriminate against any scholar on the basis of race or colour and that they support the educational policy and standard prescribed by the government,

* competent educational administration by the creation of a central education department with regional offices in order to ensure a uniform, efficient educational system throughout Namibia,

* the creation of representative bodies at schools by involving parents and representatives of local communities in the education of their children.

18. HOUSING AND COMMUNITY DEVELOPMENT

Safety for a person and his family is a primary need. One can only feel free and safe when living in a house, where oneself, ones family and ones possessions can be protected.

A house must also be affordable. A monthly payment should not cause the owner of a house financial difficulty. For this reason a DTA government will strive towards the provision of low-budget housing and the promotion of house ownership.

The DTA accepts the following objectives as defined by the Transitional Government:

(a) Low-budget housing

Low-budget housing is the housing or accommodation facilities provided to families in urban areas who do not have the means of obtaining suitable housing for themselves (excluding those people who qualify for welfare housing) and whose needs for accommodation can only be fulfilled if some or other form of public assistance is made available by means of:

* subsidies in the form of loans to local authorities for the provision of infrastructure services or to individuals at interest rates lower than prevailing market rates, and/or

* special schemes, procedures, etc. designed by the authorities concerned and which aim to lower the costs of such housing and consequently also decrease the cost for the home buyer.

(b) Home-ownership

Considering the fact that, in spite of the provision of subsidised housing to the low-income population, the primary responsibility for the provision of housing lies with the head of the family, it is the purpose of the central authority to ensure that this responsibility is understood and accepted. To achieve this goal, a policy of home-ownership for all is implemented in all urban settlements.

The security that is achieved by means of home-ownership will promote a feeling of belonging in the urban areas and will encourage a pride in home-ownership, which will encourage more people to extend, improve and maintain the houses themselves. Home-ownership must be encouraged as being a valuable investment for all income groups for the future.

Participation in the housing process must be accomplished, in other words the community must partake in decision-making, planning and implementation.

(c) Community development

Community development including education and training, is an integral part of the housing process. This process must be aimed at inter alia accomplishing acceptance of and understanding for the necessity of a policy.

The peoples' self-help inputs must be utilised, that is to say their willingness and ability to build themselves, supervising building, manage the building process or to upgrade and extend houses.

19. HEALTH

The DTA acknowledges that the health needs of the people of Namibia are vast and that these must be satisfied with limited resources. Health care systems developed in Namibia to date, are extensive and well-developed compared to other developing countries and despite serious problems of inequality and maldistribution of resources and facilities, the DTA is convinced that these systems are valuable national assets that must be strengthened and enhanced to benefit all the people of the country.

The DTA policy on health aims to redress areas of weakness in the existing health care systems in a positive manner, while utilizing its strengths to improve health care in Namibia in a manner that will promote the ideal of "health for all Namibians by the year 2000".

Health Administration Organisation

The DTA is committed to a unitary system of health administration for Namibia, which shall be embodied in the Department of National Health and Welfare. The aforementioned system shall be based on the principle of,

*   centralised strategic planning,

*   centralised coordination, and

*   maximum decentralisation and delegation of actual services rendered, on the basis of districts and regions to allow for the optimal and appropriate solution of the unique health problems encountered in the various regions of Namibia.

Provision of health care shall be provided to all Namibians, irrespective of colour, race, creed or religious affiliation.

Primary Health Care

The DTA subscribes fully to the Alma Ata Declaration of Primary Health Care and is committed to developing primary health care as the central theme of a comprehensive health care system for Namibia. The crucial aspect shall be that of mother and child health care, incorporating preventive and promotive health service like expanded immunization programs, health education, child spacing programs, etc.

Manpower Development

The DTA acknowledges that the people of Namibia are its greatest asset and is committed to strengthen health services through the active development of health workers. This will entail the establishment and development of appropriate and practical training courses and curricula, both on an in-service basis and in conjunction with academic institutions in Namibia, providing career-development opportunities for Namibian health workers.

The urgent need for the appropriate training of various categories of subprofessional health workers to complement and relieve the load on scarce professional health workers shall receive urgent attention.

Intersectoral Actions for Health

The DTA acknowledges that optimal health care for Namibians is intimately related to the dynamic interactions between health services per se and other sectors such as education (especially female literacy), agriculture (optimal nutritional provision), housing (elimination of overcrowding), provision of adequate sanitation and water affairs (provision of potable water).

The DTA is committed to the structuring of appropriate intersectoral programs and actions to facilitate the development of health services throughout the country.

Health Funding

The DTA is committed to a health care system where the state shall accept the responsibility of providing basic medical services with an emphasis on primary health care to all Namibians and in particular to disadvantaged communities. Individuals and communities shall be encouraged and educated to contribute within their means towards the costs of services by way of realistic sliding scales of fees with the provision that no one shall be refused any service on the grounds of not being able to pay a particular fee.

The DTA shall strive to fund public or state health services within the ambit of available resources, in accordance with guidelines set out by the World Health Organisation for developing countries.

The important role of private health care is acknowledged and the DTA is committed to promote private health care as a complementary adjunct to those services provided by the state. Private health care services must however, prove their own viability and must contribute to the health of Namibians in real terms.

Regional and International Cooperation

The DTA accepts that health threats to communities transcend international boundaries and is therefore committed to establishing constructive relationships with all its neighbours in the field of regional and international health promotion.

Namibian membership of the World Health Organization will be pursued after independence to ensure this country plays its full role in WHO, as well as receiving benefits of membership.

20. THE WOMEN OF NAMIBIA

The DTA is committed to :

* The creation of a Department of Women's Affairs which will act as a watchdog in respect of any form of discrimination against women in any sphere of the society in an independent Namibia. Experience has shown that the position of women in independent states in Africa has not really changed, despite lip-service in respect of ideals such as equality before the law and protection against discrimination. A Department of Women's Affairs will guard against this in Namibia.

* The recognition and expansion of the role of women in all spheres of society in an independent Namibia.

* The creation of a legal power for women in terms of which women will enjoy equal status before the law, with special reference to matters such as divorce, succession, the signing of contracts, etc.

* The mobilisation of the women of Namibia to undergo the training necessary to enable them to take their rightful place at all levels of society, including the government service, commerce and industry, agriculture and the professions.

21. SPORT

The DTA recognises the important role that sport plays in every community and in the national domestic field. Sport is important in the development and education of people and especially of young people. The DTA appreciates the value of sport as a necessary physical activity, as well as its value as a bridge builder and as an interaction that guides and improves human relations.

A DTA government will therefore support and expand sport on all levels and throughout the whole of Namibia with all possible means at its disposal.

The DTA believes that,

* sport forms its own circle within the community, as for example the church does, and that sport must therefore be allowed to function without unnecessary interference by the state.

* it is a government's duty to create the physical infrastructure for the healthy pursuit of sport. But it is the sports administrators' and participants' right to consider and decide how they must organise sport so as to ensure maximal participation and achievement.

The DTA will, according to its general policy of non-discrimination, not allow any discrimination whatsoever against any person on any sports terrain, or that sport be misused in politics, be it on a national or international level. The DTA will endeavour that no future government should prescribe to sport with whom liaisons should be undertaken or with whom not.

The DTA places a high premium on international competition and will fully support sports bodies to gain membership on international bodies.

The DTA is realistic on the necessity of sport relations in the Southern African region. Relations need to be extended and established on a non-racialistic basis. Therefore the DTA always will advantage the practice of free sport and the extension of ties amongst members of the sport fraternity.

22. NATURE CONSERVATION AND TOURISM

The DTA of Namibia firmly believes in conservation of nature as a renewable natural resource and the wise exploitation of this resource to the benefit of the people of Namibia.

We believe that our plant and animal diversity should be protected by law and exploited in such a way that will be to the benefit of coming generations.

We believe and subscribe to the Charter and principles of the International Union for the Conservation of Nature and Natural Resources (IUCN) and its World Conservation Strategy.

We are committed to the education of our people in the benefits of conserving our beautiful nature and believe that such facilities should be created and expanded so that every child in Namibia will have the opportunity to enjoy and therefore be proud of their environment.

In order to ensure the wise utilisation of our nature we believe that thorough research must be done to inform the decisions that we take.

In recognition of the fact that tourism is a renewable source of income for Namibia, we will expand existing tourist facilities and strive to maintain the stability which makes this country attractive to tourists.

Through these policies we will ensure that conservation is for the people of this country and for others to enjoy with us.

Thus the DTA will provide for,

* a semi-autonomous national conservation body which will have control over the following with respect to nature conservation:

* Management

* Law Enforcement

* Research

* Communications and Education

* Resorts Management

* The tourism functions of the Government Service

* A budget subsidised by the Central Government and supplemented by own income.

Support to the Private Sector in the creation of private game reserves and amenities as well as services for tourists outside reserves and facilities will fall under the national body.

A statutory board will be appointed by the government with the powers to coordinate all actions which may involve exploitation of nature or which may have an effect on environment. This body will ensure that no actions are taken by the government or private sector without a proper environmental assessment.

Conservation will be fully integrated into development projects in the rural areas, with the emphasis on the utilisation of resources such as wildlife to the direct benefit of local communities.

The DTA will create means by which to educate our young people in conserving our valuable natural resources.

23. INFRASTRUCTURE

Namibia has a well-developed infrastructure and a future government should not allow this infrastructure to fall into disrepair. Maintenance of the existing infrastructure will, however, entail considerable state expenditure. As in the past these maintenance requirements will compete with the large demand for social services. Further development in respect of for instance water supply will have to be done, while extension of the electricity network could be of great benefit to Namibia.

Funds will have to be found to complete the already planned water and power network, so that more farmers can become established and industries and communities can be supplied with water.

A very high priority for the DTA is the connection of our power and transport networks with those of our neighbouring states. Here we think especially of the linking up of our power networks with those of Angola and Zambia and our road and rail networks with those of Botswana.

As far as our transport corporation and post and telecommunications are concerned, they must be run on a business basis as soon as possible, so that they no longer have to rely on state funds.

24. RECONCILIATION

Reconciliation is in all probability the cornerstone on which the DTA is built. Since its inception, the DTA has strived to coordinate people from different groupings in our country into one large organisation. This was no small task because the prejudices and antagonism which has grown over the decades between ethnic groups, especially between blacks and whites, were very deep-seated. However, we succeeded in bringing together all the groups into one political organisation. We even succeeded in accomplishing cooperation between black and white, which is responsible for the fact that the independence process is proceeding without major disruptions. This is because the DTA has proved that black and white can rule together, administrate together, live together, work together and play together, and yes, even fight together without creating an uncontrollable situation.

It is truly so that we have never before been closer together - thanks to the DTA.

The fact that other parties are suddenly climbing onto the bandwagon of reconciliation is proof that we have been successful. When we started with it, there were demonstrations in front of the Turnhalle and tomatoes, eggs and even stones were thrown at us.

Together we can build up this country, but first we have to see one another as compatriots and not try to protect ourselves from one another.

Today the people of Namibia know that their security lies in the extent to which they provide security for one another.

The DTA wishes to see Namibia develop in this spirit and tradition.

Quelle: DTA-Hauptquartier, Windhoek

NAMIBIA,
IS YOUR FUTURE SAFE?

Comrades, compatriots, men and women of the People's Liberation Army of Namibia, sons and daughters of Namibia and friends.

For 105 years we have suffered under colonial oppression, foreign domination and fascist military occupation. First as oppressed people under German rule and later under the racist Pretoria regime. As we have been toiling over the years, we have been unable to know the truth. Because we were subjected to the lies of the occupationist regime and dishonest politicians.

We were the victims of deception of both warring sides of the conflict. Many people know about the evils committed inside the country and abroad. But for the sake of either "liberation" or "democracy" they kept quiet. Comrades and countrymen the time has come for the truth to be told: The elections are to be held soon. You must know the truth to prevent our beloved fatherland from being ruled by dishonest people because they will bring suffering to us.

Time and again you have been warned, but you didn't pay attention. Here are some truths to think about. If you don't believe it you are going to pay a heavy price in the not too distant future.

Did you know that the killing, torturing and detention of the first Namibians in foreign countries started as far back as 1974? The mass arrest of the so-called "spies" by the "first national movement", Swapo, started in 1980 in Angola. The first power struggle in the "first national liberation movement" started in 1964 as well as the internal strive and nepotism.

The Kwanyama language was to be spoken by all in the Swapo camps and this led to the Kwanyamas believing that Swapo was theirs. Forcing everybody in the Swapo camps to speak Kwanyama only led to the Kwanyama believing that Swapo is for the Kwanyama alone. Anyone who was not an Owambo was discriminated against and was suspected as a spy.

Anyone who did not favour Hamutenya and Auala was discriminated against and was accused to be a spy. Swapo betrayed the struggle for the liberation of Namibia by forcing more than 75 percent of Plan-fighters to fight against Unita who was not occupying or threatening our country.

Swapo who called young Namibians to go and join the struggle abroad, forced the young Namibians to fight a senseless war against Unita instead of fighting against South African troops.

Many of them were killed and others crippled for the rest of their lives. Swapo did this to follow the communist policy of internationalism. It means that socialist countries must send their soldiers to go and fight even in countries where they don't have any interests.

This means that under a Swapo government Namibian soldiers will be sent to fight in Angola. Mozambique, and probably to Ethiopia and Chad. Why should Namibians die in wars that have nothing to do with our country? Why should our young men be turned into dogs of war?

Swapo detained about two thousand innocent Namibians in other countries.
.   What do you think will they do if you let them come to power in Namibia? According to article 20, page 26, paragraph 4 of the Swapo manifesto, they will impose a one party state on Namibia should they win the elections. This will mean that Swapo in general and Swapo leaders in particular will be above the law. To criticize them will mean either to be put in the dungeons or to be shot by firing squad. That is what they did in Angola and Zambia and that is what they will do in Namibia if we let them come to power.

Article 7, page 8, paragraph 5 of the Swapo Manifesto says that Swapo believes in the moral superiority of socialism over capitalism. This means nationalising all private property including businesses. Cuca shops will be closed down in the north and the bigger businesses will be taken over by the state and this will include the bigger businesses in Owambo.

Toivo ya Toivo was betrayed by Nujoma and spent 16 years in a South African jail on Robben island. Nujoma's briefcase was taken by arrangement from his hotel room in london and the documents in there were used against Toivo in court. How many more people will be betrayed by Nujoma?

According to Nujoma the Academy in Windhoek is not a university and the people trained there cannot match Namibians who have been trained by Swapo. The Academy is a university whose examinations are set and marked by Unisa, a university whose standards are of the highest in the world.

1.   You are loyal members of Swapo who served in the movement for a long time. but when you come home, you cannot live and stay where you want. You cannot visit your families and relatives freely, especially when they belong to another party other than Swapo. Do you think that this is freedom? Even after independence under Swapo, your situation will not change.

2.   You are qualified engineers, medical doctors, technicians teachers even scholars for that matter. What guarantees did Swapo give you for employment. Where are your diplomas and certificates? Why don't you have your diplomas and certificates with you? It is clear that Swapo is jealous of you if you earn money. They do not trust you if you are educated. Why all this jealousy and mistrust? Now this party keeps the papers and you are starving. Why the suspicion if you are loyal party cadres?

3.   When you were in Angola and Zambia you were told that you will receive money, houses and food from the party. What is the situation now? Do you receive regular food rations from Swapo? And do you think Swapo does not have money? Swapo do have money but they use it only to buy houses and expensive estates for the top brass.

4. On the 8 October this year, there was a church service devoted to the returnees, detainees and Untag's arrival in Namibia. The church was almost empty. Where were those returnees to glorify the Almighty? Compare the one hundred and fifty on that day with the funeral of advocate Anton Lubowski a week before when the church was packed to capacity. And another thing: On Lubowski's funeral day there were Swapo security boys in the church patrolling even the altar just because Nujoma was around. Do you think this party has respect for God and his clergy? Do not fall prey this time. The lessons of the past where christians who suffered at the hands of dictators, should be a serious warning to you.

5. Nujoma preaches reconciliation and forgiveness, but the Lubango radio says "A luta continua". It is calling Namibians puppets, enemies, collaborators and spies. Once Swapo is in power, all former Koevoet members, policemen, former detainees and even civil servants will disappear one by one. This is and will be the official policy to eliminate opponents.

6. It is said that Swapo and the church is one. But just elect Swapo and you will see what steps they are going to take against the church. Persecution will definitely be carried out immediately and some if not all the churches will be closed down. Think of this, when you cast your vote if you are a good christian. Swapo says there is no God. They are using the churches and the clergy just to promote their own political objectives when they have reached it they will drop the churches and get rid of them.

Many of you have just returned from exile. You have seen that our country is well developed and that it has changed a lot since you left. It is not necessary to elaborate on the changes. They are obvious. All that we know is that we must not allow confidence in our economy as a whole to be destroyed, especially the infrastructure so as not to facilitate the outflow of capital. If that happens we shall have to start from scratch all over again.

We must take part in the process where all Namibians will have equal chances of participation, especially by workers of big companies and mines. This will ensure that they get a share of the profits made by them as co-owners of those mines and companies, there will be no need for them to go on destructive strikes against their own companies or mines.

In this way we will enhance productivity and develop an economy capable of making Namibia an agro-industrial power within ten years or so. The slogan of redistribution of wealth propagated by Swapo is a patent lie.

These leaders have filled their swiss bank accounts to capacity over the years. The sharing of wealth is nothing but mere rhetoric, it will only bring low productivity and economic ruin. We will even become poorer than before. Mixed economy and socialism as put forward by some parties manifesto's, is just an eye wash.

Elect a party with a clean past, vote for a party which will not establish dictatorship and the abuse of power. Because that will make us suffer even more than what we had to experience under foreign domination. Swapo leaders, the people of Namibia is challenging you to come out and tell them about your fat bank accounts in Switzerland while your ordinary members are starving.

Already you have bought luxurious villas and other estates for yourselves which is worth millions of rands, while your members are living in overcrowded houses.

The elections are drawing near. Remember your vote is secret. Only you know which party you will vote for. The election is coming closer and this is the only chance you have to vote for the right party so that you can guarantee your own security as well as true democracy.

Saamgestel en uitgegee deur die DTA, Posbus 173, Leutweinstraat, Windhoek, en gedruk deur Die Republikein Drukkery, Posbus 3436, Marconistraat, Windhoek. Quelle: Flugblatt, gefunden in Ondangwa, 8.11.1989

DTA vs Swapo in Caprivi

See the difference!

Edward Ndopu and Eve Vosloo

"KATIMA MULILO has never seen anything like this," a resident of the border town on the banks of the Zambezi River told us as a jubilant **procession of DTA supporters dressed in the party's red, white and blue and stretching for kilometres walked and sang and danced and drove through its streets on Saturday, creating a carnival atmosphere.**

They were following a bakkie on the back of which stood DTA senior vice-president, Mr Mishake Muyongo, and chairman, Mr Dirk Mudge, and it was obvious that in this, Muyongo's home town, the residents were out to give them a rousing welcome.

The occasion was two of the last big rallies to be held before the election of a Constituent Assembly takes place between November 7 and 11.

As in Rundu the previous week, Namibia's main political rivals, the DTA and Swapo, held rallies on the same day in Katima, and again there were apparently no incidents as there were at Oshakati where 120 people were hospitalised after violence and car accidents when a Swapo rally and a DTA funeral were held on the same weekend.

The rallies, which most observers thought were about the same size, could not have been more different.

The Swapo meeting took place inside a shiny new two-metre fence. Security, as at the other "Star rallies" in Windhoek, Oshakati, Swakopmund and Rundu, was very tight. Everyone who went in was searched and several journalists and photographers were turned away by aggressive Swapo security police for not having Swapo press accreditation. They were told their ordinary accreditation was not enough. Others, however, using the same accreditation, were allowed in.

Swapo president Sam

Nujoma was whisked to the meeting from the airport where he was flown in by Lear Jet, and whisked out again, and according to local residents, all his security men and many supporters were bussed in from Owambo.

The DTA rally was held at the Ngwezi Sports Field, an open stretch of ground, under a huge open-sided marquee. There was no security at all and people came and went and climbed onto the platform where the leaders were sitting or the press platform under them at random and at will.

People, many of whom had gone home for lunch after the procession, moved in and out of the rally freely, while thousands crowded together under the shade of the marquee.

The carnival atmosphere continued at the DTA rally when Mr Muyongo led the people in singing before he started his speech.

"Sons and daughters of the soil," he said. "We are on the eve of elections that will bring us true freedom and independence and it is the last time before the elections that we will have the opportunity to address you in such numbers.

"But today is also a day of sadness because I can't help thinking of all those who died fighting for our freedom and all those who died in the dungeons of Swapo. The sadness of it is that there are still misguided Namibians who have not seen the light and who believe the empty Swapo promises that are made to them.

"Apart from the DTA

there are nine other parties in this election. They are also promising you the heaven and the earth. I am afraid they are only idle words and empty promises because if there's no money they will not be able to give you anything.

"A car only runs if it has petrol in it and the fuel we need for a strong economy is the money and the know-how. If we do not have these the country will go to ruin.

"We must have a stable, democratic government that will create confidence. Only then will foreign investors be prepared to invest in Namibia and only then will people with knowledge and expertise come here because they see the opportunities we have created for them.

"If you don't believe me look at Zambia and Angola and other African states where Swapo's leaders have been living. There they arrest and kill and torture their opponents and their own supporters just like Swapo. Be careful of hyenas in sheep's clothing.

"Those countries are among the poorest in the world. They have let the economy run out of fuel. They have borrowed so much money that no-one wants to lend them any more. These countries are slowly bleeding to death and there are thousands of Africans starving because they do not have money to buy food or even the means to produce their own.

Mr Muyongo said foreign investors would be frightened off by a Swapo government as it wanted to

institute a socialist system which all the iron curtain countries in which people had lived under socialism for 40 years were trying to tear it apart because it did not work.

He said he and DTA chairman Dirk Mudge had visited Austria and Germany and the International Monetary Fund and they had assured them they would invest in Namibia if it had a stable democratic government, not a socialist dictatorship.

He said people should vote for the DTA and not for Swapo because the DTA would create a stable democratic government while Swapo was interested only in violence and would introduce socialism which would bleed the country dry.

He also said Sam Nujoma was not interested in the people of the Caprivi and had to bring in thousands of supporters from Owambo to boost his numbers.

"Swapo also has the worst military and human rights record of any liberation movement," he said.

"In Swakopmund he released two white doves. We are not interested in him releasing stupid birds. Why doesn't he release the people Swapo is still holding instead."

On the mystery surrounding the death of the so-called Acting Vice President of Swapo, Mr Brendan Simbwaye, the DTA Senior Vice President stated that somebody "somewhere in Swapo" should explain to the Namibian people what exactly

122

had happened to Mr Simbwaye.

"We want to know where he (Mr Simbwaye) was killed and where he was buried because he was our leader. I hope Swapo and South Africa will tell us the story since they are good bedfellows," he said.

Mr Muyongo also took to task Chief Moraliswane, a local chief representing the Masubiya tribe in the Caprivi, for fomenting rumours that some of his children had been incarcerated by Swapo in Angola.

As a traditional chief, Moraliswane should consider the fact that when the people of Caprivi talked about "his sons having been arrested by Swapo" this did not refer to his own sons as such.

"We meant the people, all the people, are his sons - not his sons alone."

Mr Muyongo issued a warning to Swapo leaders in the area who were involved in "training" school children "to shoot and lay grenades".

"I say to that organisation - to careful, don't touch fire."

He called on "every" political leader in the country "not to start havoc".

"Let us use our heads. If you have failed to organise the people, don't resort to dirty tricks because you are preparing your coffin. The DTA is aware of what tactics they do at every stage," he said.

Mr Muyongo emphasised that when the DTA "preached peace" it was not "a sign of weakness" but rather because the DTA leaders were "using their heads, not bullets.

"That is the best weapon we have. We are going to use bullets when we are going to be at war with another country," he said.

At the same rally, DTA chairman Mr Dirk Mudge said: "Today we have two rallies in Katima Mulilo. One is being addressed by Sam Nujoma and the other by Mishake Muyongo. I want to tell you the difference between these two men."

"Mishake Muyongo lives in this town. He has been here on many occasions and you have had the opportunity to shake his hand. He took part in a procession through the town and he is not wearing a bullet-proof vest.

"After this meeting every one of you will be able to shake hands with him. You can come within one metre of him. You can also stand behind him. There's no reason for him to be afraid of his own people.

"If you go to the Swapo meeting you will find that there is a fence between him and the people. No-one can get within 15 metres of him. You will not be allowed to shake hands with him. You can't get near enough to

recognise his face.

"That's because he is afraid. He is afraid of his people because he has a guilty conscience." (There was loud applause from the crowd at this statement.)

"But," said Mr Mudge, "Let me tell Mr Nujoma he need not be afraid of the DTA because the DTA never killed any of its opponents. We can be proud of ourselves and our party because we are building a nation. We are bringing people together.

"The DTA brought the people of the Caprivi together with all the other people of Namibia.

"The DTA has identified the problem in this country - racial prejudice. We have identified the problem and we are in the process of solving that problem.

"This country must be free after independence. The people have suffered enough and we of the DTA can't allow a party with a bad reputation to take over the government of this country.

"You know how things have deteriorated in Zambia. You know that people are coming across the river to look for food. It's because they have no democracy, a one-party state, a socialist system that people are poor and hungry.

"We have had apartheid in this country and we must get rid of it, but we don't want to swop one type of

discrimination for another."

The DTA rally was opened by a former Swapo detainee, Elizabeth Simasiku who told of her experiences while in detention.

She said that Sam Nujoma had said he would prove his allegations against the so-called South African spies in court but had thus far not done so.

She also said the Swapo children who are in East Germany were the children of the missing Swapo detainees.

At the Swapo rally held at the Kizito College grounds, Mr Sam Nujoma told his mostly Owambo audience (bussed in from Northern Namibia) that allegations that his party was still holding detainees in Angola were not true.

He explained to his unenthusiastic crowd that the United Nations Mission on Detainees (UNMD) to Angola and Zambia had disproved rumours that he was keeping Namibians in detention in those countries.

Mr Nujoma also said that it was the intention of his party to boost fishing activity on the Zambezi river and to extend Namibia's territorial waters if he was voted in as president.

Report by Edward Ndopu and Eve Vosloo. 27 Edison Street. Windhoek.

Quelle: Times of Namibia, 30.10.1989

U D F ELECTION MANIFESTO

Preamble

Historical background

For decades. Mother Namibia — not unlike a hen with her chickens — sheltered her children under her wings.

The desolate appearance of Namibia confused many slave traders who hunted the blacks of this continent and this prevented our forebears from being sold in bondage to the rest of the world. In this way, nature protected us, but what did man do to us?

(a) White Domination

Namibia is probably the only country where:

the Western obsession with colonialism;
disregard for human rights;
urges of oppression and
the rape of natural resources

were allowed to, for more than 10 decades, gnaw away like a cancer at the country and its peoples.

Namibia is the country of the Namibian nation which was forcibly occupied by, first the German Imperialists from 1884 and then by South Africa up till today. These occupations were characterised by an extermination policy in the case of the Germans and the de-humanisation of the apartheid policy of South Africa. Social and economic development was accompanied by the enslavement of the Namibian masses.

This fact led to resistance and the demand that development should include the development of the people themselves and the right to unconditional self-determination.

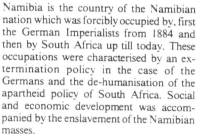

In that spirit, the UDF of Namibia rejects in total the illegal and immoral presence of the South African regime in our country. We demand unconditional independence and the unconditional right to national self-determination.

(b) Image of Black Domination

It must be said without fear or favour that SWAPO had made significant strides in various aspects of the struggle. In this

connection. SWAPO had been able to mobilize the international community to support the aspirations and struggle of the people of Namibia. Despite its UN recognition as the "sole and authentic" representative of the Namibian people. the external wing of the organisation had been practically bogged down to a permanent crisis from which it could not extricate itself. This is due to the totalitarian way in which the tribalistic, hypocritical and tyrannical clique headed by the monolithic president is steering the movement. These are leaders who hold the real power and who have indeed succeeded to lead the organisation into the abyss of disgrace and self-destruction.

With the autocratic and tyrannical leadership at the helm of power, the organisation is intrinsically undemocratic and dictatorial. This leadership is resolved to maliciously defame, blackmail and intimidate any person or member who attempts to question what he or she conceives as improper. More often than not, this tyrannical behaviour takes on violent forms such as imprisonment and killings.

(c) **DTA**

The South African racist authorities have, throughout the colonial history, imposed various divisive structures and reactionary groupings on the Namibian people. All these entities perpetuate South African colonial presence and domination. Despite attempts by the DTA to distance itself from Pretoria, its recent performance under the garb of the "government of national unity" have proved incontestably that it is unable to introduce tangible changes which could benefit the Namibian masses. This inability to "deliver the goods", has disqualified the DTA to be trusted with the sacred mandate of leading Namibia to genuine national independence.

(d) **UDF of Namibia**

From the mistakes of the past. the UDF has learnt that division was at the root of our weakness.

Unity, is therefore the credo of the UDF in its final quest for total freedom and self-determination.

It is a challenge for the UDF to now achieve reconciliation and lasting peace, particularly between the two fighting extremities, to whit black and white.

**OUR FUTURE
IS IN OUR HANDS.**

VOTE UDF AND BREAK THE CHAINS

LET US UNITE IN THE YEAR OF THE UNITED DEMOCRATIC FRONT OF NAMIBIA 25 FEBRUARY 1989

BLUE

Symbolises our policy in respect of Religion.

We acknowledge our profound thankfulness for the Supreme Guidance of God Almighty in the determination of the destiny of nations and peoples.

Therefore the UDF seeks to enshrine freedom of conscience and that the profession and free practice of religion shall be guaranteed. No one may, subject to law and order or the rights of others, be submitted to measures restricting the excercise of these freedoms.

WHITE

Symbolises peace.

After violent struggle against foreign domination for more than 100 years:

— struggle against German imperialism
— struggle against South African colonialism
— struggle against racial discrimination
— struggle against war at our borders

the UDF seeks to bring about a climate which will be conducive for peace and stability where Namibian people will live together in happiness and harmony.

GREEN

Symbolises prosperity in the whole of Namibia.

All Namibians must be in the position to enjoy the fruits of their labour and skills. No privilege shall be allowed on the grounds of race, colour, creed, sex, political affiliation or social status.

THE FIST is no token of violence.

Neither is it a SWAPO symbol.
IT SYMBOLISES UNITY.

Since Namibia had been a racially and ethnically divided nation for decades, unity is a priority.

The UDF seeks to unite all Namibians — irrespective of race, colour, language or creed —into one solid unified entity.

ECONOMIC POLICY

It is a fact of life that the majority in this country happens to be black.

And that the blacks are the poorest while the wealth of the country rests within the hands of the white minority. It is not just by chance that things are what they are today. This is the logical consequence of the status quo with its racial discrimination.

The UDF seeks to redress the unequal distribution of wealth for the upliftment of the political and socio-economical conditions of the majority of the under-privileged Namibians.

In order to redress the fate of the oppressed and under-privileged Namibians in a dynamic manner, the UDF of Namibia shall promote the establishment of a Development Bank for this purpose as a particularly urgent priority in an independent Namibia.

The UDF supports a mixed economy for Namibia which provides for the private sector on one hand and a public sector economy (with a limited macro-planning function) on the other. This economic structure can also accommodate the interests of multi-national, co-operative and small business institutions persons. The State should be in a position to play a regulatory role in this structure to prevent the occurrence of unnatural economic tendencies such as monopolies and other phenomena that will undermine the economic structure.

NAMIBIA'S NATURAL RESOURCES

Our natural resources belong to the Namibian people. On this principle all colonial contracts should be immediately reviewed and new ones negotiated on such points as:

progressive maximising taxation on profits of multi-national companies, and

determining the percentage of profits to be ploughed back into education and industrial development.

LAND TENURE

There shall be private, co-operative, parastatal and state ownership of property.

Land Reform

All idle and under-utilised land will be repossessed by the state (with an appropriate compensation) and will be re-distributed appropriately to the landless majority. The state will assist the farmers, especially the small peasant farmers. The proposed Development Bank will play a major role.

The state will discourage farmers from owning more than two economical units of agricultural land by levying progressive taxation as from the third unit.

The state will determine the size of such an economic unit.

The UDF seeks to create an effective industrial policy.

LABOUR MARKET

The UDF regards the formation of trade unions as a fundamental right of workers and fully respects the RIGHTS OF TRADE UNIONS to be independent of the government of the day. The UDF will pay special attention to important labour issues such as health and working conditions, workers' education and training and assistance programmes and will keep impressing upon employers — both in the private and in the public sectors — the need to treat their employees with dignity and a sense of social responsibility.

THEREFORE WE GUARANTEE THE FOLLOWING RIGHTS:·
The right to form independent trade unions;
The right to work;
The right to strike;
The right to a minimum living wage, annually adjusted for inflation and cost of living increases.

SOCIAL POLICY (Housing)

The UDF-led government will strive to provide every citizen with adequate housing.

EDUCATION

The UDF seeks to bring about a relevant non-racial education system.

Education which must reflect and address the objective situation in Namibia.

The system must be based on the principle of democracy and universitality.

Education will be free and compulsory on primary level and be subsidised on secondary, tertiary and university levels. The UDF-led government will strive to provide the necessary facilities in order to be able to implement its intentions.

The new government will especially assist the young to realise its full potential.

It will also:—

bring about parental participation in decision-making;

be an independent examination board;

provide adult and informal education programmes;

provide technical schools to promote production-related skills;

teach in the English medium.

LANGUAGE POLICY

English shall be the official language of the country or the state. All other national languages are equal before the law. Local authorities shall have the discretion to apply any appropriate language to facilitate communication.

HEALTH

The UDF seeks to establish a comprehensive health service with better staffed and equipped personnel. There will be a proportionate distribution of spending on health in urban as well as in rural areas.

Health services will be provided free to scholars and to old-age pensioners while the service to the public will be subsidised to facilitate the best possible medical care in the country.

GOVERNMENT STRUCTURE

Namibia shall have a stable multi-party democracy with regular elections. There shall be a Parliament consisting of a National Assembly and a Cabinet whose term of office will be a period of five (5) years. The Parliament shall be the sovereign legislative authority in and over Namibia.

The country shall be divided and sub-divided into district, municipal and village units. The principles of a constitutional democracy shall apply to all organs of the state.

An independent judiciary will safeguard the interests of all Namibians. The judiciary shall interpret the constitution and not make its own laws.

The government will appoint an independent ombudsman to investigate individual complaints against authorities.

Constitutional changes shall be made only with a two-thirds majority of Parliament voting in favour of such an amendment or through a popular referendum.

The government of the day shall be voted out during its term of office only through a vote of no-confidence by two-thirds of the members of Parliament.

An Executive President will be the head of state, vested with some own executive and otherwise mediating powers. He may be elected by Parliament or in a direct election. The President shall have the power to appoint a Prime Minister.

All Namibians will have equal opportunities in all spheres of life and should be allowed to participate and identify with the political leadership of the nation.

The Public Service shall be supervised and controlled by a Central Public Service Commission. Judicial recourse to a competent Constitutional Court shall be open to all at all times for any unconstitutional infringement of fundamental rights of individuals and communities. Namibians must be protected by the state against all undemocratic, totalitarian, violent, racist threats or group domination.

Political participation will be representative and democratic through equal, free, general and secret ballot on the basis of one man, one vote.

Fundamental rights will be guaranteed by the DECLARATION OF RIGHTS of the UDF of Namibia. The fundamental rights recognized universally must be granted to all Namibians as well, so that their human dignity will never be offended again by any authority in our country.

The Bill of Fundamental Rights includes, inter alia,

* freedom of speech and press
* freedom of speech and conscience
* freedom of association and assembly
* freedom to know the conduct of the government (Namibia shall have freedom of an Information Act)
* freedom to own property
* freedom from arbitrary arrest and torture and a right to a speedy trial.

EQUALITY

There shall be total equality between the sexes

There shall be a free and independent press without fear of government harassment.

POLICY ON WALVIS BAY

The UDF regards Walvis Bay, the islands and the Orange River as integral parts of Namibia and will fight relentlessly to repossess them.

Compiled and issued by:

The Secretariat
United Democratic Front of Namibia
Cor. Bülow and Karsch Streets   WINDHOEK

© Windhoek Printers-9-5122

Quelle: UDF-Hauptquartier, Katutura / Windhoek

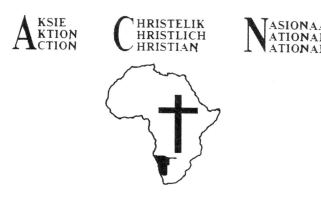

A KSIE KTION CTION C HRISTELIK HRISTLICH HRISTIAN N ASIONAAL ATIONAL ATIONAL

MANIFESTO
435 ELECTION

1. **NAME:** The name of the organisation is ACTION CHRISTIAN NATIONAL.

2. **PRINCIPLES:**

   2.1 The ACN acknowledges the sovereignty and guidance of the Triune God, also as the source of all authority in the destiny of peoples, nations and states.

   2.2 The ACN accepts the diversity of peoples and or population groups, their interdependence, their right of selfdetermination and joint authority.

   2.3 The ACN also accepts that the moral law with regard to Christian charity must be practised within the political structures, as opposed to any form of domination.

   2.4 The ACN stives for the necessary balance between rights and responsibilities of both the individual and the group.

   2.5 The ACN accepts a Christian, democratic and free enterprise system.

PROGRAMME OF ACTION
CONSTITUTIONAL POSITION

1. Action Christian National (ACN) strives for a sovereign independent state (Republic) in which.
   (a) the principles of the ACN will be incorporated,
   (b) the constitutional structure would be in accordance with the composition of the population, geographical framework, and local as well as regional requirements,
   (c) the wellknown constitutional systems in which the protection of group rights, viz. jurisdiction in and over own territory, an autogenous federal system of group representation and autonomy over own affairs, could be incorporated.
   (d) an effective civil service where, depending on the particular system. appointments, promotions and transfers are made according to merit.
   (e) decisions regarding citizenship be determined by means of the final agreement on a constitutional model.
2. ACN considers it of the utmost importance that the population of South West Africa maintain friendly relations with its neighbouring states. and particularly with the Republic of South Africa. Furthermore, this organisation intends to enter into economic, cultural, military and other agreements on a specific basis and conditions. These would be acceptable to all the relevant parties and would be of such a nature that the best interests of the territory and its people would be served.

NATIONAL SYMBOLS

ACN believes that an own name, flag and national anthem for the country would reflect the final agreement on a constitution and would serve to promote the national feeling of loyalty and not be detrimental to it.

IMMIGRATION

ACN insists that on the part of the government. steps be taken to ensure that no undesirable persons enter the country, and that immigration be limited to elements which could readily be assimilated into the population which has already developed in South West Africa, and which could not be regarded as a burden or a danger to the community.

LANGUAGE RIGHTS

ACN wishes to nurture a spirit of mutual trust and co-operation between all groups. This organisation would thus ensure that the existing language rights in regard to the various groups insofar as the State is concerned, or to the extent which the State has influence in this regard, be maintained and promoted.

LABOUR RELATIONS

ACN will work towards peaceful labour relations, for fair and equal pay for equal work and on merit. This organisation would also strive towards full employment according to the principles of free enterprise, private initiative and healthy competition in all sectors.

ECONOMIC AND FINANCIAL POLICY

1. GENERAL: The three major industries, agriculture, the exploitation of mineral resources and fisheries in South West Africa is recognised as the basis for the lasting material welfare of the country. This, together with the simultaneous development of commerce and industry should be conducted in such a manner so as to promote lasting prosperity for the country.
2. AGRICULTURE: While the interests of the various sections of the population should all enjoy the attention and care of the Government, the existence and welfare of the rural population should be the subject of particular endeavour and dedication. By applying a progressive settlement policy, the establishment on a healthy basis, of an autonomous and self-supporting class of private landowners, should be encouraged. The ACN namely envisages an independent and prosperous farming

community and therefore insists on the effective encouragement and support for the agricultural sector as a whole by the State. This would include sufficient protection against competition from elsewhere: exploitation by a middleman, as well as an effective system of marketing, agricultural credit and agricultural education. ACN believes that the striving for the above will be an evolutionary process. The necessary recognition would be given to the first and third world standards and customs. The right to exclusive control and administration, particularly in regard to financing, information and administration would be respected against the background of the ACN's standpoint and principles.

3. THE MINING INDUSTRY: ACN will work towards encouraging the exploitations of our mineral resources in every respect, with due cognisance of the welfare of the worker and the claim of the State to its fair share of the mineral ricnes of the country.

4. SECONDARY INDUSTRIES: ACN aims to vigorously promote all viable secondary industries, including sufficient protection for and due recognition of the interests of the local consumer.

5. FINANCIAL POLICY: ACN promotes a sound and fair financial policy which would take the necessity of good financial management in the administration into account. The ACN would also promote a fair distribution of the tax burden; the application where practically possible, of short term assets, to expand the permanent resources of the country to result in a stable economy.

ACN recognises the right of any individual or group to, on the basis of free enterprise, private initiative and effective competition, generate its own funds to maintain or promote standards of his particular choice.

EDUCATION

ACN believes that:

(a) education should be Christian in character and that the Bible should form the cornerstone of Christian education.

(b) the system of education should recognise, honour and promote the communal educational interests on a national level as well as the autogenous elements within this national context.

(c) each group authority have the right, powers and responsibility to effectively control, protect and promote its own education.

(d) the control of the parent over his children and his right to participation, the right to object, and choices in regard to the education of his children be acknowledged.

(e) the principle of free association be recognised and applied, and the wishes of the parents be taken into account in this regard, insofar as it does not conflict with the rights and freedom of others.

(f) the communication of cultural values in education be recognised and the cultural identity in ethnic allegiance be regarded as a non-negotiable possession.

(g) the maintenance of standards and sound edcuational principles are vitally necessary.

(h) the provision, control and administration of multi-cultural schools should not be the responsibility of group authorities.

(i) the politicization of education is unacceptable.

HEALTH

ACN envisages the establishment of a comprehensive and effective system for the protection and promotion of health in general. The ACN is convinced that a patient has the best possible chance of a speedy recovery when nursed in an atmosphere which is restful and acceptable to the patient. Thus, group authorities should have the right, powers and responsibilities to supply and maintain its own nursing service.

LOCAL AUTHORITIES

Peace and prosperity is of the utmost importance to the ACN and that is why this organisation strives towards the establishment of independent local authorities with the largest possible measure of autonomy for each local community which, according to its nature, needs and abilities, forms a strong homogenous unit.

Compiled and distributed by D. de Klerk, 4 Kepler Street, Windhoek.

Quelle: ACN-Hauptquartier, Windhoek

The 1989 Election Manifesto of The National Patriotic Front of Namibia (NPF)

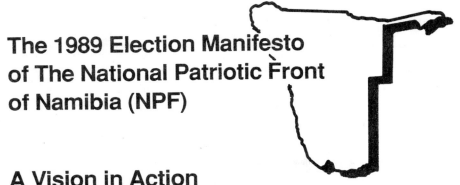

A Vision in Action

Introduction

The National Patriotic Front of Namibia (NPF) was formally established at a public meeting on the 11th March, 1989 at the Showgrounds in Windhoek by SWANU – the South West Africa National Union, CANU – Caprivi African National Union of Namibia and ANS – Action National Settlement, as a joint vehicle to face the challenges posed by the implementation of the Namibian Independence Settlement Plan, also known as Resolution 435, and to build together a new Namibia after the elections.

The National Patriotic Front represents various patriotic and legitimate interests, concerns and points of view and is therefore a unique voice of reason and common sense and a reliable force for meaningful and responsible change in our society and for an independent Namibia which is truly free and a place of happiness and prosperity for all its people.

OUR VISION OF A NEW NAMIBIA

OUR FUNDAMENTAL MISSION AND GOAL is the establishment of a new country and a new society based on equal rights and opportunities for all and where no one racial or ethnic group dominates and an economy characterized by prosperity based on growth and development.

Therefore, our MOTTO is: RECONCILIATION – DEMOCRACY – DEVELOPMENT and our symbol is an OPEN HAND OF FRIENDSHIP.

To achieve that noble goal, we believe that we should not only welcome our country's accession to National Independence – a goal and an objective for which so much lives and property have been sacrificed – but we should also work hard to ensure that our country remains truly independent from all forms of outside control and domination. Political independence must not become a mere formality, an end in itself, or the privilege of a few, but an instrument for national unity, political stability, peace (an end to the war and all forms of violence and intimidation) and prosperity, friendship and peaceful co-existence with foreign countries. With the achievement of independence, the quality of that independence is the crucial issue that concerns the NPF in the coming election campaign.

A truly independent and free Namibia must be a nation which has common values about the following fundamental principles:

(a) DEMOCRATIC GOVERNMENT based on a constitution which guarantees the rights of the people and determines the functions of the State.

(b) RESPECT FOR THE PEOPLE as the holders of supreme power.

(c) The RULE OF LAW and the consistent application of the law and equality of all before the law.

(d) Political pluralism in the form of a MULTI-PARTY DEMOCRACY which allows the freedom of expression of different and opposing ideas and points of view by individuals and political parties and their right to compete for political power in a process of regular free and fair elections.

(e) A BILL OF FUNDAMENTAL RIGHTS which defines the fundamental rights and liberties of the citizens and establishes mechanisms for their protection against possible infringement by the State or the government of the day.

(f) REJECTION OF ALL FORMS OF DICTATORSHIP which allow the government of the day to have a monopoly of deciding what is true and what is wrong or false in society. (Dictatorial regimes and organizations concentrate power and the use of force in the hands of one or a few leaders who rule without much regard for the will and opinion of others and use the instruments of force to silence and even to assassinate deserters and opponents.)

(g) A system of government based on the SEPARATION OF POWERS between the three branches of the Government – the Executive (the Cabinet), the Judiciary (the Courts) and the Legislature (the Parliament), where the Legislature has the power to create laws, the Executive to enforce them and the Judiciary adjudicating legal issues and interpreting the Constitution.

(h) The institution of OMBUDSMAN to probe into public grievances about the activities of both government and private institutions.

The National Patriotic Front fully accepts the 1982 Constitutional Principles of the Western Five for an independent Namibia and recognizes it as the internationally agreed upon framework for the Constitution of an Independent Namibia and regards the provisions contained in paragraph 35 of the Report on Namibia of the UN Secretary General of January 23, 1989, to the UN Security Council as binding on all the participating parties in the coming election. These provisions are four agreements and they are:

The agreement that the confinement to base of Swapo forces in Angola and Zambia will be monitored by Untag; the informal understandings (including the "check list") reached in 1982 on the question of impartiality; the principles concerning the Constituent Assembly and the Constitution of an independent Namibia; and the agreement that the elections will be held on the basis of a system of proportional representation, comprise, together with UNSCR 435, the United Nations Plan for Namibia.

The Building of a Nation and the Decentralized Unitary State

The Patriotic Front stands for a government based on GRASS-ROOT DEMOCRACY – a government taken to the people – by the decentralization of a number of functions, powers and duties to regional and local units. Decentralization is not the same thing as the fragmentation of our country into separate ethnic and racial homelands and entities.

The National Patriotic Front is determined to use the SPIRIT OF NATIONAL RECONCILIATION – which means to forget or put aside past differences and conflicts – to establish a sense of national identity, national pride and national purpose and to have the differences of language, culture, ideology and religion within our society also help us define what binds us together as a people and make us one nation in one indivisible country. The goal of the NPF is to integrate sectional, local and regional aspirations with the larger goals of the nation as a whole.

Broad Outlines of the Socio-economic and Cultural Objectives of the National Patriotic Front of Namibia

The primary of objectives of our socio-economic and cultural policies will be to create a society of PROSPEROUS and HARMONIOUS people and communities.

For the ordinary man in the street we propose a strategy which will provide basic needs – FOOD, SHELTER, CLOTHING AND EMPLOYMENT. For the relatively well-to-do we appeal to their conscience to recognize the fact that poverty on the part of some of their countrymen and neighbours could very well become a disaster for their own well-being. We must all unite to work and to make sacrifices for the good of all.

The NPF believes that a NAMIBIAN-STYLE MIXED ECONOMY where elements of both the private and public sectors, cooperative and collective ownership and foreign investments interplay and complement one another and operate within the context of the democratic political system will bring about economic growth and development, diversify our economic relationships and lessen our dependency on foreign countries.

Although our country faces many problems which are crying for solutions, the National Patriotic Front believes that the following problem areas are a MAJOR CONCERN TO OUR PEOPLE at the present moment and should therefore be regarded as an immediate priority.

1. The Fight against Unemployment – Job Creation

We recognize that so many things in life, including one's dignity, depend on having a job and an income. The NPF proposes, inter alia, to take the following measures and steps to establish an appropriate business environment to deal with this problem.

1.1 Protecting political STABILITY.

1.2 Revising and amending our TAX LEGISLATION to encourage individuals to work harder, companies to invest and create work and training opportunities, and small business to develop and expand. Maximizing ways and means of controlling tax collection and dealing with tax-dodgers.

1.3 Encouraging market forces through DEREGULATION – doing away with laws and regulations that inhibit economic initiative and growth.

1.4 Trimming GOVERNMENT SPENDING where necessary.

1.5 Instituting a PROGRAMME OF NATIONAL SERVICE FOR COMMUNITY DEVELOPMENT where school leavers and others will undertake projects in areas such as literacy training of our illiterate communities, agricultural counselling, primary health care, community development, etc., to get our unemployed young people off the streets.

1.6 Organizing a programme of combating BUSH ENCROACHMENT to provide charcoal and other products for the community.

1.7 Negotiating with South Africa the need to introduce some tariffs to PROTECT some of our industries from South African competition.

1.8 MOBILIZING CAPITAL by requiring local financial institutions to deposit funds in government stock or treasury bills as a means of stopping the drainage of funds earned in Namibia and using these funds for development projects.

1.9 Negotiating with concerned parties the allocation of FISHING CONCESSIONS bearing in mind our own national interest and the role of our own people in the fishing industry and declaring a 200 nautical mile economic zone.

1.10 Persuading and impressing upon mining and other foreign companies to make greater CONTRIBUTIONS TO THE DEVELOPMENT of our country and the education, training and promotion of their Namibian employees.

2. Housing

The Public Sector, the Private Sector and the individual should all combine to solve this problem. LOW-INTEREST LOANS, TAX CREDIT for funds spent on housing projects, SUBSIDIES where necessary and the individual's duty to satisfy his needs and those of his family are conceivable instruments to tackle the housing problem.

3. Welfare – Social Security

The people will be protected against FINANCIAL HARDSHIP which may result from illness, disability, childbirth, old age or death of the family breadwinner, depending on the merit of such cases. There shall be EQUAL OLD-AGE PENSIONS FOR ALL.

4. Health Services

There will be no racial or ethnic discrimination or distinction in all our medical services and facilities. Greater financial support will be given to improve and expand our current medical services and facilities to meet the goal of 'HEALTH FOR ALL' declared by the World Health Organisation. We shall IMPROVE THE SERVICE CONDITIONS of our health personnel where necessary.

People who prefer private health facilities – hospital or wards – will have to pay extra for that.

Health Education shall form part of the school curriculum to instil a sense of importance in health problems, especially preventive health.

We shall expedite the process of setting up our own Medical and Dental Council.

5.   Labour Relations

The NPF welcomes the efforts so far to modernize labour relations in Namibia and will base its labour policies on the recommendations of the Wiehahn Commission of Inquiry into Labour Matters in Namibia which, in a broad sense, are the Namibianization of the principles of the International Labour Organization. In a nutshell, the NPF regards the formation of trade unions as a fundamental right of everyone and fully respects the RIGHT OF TRADE UNIONS to be independent of the government of the day. The NPF will pay special attention to important labour issues such as health and CIVILIZED WORKING CONDITIONS, workers EDUCATION AND TRAINING, ASSISTANCE PROGRAMMES and will continuously keep on impressing upon employers, both in the public and private sectors, to treat their employees with a sense of DIGNITY and SOCIAL RESPONSIBILITY.

6.   Education

6.1   Race and colour, religion and ethnic origin will not play a role in the admission of pupils to any school in our country. Only the language medium and the ability of the pupil to cope with instruction and the curriculum will be the CRITERIA FOR ADMITTING PUPILS to any school in Namibia.

6.2   There will be ONE DEPARTMENT OF EDUCATION and a single system of education in Namibia.

6.3   The education curriculum must also reflect the NEEDS and REALITIES OF NAMIBIA and include studies about Africa and the rest of the world.

6.4   Our schools must provide the population with ECONOMICALLY relevant skills to meet the needs of an increasingly technological labour market. Science, mathematics and foreign languages will be given special consideration in all our schools.

The maintenance and development of HIGH STANDARDS must be the cornerstone of our education policy. Tougher standards, better instruction, class innovations, better textbooks, reduced classes, better facilities, improving the working CONDITIONS OF TEACHERS and respect for their work and encouraging better qualified students to become teachers, must be used as instruments to help us meet that objective.

6.5   PRIVATE SCHOOLS shall be permitted but shall be subject to the educational requirements of the State and may not offer inferior education to that provided by State schools.

6.6   In terms of the FREEDOM OF ASSOCIATION provided for in the Bill of Rights citizens will be free to establish private institutions, for example,

Cultural Councils, to satisfy their particular needs such as the promotion of their languages, cultures and traditions, provided such institutions shall not act in any manner which, in any way, is contrary to any of the provisions in the Bill of Rights. Such institutions, as in the case of private schools, may apply for State assistance where necessary and shall qualify for such assistance to such an extent as they provide services that would otherwise have been provided by the State.

6.7   There shall be a special EDUCATION FOR THE DISABLED who shall enjoy equal status with the rest of the students.

6.8   The MEDIUM OF INSTRUCTION shall be the vernacular (mother tongue) at the pre-primary and primary levels in all State schools. However, English shall be the medium of instruction at all levels of education (running parallel with the vernacular at the pre-primary and primary levels) in order to expedite English as the official language of Namibia. Afrikaans will continue to serve as the lingua franca during the transitional period. All the national languages of Namibia will be freely used wherever necessary.

6.9   Religious instruction will not be compulsory and there will be NO DISCRIMINATION IN RELIGIOUS TEACHING as between the various religions in our country and the world.

6.10   PRE-PRIMARY education will be free and PRIMARY education will be free and compulsory.

6.11   The LIBERTY OF PARENTS, and where applicable, legal guardians, to choose for their children the type of school and direction of education will be respected and protected.

7. Farming, Landownership and the Development of the Underdeveloped Areas

Our main objective in the agricultural field is to OVERCOME THE PRESENT IMBALANCE between trained and relatively prosperous farmers and predominantly un-trained, poor communal farmers, or sub-farmers (bywoners) and to raise agricultural productivity by all sections of our agricultural community.

The following MEASURES and STEPS will be considered to achieve that object:

7.1   The State will PURCHASE UNDERUTILIZED FARMLAND and lease it to potential farmers on the condition that the land is used productively.

7.2   The State will encourage the creation of CREDIT INSTITUTIONS to help promising but needy farmers on reasonable terms.

7.3 The State will impose a TAX ON FARMLAND to discourage people from holding too many farms for the purpose of tax avoidance.

7.4 The State will encourage the introduction of a SYSTEM OF COOPERATIVE LANDOWNERSHIP to serve as a TRANSITIONAL MEASURE between the communal system and a fully-fledged separate right-of-ownership system coupled with the provision of meaningful training and guidance. Such a system would make provision for PLANNED DIVISION of the present communal areas into large economic units where PROPRIETARY RIGHTS are given jointly, in undivided SHARES, to residents of a certain area. Extension services and agricultural guidance will be provided to the cooperative jointly and the cooperative could do marketing of the products on behalf of the members. Each farmer would, however, make progress or fall behind according to his own ability and achievements. In this way a commercial substructure would be introduced whilst the various farmers pass through the different stages of skill and expertise.

7.5 PRIVATE DEVELOPERS can, through a scheme of leasing land, help develop the communal, underdeveloped areas.

7.6 The overall objective of our policy on farming, landownership and the development of underdeveloped areas is the JOINT DEVELOPMENT OF OUR MATERIAL AND HUMAN RESOURCES.

7.7 There can be no DEPRIVATION AND/OR NATIONALIZATION of private, cooperative and collective property without prior consultation and just compensation. Deprivation and/or nationalization can only take place in the national interest.

8. Crime Prevention

8.1 Our cities and towns must at all times be PROTECTED FROM ALL FORMS OF CRIME.

8.2 CATTLE THEFT, a growing problem on the farms and rural areas, must be firmly combatted by means of a LEGISLATION which punishes cattle thieves to long jail terms without an option of paying a fine.

9. Equality of Men and Women

Our WOMEN compatriots shall enjoy EQUAL RIGHTS with their male compatriots in all spheres of public life and discrimination against them shall be forbidden by LAW.

10. The Youth

The youth, as the future of our country, shall be given SUPPORT, irrespective of race and colour and ethnic origin, in all their endeavours TO BECOME STRONG AND HEALTHY AND CAPABLE LEADERS of tomorrow.

11. Traditional leaders

The NPF shall propose the creation of an ADVISORY CHAMBER OF TRADITIONALY LEADERS as a means of integrating our traditional leaders into our political system and enabling the government to make use of their advice and options in the process of nation-building.

12. Walvis Bay

The NPF will negotiate with South Africa the USE by Namibia of WALVIS BAY in the interim period and a PEACEFUL RETURN to Namibia of the enclave and all the offshore islands.

13. Defence and Security

We need security forces to PROTECT and DEFEND our laws, our democratic system of government and the fruits of the labour of our people.

The present South West African Police will become the POLICE FORCE OF NAMIBIA and will continue to exercise responsibility for internal security, the maintenance of law and order and the prevention, investigation and solution of crimes.

We shall establish our own Defence Force – The NAMIBIAN DEFENCE FORCE – and, as a demonstration of our spirit of National Reconciliation, all Namibians, from both sides of the military components, who are qualified for a military career, will form the backbone of our Defence Force.

Our Security Forces will be given the necessary support and encouragement to have pride in their work and to serve the people correctly and wholeheartedly.

14. Public Service Commission

Our country shall have an IMPARTIAL PUBLIC SERVICE COMMISSION whose powers and functions shall be defined by law.

15. The Namibianization Process

An independent Namibia must make a conscious and constant effort to have its OWN PEOPLE EDUCATED AND TRAINED AND PROMOTED in important positions in the administration and the economy of our country to achieve the goal of maximising our degree of self-reliance in the shortest possible time.

16. Foreign Policy

An independent Namibia must be a truly NEUTRAL AND NON-ALIGNED NATION – with no foreign military bases on its soil and not belonging to military blocks.

Our foreign policy will be "Friendship and Independence in Foreign Affairs and Peaceful Co-existence with our Neighbours!", maintaining economic and other contacts with foreign countries on the basis of mutual benefit. PEACEFUL CO-EXISTENCE and FRIENDSHIP, however, shall not mean that our country will keep silent about the violations in our neighbouring countries or elsewhere in the world, of the values and principles for which our country stands. We must never allow ourselves to be used by foreign powers, or to become responsible to anyone other than those who elected us. We must not involve ourselves in proxy wars or disputes. Our foreign policy goal must be to maximise the circle of friends and partners and to minimize or eliminate the number of enemies and opponents.

Summary and Conclusion

It is clear that the NPF IS A VOICE OF REASON AND COMMON SENSE and without its participation in the determination of the constitutional future of Namibia, our country will be robbed of a fundamental asset concerning its future.

The NPF does not only identify problems facing our country, but seriously attempts to also suggest practical alternative solutions.

And there is no doubt that the NPF is in the hands of leaders who know what they are talking about and who can be relied upon to bring about meaningful and responsible change to this country and who are supported by a vast reservoir of very capable functionaries.

NPF

SUPPORT THE NPF FOR A BETTER TOMORROW BASED ON RECONCILIATION, DEMOCRACY AND DEVELOPMENT.

Quelle: NPF-Wahlkampfbüro, Windhoek

NAMIBIA NATIONAL FRONT

WHAT IS THE NNF ?

NAMIBIA NATIONAL FRONT (NNF).

What is the NNF ?

The Namibia National Front (NNF) is a progressive political power bloc, vehemently opposed to any and every form of racial segregation, apartheid and colonial domination.

The NNF is an electoral alliance of several political parties with deep roots in the struggle for national liberation and independence from South African rule. The following parties currently constitute the NNF:

1.	The South West Africa National Union (SWANU), leader Adv. Vekuii Rukoro, headquarters in Windhoek.

2.	The Namibia Independence Party (NIP), leader Mr Albert Krohne, headquarters in Keetmanshoop.

3.	The Rehoboth Volksparty, leader Mr Arrie Smith, headquarters in Rehoboth.

4.	The United Namibia People's Party (UNPP), leader Mr Hizipo Shikondombolo, headquarters in Oshakati.

5.	The Mmabatho People's Party, leader Mr Michael Simana, headquarters in Gobabis.

The NNF's Constitutional Proposals

*	The NNF is a non-racial and anti-racist electoral alliance which rejects any system of government based on "race" or ethnicity and which believes that the national unity of all Namibians must form the basis of the new nation.

* The NNF proposes an independent Namibian state with its national unity and territorial integrity secured and which shall include the Port of Walvis Bay and the Islands off the coast as an integral part of Namibia.

* An independent Namibia shall have the freedom and the rights of the individual guaranteed by a Bill or Charter of Fundamental Human Rights which will be rigidly entrenched in the Constitution. The Bill of Rights will be binding on all judicial, legislative and administrative authorities and will be enforceable by the Courts.

* The Constitution will furthermore entrench the powers of the Courts of the land and, to ensure complete independence and impartiality, the judges of the Supreme Court will be appointed on merit and enjoy security of tenure and will not be subject to any form of control or interference by the legislative or executive authorities.

* A uni-cameral (single-chamber) Parliament will be the supreme legislative and administrative body and will be entrusted with all matters of national interest affecting the country and its people

* An Executive President,who will be the Head of State and Head of Government,will be elected by Parliament to perform such functions as may specifically be entrusted to him/her by Parliament. The executive authority will vest in a Cabinet of Ministers, headed by the President, all of whom must,at all times, enjoy the confidence of Parliament.

* Unqualified universal adult suffrage is proposed with a common voters' roll for all the inhabitants of the country. Most of the members of Parliament will be directly elected through a system of Proportional Representation,while a few seats will be reserved for special interest groups.

* Regional Councils are also proposed which would have the power to deal only with matters of purely regional concern to all the residents of each particular region.

* Municipal Councils will be elected by the permanent adult residents of any town or city who are the owners or bona fide occupiers of any dwelling in that town or city.

THE NNF's ECONOMIC POLICY.

The following is a summary of the main aims and principles of the NNF's economic policy for the first 5 to 10 years after independence:

* To aim towards a fair re-distribution of wealth.

* To draw up a Development Plan which will serve as a guideline for all social and economic initiatives for both the public and the private sector.

* To expropriate only in very exceptional circumstances, when it is clearly in the national interest and then only against the payment of fair compensation.

* To encourage private enterprise in general but to guide and assist it in such a manner that the gap between rich and poor and Black and White will be eliminated in the shortest possible time.

* To guard against unhealthy monopolistic conditions and other forms of abuse, including corruption.

* To give a high priority to the creation of employment opportunities.

* To encourage the formation of truly independent Trades Unions for the defence of the interests of all workers.

* To establish centres for training in skills such as agriculture, animal husbandry, engineering, administration, etc.

* To provide assistance to those who by reason of age, inadequate education, infirmity or other disability are unable to help themselves.

* To establish a State Development Bank to stimulate and assist in the financing of industrial, commercial and agricultural enterprises.

* To establish a State Mining Corporation to encourage the development of the mining industry and to purchase a minority share-holding in existing and future mines.

* To introduce a system of progressive taxation on farmland so as to discourage the ownership of excessive farming land.

* The state shall assist those farms which cannot be developed to their maximum potential through lack of management ability or financial resources on the part of the owners.

* To purchase or acquire farming land through the medium of the Agricultural Development Bank for sub-division and re-sale or re-distribution to private or co-operative owner-occupiers.

* To require that all meetings of Directors of companies incorporated in Namibia are held in the country and that a certain percentage of Board positions be allocated to Namibians.

* To enforce a 200 nautical mile (300 kilometre) off-shore fishing limit and to maximise the long-term yield of fish.

* To review the current regulations on the movement of capital in and out of the country.

* To encourage foreign investment on the basis of a partnership agreement with the state or with the private sector insofar as

this accords with the developmental needs and priorities of Namibia.

* To foster trade with our neighbours, to build a rail-link with Botswana and Angola and to build additional harbours at Luderitz and other suitable places in order to further develop trading routes.

* To stimulate economic growth among the poor through the expansion of the informal sector with special incentives to producer co-operatives and low-interest loans to small businesspersons.

* The state shall establish the necessary infra-structure, through a comprehensive programme of community-development, to promote the growth of the rural areas and to prevent the present drift to the towns.

* To reduce state expenditure by, for example, reducing the civil-service and by having a relatively small professional army and replacing the bulk of the existing army with a para-military police force.

THE NNF's ELECTION MANIFESTO.

The NNF's basic election platform is made up of these planks:

* DEMOCRACY, that is, a stable multi-party constitutional democratic system of government in a single, secular state.

* NATIONAL UNITY, that is, the state shall be unitary and shall not be composed of any administrative structures which have a tribal, ethnic or "racial" basis.

* LIBERTY, that is, constitutionally-guaranteed basic human rights and fundamental freedoms.

* LAND, that is, the return to the people of Namibia of all their natural and national resources and assets from which they have been alienated. This includes Walvis Bay, the Islands off the coast, the waters of the Orange River, the land previously occupied by the traditional owners in pre-colonial times and the country's mineral wealth.

* PROSPERITY and SOCIAL JUSTICE, that is, the state-sponsored and planned improvement in the standard of living and the quality of life, with particular attention to correcting the gross inequalities between Black and White which have been produced by the apartheid, colonial and ethnic systems of government.

Published and distributed by Dr Kenneth Abrahams, NNF Secretary for Publicity and Information, P.O.Box 21075, Windhoek 9000.

Tel: 061-34813. Erf 4850, Kanna St, Khomasdal.

Quelle: NNF-Hauptquartier, Khomasdaal / Windhoek
****

Confidential to
PLAN MEMBERS
FROM ONGANDJERA

I would like to make known to all the **PLAN FIGHTERS from Ongandjera** that due to the fact that Our Country's natural resources had been plundered by the Multinational Mining Companies in defiance with the UN Resolutions, SWAPO will not be able to compensate all of you as per promise.

The only people who will get their full pay are you, **my people from Organdjera.** This is a top secret that you must keep to yourselves. Remember you're **the eyes of the party.** Charity begins at home. You're the people who had been taking good care of parents mothers and deserve this special attention therefore.

As per promise you'll each get your **R6000.00** at a place that will be announced to you latter. I'll see to it that you're well provided for soon after the seizure of power by us.

The security personel will be composed of you and **you'll hold key positions in the rest of the government.**

Don't trust anyone even if it is your wife, if she is not from Ongandjera, she is just not ours. That is how our ranks were infiltrated by South African spies because we were not careful enough. Now is the right time for us to act correctly and responsibly.

The war victims must only be kept on the line. Only after the election after they've voted for us can they be told to just be happy with the food all returnees are receiving from the **RRR** or **CCN,** in conjunction with the **UNHCR.**

Published by Swapo News Services (Pty) Ltd. C/o Goethe and Grimm Streets, Windhoek. Printed by John Meinert (Pty) Ltd. Stuebel Street, Windhoek. Edited by Sam Nujoma

Quelle: Flugblatt, gefunden in Ondangwa, 8.11.1989

THE SWAPO RUSH FOR PASSPORTS

WHY ARE SO MANY SWAPO SUPPORTERS RUSHING FOR PASSPORTS TO RUSH OUT OF THE COUNTRY?

ABOUT 3 000 OF THOSE SWAPO PEOPLE WHO RETURNED ONLY A FEW MONTHS AGO ALREADY HAVE BRAND-NEW PASSPORTS TO LEAVE AGAIN -- WHY?

THEY WILL PROBABLY VOTE AND FLY AWAY AS SOON AS THEY HEAR THAT THE DTA HAS BEATEN SWAPO.

THERE ARE EVEN STRONG RUMOURS HERE IN OWAMBO THAT SWAPO LEADERS SUCH AS SAM NUJOMA HIMSELF AND THEO-BEN GURIRAB WILL BE THE FIRST TO LEAVE.

THEY DO NOT WANT TO BE HERE WHEN SWAPO LOSE. THEY FEAR THAT:

* SWAPO WILL NOT WIN OUTRIGHT

* SWAPO WILL NOT EVEN GET A SIMPLE MAJORITY
  IN FACT, SWAPO WILL BE DEFEATED - BY DEMOCRACY

AND THE LEADER OF DEMOCRACY IN THIS COUNTRY IS THE DTA OF
NAMIBIA!

DO NOT VOTE FOR LOSERS, VOTE FOR THE ONLY WINNERS...
VOTE FOR THE DTA

OUR LEADERS ARE STAYING TO BUILD ONE NAMIBIA, ONE NATION!!!

Quelle: Flugblatt, gefunden in Ondangwa, 8.11.1989

CODE OF CONDUCT

FOR POLITICAL PARTIES DURING PRESENT ELECTION CAMPAIGN

On Tuesday 12 September 1989 nine Namibian political parties signed an agreement among themselves. It establishes a Code of Conduct which they have pledged to respect during the coming electoral campaign. They have also agreed to issue directives to their members and supporters to observe this Code, and to take other necessary steps to ensure that its terms are respected. They, and I, have also agreed to publicise this Code throughout Namibia by all the various means at our disposal.

I have been deeply impressed by the attitudes of restraint, constructiveness and flexibility shown by the parties in concluding this agreement. It is an important and historic achievement on the long road that has led to the prospect, soon to be realised, of free and fair elections for an independent Namibia. It is also a significant step towards national reconciliation.

Martti Ahtisaari, Special Representative of the Secretary-General

An essential part of free and fair elections is freedom of political campaigning. Everyone has the right to put forward their political principles and ideas, without threat or fear, to every other person, without exception. But freedom of political campaigning also carries responsibilities, including the duty to accept every other person's freedom to campaign.

The Namibian political parties whose names are subscribed to this document, meeting together in Windhoek under the chairmanship of the Special Representative of the Secretary-General of the United Nations on 12 September 1989, have agreed as follows:

▶ 1. Intimidation, in any form, is unacceptable and will be expressly forbidden by the parties in directives to their members and supporters.

▶ 2. Party leaders will instruct their members and supporters that no weapon of any kind, including any traditional weapon, may be brought to any political rally, meeting, march or other demonstration.

▶ 3. Parties will notify UNTAG-CIVPOL as well as SWAPOL in advance of their planned meetings and other rallies.

▶ 4. All practical steps will be taken by parties to avoid holding rallies, meetings, marches or demonstrations close to one another at the same time. Party leaders undertake to co-operate in applying this principle in good faith and in a reasonable spirit should any coincidence of time or venue arise.

► 5. Speakers at political rallies will at all times avoid using language which threatens or incites violence in any form against any other person or group of persons. Parties will not issue pamphlets, newsletters or posters, whether officially or anonymously, which contain inflammatory language or material.

► 6. All parties will consistently emphasize, both to their supporters and also to voters in general, that there will be a secret ballot, and that consequently no one will know how any individual may have voted.

► 7. Party members and supporters will not disrupt other parties' rallies, meetings, marches or demonstrations.

► 8. Party members and supporters will not seek to obstruct other persons from attending the political rallies of other parties.

► 9. Party members and supporters will not plagiarize symbols of other parties, or steal, disfigure or destroy political or campaign materials of other parties.

► 10. Party leaders will use their good offices to seek to ensure reasonable freedom of access by all political parties to all potential voters, whether they be at farms, on state-owned properties, in villages, or at secondary reception centres. They will also seek to ensure that such potential voters wishing to participate in related political activities have freedom to do so. This may, where necessary, take place outside working hours.

► 11. Parties will establish effective lines of communication to one another at headquarters, regional and district levels, and will appoint liaison personnel who will be constantly on call to deal with any problems that may arise.

► 12. Parties will meet on a fortnightly basis under the chairmanship of UNTAG regional directors or centre heads to discuss all matters of concern relating to the election campaign. A standing committee of party leaders at headquarters will meet on a fortnightly basis under the chairmanship of the Special Representative or his Deputy to deal with such matters on a nation-wide basis. An observer from the Office of the AG will be invited to attend the meeting of the standing committee. Emergency meetings will be convened as and when necessary.

▶ 13. All allegations of intimidation and other unlawful conduct in the election campaign will be brought to the attention of the nearest UNTAG-CIVPOL and SWAPOL stations or patrols.

▶ 14. Party leaders will issue directives to their members and supporters to observe this Code of Conduct, and take all other necessary steps to ensure compliance.

▶ 15. It is stated in the Settlement Proposal that: "The elections will be under the supervision and control of the United Nations in that, as a condition to the conduct of the electoral process, the elections themselves and the certification of their results, the United Nations Special Representative will have to satisfy himself at each stage as to the fairness and appropriateness of all measures affecting the political process at all levels of administration before such measures take effect." Party leaders undertake to honour the outcome of free and fair elections so certified by the Special Representative of the Secretary-General of the United Nations.

▶ 16. The Special Representative and party leaders undertake to publicise this Code of Conduct throughout Namibia by all means at their disposal.

The Namibian political parties whose names are subscribed below accept and endorse this Code of Conduct as binding upon them. They agree that alleged violations will be brought to and considered by the Standing Committee referred to in paragraph 12 above.

NAME OF PARTY	NAME OF REPRESENTATIVE	SIGNATURE
Action Christian National	J.M. de Wet	
Democratic Turnhalle Alliance	F.J. Kozonguizi	
Federal Convention of Namibia	H. Diergaardt	
Namibia Christian Democratic Party	W. Adam	
Namibia National Front	I. Uirab	
National Patriotic Front of Namibia	E. van Zijl	
South West Africa People's Organization	H.G. Geingob	
SWAPO-Democrats	for A. Shipanga	
United Democratic Front	Justus Garoeb	
Christian Democratic Action	E. Neef	
Namibian National Democratic Party	P. Helmuth	

In the presence of the Special Representative of the Secretary-General,

Martti Ahtisaari

UNTAG Headquarters,
Windhoek, 12 September 1989

UNTAG

Quelle: Plakat, UNTAG-Hauptquartier, Windhoek

IT'S EASY TO VOTE

Every person who has registered can vote.

MAKE YOUR OWN DECISION.

Mark an X next to the party of your choice. Vote for only one party.

Quelle: Plakat, UNTAG-Hauptquartier, Windhoek

Party	Abbreviation	Symbol	Vote
AKSIE CHRISTELIK NASIONAAL	ACN		
CHRISTIAN DEMOCRATIC ACTION FOR SOCIAL JUSTICE	CDA		
D.T.A. VAN NAMIBIË	DTA		
FEDERAL CONVENTION OF NAMIBIA	FCN		
NAMIBIA NATIONAL DEMOCRATIC PARTY	NNDP		
NAMIBIA NATIONAL FRONT	NNF		
NATIONAL PATRIOTIC FRONT OF NAMIBIA	NPF		
SWAPO-DEMOCRATS	SWAPO-D		
SWAPO OF NAMIBIA	SWAPO		
UNITED DEMOCRATIC FRONT OF NAMIBIA	UDF		

Stem slegs vir een party

Stem deur 'n X te maak in die vierkant teenoor die kenteken van die party vir wie u wil stem.

Vote for one party only

Record your vote by a X in the square opposite the symbol of the party for which you wish to vote.

Quelle: Official Gazette, 13.10.1989

Commission On Independence For Namibia

1400 Eye Street, N.W. • Suite 400 • Washington, D.C. 20005 • (202) 371-1212 • FAX (202) 842-3211 • P.O. Box 30738, Windhoek 9000

Report of the
First Observer Mission
of

THE COMMISSION
ON INDEPENDENCE FOR NAMIBIA

July 1989

A Project of the Lawyers' Committee for Civil Rights Under Law

EXECUTIVE SUMMARY

Our delegation visited Namibia from June 18 to 25, in order to study first-hand the events during the early phase of Namibia's transition to independence through free and fair elections under Resolution 435.

We spoke with a wide range of individuals across the political spectrum, with representatives of the major parties, church leaders, union members, the Administrator General and his staff, Martti Ahtisaari and other officials of the United Nations Transition Assistance Group (UNTAG), as well as ordinary Namibians. We spent time in Windhoek, Katatura, Khomasdal, Rundu, Oshakati, Oniipa and Ongwediva.

We left Namibia with a mixture of admiration and deep disquietude - admiration for the determination of the Namibian people to achieve their long-delayed independence and disquietude over the tremendous and unnecessary obstacles to the free and fair elections scheduled for November.

On the basis of our observations, the following are our major concerns.

I.

The continued operation of former Koevoet personnel in the north, under the banner of the South West Africa Police (SWAPOL), creates dangers, real and perceived. Former Koevoet members, once described by one of their own as exterminators, symbolizes the terror of the past war in the north. They still drive their dreaded Casspirs. On one day last week (June 13) 80 were counted passing in front of the Ongwediva refugee reception center. They still carry automatic R-4s. They still operate primarily from their former bases. It is a travesty to suggest that they now constitute legitimate civilian police.

We heard credible reports of assaults, death threats, violent disruptions of meetings, and sexual assault. We also heard credible reports about night raids and Koevòet moving from house to house and village to village searching for returnees and their families to intimidate and harass.

It is essential that the conservative estimate of approximately 1500 former members of Koevoet be dismissed promptly from SWAPOL. There can be no place in a police force for anyone who was a member of such a notorious and ruthless organization. Their continued deployment in the police constitutes a flagrant violation of the letter and the spirit of Resolution 435. General Hans Dreyer, who was the founder and leader of Koevoet, should be removed from his current post as commander of police in the northern area.

In addition, the use of Casspirs should be banned. They conjure up the terror of the past. They were the means and the symbol of intimidation. They have no legitimate policing function today.

Considering the provisions and spirit of Resolution 435, we are concerned that law and order, for which the AG has "primary" but not exclusive authority under 435, is not being administered with the same "impartiality" that the AG has long demanded of the United Nations for Namibia.

II.

UNTAG is not presently capable of defusing the atmosphere of intimidation that pervades much of Namibia. It is woefully understaffed and inadequately equipped to fulfill the responsibilities of its mission. There are too few police monitors to accompany each SWAPOL patrol. They are not authorized to participate directly in police investigation of complaints and when SWAPOL declines to carry out many investigation of serious complaints, UNTAG cannot compel it to do so. These limitations have confused, angered and demoralized Namibians.

III.

The basic structures of apartheid still exist in this country in the form of AG8, which acts as a continuing impediment to free and fair elections. It should be promptly repealed. Those who fled Namibia to escape apartheid are returning to find its key structures still embedded in their country's laws.

IV.

The laws governing the whole electoral process have been delayed far too long. They have not been promulgated at this late date, only 10 days before the scheduled start of the electoral cam-

paign. This has made it impossible for the political parties to
commence the kind of organizing and educational activities which
are an essential part of free and fair elections.

V.

The law governing voter registration is seriously flawed. This
is no ordinary election. It is an election which will determine
the future structure of a newly independent nation. The laws
that define voter eligibility should limit the vote to those for
whom the South West Africa Mandate was established by the League
of Nations, i.e., bona fide Namibians. Eligibility should not be
extended to civil servants or military personnel temporarily
seconded to Namibia by South Africa as part of its occupation
administration.

Citizens should register and vote in their district of residence
or work. The law, which permits registration and voting anywhere
in the country, makes it virtually impossible to check the
eligibility of voters - certainly in the absence of a national
voters' roll.

VI.

The widely discussed plans for the conduct of the voting are even
more troubling. The approximately 40% of the electorate that are
illiterate would be able to receive help in marking their ballots
only from the government employee who is the chief election
official at the polling site. Ballots would be placed in sealed
numbered envelopes which could be traced to individual voters.
Given South Africa's illegal domination of Namibia, these
provisions, if promulgated into law, would destroy public
confidence in the secrecy of the ballot. They create a massive
opportunity for conversion of the election.

The plan to transport all ballots to Windhoek rather than count
them at the polling locations is fraught with danger and is an
invitation to fraud. The presence of UNTAG officials at the
polling stations, during the vote count and during transit will
clearly not cure these defects. Furthermore, it is understood
that the counting of the ballots in Windhoek will take as long as
two weeks, a delay that is likely to lead to unrest and a lack of
faith in the results.

VII.

There are certain basic safeguards to free and fair elections.
One is fair access to the media by all political parties. This
is a critical requirement in a country like Namibia, where the
government has a monopoly over television and radio and where 40%
of the population is illiterate. Consequently, special measures
must be taken to ensure impartiality. In particular, the ethnic
radio stations reach a constituency with little access to other
sources of information. They must be monitored carefully to
guarantee even-handed coverage of all election issues.

VIII.

Another area calling for special measures relates to access by
bona fide representatives of political parties and by UNTAG to
the approximately 30% of the work force who work and live on
large farms. Access to these workers has been strictly controlled by farm owners, who dominate the lives of their laborers
and who may seek to control their political choices.

* * * * * * *

In spite of all the problems, there is an enthusiasm in this
country about impending independence that is infectious. And,
during our visit we were privileged to witness rare moments in
history. For example, the day that we visited the returnee
center at Ongwediva as thousands of people gathered to joyously
welcome home the returnees - the brothers who embraced after 15
years apart, the cousins reunited after one had disappeared
without a trace.

We were also tremendously impressed by the efficient and humane
operation of the reception camp at Ongwediva by the U.N. High
Commission for Refugees (UNHCR) and the Council of Churches of
Namibia. We also pay our respects to the many UNTAG people who
are clearly trying to do their best under severe restrictions and
with limited resources.

On the basis of our observations, however, we conclude in general
that the U.N. "supervision and control" of South Africa's role in
the transition period to date has failed to produce the conditions which are the prerequisites to the free and fair elections
called for in Resolution 435. The process is currently being
undermined in various ways which would either inhibit the making
of a free and fair choice by Namibians or allow the possibility
of fraud in the electoral process itself.

Quelle: Report of the First Observer Mission of The Commission on Independence for
Namibia; Windhoek, July 1989, S. i-iv (Büro Windhoek)

158

Preparing for a Free Namibia: Elections, Transition and Independence

The Report of the
Commonwealth Observer Group on Namibia

Windhoek, Namibia   10 October 1989

SUMMARY OF CONCLUSIONS

As we write, a process of historic proportion is entering its penultimate phase. There are precisely four weeks before polling commences, and much remains to be done before an acceptable poll can take place. Coming as we did at this stage of the preparations there are and have been special opportunities for a group such as ours to contribute to the process, bearing in mind at all times both our mandate and the circumspection required if we were to discharge our role.

Against the background of war, tension and mistrust in which this election takes place as well as the imperfect compromise reflected in the division of responsibilities between the Administration and the United Nations it is not surprising that so many steps have been the subject of dispute, hard negotiation, and widespread criticism. This combined with the events of 1st April meant that the United Nations Transition Assistance Group (UNTAG) got away to a slow start, but that has changed. Some criticism has inevitably been unhelpful or geared to partisan advantage, but we have seen that most of it has been constructively motivated and genuinely helpful in its effect. The United Nations itself has received some criticism and has been able to draw on some of it to make needed changes. We were struck by the comment of one highly-motivated Namibian group that it has restrained its criticism of the United Nations because it was so important to maintain the United Nations' "moral authority" as the guarantor of the Resolution 435 process. We fully share that concern, but would also express our confidence in the great trust that the United Nations has gained among Namibians, and our judgement that by being open to criticism and needed changes, the United Nations can only maintain and enhance its authority and usefulness, to Namibians and the world. We were deeply impressed by the United Nations' achievement in transforming a heavily-militarised country into a comparatively peaceful society. Its work, too, in repatriating the refugees, and continuing to care for them, has deservedly received praise from all quarters.

We found widespread evidence of increasing confidence in

UNTAG as the various parties have progressively better understood its role, and have seen the United Nations slowly asserting its authority over the South African-appointed Administrator-General.

Progress has been made, but the process remains so delicately poised that at this stage we cannot pronounce definitely upon the prospects for a free and fair election actually taking place, not to speak of the success or otherwise of the implementation of the further phases of Resolution 435. To do so would be to enter the realms of conjecture. We can, however, on the basis of our observations, do three things.

First, we can offer an assessment of the progress made to date, with a view to its impact on the prospects for free and fair elections.

Second, we can extract any lessons we see which may be relevant for the future of the process. We distilled some such suggestions part way through our visit, and we wrote to the Special Representative on 3 October (see Annex II) in the hope that these might be of practical assistance. We discussed these and other matters with him on 9 October. We also left an Aide Memoire with the Administrator-General on 10 October (see Annex III).

Third, we can look ahead to the further stages of campaigning, polling, and of the Constituent Assembly. Beyond that we can look to the governance of the country and its preparation for a healthy transition to independence. In so doing we can try to identify points for special vigilance, anticipate potential problems, and suggest approaches which might avoid or alleviate them.

In going about our task we have had opportunities to meet, formally and informally, with both the Special Representative and the Administrator-General and with members of their staffs at various levels. Our discussions have been cordial and we believe that we may have assisted their thinking on a number of important matters. We also travelled the length and breadth of the country. As we went we met officials, party leaders and workers, community leaders, and ordinary voters. Of special significance was our visit to Walvis Bay, whose early integration into a free and indepedent Namibia will be essential to its well being.

The progress made to date has been substantial, but difficult. After many early problems, the final registration was high and the parties have told us that they were generally satisfied. Despite inefficiencies and frustrations for many potential voters (particularly with mobile registration stations) we did not find hard evidence of any significant attempt to prevent or compromise the process. There is some lingering resentment with the law itself which allowed people (mainly South Africans resident in the Republic, who would normally not be considered Namibians) to register to vote.

One matter for concern is the delay in the Administrator-General's promulgation of the election law. Even as we report (10 October) this law - due out on 12 May - has still not been published. Necessarily, this has created doubts and uncertainties, and undermined confidence in, and jeopardised the efficiency of, the election process itself. Already the alarming delay in promulgating the law governing the election process has prevented the finalising of training manuals and the commencement of the training of election officials. It also has handicapped the political parties, if they are to take full advantage of the opportunities we expect the law to provide for them to satisy themselves as to the integrity of the process by participating in it - a participation which we see as providing an important safeguard both for the Special Representative and the Administration. Even if the election law is promulgated immediately, valuable time has already been lost.

Practical lessons must be drawn and applied from the start-up problems with the registration process, which if repeated in the much shorter voting period have the potential seriously to flaw the process.

We have also expressed deep unease about the physical arrangements for the ballot. The time now apparently allowed for the through-put of voters in static stations is substantially less than that planned for in such other African countries as Ghana, The Gambia and Botswana - the latter allowing more than twice as long as the Administration here, with both polling staff and voters well familiar with a simpler polling process, and with a much higher rate of literacy. We have strongly urged both UNTAG and the Administration to review their projections in this light and most importantly to conduct joint tests, and simulations under field conditions. As we report, these field simulations have still not taken place.

There is a real need to guarantee the secrecy of the vote and the integrity of the polling procedures. We are happy to note the efforts of UNTAG to this end.

A dominant issue overhanging the possibilities for free and fair elections remains the issue of intimidation and violence. The campaign will be keenly contested by parties whose supporters have no previous experience of the political process and are still readjusting from a state of war to an uneasy and incomplete peace. The situation is fragile and calls for policing which is impartial, skilful and firm. The South West African Police (SWAPOL) is ill-equipped both in fact and in perception to undertake these roles, so that the performance of UNTAG's police monitors will be particularly critical. By their own assessment, SWAPOL's commanders do not have the capacity to maintain law and order in the whole northern region. But the Administration's notion of bringing in reinforcements from South Africa is clearly unacceptable. This under-capacity demands urgent but appropriate remedial measures, specially in the light of recent trends in Ovamboland - both of violence and its inadequate handling by the Administration - to which we were witness. Ex-Koevoet elements remain an insidious and explosive presence - and in spite of repeated international efforts to defuse this threat, the Administration has clearly acted irresponsibly and in bad faith in responding. We cannot overemphasise the need for UNTAG to have the capacity to cope with this menace.

Above all, it is central to the elections for voters to be able to journey to the polls and cast their ballots in safety and in the conviction that their vote is secret. This in turn calls for considerable work on the part of all involved - the political parties, the Administration and the Special Representative - to impress upon the people that, notwithstanding the past conduct of the civil service, their vote will be known to no-one. We were encouraged by plans to this end.

Perhaps crucially, there is the position of the South African Government. It has never been, and still is not, a willing and impartial partner in the execution of Resolution 435. The obstructive tactics, and belated, grudging concessions of its Administrator-General have placed innumerable and needless obstacles in the path of the Special Representative in particular, and the political process in general. The withdrawal of its own troops proceeded to schedule, and was televised around the world. Otherwise every single step to be taken has encountered resistance, evasion and actual delay. That today the process hangs by such a slender thread, and cannot be regarded as secure, is attributable very largely to South African intransigence for its own sake. South Africa, too, has proceeded in a manner calculated to retain both the ability to cause the whole process to miscarry or, perhaps more sinister, actively to destabilise the government which eventually emerges.

Initiatives on the part of its Administrator-General, too, have been taken in South Africa's interests, and not those of the people of Namibia.

That said, we have taken account of the fact that the tragic events of 1 April could have been used by South Africa as justification for it to withdraw from the process altogether. In the light of all we have seen and heard, we conclude that the South African Government remains of the view that it is at present in its national interest to allow the process to proceed to the point where a Namibian government emerges which the international community can recognise. Its ultimate intentions are unclear, but all its options have been kept open.

Once Namibia's Constituent Assembly is established by the Namibian people through a process of free and fair elections, it will have the destiny of the country in its hands. The final stages of Resolution 435 - the declaration of independence and construction of a new government - will be shaped by its deliberations. There will be continuing and vital functions for UNTAG in this phase both to assist the Assembly and to supervise and control the process of transition. The Administrator-General, contrary to his proposal in his first Draft Proclamation on the Constituent Assembly, has no claim whatsoever to predetermine or judge the work of the Assembly. He should, in fact, be even more strictly limited to the maintenance of law and order, the provision of all required support to the Assembly and the day-to-day administration of the business of government and the management of public assets in the interests of the territory's citizens. It is the responsibility of South Africa and the Security Council to ensure that these responsibilities are respected by the Administration, and that in particular no steps are taken that would tend to strip the new nation of its assets or skills.

The assurance of the binding inclusion of the constitutional principles of 1962, which are an integral and uncontested part of the package of the Resolution 435 settlement plan is a matter for both the Constituent Assembly of Namibia and the United Nations, through the Security Council, to accomplish.

As Namibia prepares for transition to independence, its

162

economic prospects include both negative and positive factors which call for some immediate international measures and concerted assistance planning. South Africa's slashing of budgetary support, and taking of measures that would encourage the exodus of the civil servants with their pension funds, represent an economic "scorched earth" policy wholly inconsistent with the terms of Resolution 435 and the norms of civilised international behaviour. The United Nations and its members cannot for one moment accept such steps, and it is the Special Representative's right to ensure that what should be a purely caretaker Administration makes no prejudicial changes (including privatisations) before independence.

Beyond these problems the country's prospects are encouraging, given appropriate and timely assistance from the world. Business and farm leaders are prepared for new national development efforts, and Namibia can quickly benefit from the lifting of sanctions that affect its trade and investment and from international acceptance of its fishing zones. We have identified a good number of practical assistance possibilities that would have major benefit, and to which Commonwealth countries in particular might address themselves.

Finally, the international community must be prepared to follow through on its commitment to secure the return of Walvis Bay and the offshore islands to Namibia, if the country's independence is to be effective.

The people of Namibia have already demonstrated the depth of their desire to participate in the democratic process. Many travelled long distances and waited for lengthy periods in order to register. The turn-out for registration was impressive and provided conditions allow it, we would expect a most substantial turn-out for the vote.

There will be many governments and organisations observing the poll itself. We have done our part in support of the United Nations whose responsibility it will be to certify whether or not free and fair elections have taken place and would not see a Commonwealth presence over the period of the poll as adding significantly to international scrutiny. However, if there is a desire for the Commonwealth to play a continuing role on the ground in Namibia, we would recommend that this might usefully be undertaken by a small mission visiting the country at an appropriate time shortly after the elections to discuss the full range of transition issues in the post-election phase.

In the prevailing environment in Namibia, it will take unstinting commitment by the people's leaders in support of the Special Representative and his staff's own dedicated efforts to sustain the process through to a successful conclusion. As of today we believe this to be possible, and we would respectfully take this opportunity, through our Commonwealth leaders, to appeal in particular to the political leaderships not to allow this historic opportunity for their emerging nation to slip from its grasp.

Windhoek,
Namibia

10 October 1989

Quelle: Preparing for a Free Namibia: Elections, Transition and Independence. The Report of the Commonwealth Observer Group on Namibia, Windhoek, 10.10.1989, S. ix-xiii (Commonwealth Secretariat, London)

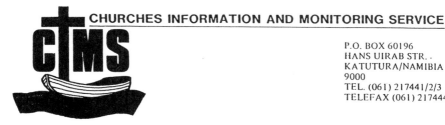

CHURCHES INFORMATION AND MONITORING SERVICE

P.O. BOX 60196
HANS UIRAB STR. .
KATUTURA/NAMIBIA
9000
TEL. (061) 217441/2/3
TELEFAX (061) 217444

CIMS UPDATE

(Compiled from field reports for the period until 20th October)

24th October 1989

COUNCIL OF CHURCHES IN NAMIBIA

THE POLITICAL CAMPAIGN

With the end of registration on 23rd September, the political
campaign for the November elections began in earnest. Flags,
posters, the wearing of party colours, party hand signals and the
singing of political songs are the major ways that people have
demonstrated their allegiances. There has been a rapid increase
in political literature as part of the drive for voter education,
as well as the appearance of smear posters directed at SWAPO.

A number of examples of smear leaflets have been identified from
Caprivi.

"SWAPO congratulations on all your new cars!! A quick calculation
shows that your new cars and bakkies in the East Caprivi has a
total worth of more than one million rand!!..........The SWAPO
leaders are incompetent with money. They are wasting their money
on bakkies, while they should be saving it for the future of
Namibia!!"

"I have heard that SWAPO is a Communist party and the Caprivians
do not want Communism.......If SWAPO is not a communist organisation, why do you concentrate your influence on young people? That
is also what Lenin did in 1917!! And the consequences....Cambodia
used the youth to kill the masses..." Your Concerned Mask.

Leaflets attacking SWAPO's Sam Nujoma, who was described as
"chief liar and deceiver in Africa, its lowest educated leader
who will tell beautiful stories and make lots of false
promises..." were dropped from a plane in Khomasdal in large
numbers around the time of the first SWAPO star rally which
Nujoma addressed on 24th September. The author's name was not
given.

Incidents of defacing the posters of the opposition are common-place. SWAPO put up 270 posters announcing the rally they planned to hold in Khomasdal, Windhoek, but in the end only 50 remained. There are also examples of political flags on houses being replaced overnight by those of the opposition.

Political parties in Owambo have developed detailed plans for the rest of the campaign period. DTA for example plan to hold a total of 29 rallies in the region during October. But the most significant event and the largest rally by far was the SWAPO Star rally held on 7th October when Sam Nujoma returned to Owambo for the first time from exile and addressed a crowd of 70,000.

In the South, in the Mariental district DTA flags are seen in many places, particularly in low income areas in Gibeon. CIMS observers report that it would appear that the DTA have been successful in winning the poor to their side, with reports of incentives being offered. DTA, in common with other parties, offer transportation to rallies, and undertake errands for their supporters. There are also claims of material assistance being given.

Access to voters is a critical issue for political parties at this stage of the campaign. In Tsumeb, the unions complained that Tsumeb Corporation had refused permission to SWAPO to put up posters in the compound or to allow SWAPO flags. But DTA is treated differently. "If you go to the hostel, they ask if you are DTA. If you say yes, they give you a T-shirt. If you refuse they can dismiss you. They are for one party." However, the company has allowed SWAPO supporters to wear T-shirts.

By contrast, SWAPO in Tsumeb report that they no longer have problems of gaining access to farms to speak to farm workers. Explanations of the SWAPO manifesto on land reform had led to a relaxation in attitudes. Of the other political parties in the district visited by CIMS observers only UDF reported difficulties. The unions, however, painted a far gloomier picture. Workers, they said, do not know when they will get permission to go and vote.

UNTAG have continued to hold regular meetings with the political parties. These have generally been reported to be helpful. DTA, however, did not attend the meeting following the first weekend of rioting in Owambo on 5th October. DTA was also the only party not represented at a meeting UNTAG convened with political parties in the Windhoek region in mid-September. .

The UN has come under increasing criticism from the DTA and the smaller political parties, on the issue of impartiality. In Tsumeb the DTA officials complained they had lost faith in their impartiality because of SWAPO intimidation. He quoted the example of a DTA supporter, who works as a security guard, who was seriously injured in an incident in May. Although SWAPOL and UNTAG took statements, they had taken no action.

VOTER EDUCATION

There is considerable concern at the long delay in finalising the electoral law which has delayed plans for voter education. The law was finally published on 13th October leaving just over three weeks to inform the public as to how precisely voting would take place. The majority of recommendations made by the Council of Churches in commenting on the original draft proclamation have been incorporated. In the final proclamation, the secrecy of the ballot is assured and the final result of the election will now be known much earlier, now that counting will be undertaken at district rather than national level.

In advance of the publication of the proclamation, political parties and UNTAG had begun to try and familiarise people with mock ballot papers listing the ten registered parties and instructing people on how to mark the ballot against the party of their choice. This included efforts by SWAPO to undertake voter education programmes amongst farmworkers. In Otjiwarongo, SWAPO has prepared a memorandum directed to the Farmers' Union to try to arrange for an all party meeting in an attempt to get farmers to cooperate with the different political parties.

There have been reports of confusion about the significance of marking the ballot with a cross. A CIMS observer visiting villages in Kavango heard two DTA campaigners explaining to voters that "if you don't like DTA, make a cross behind DTA". UNTAG has confirmed that any mark on the ballot paper is acceptable so long as it is in the correct place.

The need to inform women was particularly noted. Women by and large have been aware of the importance of registration for voting. However, SWAPO Women's Council noted that where political loyalties within the family were divided, women were open to threats from their husbands if they did not vote the same way. In these circumstances it was important to stress the secrecy of the ballot.

Political parties have warned of the difficulties in getting 700,000 people to the polls in just five days. This will be much harder than the registration process spread over several months. The need has been expressed for adequate translators and interpreters at the polling stations who can translate in languages other than Afrikaans and English.

Local pastors in different parts of the country have expressed interest in attending workshops which will help them explain in an impartial way to their congregations the election process. With the start of the voter education campaign, UNTAG had been invited to churches to explain the voting procedures.

INTIMIDATION AND SECURITY

Incidents of intimidation, which have been noticeable in the north of the country, represent the greatest threat to free and fair elections. Intimidation takes two forms: intimidation by members of the security forces and their former members, and by members of political parties. The two types are becoming increasingly confused as DTA claims that most of the former members of Koevoet have joined the ranks of their supporters. Most intimidation incidents are the result of conflicts between DTA and SWAPO supporters with the majority of incidents being regarded as a result of DTA provocation.

Violence in Owambo

Following a period of relative calm, violence erupted in Owambo over the weekend of 30th September-1st October, and was repeated the following weekend, 7-8th October. However, there were no reports of incidents during the weekend of 14-15 October and 21-22nd October.

On the morning of Saturday, 30th September, 900 members of Koevoet were "demobilised" at the SWAPOL headquarters in Oshakati. Later in the day, a DTA mobiliser, Lukas Pedro, was beaten to death outside a cuca shop by a group of people said to be SWAPO supporters. SWAPO and DTA gave CIMS observers conflicting reports of what happened but at some stage during the proceedings prior to the killing a grenade - a "smoke grenade" in the DTA version and a "hand grenade" according to SWAPO was thrown into a crowd of people said to be SWAPO supporters.

When news spread of the killing, DTA supporters began to take revenge ordering people to remove SWAPO flags from their houses, pulling down some and burning others. CIMS observers reported many people beaten up, cars damaged and houses attacked. On Sunday 1st October, 29 people were treated at Oshakati hospital, of whom 8 were admitted. Although the situation calmed down over the next few days, the atmosphere remained tense. There were no reports of retaliation by SWAPO supporters. However, it was noticeable that many people removed SWAPO flags from their houses and these were only put back as news spread of the rally which Sam Nujoma would address on 7th October. It was widely believed that former Koevoet members, "demobilised" on 30th September, were behind the violence.

CIMS observers detailed several examples of incidents of intimidation on Sunday 1st October:

- A boy, fleeing a group of DTA supporters, took refuge in the house of Lukas Simon and Martha Johannes in Ongwediva. The DTA supporters followed him into the house and began to beat up the boy and the couple. The woman was hit on the head with a stone and received injuries to her right arm and back; the man received a blow to the head and an arrow wound in the arm. Their house was burned down. The next day CIMS observers visited the couple in hospital.

- UNTAG did not escape attack. An American visitor, who had been filming a group of DTA supporters, was chased by the group and after a half hour car chase took refuge in the office of the UNTAG police monitors in Oshakati. The group followed him in, hit two of the police monitors, punched another and a scuffle ensued. The video camera was stolen.

- At 4 in the afternoon, Erastus Ingo was sitting with two friends outside a shop in Oshakati. A crowd of around 50 people wearing DTA shirts arrived at the shop carrying pangas, knobkerries, stones and bottles. SWAPO posters were removed, furniture smashed, and three people were beaten up. Ingo's skull was fractured in two places, his eye injured and he lost teeth. Commenting on the incident he said it was clear that the aggression resulted from his sympathy for SWAPO. He received hospital treatment but did not plan to report the case to UNTAG or SWAPOL.

The following weekend — on Saturday, 7th October Sam Nujoma addressed a rally in the north for the first time since his return from exile. Despite the events of the previous weekend, the SWAPO rally passed off peacefully. However, violence broke out on the Saturday evening and continued throughout the weekend. Gunfire and explosions were heard in and around Oshakati especially in the late afternoon and evening.

The following incidents were reported by CIMS observers:

— 15 people were treated in Oshakati hospital after a grenade exploded at a school in Ondangwa. Those injured were all aged between 18-22;

— 5 people were injured in another incident at a senior secondary school;

— 12 were treated at Oshakati hospital after a grenade exploded at a place between Ondangwa and Oshakati;

— on Sunday evening, 15 were injured, and two women died, after a hand grenade was thrown into a crowd singing SWAPO songs;;

— in addition, a security policeman died in what appears to have been a domestic dispute.

With the exception of this last incident, in all cases the victims of violence were SWAPO supporters.

In addition, CIMS observers gave detailed accounts of incidents which they witnessed for themselves. The following are two examples:

— a man, wearing SWAPO colours lying on the ground as a result of an earlier unprovoked attack by DTA supporters, was further kicked and his head stamped on. The CIMS observer took him to hospital where he met an unsympathetic response from the doctor, who assumed that the victim was drunk. The doctor had to be persuaded to examine for fractures;

— a DTA supporter, with a phosphorus bomb in his hand, threatened to throw it into a crowd of SWAPO supporters. Earlier, a neighbouring house belonging to Mrs. Tuufilwa Ndenwene had been burnt down. The South West African police had been called and UNTAG had arrived and left again, but SWAPOL never appeared.

— UNTAG was once again the subject of attacks. In one incident, after the funeral of Lukas Pedro in Ongwediva, CIMS observers witnessed DTA supporters chasing and stoning an UNTAG vehicle, shouting "UNTAG, UNTAG".

In commenting on the events of the two weekends, CIMS observers remarked that the pattern of intimidation suggested some organised action. They related this to the "demobilisation" of Koevoet on 30th September. DTA supporters were responsible for

most incidents and no evidence could be found of aggression against DTA supporters. However, the DTA leadership told CIMS observers that they were "trying to calm their people down". It is worth noting that the funeral of Lukas Pedro, which was attended by DTA leader, Dirk Mudge, passed off peacefully. But as soon as it was ended, and the crowd began to disperse, the first flare rocket was fired. CIMS observers gained the impression that the violence was not officially inspired although they felt the leadership might have been able to do more to prevent the violence and intimidation.

By comparison, SWAPO supporters demonstrated considerable restraint. On Friday 6th October, a group of SWAPO supporters were successfully diverted from marching on the DTA office in Oshakati.

SWAPOL did not play an active role in maintaining law and order. They are seen as partisan and many are believed to be DTA supporters. Several policeman were seen by CIMS observers to give DTA salutes to passing DTA cars. Most of the disbanded Koevoet members are believed now to be active DTA supporters. Although they are supposed to have been disarmed, they are seen carrying knives and sticks quite openly. There is a rumour that on demobilisation they were each given 8 hand grenades. Former Koevoet members were seen consuming considerable quantities of alcohol over the weekend of 7/8 October.

In addition to events in and around Oshakati, there were incidents in the border area. Uniformed men, believed to be UNITA soldiers killed a man, Jonas Mweuhanga, on 2nd October. On 11th October, CIMS observers received information that another group of uniformed soldiers had crossed the border and had robbed villagers.

Kavango

Several examples of intimidation by DTA supporters have been received from Kavango where several officials of the party are former members of the army (SWATF) demobilised, but on full pay until the end of November. Many DTA supporters hold weapons. On 11th October a fight broke out at a cuca shop at Kahenge provoked, it is alleged, by some DTA supporters which resulted in several people receiving injuries. Meanwhile DTA officials, including former 202 batallion member, Bernhard Nekaro Haikera looked on. When challenged to stop his people from stoning SWAPO supporters, he replied that if the crowd did not disperse he would shoots. Whereupon he produced a pistol which he fired twice in the air.

- On 18th September, Kudumo Linyando, was stopped by a man and asked why he was wearing a SWAPO T-shirt. He explained that it was the T-shirt of his choice and walked on. A few moments later he was grabbed by his shirt and kicked and punched resulting in the need for hospital treatment.

- On 1st October, a group of friends met near a shop in Kangweru. They were approached by a group of DTA supporters singing anti-SWAPO songs and shouting anti-Nujoma slogans. They wanted to know what the group of friends were talking about. When they failed to get a response quickly enough the DTA supporters attacked the group with sticks and slapped their faces resulting in one woman losing consciousness briefly.

Both these cases have been reported to the O'Linn Commission on Intimidation.

- Another incident from Kavango occurred at Omega, the settlement made up of demobilised members of Batallion 201. A man called Joseph Thihupa had the DTA T-shirt he was wearing ripped after he had spoken to man known to be a SWAPO supporter who was visiting a relative. To make this visit the SWAPO supporter, Bonifatius Mungeli, had obtained permission to enter the area from ex-SADF Major Mr. Taylor. The implication was that Omega was an area where only the DTA could campaign and where former military personnel acted as if it was a military area.

- There have been several reports of people in the area being forced to "register" although voter registration ended on 23rd September. It appears that people are forced to take out DTA membership cards.

When a serious disturbance broke out at Kahenge in Kavango on 11th October between rival party supporters, the police were approached and asked to help take the injured to hospital. The police refused to help take SWAPO members to the hospital saying that "SWAPO was their enemy".

Caprivi

The CIMS observer team visiting the area in early October reported that the situation was relatively calm. However, 19 cases of intimidation were reported from SWAPO and 3 from DTA. A common complaint is the occupation of a particular area to hinder another party from holding a political meeting. This happens only in the absence of UNTAG. Although all-party meetings have been held regularly under the chairmanship of UNTAG, cases of intimidation are not decreasing.

Another form of intimidation occurs through the distribution of leaflets from various sources designed to confuse people. A so called News Update / Intern includes press cuttings mainly from the Times of Namibia; leaflets signed by "Concerned Mask" attack SWAPO and the CCN; unsigned leaflets attack SWAPO and SWAPO members; and leaflets are also produced by the Concerned Parents Association.

The demobilisation of SADF and Koevoet has led to some security concerns. There are weapons, which have not been handed in, and there are believed to be hidden arms caches. On 3rd September, for example, a hand grenade exploded on a playground. UNTAG estimates the number of civilians in possession of firearms in Katima Mulilo to between 600 and 800. Former Koevoet members from West Caprivi are patrolling the Zambian border. Former SADF soldiers are working for the administration as doctors, administrators and teachers. Former SADF soldiers have formed an association Kopano Ya To. Members describe this as a cultural organisation while others see more sinister motives including the possibility at some later date of speedy remobilisation. Some members are actively campaigning with DTA.

The CIMS observer team were told about a police camp 2 kilometres east of Kalimbeza village near the Zambezi river. This was not included on the list of SWAPOL bases provided by UNTAG and there was no sign of an UNTAG monitoring presence. It was said that this camp had been used to detain and torture political prisoners. About 5 kilometres the other side of Kalimbeza is the Nambweza Youth Camp. CIMS observers were told that this camp was run by the SADF and provided political education. It has not been used since May 1989 but someone is looking after the place and there are still beds in the dormitory.

CIMS observers also note with suspicion the NAMWI Foundation. Founded in 1986 in what used to be a recreation centre for SADF soldiers, it now runs a community centre. The Executive Secretary proudly displayed a T-shirt which read "Caprivi Riot Unit — Striving for Peace." Although claiming to be an apolitical non-governmental organisation, there are hints of links with the SADF.

Tsumeb

From Tsumeb, CIMS observer reported a disturbing incident which took place on 17th October. Mrs. Meila Nghidinwa, a returnee, reported that she was walking home with a friend at 7.30 pm when she was confronted by two men wearing grey uniform. She believes they were members of koevoet. She was questioned aggressively about where she was going. She explained that she was going to her father's house. When she attempted to walk on she found her way blocked by the two men who drew a pistol on her. "Do you know our job?". She managed to push away the pistol which fell to the ground and ran to a friend's house.

A serious incident of another kind from the Tsumeb district concerned workers at the Henning Crusher Company. The manager told the foreman that the workers must go to a DTA rally. Some workers resisted because they were not DTA members. They refused to go. The manager said "This is not a SWAPO company" and six SWAPO workers were fired on 8th July. The case has been taken to the O'Linn Commission. The six workers are staying with friends as they have been evicted from their houses which are owned by the municipality but rented by the company for their workers.

Otjiwarongo

Following the stoning to death of a white policeman last month in the single quarters in Otjiwarongo, the municipality has decided to demolish the flats and has given inhabitants eviction notices as from 31st October. The Orwetoveni single quarters with dormitories designed to accommodate 20 - 40, now house many more. The area is a SWAPO stronghold. The CIMS team observed that the place was rapidly developing into a slum and throwing people out on the streets was not the solution.

Katutura

On 26th September, the DTA held a march in Katutura. It started around 6 pm and covered a distance of four kilometres. According to the DTA, 300 set out in cars and on foot but that by the end 1,000 had joined the march. Trouble broke out as the marchers, shouting anti-SWAPO slogans passed through strong SWAPO districts of Katutura. Stones were thrown at houses and a number of people were injured two seriously. According to UNTAG 34 houses were damaged and nine people were injured and treated in hospital. The injured included a 20 year old man who received multiple injuries and a child of two admitted with a depressed fracture of the skull.

A CIMS staff member was a witness and a victim of the events. At

around 7.45 he came across the march. He witnessed one car with
DTA stickers chasing people. His car was surrounded by DTA
supporters who wanted to pull him out. He ordered the other
occupants to lock their doors. He observed that the crowd was
unruly and although he had no proof, they behaved as if they were
under the influence of alcohol. Whilst they surrounded his car,
they stoned his rear window and damaged the boot with a metal
instrument. "They did not throw stones from a distance but
smashed the car window from close range". A woman in the car
needed hospital treatment and the incident was reported to the
police. Damage to the car was estimated at R1,000.

In the wake of these events controversy broke out as to whether
or not the DTA had permission to march in terms of AG 23. It was
reported later in the media that permission had been obtained for
driving through Katutura with loud speakers and not for a rally
or march. DTA was later refused permission to hold a second
march in the same area two days later. In a TV interview, the DTA
claimed that, if the elections were to be "free and fair", every
party must have access to campaign in any area and there must not
be "no go areas" for any party.

The role of SWAPOL and UNTAG also came in for criticism. SWAPOL
were blamed for failing to stop the violence and UNTAG for failing to intervene. A frustrated UNTAG police monitor maintained
UNTAG was always being blamed for not intervening yet had powers
to monitor not control such events. He reported that five UNTAG
monitors had witnessed and filmed the events.

There were also suggestions that many of the marchers were out-
siders. It was rumoured that buses with South African registration plates had been seen bringing people into Katutura. CIMS
observers could not confirm this although they did observe vehicles with RSA number plates outside the Katutura office of the
DTA.

The South

A CIMS team visiting the Mariental district reported that the
region was comparatively peaceful and lacking incidents of intimidation such as are found in the north. There are nevertheless
exceptions and they identified a number of cases of workers,
dismissed for wearing T-shirts of SWAPO affiliated unions. These
cases had not been reported to UNTAG but were being taken up with
the Legal Assistance Centre in Windhoek. " The primary difficulties in the South lie in the almost feudal relationships of
servitude and poverty in which farm workers are held."

On 13th October the Council of Churches issued a press release
calling for restraint on the part of political parties in the
last period of the election campaign.
 "...we regret the fact that hardly a fortnight after the signing
of the Code of Conduct, a pattern of sporadic acts of intimidation had emerged.

We believe that it is our prophetic duty to remind our sisters
and brothers that intimidation does not only threaten the holding
of free and fair elections, but could create conditions for a
civil war — something which is too ghastly to contemplate.

172

The member churches of the CCN urged the Administrator-General to
exercise his powers to ensure a climate of peace and tranquility
is achieved; urged the UN Special Representative to "effectively
exercise his supervisory powers" and ensure that SWAPOL carries
out its duty of maintaining law and order in accordance with
universally accepted standards of policing. The police must not
be allowed to deliberately close their eyes and ears in the face
of intimidation and violence. Finally the CCN urged political
leaders to not lose sight of their collective responsibility to
"build a nation from the ashes of destruction of apartheid."

RETURNEES

The number of returnees in secondary centres in the Mariental
district had reduced by the time a CIMS team visited in late
September. Many had stated that they were frightened to return
to their homes in the north for fear of Koevoet. A professional
social worker found the reasons for their reluctance to move on
often more complex. Some had practical problems, for example
their luggage had been lost, some had problems tracing relatives
although 50% were later able to locate family. But in addition
there were fears and anxieties arising from fifteen years of
living in settlements as refugees which created problems in
adapting to fending for themselves on return to Namibia.

The same CIMS team were told that the fate of SWAPO detainees was
still a hot political topic. Local people were not convinced by
the explanations which they had received from SWAPO to date.

Quelle: Churches Information and Monitoring Service (CIMS), Katutura / Windhoek:
Update, 24.10.1989 (Büro Katutura)

STATEMENT BY INTERNATIONAL OXFAMS' DELEGATION
TO OBSERVE VOTING IN THE NAMIBIAN ELECTIONS

Windhoek, 10th November 1989

In the face of an electoral process which frequently made it difficult for voters to exercise their democratic right to cast their vote for the party of their choice, the people of Namibia have shown a remarkable determination to participate in determining their own future for the first time. This was the overriding conclusion of the International Oxfam Observer Mission at the mid-point in the voting process. Some of the members of the Mission also observed the registration process in July.

Over the past three days, mission members have fanned out across the country, observing static and mobile polling stations in every part of the country, and having meetings with representatives of UNTAG (including the Special Representative Maarti Ahtissari), representatives of the Adminstrator General and the political parties, as well as with Namibians of all races.

We congratulate all the parties concerned that an election under international supervision is occurring at all. We conclude that, in formal terms at least, an environment exists in which a secret vote may be cast. But in parts of the country we found disturbing flaws in the process.

Many of the difficulties are the result of UN Resolution 435, setting out the terms by which Namibia would attain its independence from South Africa. As many observers then said, and others witnessed during the often unsatisfactory registration process, UNSCR 435 made a genuinely democratic election virtually impossible. It has been a consistent and deeply held concern that the colonial power, South Africa, should run the electoral process with UN in a <u>supervisory</u> rather than a <u>controlling</u> role.

A further concern was the small number of polling stations for so many people over such transport deficient territory. It is a tribute to the efforts of the political parties that such a large proportion of the voting population have already cast their votes.

The major flaws which we have personally observed at the end of 3 days of polling include:

1. The inadequate number of polling stations, especially in Ovamboland, Swakopmund and a number of other areas. Some polling stations have had to accomodate several thousand voters. Many of these voters have travelled whom after travelling very long distances and stood in the blazing sun for hours and hours. They could not vote and had to try to make arrangements to return the next day and possibly the day after. These conditions struck us inhumane and unjust but people were prepared to endure them in order to vote. Mobile polling stations have made a great effort to reach voters. In the end, in much of the country only the heroic determination of tens of thousands of Namibians to exercise their rights even in the face of seriously adversity has

led to such a high rate of voting at this stage.

2. The inadequate preparation of the AG's Office and its staff
has been evident in a number of ways. There has been
inconsistencies in the application of the law, for example the
interpretation of what constitutes a tendered ballot varied
greatly from one electoral district and polling station to
another. After our observers raised the issue at Engela, polling
officers rectified their procedures.

3. In the north especially, the ability of the AG's staff to
conduct the process competently must be questioned when the
widespread shortage of ballot papers forced the closure of a
number of polling stations for varying periods of time. We
question whether it is coincidental that such shortages occurred
in an area where support for SWAPO is extremely strong.

4. The relationship between the AG and UNTAG officials varied
widely between electoral districts and polling stations.
Sometimes there was a remarkable degree of cooperation between
the two. In other cases there was a distinct sense that the AG's
officials ran the show with UNTAG playing a subordinate role.

5. The role of polling agents and observers was interpreted with
wide variation from place to place. Often party polling agents
were placed where they could not properly watch the voting
process. Sometimes observers were warly welcomed inside polling
stations. In other cases access was restricted to brief periods
of time and observers felt unwelcome.

6. In some places, such as Leonardville and Swakopmund, polling
stations were located in the magistrates court buildings, a
symbol in itself of the colonial apartheid regime. In
Leonardville the polling station was in the magistrates court
itself, attached to the police station, and armed white SWAPOL
constables wandered in and out of the polling station in full
view of all the voters, chatting openly with AG officials. In
Swakopmund no polling station was set up in the large African
township.

7. In some places all communication with voters was by white AG
officials who spoke Afrikaans, with UN officials having no way of
understanding what has been said. In those parts of Namibia that
are akin to the Transvaal or old Mississippi, this made a mockery
of the whole process.

8. In the south and in Windhoek, the phenomenon of South
Africans voting constituted a major departure from democratic
processes. The very setting up of a polling station at the
airport to accomodate South Africans flying in to vote and flying
immediately out again is the essence of injustice and smacks of
racism, given the poor distribution of polling stations
elsewhere. When black Namibians living in Walvis Bay have faced
obstacles voting, white Namibians who live in South Africa have
been facilitated through the provision of buses from the Republic
and special polls of convenience.

9. We have observed that the Churches of Namibia continue their
crucial role of supporting the voting process and encouraging
Namibians to participate.

Our criticisms of this flawed process are doubly significant since the election outcome may prove to rest on a small number of voters. Yet the outcome will determine such central issues as future political alignments and the possibility of true national dialogue and reconciliation. It is absolutely crucial for the Namibian people to finally be confident both in the voting procedures and the count which is still to come.

As for the International Oxfam group we intend
to maintain and strengthen our commitment to an independent Namibia. Individual Oxfams are actively discussing with their NGO partners in the country support for appropriate development initiatives which have a vital part to play in the future of independent Namibia

Quelle: Oxfam Büro, Windhoek

STATEMENT BY THE INTERNATIONAL OXFAMS DELEGATION TO OBSERVE VOTING IN THE NAMIBIAN ELECTIONS

WINDHOEK 15 NOVEMBER 1989.

The international Oxfam observer team views the election in Namibia as a triumph for the Namibian people. It has already pointed out that the under resourcing of the UNTAG exercise resulted in election arrangements which were sometimes less than optimal. We congratulate the staff of UNTAG on the very hard work they performed with devotion in difficult circumstances with significant constraints. The election has provided many valuable lessons on the need for better UN resourcing and on organization and procedures for any future exercises in other countries.
We were highly impressed with the commitment and contribution of the nationals from each of our own countries working throughout the UNTAG structure. They will add significantly to international understanding and solidarity.
The Administrator-General's staff at the polls acted, on our observation, in most instances with propriety, fairness and a necessary degree of flexibility under difficult circumstances. There were a great many instances of effective and cordial integration between the election officials and the UNTAG teams.
While aspects of the process can be criticized, as we have done, the achievement of a 97% vote in a voluntary poll with a very low proportion of spoiled votes in an electorate which in the majority is illiterate, means that the people knew how they wanted to vote, and were determined whatever the difficulties and inconvenience to cast that vote. The conclusion is that the election has expressed the will of the Namibian people.
Following the election, the parties generally have expressed their concern to co-operate in the achieving of a constitution within the UN principles laid down in 1982. That augurs well for the setting up of a government and the achievement of independence at an early date.
An early issue to be resolved is that of the detainees, and the international aid and human rights organizations expect this to be dealt with promptly in accordance with internationally accepted human rights principles.
The Oxfam movement has for years been involved in substantial aid projects with the people of Namibia, through the CCN, the National Liberation Movement and community aid organizations. We intend not only to continue but to consolidate that commitment. We stand ready to co-operate with the new government, its agencies, the CCN and other non-governmental agencies to assist in the development of an independent Namibia.

THIS DELEGATION INCLUDED REPRESENTATIVES FROM OXFAM CANADA, OXFAM AMERICA, OXFAM UK AND EIRE AND COMMUNITY AID ABROAD (AUSTRALIA).

FOR INTERVIEWS PLEASE CONTACT: DON DUNSTAN AND/ OR MEYER BROWNSTONE, TEL: 33624 OR 32239

Quelle: Oxfam Büro, Windhoek

Windhoek - city of queues

BY DAVID LUSH AND SAPA

WINDHOEK WAS a city of queues yesterday as voters flocked to the polls to cast their ballot, many for the first time in their lives.

When the capital's twelve polling stations opened at 07h00, thousands of people were already gathered outside, the queues - all more than half a kilometre long - snaking into the distance.

In Katutura, one of the first to vote was Swapo President Mr Sam Nujoma and other top party officials who arrived at the Hakahana polling station soon after it opened at 07h00.

"Today we are finally burying apartheid colonialism," said Mr Nujoma as he was ushered into the polling booth after queueing for about 15 minutes, giving a power salute to the crowd of waiting voters which stretched for more than two kilometres around the polling station.

Wearing a dark pin-striped suit and flanked by Swapo secretary-general, Mr Andimba Toivo Ya Toivo, Mr Nujoma walked into the station, produced his registration card and identity document, was given a ballot sheet and then disappeared into the polling booth before emerging again to drop the paper into the ballot box.

Asked whether he felt his was the least secret vote in the country, Mr Nujoma laughed and said the whole world knew who he would vote for, but "it still remains a secret as no one saw me make my cross".

A handful of voters slept the night at the Khomasdal polling station, while first to vote at Katutura's St Barnabas School, Mr Karl Mbaha, said he had been queuing since 04h00.

"I couldn't sleep I was so excited," said Mr Mbaha clutching a Swapo flag, surrounded by camera crews and inquisitive journalists. "But I didn't expect there to be so many newspaper people here."

When the polling station opened its doors, Mr Mbaha was ushered in by an election official who brusquely ordered that the flag be left outside.

Mr Mbaha emerged a few minutes later with a large smile on his face and obviously feeling good about voting for the first time in his life.

He said he had spoiled his ballot paper by making the cross too big, but was given another one and succeeded with the second attempt. However, he was confident his vote would be counted and that it was secret.

A blind man Mr Gideon Kephas was also among the first to vote at St Barnabas. Mr Kephas said the voting process was explained to him by election officials and he was then guided by his friend who had come with him to the polling station. Mr Kephas also felt his vote was secret.

Elsewhere in the township, the queues were soon almost encircling the Career Training Centre in Soweto and Goreangab School. First in line at the former was Mr Magano Peter who queued with his family of six from two in the morning because, he said, he had to go to work in the afternoon.

Several Katutura businesses closed down for the day so that staff could vote while the township's Single Quarters, usually a hive of activity, was almost deserted with market stalls left standing empty and unattended.

There was no escaping the polling station crowds in Windhoek city, as many township residents found out. There were a few shocked residents in "white city" as convoys of vehicles ferried Swapo supporters from the locations to polling stations in Eros, Olympia and Pioneers Park.

In Olympia, the queue soon wrapped itself several times around the polling station car park, voters taking three hours and more to cast their ballot.

By 11h00 the savage summer sun was taking its toll on voters who craved, many to no avail, for refreshments. It is illegal for political parties to provide voters with food and drink and few private businesses appeared to be taking advantage of a potentially captive market.

However, Swapo Election Director, Mr Hage Geingob, was confident

his party's supporters would not be put off by the heat. "Our people are fighters and they are strong," he said, marvelling at the size of the queue at Olympia polling station. "They stand all day at rallies without water so they should be allright here."

In the city centre, queues developed both outside the railway station polling centre and inside surrounding take-away stores selling cool drink.

Two hours after the polls opened, the queue of voters had wound its way through the station car park and up Barnhoff Street to oposite the police station.

Voter Ms Fenny Tobias came in from Katutura at 06h30 in a bid to escape the crowds, only to find the queue for the railway station centre already half-way up Barnhof Street. Three hours later she was still 100 metres away from the ballot box.

Ms Tobias said she had gone to the Department of Civic Affairs to find out where the polling stations were only to find hundreds of people wanting the same information. There was no notice giving details of where to vote but they were eventually pointed in the right direction by a helpful security guard, said Ms Tobias.

(Report by David Lush of 104 Leutwein Street, Windhoek and Sapa.)

Quelle: The Namibian, 8.11.1989

ELECTION FEVER ON THE WESTERN FRONT

VOTERS from Windhoek through to the coast at Swakopmund have been streaming to the polls in unexpectedly high numbers since the start of the voting on Tuesday. In Okahandja on Tuesday, many voters succumbed to the heat as thousands made a point of reaching the polls as soon as possible.

Election officers in Okahandja, Karibib, Usakos, Arandis and Swakopmund have all been caught off guard with the onslaught of voters.

With little provision being made for the masses to withstand the intense heat in the interior, contigency plans had to be made providing potensial voters with basics such as water, and in many cases medical aid.

Against the expectations, no serious cases of intimidation in the above mentioned areas have thus far been reported save odd incidents of alcohol related violence.

At some polling booths, confusion was evident with regard to the provisions of AG 19 (Note the one prohibiting part party politics within 500 metres of voting points).

In places such as Karibib and Usakos, Swapo officials complained of the non-compliance of certain parties such as the UDF and the DTA.

In these areas no Swapo colours of whatever nature were evident, not even on the voters themselves whereas the DTA and the UDF openly flaunted their colours close to the polling booths.

However in Arandis the scenario was totally different. Of the 1246 voters who passed through the polling station, Swapo badges, shirts,

caps and scarves were evident on virtually every voter.

A Swapo official in the mining town, Joseph Ekandjo, said on inquiry that the party had been assured by both the officials of the AG and Untag that there would be no problem should interested voters wear their party colours.

In Swakopmund, where in the region of 7000 voters cast their ballots on the first day, an atmosphere of live and let live has prevailed since polling. A prominent businessman in the town, Mr Hannes van der Merwe said he had waited for 13 hours before casting his vote.

He maintained that a spirit of co-operation was the order of the day with many people suffering from fatigue after the long wait.

"There was nothing provided for the people. No drinks, no toilets and no feeding points", he said.

"The only guys who helped us were the SWAPO guys who gave us water" he said. "It gave me hope for the future" he added.

Officials in the voting process approached so far have all been full of praise for the manner in which Namibians have conducted themselves.

An Untag official at one polling station in Swakopmund said he did

not know of another country in the world where potential voters would withstand such intense heat and still be there to vote at the end of the day.

At most polling stations, the officials on duty have been accommodating in allowing voters to cast their ballots after the 7pm deadline.

In Swakopmund, one polling station only closed its doors at 10pm. While this caused a tremendous strain on those manning the station - most only got to sleep after 1pm and have to be on duty at 6:30 am the next morning - the general feeling was the voter turn-out would decrease as the week progressed and that the processing of voters would improve.

On Monday in Swakopmund, the first hour saw only 80 voters emerge while the second hour saw an improvement of up to 120 voters.

The anticipated problems with voters from Walvis Bay never materialised with most eligible voters crossing unhindered on Tuesday and Wednesday.

The head of the SWAPO office in Swakopmund, Mr Ben Amadhila, expressed his satisfaction at the way things were progressing and said that despite the fears generated after the registration period, it seems that Namibians at the coast were conducting themselves in admirable

fashion.

While many are taking the elections here seriously, there are several people who are taking the most of the opportunities to make a bit of extra cash.

One woman outside the polling station at the Swakopmund Sport Club boasted of having sold 20 cases of apples in the first day (40 cents an apple) while others have been selling cold drinks at healthy profits to the dehydrated. As has become common place, the DTA have again stolen the show as far providing free (and not so fair) food is concerned.

In Okahandja, Karibib and Usakos, the party announced open season for the entire election week with all and sundry being provided with braai packs of sausages and most as well bread and refreshments from 7 am to 7 pm every day - again giving credence to the saying "We eat at the DTA, but we vote for X".

The elections proceedings were thus far best summed up by a Swapo observer at the Arandis polling station who looked up at the face of a Namibian placing his ballot in the box and said "So this is what free and fair elections look like".

Quelle:

The Namibian, 10.11.1989

'Friends of SA' ferry whites en masse

A LOAD of 40 buses crossed the border between South Africa and Namibia to ferry the South African citizens to cast their controversial votes in Namibia independence elections. According to unofficial sources, about 2200 people voted on the first day of the elections in this border town.

Of this number, over 90 per cent of them were transported in from South Africa at great financial cost.

An organisation known as 'Friends of SA', an 'apolitical' group, is bearing the financial costs of this project.

According to one of the officials of this controversial 'apolitical' grouping, voters, irrespective of their political affiliations or colour, could make use of the transport to come and vote. But as far as this reporter could establish, all those who made use of this facility were whites.

This reporter also learned that different institutions, ranging from political parties in Namibia to business people, were sponsoring the project.

This organisation, 'Friends of SA', was called into being with the clear purpose of ferrying whites from South Africa. The voting by South African citizens, an estimated 10 000 of them, was opposed to the last minute by certain major political parties.

One of the chief organisers said that the luxury buses would be running until the last day of elections to ensure that all eligible SA citizens had the chance to vote. He said the project was initiated with the help of interested political parties and business people.

The SA citizens were provided with food and all the help they needed.

Information reaching us in Karasburg indicated that about 170 sheep were slaughtered to feed the South Africans coming to vote in Namibia, and that more would be slaughtered as the influx was expected to reach its peak by the weekend.

Although the names of specific political parties was not mentioned, it was obvious that the DTA, ACN and NPF were three parties well-represented among the people who travelled to Namibia.

Posters reading 'DTA country' were displayed at the entrance to the tarred roads near the SA border.

(Report by Da'oud Vries, 104 Leutwein Street, Windhoek).

Quelle: The Namibian, 10.11.1989

Clashes in Owambo

OSHAKATI - Supply problems and the first incidents of inter-party clashes characterised voting in the populous north of Namibia on the third day of the five-day election for a Constituent Assembly.

A number of polling stations had to close down for large parts of the day because they had run out of ballots, ballot boxes, envelopes for tendered votes and the fluorescent emulsion used to mark voters' hand.

Election officials said the materials were available in the north, but they had been sent to wrong places, because planning had been done on the basis of registration statistics. In reality people voted at different places from where they registered. Two incidents of inter-party violence, neither serious, were reported.

At Ohangwena Sapa witnessed an exchange of insults and threats, as well as minor scuffles, between supporters of Swapo and the DTA, who threatened each other with firearms. The incident was apparently sparked when Swapo supporters grabbed papers from a DTA vehicle. Police arrived and the people involved dispersed peacefully, police sources said later.

Unconfirmed reports from Engela said UN police had to intervene when supporters of Swapo and DTA threatened each other with firearms. No actual fighting occurred. Police have been unable to confirm the incident.

Voting proceeded at a much slower rate on Thursday, mainly because 75 percent of the registered voters in the Owambo region had voted on the first two days of the election.

Election officials at some smaller polling stations said they had had to close down several times because they had run out of materials.

On the whole, however, the election went on smoothly and peacefully and UN Special Representative Martti Ahtisaari said he was very satisfied when he visited the north.

The Namibian constitutional election was a great success in the northern region of Owambo on Wednesday, Untag spokesman Hugo Anson said yesterday morning.

Mr Anson said about 87 000 voters cast their ballots Wednesday, while about 9 500 did so on Tuesday. This means that a total of at least 182 000 of Owambo's more than 248 000 voters have made their choice of who they want to represent them in the body which is to write an independence constitution for Namibia.

With the result of 10 polling stations still outstanding, this means that about 75 percent of Owambo's traditional Swapo-supporting voters cast their ballots on the first two days.

Mr Anson admitted there had been problems at some polling stations with supply of election material, mostly ballots and ballot boxes. He said these problems were being addressed urgently

Report by Pierre du Plessis, Sapa, Strauss St, Windhoek.

Quelle:

Times of Namibia, 10.11.1989

Voting went smoothly in the south

IS THE south Democratic Turnhalle Alliance country? This was the question asked by many foreign observers. Before the actual process of voting started on Tuesday, the organisation started hosting parties all over the south in an attempt to show some muscle.

In Keetmanshoop, when the DTA's noisy sound system was activated, young children started streaming to the tent which was just a few metres from the house of the DTA's fourth man, Mr Daniël Luipert.

The show went on until midnight with Mr Barney Barnes and Mr Luipert occasionally reminding the crowd to cast their vote for the DTA. This was notwithstanding the fact that 90 per cent of the people who were partying were children not eligible to vote.

The Namibian was told by a restaurant worker that the DTA ordered 6 000 hamburgers and hotdogs from Trek Restaurant in Keetmanshoop. Because of this order the restaurant workers had to report for duty at 04h00 in the morning.

Mr Barnes and Mr Luipert were first to vote with their supporters queuing behind them in the black township of Keetmanshoop.

Throughout the whole process of voting only a few serious incidents of intimidation or election malpractices were reported in the south.

The atmosphere in Aroab was very quiet on Monday except for a Swapo voters education team which visited the village.

In Karasburg, The Namibian was told by polling agents of different parties that the DTA organisers made themselves guilty of serious election malpractices. In one such incident a "blind" man's vote was disqualified when it was discovered that he was not blind after all.

According to a Swapo polling agent, a man with dark glasses was brought in by a DTA organiser. The man was said to be blind on which the electoral officers suggested that he be helped in the polling booth. When the two went in, the Swapo agent heard the DTA organiser telling the "blind" man to put his cross where the two fingers were.

After the cross was made and the ballot paper was just about to be put in the box, the Swapo agent said he knew where the cross was made and that it was made by the "blind" man.

When the paper was opened it was

discovered that it was a DTA vote and that the "blind" man made the cross himself.

It also became clear that the man was not blind, but that the DTA organiser just wanted to make sure that the vote was for the Alliance.

In Ariamsvlei there was a huge influx of South African citizens ferried in with buses to vote. Of the buses which invaded Namibian soil were NPF, ACN and DTA stickers. The voting process went smooth with people occasionally reminded to fill their stomachs with the free food

which was provided by an "apolitical" group called Friends of South Africa.

This dubious organisation was also involved in the process of voting by making certain arrangements which were regarded by Untag as smoothing the process.

An Untag official said he did not have any problems with the organisation as long as it did not interfere with the free and fair motto of the elections.

Both Untag and Administrator-General election officials expressed

their satisfaction with the process.

The only thing which they discovered was the lack of understanding by the local voters as to how to make their mark. They said they discovered that the locals were not informed or were not clear about the voting procedure.

They complained that some voters - instead of putting their crosses on the the ballot paper - made it on an example paper which was put in the booth to explain the process to the voters. As a result of this the paper had to be removed from the booths to

prevent confusion.

In Lüderitz, despite a few registered seamen who were still on the sea, most people had a chance to vote.

Generally, despite ignorance of the voters and a few election malpractices, the process was concluded satisfactorily.

(Report by Da'oud Vries, 104 Leutwein Street, Windhoek.)

Quelle:

The Namibian, 13.11.1989

NEARLY 100 % POLL
and Ahtisaari declares the election free and fair

A TOTAL of 95,55 per cent of registered voters had cast their ballot when the polls finally closed on Saturday night.

Soon afterwards, the UN Special Representative Mr Martti Ahtisaari declared the voting procedure free and fair, a decision echoed by the Administrator General, Mr Louis Pienaar.

Although the figures for the numbers of voters from 36 isolated polling stations in the north of the country were still outstanding, Saturday's final turnout tally was high by any standards.

Windhoek had the second lowest turnout of voters throughout the whole country with 90,7 per cent of the registered voters casting their ballot, although this relatively low figure could be explained by the fact that people working in the capital could have returned to their home regions to vote.

Damaraland, for example, had a 101,6 per cent turnout while 100,5 per cent of Rehoboth's registered voters cast their ballot.

East Caprivi had the lowest figure of 89,6 per cent.

The biggest turnout of voters was in Luderitz with 110,9 per cent, but this was due to the hight number of migrant workers living in the region, 23,7 per cent of votes cast being tendered ballots (votes cast by those of people who had registered elsewhere in the country).

Voting on the final day was slow, with only 0,77 per cent of the registered voters turning out in the far north. The only noticeable exception was Karasburg (26,7 per cent), no doubt explained by the cavalcade of voters bussed in from South Africa.

The voting process was declared a resounding success by both Untag and the Administrator General, giving his stamp of approval yesterday after Mr Arhtisaari's announcement on Saturday that, up until now, the election had been free and fair.

"We are completely satisfied that it (the voting) was free and fair," said chief spokesperson for the Administrator General, Mr Gerhard Roux. "We are completely satisfeid that every Namibian permitted to do so had an opportunity to vote. And we are completely satisfied that those Namibians who were qualified and live outside the border, had the opportunity to vote."

South African Foreign Minister, Mr Pik Botha, was also pleased with

the "successful conclusion" of "the most important phase of the independence process".

"The South African Government stands ready to recognise the results as certified by Mr Ahtisaari, and is ready to work constructively with the future government of Namibia.

"Southern Africa is entering a new phase where the emphasis will be on economic co-operation, and where ideological differences will be pushed to the background.

"Namibia's independence is of great historic importance for the whole of Africa; it is the last country of the colonial era to gain independence. I am thankful that the election in this particular country, with its many contrasts and turbulent history, took place peacefully."

Of course, the counting of the ballots still has to take place before Mr Ahtisaari can declare the result and entire election process as being free and fair.

The ballot counting was due to start at 07h00 this morning and the final result is expected to be an-

nounced sometime on Wednesday, although results from the regional centres (a tally of which will make up the final result) should start coming through as from later today.

Mr Roux made another appeal for calm. "A heavy strain will be put on all of us in the next three days, with a mounting fervour coming in the wake of results being announced.

"This is all the more reason why

we should aèt with restraint. We have come a long way over a difficult road. We must not stumble at the last hurdle."

(Report by David Lush, 104 Leutwein Street, Windhoek.

Quelle:

The Namibian, 13.11.1989

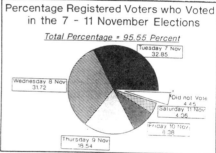

Percentage Registered Voters who Voted in the 7 - 11 November Elections

Total Percentage = 95.55 Percent

Tuesday 7 Nov 32.85
Wednesday 8 Nov 31.72
Did not vote 4.45
Saturday 11 Nov 4.06
Friday 10 Nov 6.38
Thursday 9 Nov 18.54

DISTRICT	Registered Voters	Percentage Registered who voted	Ordinary Votes	Tendered Votes	Total	Percentage Tendered Votes
01 BETHANIE	2464	95.05	2023	319	2342	13.62
02 DAMARALAND	15127	101.61	12998	2372	15370	15.43
03 GOBABIS	19250	94.84	16156	2101	18257	11.51
04 GROOTFONTEIN	20510	96.80	16243	3610	19853	18.18
05 HEREROLAND	16317	97.42	13157	2739	15896	17.23
06 KAOKOLAND	13546	92.79	10108	2461	12569	19.58
07 KARASBURG	18257	103.27	14435	4419	18854	23.44
08 KARIBIB	6955	96.46	5648	1061	6709	15.81
09 KAVANGO	64156	94.65	53398	7325	60723	12.06
10 KEETMANSHOOP	20039	96.80	17310	2087	19397	10.76
11 LUDERITZ	10740	110.99	9088	2832	11920	23.76
12 MALTAHOHE	2635	98.29	2266	324	2590	12.51
13 MARIENTAL	14630	96.64	11879	2260	14139	15.98
14 OKAHANDJA	11233	93.33	9036	1448	10484	13.81
15 OMARURU	6008	96.45	4842	953	5795	16.45
16 OOS-CAPRIVI	28096	89.60	23045	2128	25173	8.45
17 OTJIWARONGO	13287	92.90	10276	2067	12343	16.75
18 OUTJO	7219	96.01	5868	1063	6931	15.34
19 OWAMBO	248272	96.59	226294	13511	239805	5.63
20 REHOBOTH	17346	100.50	14848	2584	17432	14.82
21 SWAKOPMUND	25363	95.31	19759	4414	24173	18.26
22 TSUMEB	14651	95.05	12244	1682	13926	12.08
23 WINDHOEK	105382	90.71	83829	11763	95592	12.31
TOTAL	701483	95.55	594750	75523	670273	11.27

The final tallies at the close of voting on Saturday (excluding figures from 38 isolated polling stations which were still to report back.)

FREE AND FAIR ELECTIONS mean...

ACCEPTING THE RESULTS

The Namibian elections have been unique. Never has so much care been taken to ensure that national elections were free and fair. The eyes of the world have been on Namibia as UNTAG has supervised and controlled each stage of the process.

All Namibia's political parties signed the Code of Conduct. In it, they promised to honour and accept the results of the elections, provided the Special Representative, Martti Ahtisaari, certifies that they have been free and fair.

Mr. Ahtisaari first has to judge if the process of polling has been free and fair. Then he has to decide if the counting has been free and fair.

The political leaders you elect will work together within the framework of the Constituent Assembly, no matter how many seats their parties win. They will adopt the Constitution drawn up by the Assembly, on behalf of all Namibians.

Your vote has been your free choice for your country's future. The election results will be the sound of the democratic voice of all the people of Namibia.

YOUR PARTY ACCEPTS THE OUTCOME OF FREE AND FAIR ELECTIONS... IT ACCEPTS THE WILL OF THE NAMIBIAN PEOPLE

Quelle: The Namibian, 13.11.1989 (Anzeige)

People of Namibia vote for freedom from colonial rule

BY GWEN LISTER

NAMIBIANS took to the streets yesterday in several towns and in the capital to show their support for the victors in the Namibian independence elections, Swapo.

After a long night, during which very few Namibians slept at all, the final two results in the polling districts of Ovamboland and Kavango swept Swapo of Namibia to a clear majority in Namibia independence elections, giving the movement a total of 41 seats in the 72-member Constituent Assembly.

Namibian self-determination became a reality after many decades in the historic election outcome yesterday.

DTA posters and placards rapidly began to disappear and little evidence of DTA supporters was seen in the streets of the capital yesterday.

Shortly after the Ovamboland result became known at mid-morning, giving Swapo its majority,

the Administrator-General, Mr Louis Pienaar, invited the Swapo President, Mr Sam Nujoma, to the Tintenpalast, where he congratulated him on his movement's victory.

Ballot counting on Monday night was delayed by various problems; thus far unexplained power failures in the far north and in Windhoek itself resulted in a delay as well as problems with the verification of the more than 96 000 tendered ballots.

At 19h00 last night, the final election result was announced by the AG's chief spokesperson, Mr Gerhard Roux, on behalf of the chief electoral officer, Mr A.G. Visser. The total votes polled by each party are as follows: ACN 23 728 (three seats); CDA 2495; DTA 191 532 (21 seats); FCN 10 452 (one seat); NNDP 984; NNF 5 344 (one seat); NPF 10 693 (one seat); Swapo-D 3 161; Swapo of Namibia 384 567 (41 seats); and

the UDF 37 874 (four seats). The total number of votes polled was 670 830.

Late this morning, the counting point at the Windhoek Showgrounds was a hive of activity, with very tired workers beginning to flag after a long day and night of counting ballot papers.

At 20h00 last night, the United Nations Special Representative, Mr Martti Ahtisaari, certified the electoral process in Namibia as being free and fair at each stage, and that it had been conducted to his satisfaction.

Adding that he had considered all aspects of the process, with particular reference to proper and timely tabulation and publication of voting results as required by the Security Council, Mr Ahtisaari felt that the election had "given the whole world a shining lesson in democracy".

He added that there had been no

losers, and that the people of Namibia as a whole had been victorious, united in their dedication to peace, reconciliation and the future.

Throughout the country, it was without doubt Swapo's day, and by the time of going to press last night there had been no reports of any major acts of intimidation in retaliation for the final result.

At the time that final election results were coming through yesterday, the Swapo President said that he was "grateful and proud that the Namibian people had elected Swapo to office". In an interview with Nampa, Mr Nujoma added that many lives had been sacrificed to ensure the arrival of the historic day of victory.

Reaching out a hand of reconciliation to other parties with seats in the Constituent Assembly, he said that he hoped other parties would play a positive role in their contribution to the drafting of a national independ-

ence constitution.

Mr Nujoma did not forget the United Nations Transition Assistance Group, and added that he thanked Untag for having come to this country under the directives and mandate of the UN Security Council.

He assured the UN Special Representative of full cooperation from Swapo and the Namibian people. Mr Nujoma also thanked the Organisation of African Unity (OAU) for their special role in the liberation of Africa, and in particular, Namibia.

He experienced gratitude to the African heads of state to this end.

Mr Nujoma would host a press conference at 10h00 today.

Quelle:
The Namibian, 15.11.1989

Swapo 57,32% DTA 28,55% UDF 5,64% ACN 3,53%
•No total power
Triumph for democracy!

Deon vd Merwe THE DTA leadership late yesterday acknowledged Swapo's electoral victory and said that as democrats the Alliance accepted the will of the people in the interest of Namibia's early independence.

Addressing a press conference, the Senior Vice President of the movement, Mr Mishake Muyongo and the Chairman, Mr Dirk Mudge said the DTA wanted to impress upon Swapo the great responsibility which now lay with the party. It assured Swapo that for its part the DTA would co-operate in every endeavour for the good of the country and its people.

"We congratulate you as the overall winner. A great responsibility now rests with you. The DTA will not play a negative role — but we will strictly guard the interests of our country," Mishake Muyongo said.

The DTA leaders said they wished to put the minds of their supporters, as well as other people in the country, at rest. The result of the election in Namibia should not be viewed as the end — but rather as the beginning of a new and independent Namibia free of colonialism and apartheid.

Both Messrs Muyongo and Mudge reiterated their firm conviction that the independence process should not be delayed unnecessarily.

They said the DTA would go to the Constituent Assembly, not align themselves with any of the other parties, but to make a constructive contribution to the business of the House,

which was to write an acceptable constitution for the soon to be independent Namibia.

Mr Mudge said he had seen various versions of the proposed Swapo constitution and although there were differences, he was sure that once consultations and deliberations got underway, much common ground would be found. Both he and Mr Muyongo said that in the main they would like to see a bill of fundamental rights and the assurance of a continued multi-party system enshrined in a future constitution.

The DTA leaders emphasised the importance of function of the Constituent Assembly. This would be the forum at which the representatives of the nation would meet, discuss, debate and by a democratic process arrive at solutions to the problems facing Namibia' immediate constitution problems.

Asked whether the though Mr Nujoma wa right in predicting inde pendence before Chris: mas, the DTA leaders sa' if the Swapo proposals the Assembly proved to b . acceptable to a two-thir majority of the 72 men bers, this was quite po- sible. Mr Mudge said h was speaking for all hi colleagues when he said that no-one relished the

though of another election in the immediate future. He expressed the hope that there would be a government formed from within the ranks of the Constitutional Assembly. If such a government was a coalition, representative of the representation in the House, and it was allowed the opportunity of governing for a reasonable time, it would give the parties time to get to know each other and to build a trust which was essential.

The DTA, and other parties, however, also had prepared documents. It would be less than democratic not to allow other parties in the Assembly an opportunity to voice their views on this most important matter. They added that the DTA would not merely rubber-stamp a Swapo constitution for the sake of convenience. Time was of the essence, but the process of preparing an acceptable constitution could be hurried along regardless of the consequences.

Mr Muyongo said in the final analysis that Namibia's constitution should be a document which was down to earth, practical and one that the majority of the people could live with.

Although the DTA did not obtain a majority, it was strongly represented and it

was in a position of preventing the majority party from acting at random where the national interest was at stake. It was the DTA's view that the interest of the country far outweighed party interests. Therefore it did not intend entering into a dispute with smaller parties which caused the Alliance difficulties during the election campaign. The DTA also hoped that the future would bring serious introspection.

The DTA leadership went on to say that all elected leaders now faced a major challenge. It was their task to build a nation from a seriously divided population. Not only black and white, but all ethnic groups must work together.

Mr Muyongo appealed to the whites in the country to stay. He said they were Namibians and sorely needed in the construction of a new and unified nation.

The leaders said the DTA would ensure that the democratic process in Namibia continued. The party was in a position to guard the interests of the people and to make sure that within the next few years, they were again afforded the opportunity of exercising their democratic right of voting for the party of their choice.

Report by Deon vd Merwe,
27 Edison Street Windhoek

Festive Swapo demo in Windhoek

Edward Ndopu

SEVERAL thousand Swapo supporters took to the streets in Windhoek yesterday in various localities of the town as a show of strength for their party's 57 percent simple majority victory in the recently concluded Constituent Assembly elections.

Kaiser Street, Windhoek's main street, was crammed with hoardes of election infatuated Swapo supporters who danced, sang and shouted Swapo slogans all along the

length and breadth of the road.

The festive demonstration was a spontaneous reaction by Swapo members to the announcement earlier in the morning that the party had swept the votes in Ovamboland by 92 percent, effectively providing it with a simple majority in the planned Constituent Assembly.

Ironically, there was a predominance of Ovambo-speaking people, drawn mostly from Katutura, outside Windhoek, in the crowds

that took to the streets who displayed contempt in their songs for "apartheid colonialism, DTA, whites and puppets".

Many onlookers could not conceal their outrage at what they loudly referred to as "an uncalled for demonstration" that sought to provoke the wrath of opposition parties.

One onlooker, Ms. Betty Gawases, expressed the feelings of several people interviewed by the Times of Namibia when she said, "We know many

of the parties like the DTA could have got the majority, but it is a fact that they lost because of one single tribe which forms the greater part of this country."

The Swapo members, who at some stages were unruly, turned the otherwise peaceful quiet of central Windhoek into an atmosphere akin to a wild carnival.

It appeared as though the Swapo membership were not told the actual result obtained by the party, about 41 seats in the Constituent Assembly, because many of them kept shouting that "two-thirds majority belongs to Swapo", amid the blaring of horns.

This behaviour annoyed pedestrians and motorists alike, who were rather inconvenienced by the Swapo mobs, who persistently shouted praise-songs in honour of their leader, Sam Nujoma.

By late afternoon yesterday, the streets of central Windhoek were, however, back to their normal relative quiet.

What remained was an accumulated, unsightly collection of litter and empty soda cans, left along the trail followed by the Swapo members.-

Report by Edward Ndopu, 27 Edison Street, Windhoek.

... But not all behaved very well

Uapi Ngava

SEVERAL businesses in the capital were yesterday vandalised when Swapo supporters, mostly teenagers, took to the streets to celebrate their party's lead of 57 percent in the independence elections that were announced yesterday. Believing that meant a victory leading to the overall and sole control of an independent Namibian state, the revellers went about singing praises to Nujoma and his lieutenants among shouts of "away with puppets ... DTA down ... Boers go to South Africa ..." At a certain department store in the capital, a doortender was severely assaulted before a group of the revellers entered the shop and pinched a few articles.

Political analysts interviewed by The Times said the irrational frenzy of excitement by the Swapo supporters could be explained in terms of the sustained depression they underwent while the Democratic Turnhalle Alliance kept the lead as the counts were released which lasted about 24 hours.

Swapo was awoken from a defeating slumber when tribalism overtook national popularity. Until then, Swapo supporters were gloomy and worried while the votes from Owambo, the party's base and birthplace in the deep north bordering Angola, were awaited.

A businesswoman told of a man who walked into her shop and demanded a job as Managing Director allegedly promised him by Sam Nujoma of Swapo in the event of his party winning.

A police officer commented that the police did not act against anyone yesterday "because such silly extravagance" (uitspattighcid) does not last long.

Another businessman said he wanted the revellers to know that his concern will not tolerate any such behaviour on his premises after witnessing the assault on his neigbour's doorkeeper.

Report by Uapi Ngava, 27 Edison Street, Windhoek

Quelle: Times of Namibia, 15.11.1989

A democratic mandate to lead Namibia

The President of SWAPO, Cde Sam Nujoma, on 15 November held his first press conference as election victor to give SWAPO's response to the election results. He made the following statement.

The Namibian people have spoken. They have given SWAPO the democratic mandate to lead Namibia to independence.

For this mandate, I would like to express, on behalf of SWAPO, profound gratitude to the Namibian people for the trust and confidence they have expressed in our organization.

I would like to state that the victory that SWAPO has won is not just a historic achievement for SWAPO. It is a victory for the whole Namibian nation.

The Namibian nation has won its long-denied right to self-determination and independence. For this reason there are no losers. We are all victors, even those that did not gain seats will have the opportunity to enjoy the fruits of independence.

With the clear majority that it has in the form of a plurality, SWAPO now has a sovereign mandate to convene the Constituent Assembly within a matter of days, to lead the Assembly in its task of writing and adopting a Constitution for independent Namibia and to set the date for independence. In so doing, we are looking forward to the co-operation of all those other political parties which have gained seats in the Constituent assembly.

The collective mandate which we have received for this purpose imposes on us the responsibility to move speedily in our deliberations, and thereby to ensure that Namibia's independence is not delayed any further.

Although we have not yet held consultations with other parties, it is SWAPO's expectation that none of the parties that has won seats has any interest in delaying the country's independence.

SWAPO has been giving considerable thought to the principles and ideas which should be included in the Constitution for an independent Namibia.

However, these notwithstanding, we are prepared to give ample time to the other parties to put forth their views regarding the Constitution.

We have no intention of imposing our views on others. And we anticipate no serious disagreements on this.

We stand ready to be guided by the democratic principle of open discussion and decision by majority.

Our legitimate preoccupation with writing the Constitution must not blind us to the pre-occupation of the Namibian people, namely, the early achievement of independence, and the establishment of a government which will address, at the earliest possible time, their pressing socio-economic problems.

SWAPO wants to reassure the nation that it will stand by its policy of national reconciliation. In this connection, we re-state our readiness to co-operate with all sectors of our society, including those in business, the Public Service, the farmers and the workers, in moving our society forward.

Specifically, I want to reassure the Civil Service that its services will continue to be needed, as will the productive efforts of all sectors of our economy.

Quelle:
Namibia Today, 18.11.1989

1982 PRINCIPLES ADOPTED

Gurirab unexpectedly proposes adoption and tension disappears

BY PIERRE DU PLESSIS, SAPA

THE first meeting of Namibia's Constituent Assembly yesterday swiftly defused what had promised to be a major stumbling block in the process of drafting an independence constitution for Africa's last colony when it unanimously adopted the 1982 constitutional guidelines as a framework for its work.

The 67 men and five women members of the Assembly, who were greeted by a crowd of enthusiastic well-wishers, as well as a sprinkling of protestors, when they arrived at the historic Tintenpalast, closed their first session by accepting the 1982 Principles as a framework.

They started their work shortly after 10h00 by electing Swapo election director Hage Geingob as chairperson of the Assembly, thus making him the first Swapo official with an office in the seat of government.

After taking over the chair from Swapo president Sam Nujoma - who was acting chairperson in his capacity as leader of the majority party - Mr Geingob urged the Assembly to ensure a speedy independence through a process of give-and-take negotiations.

Mr Nujoma told the Assembly that the most important work - nation-building, national reconciliation and socio-economic upliftment - could start only once independence had been attained.

He expressed a desire for early independence.

This sentiment was echoed by leaders of the minority parties as they took it in turn to address the House, although some warned it would not do to rush deliberations about the constitution.

Most leaders also accepted and echoed the need for national reconciliation, while stressing the importance they attached to the 1982 Principles.

These Principles, negotiated with the help of the Western powers to break the deadlock in the Namibian settlement process, have always been regarded as part and parcel of the independence plan.

But when it emerged in the course of drawing up legislation to create the Constituent Assembly that Swapo was opposed to the inclusion of the Principles in the proclamation, several parties inferred the liberation movement was no longer interested in the Principles.

This became an issue in the last stages of the election campaign, although Swapo leaders insisted they had negotiated the Principles and still supported them, but did not want them prescribed through South African legislation.

Observers predicted Swapo would deviate from the Principles - which are that an independent Namibia must be a unitary, multi-party constitutional democracy with an independent judiciary and a bill of fundamental rights - and establish a one-party state.

This fear was echoed in the speeches by minority leaders in the Constituent Assembly during the ceremonial morning session.

In the afternoon, the Assembly reconvened to appoint a committee which will draft rules and procedures for the House.

The process went ahead smoothly and it was announced the Assembly would adjourn until next Monday to give the committee time to do its work.

Then Swapo foreign secretary Theo-Ben Gurirab unexpectedly indicated he wanted to speak.

He said his intervention was in response to the emphasis on the 1982 Principles during the morning session.

DTA chairperson Dirk Mudge tried to stop Mr Gurirab, but he pressed ahead and proposed the Assembly, as part of its first session, adopt the 1982 Principles as a framework for the constitution it is going to draft.

The motion was accepted unanimously with applause by the Assembly, and the House adjourned.

Observers believe the adoption of the Principles has played a major role in eliminating distrust between the minority parties and Swapo, adding this would greatly speed up the drafting of a constitution.

There seemed to be a genuine air of reconciliation in the Assembly - members from opposing parties chatted amiably while the secret voting for a chairperson was going on - and all the party leaders stressed the need for nation-building.

With the Assembly already agreed on a guiding set of principles after only one day - and a day which most expected to be devoted to ceremony and purely practical matters - there is every chance that Namibia will be independent sooner rather than later, some observers said.

What is beyond doubt is that it will be a multi-party democracy with a bill of rights, and after that long-awaited independence, they added.

OLD HANDS AND NEWCOMERS JOIN FORCES

BY MARK VERBAAN OF NAMIBIA NEWS SERVICE

SCORES of foreign media and curious onlookers gathered outside the imposing Tintenpalast building in the Namibian capital yesterday to witness the arrival of the seven party's representatives elected to the Constituent Assembly.

The 72-member body sat for the first time at 10h00 yesterday to begin the arduous task of thrashing out a constitution for the new independent state of Namibia.

The former South African colony is now well on the road to self-determination following a successful election in which 90 percent of the electorate voted.

It was indeed a rare and strange sight to witness old political arch-enemies sitting down together in the same room, and even going so far as to shake each others' hands and give the traditional bear-hug.

Opening the session was Swapo president Sam Nujoma, as leader of the party which scored a 57 per cent majority in the UN-supervised elections under the Security Council's Resolution 435.

The Assembly was asked to vote for a chairperson, with the nominees being Swapo election director Hage Geingob, and DTA official Andrew Matjila.

Geingob was head of the UN Institute in Lusaka (Unin) during his years in exile.

Matjila, on the other hand, found nothing strange about being in the high-ceilinged chamber. He had often been there during sittings of the then National Assembly in his capacity as Minister of Education in the South African-appointed interim government.

Many of his colleagues in the interim government, which was disbanded in February this year after four years in power, were present at the Assembly sitting this morning. Local journalists were amused to note how these former ministers virtually gloated over the Swapo representatives, most of whom had spent up to 30 years in exile and had never participated in such a body.

DTA leader Dirk Mudge, in his efforts to appear an old hand at the game, spent a few minutes reading a newspaper before the session began.

Mudge was Minister of Finance in the interim government.

After the 72 members had voted for a chairperson, it was announced that Geingob had been elected to the position with 47 votes. Swapo has 41 seats in the Assembly, and observers were speculating as to which representatives from other parties had voted for the Swapo official.

Taking his position, Geingob pledged to the House that he would "execute my tasks dutifully and conscientiously".

He said that by holding the majority in the Assembly, the people of Namibia had given Swapo the mandate to "hammer out a constitution in a spirit of compromise".

"This is a trust we dare not betray," he said.

Geingob added that the three tasks which lay before the Assembly were the drawing up of a constitution, the adoption of the document by two-thirds majority, and the setting of a date for independence.

"There will be differences of opinion in vital matters, but through deliberations we should find solutions and move forward," Geingob said.

He said that as chairperson, he

would remain "as impartial as is humanly possible".

"Our country is in a state of anxious suspense regarding the outcome of our work. The challenges are great. It is now up to us to deliver Namibia from the bondage of colonialism...but we must remember that the people are waiting."

Addressing the delegates, Nujoma said Swapo was proud of being "a Namibian party which has been associated with the struggle which led to this auspicious occasion".

"On behalf of Swapo I would like to pay tribute to those countrymen and women who laid down their lives to make this day a reality," the 60-year-old leader said.

He thanked the South African Administrator-General, Louis Pienaar, for the "wonderful co-operation given to me and Swapo".

He also thanked the UN Special Representative, Mr Martti Ahtisaari, for the job done by the UN Transition Assistance Group (Untag).

"However, the prize must go to the people of this country."

Nujoma said it was incumbent on the delegates to hasten the day of independence.

"Our people have suffered and waited too long for their God-given right to self-determination and independence.

"Our task, as founding fathers and mothers of the nation, is to draw up a constitution.

"I am fairly confident that you can accomplish the task entrusted to you and not let our people down. I too will do my best," Nujoma said.

Vice-president of the DTA, Mishake Muyongo, said in his speech that the Alliance would be prepared to "co-operate constructively"

"The DTA represents a broad spectrum of the Namibian people, and this was demonstrated by the election results," he said, referring to the 21 seats captured by the Alliance.

"We are here to give and take. Namibia has been under colonial rule

for so long that we should not delay. People in this country have suffered for a long time, and they need a democratic process which can give them a prosperous and happy life," he said.

Leader of the United Democratic Front, Justus Garoëb, said the success of the Assembly depended on the willingness of the various parties to co-operate in the drafting of a constitution.

Garoëb, whose party scored four seats in the Assembly, said the "people who have suffered under colonialism for almost a century are looking with expectation at us to deliver them from racial disunity"

Assuring his party's co-operation, Garoëb said that "very serious problems still remain"

He claimed that the election had been neither free nor fair, but that the UDF remained prepared to assist in the building of a new future.

"It might still be hard to reach our goal of self-determination if such problems are to cast a shadow of doubt and mistrust," he said.

Garoëb then referred to an ongoing saga concerning alleged South African spies which were still being held by Swapo in camps in Angola and Zambia.

Although Swapo claims to have released all its prisoners, certain political parties maintain that many more are still being held.

"There is evidence that hundreds of Namibians did not participate in the election process against their will. The election was therefore not free and fair," he said.

Garoëb added: "All the unresolved problems must be dealt with by the Constituent Assembly before getting down to its work."

However, discussing the issue of whether or not Swapo is still detaining alleged spies is not part of the Assembly's mandate, and it is highly unlikely that Swapo would permit such matters to be raised before a constitution has been written and

adopted.

Garoëb said the UDF was concerned about "the fate of Namibians who have been denied the right to vote"

Hinting at a possible veto of the constitution by the UDF, Garoëb said his party has "remarkable bargaining power"

Considering the UDF has only four seats, observers are of the opinion that this statement might be something of an exaggeration.

Garoëb also said that his party supported the principle of another election which would vote a government into power. However, if a constitution is adopted by 48 members of the Assembly, it would be possible for the majority party to establish a government immediately.

Swapo does not subscribe to the notion of another election being called.

Leader of the exclusively-white Action Christian National (ACN), Jannie de Wet, said that Swapo would play a major role in the future, "and if done in the spirit of give and take, there is a bright future for Namibia".

Speaking on behalf of the ACN's three seats, De Wet said he believed the Assembly could have a result "within days".

The former Minister of Agriculture in the interim government, it is believed that De Wet is hoping for a similar position in the independent government.

While the ACN has a policy of retaining group (white) rights in the new Namibia, De Wet said the supporters and members of his party saw themselves as "part of the residents of Namibia".

"We want to be accepted and fit in as such," he said.

"We accept that South West Africa is moving into a new era, and we want to be part of this new land and its dispensation," he said.

The ACN claims to speak for the majority of Namibia's 60 000 whites.

Other representatives who made opening speeches were Moses

Katjiuongua of the National Patriotic Front (NPF), Hans Diergaardt of the Federal Convention of Namibia (FCN) and Vekuii Rukoro of the Namibia National Front (NNF). All three parties scored one seat each in the Assembly.

Katjiuongua said that Swapo, as the majority party, has to "reassure the nation that they are in safe hands and that they have security in their lives".

"The business community needs a statement from Sam Nujoma that no policy is contemplated which will ruin the economy," said Katjiuongua.

The former interim government Minister of Health and Welfare delivered a stinging and often bitter speech directed at Swapo and its president.

"It doesn't make sense to talk about national reconciliation while calling your opponents nasty names. Political mudslinging is two-way traffic," he said.

Referring to previous statements made by Nujoma regarding an investigation into the suitability of certain members of the police force, Katjiuongua said: "There are many in this country who would like to see the same thing done with Plan (Swapo's military wing) and Swapo security." He added: "The urge for independence should not blind us to the realities of this country."

Delegates elected a Standing Committee this afternoon shortly before the session adjourned. The committee is to draw up rules and regulations affecting the Assembly, which is due to meet again on Monday.

Quelle:

The Namibian, 22.11.1989

THE CONSTITUTION OF THE REPUBLIC OF NAMIBIA

188

TABLE OF CONTENTS

190

CHAPTER 9   THE ADMINISTRATION OF JUSTICE

CHAPTER 10   THE OMBUDSMAN

CHAPTER 11   PRINCIPLES OF STATE POLICY

CHAPTER 12   REGIONAL AND LOCAL GOVERNMNET

CHAPTER 13   THE PUBLIC SERVICE COMMISSION

CHAPTER 14   THE SECURITY COMMISSION

CHAPTER 15   THE POLICE AND DEFENCE FORCES AND THE PRISON SERVICE

CHAPTER 16   FINANCE

CHAPTER 17   CENTRAL BANK AND NATIONAL PLANNING COMMISSION

CHAPTER 18   COMING INTO FORCE OF THE CONSTITUTION

CHAPTER 19   AMENDMENT OF THE CONSTITUTION

Preamble

Whereas recognition of the inherent dignity and of the equal and inalienable rights of all members of the human family is indispensable for freedom, justice and peace;

Whereas the said rights include the right of the individual to life, liberty and the pursuit of happiness, regardless of race, colour, ethnic origin, sex, religion, creed or social or economic status;

Whereas the said rights are most effectively maintained and protected in a democratic society, where the government is responsible to freely elected representatives of the people, operating under a sovereign constitution and a free and independent judiciary;

Whereas these rights have for so long been denied to the people of Namibia by colonialism, racism and apartheid;

Whereas we the people of Namibia –

have finally emerged victorious in our struggle against colonialism, racism and apartheid;

are determined to adopt a Constitution which expresses for ourselves and our children our resolve to cherish and to protect the gains of our long struggle;

desire to promote amongst all of us the dignity of the individual and the unity and integrity of the Namibian nation among and in association with the nations of the world;

will strive to achieve national reconciliation and to foster peace, unity and a common loyalty to a single state;

committed to these principles, have resolved to constitute the Republic of Namibia as a sovereign, secular, democratic and unitary State securing to all our citizens justice, liberty, equality and fraternity,

Now therefore, we the people of Namibia accept and adopt this Constitution as the fundamental law of our Sovereign and Independent Republic.

CHAPTER 1

The Republic

Article 1   Establishment of the Republic of Namibia and Identification of its Territory

(1)   The Republic of Namibia is hereby established as a sovereign, secular, democratic and unitary State founded upon the principles of democracy, the rule of law and justice for all.

(2)   All power shall vest in the people of Namibia who shall exercise their sovereignty through the democratic institutions of the State.

(3)   The main organs of the State shall be the Executive, the Legislature and the Judiciary.

(4)   The national territory of Namibia shall consist of the whole of the territory recognised by the international community through the organs of the United Nations as Namibia, including the enclave, harbour and port of Walvis Bay, as well as the off-shore islands of Namibia, and its southern boundary shall extend to the middle of the Orange River.

(5)   Windhoek shall be the seat of central Government.

(6)   This Constitution shall be the Supreme Law of Namibia.

Article 2   National Symbols

(1)   Namibia shall have a National Flag, the description of which is set out in Schedule 6 hereof.

(2)   Namibia shall have a National Coat of Arms, a National Anthem and a National Seal to be determined by Act of Parliament, which shall require a two-thirds majority of all the members of the National Assembly for adoption and amendment.

(3) (a) The National Seal of the Republic of Namibia shall show the Coat of Arms circumscribed with the word "NAMIBIA" and the motto of the country, which shall be determined by Act of Parliament as aforesaid.

(b) The National Seal shall be in the custody of the President or such person whom the President may designate for such purpose and shall be used on such official documents as the President may determine.

Article 3   Language

(1) The official language of Namibia shall be English.

(2) Nothing contained in this Constitution shall prohibit the use of any other language as a medium of instruction in private schools or in schools financed or subsidised by the State, subject to compliance with such requirements as may be imposed by law, to ensure proficiency in the official language, or for pedagogic reasons.

(3) Nothing contained in Sub-Article (1) hereof shall preclude legislation by Parliament which permits the use of a language other than English for legislative, administrative and judicial purposes in regions or areas where such other language or languages are spoken by a substantial component of the population.

CHAPTER 2

Citizenship

Article 4   Acquisition and Loss of Citizenship

(1) The following persons shall be citizens of Namibia by birth:

(a) those born in Namibia before the date of Independence whose fathers or mothers would have been Namibian citizens at the time of the birth of such persons, if this Constitution had been in force at that time; and

(b)   those born in Namibia before the date of Independence, who are not Namibian citizens under Sub-Article (a) hereof, and whose fathers or mothers were ordinarily resident in Namibia at the time of the birth of such persons: provided that their fathers or mothers were not then persons:

    (aa)   who were enjoying diplomatic immunity in Namibia under any law relating to diplomatic privileges; or

    (bb)   who were career representatives of another country; or

    (cc)   who were members of any police, military or security unit seconded for service within Namibia by the Government of another country: provided further that this Sub-Article shall not apply to persons claiming citizenship of Namibia by birth if such persons were ordinarily resident in Namibia at the date of Independence and had been so resident for a continuous period of not less than five (5) years prior to such date, or if the fathers or mothers of such persons claiming citizenship were ordinarily resident in Namibia at the date of the birth of such persons and had been so resident for a continuous period of not less than five (5) years prior to such date;

(c)   those born in Namibia after the date of Independence whose fathers or mothers are Namibian citizens at the time of the birth of such persons;

(d)   those born in Namibia after the date of Independence who do not qualify for citizenship under Sub-Article (c) hereof, and whose fathers or mothers are ordinarily resident in Namibia at the time of the birth of such persons: provided that their fathers or mothers are not then persons:

    (aa)   enjoying diplomatic immunity in Namibia under any law relating to diplomatic privileges; or

    (bb)   who are career representatives of another country; or (cc)   who are members of any police, military or security unit seconded for service within Namibia by the Government of another country; or

(dd)   who are illegal immigrants:

provided further that Sub-Articles (aa), (bb), (cc) and (dd) hereof will not apply to children who would otherwise be stateless.

(2)   The following persons shall be citizens of Namibia by descent:

(a)   those who are not Namibian citizens under Sub-Article (1) hereof and whose fathers or mothers at the time of the birth of such persons are citizens of Namibia or whose fathers or mothers would have qualified for Namibian citizenship by birth under Sub-Article (1) hereof, if this Constitution had been in force at that time; and

(b)   who comply with such requirements as to registration of citizenship as may be required by Act of Parliament: provided that nothing in this Constitution shall preclude Parliament from enacting legislation which requires the birth of such persons born after the date of Independence to be registered within a specific time either in Namibia or at an embassy, consulate or office of a trade representative of the Government of Namibia.

(3)   The following persons shall be citizens of Namibia by marriage:

(a)   those who are not Namibian citizens under Sub-Article (1) or (2) hereof and who:

(aa)   in good faith marry a Namibian citizen or, prior to the coming into force of this Constitution, in good faith married a person who would have qualified for Namibian citizenship if this Constitution had been in force; and

(bb)   subsequent to such marriage have ordinarily resided in Namibia as the spouse of such person for a period of not less than two (2) years; and (cc)   apply to become citizens of Namibia;

(b)   for the purposes of this Sub-Article (and without derogating from any effect that it may have for any other purposes) a marriage by customary law shall be deemed to be a marriage: provided that nothing in this Constitution shall preclude Parliament from enacting legislation which defines the requirements which need to be satisfied for a marriage by customary law to be recognised as such for the purposes of this Sub-Article.

(4)   Citizenship by registration may be claimed by persons who are not Namibian citizens under Sub-Articles (1), (2) or (3) hereof and who were ordinarily resident in Namibia at the date of Independence, and had been so resident for a continuous period of not less than five (5) years prior to such date: provided that application for Namibian citizenship under this Sub-Article is made within a period of twelve (12) months from the date of Independence, and prior to making such application, such persons renounce the citizenship of any other country of which they are citizens.

(5)   Citizenship by naturalisation may be applied for by persons who are not Namibian citizens under Sub-Articles (1), (2), (3) or (4) hereof and who:

(a)   are ordinarily resident in Namibia at the time when the application for naturalisation is made; and

(b)   have been so resident in Namibia for a continuous period of not less than five (5) years (whether before or after the date of Independence); and

(c)   satisfy any other criteria pertaining to health, morality, security or legality of residence as may be prescribed by law.

(6)   Nothing contained herein shall preclude Parliament from authorizing by law the conferment of Namibian citizenship upon any fit and proper person by virtue of any special skill or experience or commitment to or services rendered to the Namibian nation either before or at any time after the date of Independence.

(7) Namibian citizenship shall be lost by persons who renounce their Namibian citizenship by voluntarily signing a formal declaration to that effect.

(8) Nothing in this Constitution shall preclude Parliament from enacting legislation providing for the loss of Namibian citizenship by persons who, after the date of Independence:

(a) have acquired the citizenship of any other country by any voluntary act; or

(b) have served or volunteered to serve in the armed or security forces of any other country without the written permission of the Namibian Government; or

(c) have taken up permanent residence in any other country and have absented themselves thereafter from Namibia for a period in excess of two (2) years without the written permission of the Namibian Government:

provided that no person who is a citizen of Namibia by birth or descent may be deprived of Namibian citizenship by such legislation.

(9) Parliament shall be entitled to make further laws not inconsistent with this Constitution regulating the acquisition or loss of Namibian citizenship.

CHAPTER 3

Fundamental Human Rights and Freedoms

Article 5   Protection of Fundamental Rights and Freedoms

The fundamental rights and freedoms enshrined in this Chapter shall be respected and upheld by the Executive, Legislature and Judiciary and all organs of the Government and its agencies and, where applicable to them, by all natural and legal persons in Namibia, and shall be enforceable by the Courts in the manner hereinafter prescribed.

Geographisches Institut
der Universität Kiel
Neue Universität

Article 6   **Protection of Life**

The right to life shall be respected and protected. No law may prescribe death as a competent sentence. No Court or Tribunal shall have the power to impose a sentence of death upon any person. No executions shall take place in Namibia.

Article 7   **Protection of Liberty**

No persons shall be deprived of personal liberty except according to procedures established by law.

Article 8   **Respect for Human Dignity**

(1)   The dignity of all persons shall be inviolable.

(2)   (a)   In any judicial proceedings or in other proceedings before any organ of the State, and during the enforcement of a penalty, respect for human dignity shall be guaranteed.

(b)   No persons shall be subject to torture or to cruel, inhuman or degrading treatment or punishment.

Article 9   **Slavery and Forced Labour**

(1)   No persons shall be held in slavery or servitude.

(2)   No persons shall be required to perform forced labour.

(3)   For the purposes of this Article, the expression "forced labour" shall not include:

(a)   any labour required in consequence of a sentence or order of a Court;

(b)   any labour required of persons while lawfully detained which, though not required in consequence of a sentence or order of a Court, is reasonably necessary in the interests of hygiene;

(c)   any labour required of members of the defence force, the police force and the prison service in pursuance of their duties as such or, in the case of persons who have conscientious objections to serving as members of the defence force, any labour which they are required by law to perform in place of such service;

(d)   any labour required during any period of public emergency or in the event of any other emergency or calamity which threatens the life and well-being of the community, to the extent that requiring such labour is reasonably justifiable in the circumstances of any situation arising or existing during that period or as a result of that other emergency or calamity, for the purpose of dealing with that situation;

(e)   any labour reasonably required as part of reasonable and normal communal or other civic obligations.

Article 10   Equality and Freedom from Discrimination

(1)   All persons shall be equal before the law.

(2)   No persons may be discriminated against on the grounds of sex, race, colour, ethnic origin, religion, creed or social or economic status.

Article 11   Arrest and Detention

(1)   No persons shall be subject to arbitrary arrest or detention.

(2)   No persons who are arrested shall be detained in custody without being informed promptly in a language they understand of the grounds for such arrest.

(3)   All persons who are arrested and detained in custody shall be brought before the nearest Magistrate or other judicial officer within a period of forty-eight (48) hours of their arrest or, if this is not reasonably possible, as soon as possible thereafter, and no such persons shall be detained in custody beyond such period without the authority of a Magistrate or other judicial officer.

(4)   Nothing contained in Sub-Article (3) hereof shall apply to illegal immigrants held in custody under any law dealing with illegal immigration: provided that

such persons shall not be deported from Namibia unless deportation is authorised by a Tribunal empowered by law to give such authority.

(5) No persons who have been arrested and held in custody as illegal immigrants shall be denied the right to consult confidentially legal practitioners of their choice, and there shall be no interference with this right except such as is in accordance with the law and is necessary in a democratic society in the interest of national security or for public safety.

Article 12   Fair Trial

(1) (a)   In the determination of their civil rights and obligations or any criminal charges against them, all persons shall be entitled to a fair and public hearing by an independent, impartial and competent Court or Tribunal established by law: provided that such Court or Tribunal may exclude the press and/or the public from all or any part of the trial for reasons of morals, the public order or national security, as is necessary in a democratic society.

(b)   A trial referred to in Sub-Article (a) hereof shall take place within a reasonable time, failing which the accused shall be released.

(c)   Judgments in criminal cases shall be given in public, except where the interests of juvenile persons or morals otherwise require.

(d)   All persons charged with an offence shall be presumed innocent until proven guilty according to law, after having had the opportunity of calling witnesses and cross-examining those called against them.

(e)   All persons shall be afforded adequate time and facilities for the preparation and presentation of their defence, before the commencement of and during their trial, and shall be entitled to be defended by a legal practitioner of their choice.

(f)   No persons shall be compelled to give testimony against themselves or their spouses, who shall include partners in a marriage by customary law, and no Court shall admit in evidence against such persons testimony which has been obtained from such persons in violation of Article 8(2)(b) hereof.

(2) No persons shall be liable to be tried, convicted or punished again for any criminal offence for which they have already been convicted or acquitted according to law: provided that nothing in this Sub-Article shall be construed as changing the provisions of the common law defences of "previous acquittal" and "previous conviction".

(3) No persons shall be tried or convicted for any criminal offence or on account of any act or omission which did not constitute a criminal offence at the time when it was committed, nor shall a penalty be imposed exceeding that which was applicable at the time when the offence was committed.

Article 13   Privacy

(1) No persons shall be subject to interference with the privacy of their homes, correspondence or communications save as in accordance with law and as is necessary in a democratic society in the interests of national security, public safety or the economic well-being of the country, for the protection of health or morals, for the prevention of disorder or crime or for the protection of the rights or freedoms of others.

(2) Searches of the person or the homes of individuals shall only be justified:

(a)   where these are authorised by a competent judicial officer;

(b)   in cases where delay in obtaining such judicial authority carries with it the danger of prejudicing the objects of the search or the public interest, and such procedures as are prescribed by Act of Parliament to preclude abuse are properly satisfied.

Article 14   Family

(1) Men and women of full age. without any limitation due to race, colour, ethnic origin, nationality, religion, creed or social or economic status shall have the right to marry and to found a family. They shall be entitled to equal rights as to marriage, during marriage and at its dissolution.

(2) Marriage shall be entered into only with the free and full consent of the intending spouses.

(3) The family is the natural and fundamental group unit of society and is entitled to protection by society and the State.

Article 15   Children's Rights

(1) Children shall have the right from birth to a name, the right to acquire a nationality and, subject to legislation enacted in the best interests of children, as far as possible the right to know and be cared for by their parents.

(2) Children are entitled to be protected from economic exploitation and shall not be employed in or required to perform work that is likely to be hazardous or to interfere with their education, or to be harmful to their health or physical, mental, spiritual, moral or social development. For the purposes of this Sub-Article children shall be persons under the age of sixteen (16) years.

(3) No children under the age of fourteen (14) years shall be employed to work in any factory or mine, save under conditions and circumstances regulated by Act of Parliament. Nothing in this Sub-Article shall be construed as derogating in any way from Sub-Article (2) hereof.

(4) Any arrangement or scheme employed on any farm or other undertaking, the object or effect of which is to compel the minor children of an employee to work for or in the interest of the employer of such employee, shall for the purposes of Article 9 hereof be deemed to constitute an arrangement or scheme to compel the performance of forced labour.

(5) No law authorising preventive detention shall permit children under the age of sixteen (16) years to be detained.

Article 16   Property

(1) All persons shall have the right in any part of Namibia to acquire, own and dispose of all forms of immovable and movable property individually or in association with others and to bequeath their property to their heirs or legatees: provided that Parliament may by legislation prohibit or regulate as it deems expedient the right to acquire property by persons who are not Namibian citizens.

(2) The State or a competent body or organ authorised by law may expropriate property in the public interest subject to the payment of just compensation, in accordance with requirements and procedures to be determined by Act of Parliament.

Article 17   Political Activity

(1) All citizens shall have the right to participate in peaceful political activity intended to influence the composition and policies of the Government. All citizens shall have the right to form and join political parties and, subject to such qualifications prescribed by law as are necessary in a democratic society, to participate in the conduct of public affairs, whether directly or through freely chosen representatives.

(2) Every citizen who has reached the age of eighteen (18) years shall have the right to vote and who has reached the age of twenty-one (21) years to be elected to public office, unless otherwise provided herein.

(3) The rights guaranteed by Sub-Article (2) hereof may only be abrogated, suspended or be impinged upon by Parliament in respect of specified categories of persons on such grounds of infirmity or on such grounds of public interest or morality as are necessary in a democratic society.

Article 18   Administrative Justice

Administrative bodies and administrative officials shall act fairly and reasonably and comply with the requirements imposed upon such bodies and officials by common law and any relevant legislation, and persons aggrieved by the exercise of such acts and decisions shall have the right to seek redress before a competent Court or Tribunal.

Article 19   Culture

Every person shall be entitled to enjoy, practise, profess, maintain and promote any culture, language, tradition or religion subject to the terms of this Constitution and further subject to the condition that the rights protected by this Article do not impinge upon the rights of others or the national interest.

Article 20   Education

(1)   All persons shall have the right to education.

(2)   Primary education shall be compulsory and the State shall provide reasonable facilities to render effective this right for every resident within Namibia, by establishing and maintaining State schools at which primary education will be provided free of charge.

(3)   Children shall not be allowed to leave school until they have completed their primary education or have attained the age of sixteen (16) years, whichever is the sooner, save in so far as this may be authorised by Act of Parliament on grounds of health or other considerations pertaining to the public interest.

(4)   All persons shall have the right, at their own expense, to establish and to maintain private schools, or colleges or other institutions of tertiary education: provided that:

(a)   such schools, colleges or institutions of tertiary education are registered with a Government department in accordance with any law authorising and regulating such registration;

(b)   the standards maintained by such schools, colleges or institutions of tertiary education are not inferior to the standards maintained in comparable schools, colleges or institutions of tertiary education funded by the State;

(c)   no restrictions of whatever nature are imposed with respect to the admission of pupils based on race, colour or creed;

(d)   no restrictions of whatever nature are imposed with respect to the recruitment of staff based on race or colour.

Article 21   Fundamental Freedoms

(1)   All persons shall have the right to:

(a)   freedom of speech and expression, which shall include freedom of the press and other media;

(b)   freedom of thought, conscience and belief, which shall include academic freedom in institutions of higher learning;

(c)   freedom to practise any religion and to manifest such practice;

(d)   assemble peaceably and without arms;

(e)   freedom of association, which shall include freedom to form and join associations or unions, including trade unions and political parties;

(f)   withhold their labour without being exposed to criminal penalties;

(g)   move freely throughout Namibia;

(h)   reside and settle in any part of Namibia;

(i)   leave and return to Namibia;

(j)   practise any profession, or carry on any occupation, trade or business.

(2)   The fundamental freedoms referred to in Sub-Article (1) hereof shall be exercised subject to the law of Namibia, in so far as such law imposes reasonable restrictions on the exercise of the rights and freedoms conferred by the said Sub-Article, which are necessary in a democratic society and are required in the interests of the sovereignty and integrity of Namibia, national security, public order, decency or morality, or in relation to contempt of court, defamation or incitement to an offence.

Article 22   Limitation upon Fundamental Rights and Freedoms

Whenever or wherever in terms of this Constitution the limitation of any fundamental rights or freedoms contemplated by this Chapter is authorised, any law providing for such limitation shall:

(a)   be of general application, shall not negate the essential content thereof, and shall not be aimed at a particular individual;

(b)   specify the ascertainable extent of such limitation and identify the Article or Articles hereof on which authority to enact such limitation is claimed to rest.

Article 23   Apartheid and Affirmative Action

(1)   The practice of racial discrimination and the practice and ideology of apartheid from which the majority of the people of Namibia have suffered for so long shall be prohibited and by Act of Parliament such practices, and the propagation of such practices, may be rendered criminally punishable by the ordinary Courts by means of such punishment as Parliament deems necessary for the purposes of expressing the revulsion of the Namibian people at such practices.

(2)   Nothing contained in Article 10 hereof shall prevent Parliament from enacting legislation providing directly or indirectly for the advancement of persons within Namibia who have been socially, economically or educationally disadvantaged by past discriminatory laws or practices, or for the implementation of policies and programmes aimed at redressing social, economic or educational imbalances in the Namibian society arising out of past discriminatory laws or practices, or for achieving a balanced structuring of the public service, the police force, the defence force, and the prison service.

(3)   In the enactment of legislation and the application of any policies and practices contemplated by Sub-Article (2) hereof, it shall be permissible to have regard to the fact that women in Namibia have traditionally suffered special discrimination and that they need to be encouraged and enabled to play a full, equal and effective role in the political, social, economic and cultural life of the nation.

Article 24   Derogation

(1)   Nothing contained in or done under the authority of Article 26 hereof shall be held to be inconsistent with or in contravention of this Constitution to the extent that it authorises the taking of measures during any period when Namibia is in a state of national defence or any period when a declaration of emergency under this Constitution is in force.

(2)   Where any persons are detained by virtue of such authorisation as is

referred to in Sub-Article (1) hereof, the following provisions shall apply:

(a)   they shall, as soon as reasonably practicable and in any case not more than five (5) days after the commencement of their detention, be furnished with a statement in writing in a language that they understand specifying in detail the grounds upon which they are detained and, at their request, this statement shall be read to them;

(b)   not more than fourteen (14) days after the commencement of their detention, a notification shall be published in the Gazette stating that they have been detained and giving particulars of the provision of law under which their detention is authorised;

(c)   not more than one (1) month after the commencement of their detention and thereafter during their detention at intervals of not more than three (3) months, their cases shall be reviewed by the Advisory Board referred to in Article 26 (5)(c) hereof, which shall order their release from detention if it is satisfied that it is not reasonably necessary for the purposes of the emergency to continue the detention of such persons;

(d)   they shall be afforded such opportunity for the making of representations as may be desirable or expedient in the circumstances, having regard to the public interest and the interests of the detained persons.

(3)   Nothing contained in this Article shall permit a derogation from or suspension of the fundamental rights or freedoms referred to in Articles 5, 6, 8, 9, 10, 12, 14, 15, 18, 19 and 21(1)(a), (b), (c) and (e) hereof, or the denial of access by any persons to legal practioners or a Court of law.

Article 25   Enforcement of Fundamental Rights and Freedoms

(1)   Save in so far as it may be authorised to do so by this Constitution, Parliament or any subordinate legislative authority shall not make any law, and the Executive and the agencies of Government shall not take any action which abolishes or abridges the fundamental rights and freedoms conferred

by this Chapter, and any law or action in contravention thereof shall to the extent of the contravention be invalid: provided that:

(a)   a competent Court, instead of declaring such law or action to be invalid, shall have the power and the discretion in an appropriate case to allow Parliament, any subordinate legislative authority, or the Executive and the agencies of Government, as the case may be, to correct any defect in the impugned law or action within a specified period, subject to such conditions as may be specified by it. In such event and until such correction, or until the expiry of the time limit set by the Court, whichever be the shorter, such impugned law or action shall be deemed to be valid;

(b)   any law which was in force immediately before the date of Independence shall remain in force until amended, repealed or declared unconstitutional. If a competent Court is of the opinion that such law is unconstitutional, it may either set aside the law, or allow Parliament to correct any defect in such law, in which event the provisions of Sub-Article (a) hereof shall apply.

(2)   Aggrieved persons who claim that a fundamental right or freedom guaranteed by this Constitution has been infringed or threatened shall be entitled to approach a competent Court to enforce or protect such a right or freedom, and may approach the Ombudsman to provide them with such legal assistance or advice as they require, and the Ombudsman shall have the discretion in response thereto to provide such legal or other assistance as he or she may consider expedient.

(3)   Subject to the provisions of this Constitution, the Court referred to in Sub-Article (2) hereof shall have the power to make all such orders as shall be necessary and appropriate to secure such applicants the enjoyment of the rights and freedoms conferred on them under the provisions of this Constitution, should the Court come to the conclusion that such rights or freedoms have been unlawfully denied or violated, or that grounds exist for the protection of such rights or freedoms by interdict.

(4)   The power of the Court shall include the power to award monetary compensation in respect of any damage suffered by the aggrieved persons in conse-

quence of such unlawful denial or violation of their fundamental rights and freedoms, where it considers such an award to be appropriate in the circumstances of particular cases.

CHAPTER 4

Public Emergency, State of National Defence and Martial Law

Article 26   **State of Emergency, State of National Defence and Martial Law**

(1)   At a time of national disaster or during a state of national defence or public emergency threatening the life of the nation or the constitutional order, the President may by Proclamation in the Gazette declare that a state of emergency exists in Namibia or any part thereof.

(2)   A declaration under Sub-Article (1) hereof, if not sooner revoked, shall cease to have effect:

   (a)   in the case of a declaration made when the National Assembly is sitting or has been summoned to meet, at the expiration of a period of seven (7) days after publication of the declaration; or

   (b)   in any other case, at the expiration of a period of thirty (30) days after publication of the declaration;

   unless before the expiration of that period, it is approved by a resolution passed by the National Assembly by a two-thirds majority of all its members.

(3)   Subject to the provisions of Sub-Article (4) hereof, a declaration approved by a resolution of the National Assembly under Sub-Article (2) hereof shall continue to be in force until the expiration of a period of six (6) months after being so approved or until such earlier date as may be specified in the resolution: provided that the National Assembly may, by resolution by a two-thirds majority of all its members, extend its approval of the declaration for periods of not more than six (6) months at a time.

(4)   The National Assembly may by resolution at any time revoke a declaration approved by it in terms of this Article.

(5)   (a)   During a state of emergency in terms of this Article or when a state of national defence prevails, the President shall have the power by Proclamation to make such regulations as in his or her opinion are necessary for the protection of national security, public safety and the maintenance of law and order.

(b)   The powers of the President to make such regulations shall include the power to suspend the operation of any rule of the common law or statute or any fundamental right or freedom protected by this Constitution, for such period and subject to such conditions as are reasonably justifiable for the purpose of dealing with the situation which has given rise to the emergency: provided that nothing in this Sub-Article shall enable the President to act contrary to the provisions of Article 24 hereof.

(c)   Where any regulation made under Sub-Article (b) hereof provides for detention without trial, provision shall also be made for an Advisory Board, to be appointed by the President on the recommendation of the Judicial Service Commission, and consisting of no more than five (5) persons, of whom no fewer than three (3) persons shall be Judges of the Supreme Court or the High Court or qualified to be such. The Advisory Board shall perform the function set out in Article 24 (2)(c) hereof.

(6)   Any regulations made by the President pursuant to the provisions of Sub-Article (5) hereof shall cease to have legal force if they have not been approved by a resolution of the National Assembly within fourteen (14) days from the date when the National Assembly first sits in session after the date of the commencement of any such regulations.

(7)   The President shall have the power to proclaim or terminate martial law. Martial law may be proclaimed only when a state of national defence involving another country exists or when civil war prevails in Namibia: provided that any proclamation of martial law shall cease to be valid if it is not approved within a reasonable time by a resolution passed by a two-thirds majority of all

the members of the National Assembly.

CHAPTER 5

The President

Article 27   Head of State and Government

(1)   The President shall be the Head of State and of the Government and the Commander-in-Chief of the Defence Force.

(2)   The executive power of the Republic of Namibia shall vest in the President and the Cabinet.

(3)   Except as may be otherwise provided in this Constitution or by law, the President shall in the exercise of his or her functions be obliged to act in consultation with the Cabinet.

Article 28   Election

(1)   The President shall be elected in accordance with the provisions of this Constitution and subject thereto.

(2)   Election of the President shall be:

   (a)   by direct, universal and equal suffrage; and

   (b)   conducted in accordance with principles and procedures to be determined by Act of Parliament: provided that no person shall be elected as President unless he or she has received more than fifty (50) per cent of the votes cast and the necessary number of ballots shall be conducted until such result is reached.

(3)   Every citizen of Namibia by birth or descent, over the age of thirty-five (35) years, and who is eligible to be elected to office as a member of the National

Assembly shall be eligible for election as President.

(4) The procedures to be followed for the nomination of candidates for election as President, and for all matters necessary and incidental to ensure the free, fair and effective election of a President, shall be determined by Act of Parliament: provided that any registered political party shall be entitled to nominate a candidate, and any person supported by a minimum number of registered voters to be determined by Act of Parliament shall also be entitled to be nominated as a candidate.

Article 29   Term of Office

(1) (a)   The President's term of office shall be five (5) years unless he or she dies or resigns before the expiry of the said term or is removed from office.

     (b)   In the event of the dissolution of the National Assembly in the circumstances provided for under Article 57(1) hereof, the President's term of office shall also expire.

(2) A President shall be removed from office if a two-thirds majority of all the members of the National Assembly, confirmed by a two-thirds majority of all the members of the National Council, adopts a resolution impeaching the President on the ground that he or she has been guilty of a violation of the Constitution or guilty of a serious violation of the laws of the land or otherwise guilty of such gross misconduct or ineptitude as to render him or her unfit to hold with dignity and honour the office of President.

(3) A person shall hold office as President for not more than two terms.

(4) If a President dies, resigns or is removed from office in terms of this Constitution, the vacant office of President shall be filled for the unexpired period thereof as follows:

     (a)   if the vacancy occurs not more than one (1) year before the date on which Presidential elections are required to be held, the vacancy shall be filled in accordance with the provisions of Article 34 hereof;

(b)   if the vacancy occurs more than one (1) year before the date on which Presidential elections are required to be held, an election for the President shall be held in accordance with the provisions of Article 28 hereof within a period of ninety (90) days from the date on which the vacancy occurred, and pending such election the vacant office shall be filled in accordance with the provisions of Article 34 hereof.

(5)   If the President dissolves the National Assembly under Articles 32(3)(a) and 57(1) hereof, a new election for President shall be held in accordance with the provisions of Article 28 hereof within ninety (90) days, and pending such election the President shall remain in office, and the provisions of Article 58 hereof shall be applicable.

(6)   If a person becomes President under Sub-Article (4) hereof, the period of time during which he or she holds office consequent upon such election or succession shall not be regarded as a term for the purposes of Sub-Article (3) hereof.

Article 30   Oath or Affirmation

Before formally assuming office, a President-elect shall make the following oath or affirmation which shall be administered by the Chief Justice or a Judge designated by the Chief Justice for this purpose:

"I, ..., do hereby swear/solemnly affirm,

That I will strive to the best of my ability to uphold, protect and defend as the Supreme Law the Constitution of the Republic of Namibia, and faithfully to obey, execute and administer the laws of the Republic of Namibia;

That I will protect the independence, sovereignty, territorial integrity and the material and spiritual resources of the Republic of Namibia; and

That I will endeavour to the best of my ability to ensure justice for all the inhabitants of the Republic of Namibia.

(in the case of an oath)

So help me God."

Article 31   Immunity from Civil and Criminal Proceedings

(1)   No person holding the office of President or performing the functions of President may be sued in any civil proceedings save where such proceedings concern an act done in his or her official capacity as President.

(2)   No person holding the office of President shall be charged with any criminal offence or be amenable to the criminal jurisdiction of any Court in respect of any act allegedly performed, or any omission to perform any act, during his or her tenure of office as President.

(3)   After a President has vacated that office:

    (a)   no Court may entertain any action against him or her in any civil proceedings in respect of any act done in his or her official capacity as President;

    (b)   a civil or criminal Court shall only have jurisdiction to entertain proceedings against him or her, in respect of acts of commission or omission alleged to have been perpetrated in his or her personal capacity whilst holding office as President, if Parliament by resolution has removed the President on the grounds specified in this Constitution and if a resolution is adopted by Parliament resolving that any such proceedings are justified in the public interest notwithstanding any damage such proceedings might cause to the dignity of the office of President.

Article 32   Functions, Powers and Duties

(1)   As the Head of State, the President shall uphold, protect and defend the Constitution as the Supreme Law, and shall perform with dignity and leadership all acts necessary, expedient, reasonable and incidental to the discharge of the executive functions of the Government, subject to the overriding terms of this Constitution and the laws of Namibia, which he or she is constitutionally obliged to protect, to administer and to execute.

(2)   In accordance with the responsibility of the executive branch of Government to the legislative branch, the President and the Cabinet shall each year during the consideration of the official budget attend Parliament. During such session the President shall address Parliament on the state of the nation and on the future policies of the Government, shall report on the policies of the previous year and shall be available to respond to questions.

(3)   Without derogating from the generality of the functions and powers contemplated by Sub-Article (1) hereof, the President shall preside over meetings of the Cabinet and shall have the power, subject to this Constitution to:

   (a)   dissolve the National Assembly by Proclamation in the circumstances provided for in Article 57(1) hereof;

   (b)   determine the times for the holding of special sessions of the National Assembly, and to prorogue such sessions;

   (c)   accredit, receive and recognise ambassadors, and to appoint ambassadors, plenipotentiaries, diplomatic representatives and other diplomatic officers, consuls and consular officers;

   (d)   pardon or reprieve offenders, either unconditionally or subject to such conditions as the President may deem fit;

   (e)   negotiate and sign international agreements, and to delegate such power;

   (f)   declare martial law or, if it is necessary for the defence of the nation, declare that a state of national defence exists: provided that this power shall be exercised subject to the terms of Article 26(7) hereof;

   (g)   establish and dissolve such Government departments and ministries as the President may at any time consider to be necessary or expedient for the good government of Namibia;

   (h)   confer such honours as the President considers appropriate on citizens, residents and friends of Namibia in consultation with interested and relevant persons and institutions;

(i)   appoint the following persons:

    (aa)   the Prime Minister;

    (bb)   Ministers and Deputy-Ministers;

    (cc)   the Attorney-General;

    (dd)   the Director-General of Planning;

    (ee)   any other person or persons who are required by any other provision of this Constitution or any other law to be appointed by the President.

(4)   The President shall also have the power, subject to this Constitution, to appoint:

    (a)   on the recommendation of the Judicial Service Commission:

        (aa)   the Chief Justice, the Judge-President of the High Court and other Judges of the Supreme Court and the High Court;

        (bb)   the Ombudsman;

        (cc)   the Prosecutor-General;

    (b)   on the recommendation of the Public Service Commission:

        (aa)   the Auditor-General;

        (bb)   the Governor and the Deputy-Governor of the Central Bank;

    (c)   on the recommendation of the Security Commission:

        (aa)   the Chief of the Defence Force;

        (bb)   the Inspector-General of Police;

        (cc)   the Commissioner of Prisons.

(5) Subject to the provisions of this Constitution dealing with the signing of any laws passed by Parliament and the promulgation and publication of such laws in the Gazette, the President shall have the power to:

(a) sign and promulgate any Proclamation which by law he or she is entitled to proclaim as President;

(b) initiate, in so far as he or she considers it necessary and expedient, laws for submission to and consideration by the National Assembly;

(c) appoint as members of the National Assembly but without any vote therein, not more than six (6) persons by virtue of their special expertise, status, skill or experience.

(6) Subject to the provisions of this Constitution or any other law, any person appointed by the President pursuant to the powers vested in him or her by this Constitution or any other law may be removed by the President by the same process through which such person was appointed.

(7) Subject to the provisions of this Constitution and of any other law of application in this matter, the President may, in consultation with the Cabinet and on the recommendation of the Public Service Commission:

(a) constitute any office in the public service of Namibia not otherwise provided for by any other law;

(b) appoint any person to such office;

(c) determine the tenure of any person so appointed as well as the terms and conditions of his or her service.

(8) All appointments made and actions taken under Sub-Articles (3),(4),(5),(6) and (7) hereof shall be announced by the President by Proclamation in the Gazette.

(9) Subject to the provisions of this Constitution and save where this Constitution otherwise provides, any action taken by the President pursuant to any power vested in the President by the terms of this Article shall be

capable of being reviewed, reversed or corrected on such terms as are deemed expedient and proper should there be a resolution proposed by at least one-third of all the members of the National Assembly and passed by a two-thirds majority of all the members of the National Assembly disapproving any such action and resolving to review, reverse or correct it.

(10) Notwithstanding the review, reversal or correction of any action in terms of Sub-Article (9) hereof, all actions performed pursuant to any such action during the period preceding such review, reversal or correction shall be deemed to be valid and effective in law, until and unless Parliament otherwise enacts.

Article 33   Remuneration

Provision shall be made by Act of Parliament for the payment out of the State Revenue Fund of remuneration and allowances for the President, as well as for the payment of pensions to former Presidents and, in the case of their deaths, to their surviving spouses.

Article 34   Succession

(1)   If the office of President becomes vacant or if the President is otherwise unable to fulfil the duties of the office, the following persons shall in the order provided for in this Sub-Article act as President for the unexpired portion of the President's term of office or until the President is able to resume office, whichever is the earlier:

(a)   the Prime Minister;

(b)   the Deputy-Prime Minister;

(c)   a person appointed by the Cabinet.

(2)   Where it is regarded as necessary or expedient that a person deputise for the President because of a temporary absence from the country or because of pressure of work, the President shall be entitled to nominate any person enumerated in Sub-Article (1) hereof to deputise for him or her in respect of such specific occasions or such specific matters and for such specific periods as in his or her discretion may be considered wise and expedient,

subject to consultation with the Cabinet.

CHAPTER 6

The Cabinet

Article 35   Composition

(1)   The Cabinet shall consist of the President, the Prime Minister and such other Ministers as the President may appoint from the members of the National Assembly, including members nominated under Article 46(1)(b) hereof, for the purposes of administering and executing the functions of the Government.

(2)   The President may also appoint a Deputy-Prime Minister to perform such functions as may be assigned to him or her by the President or the Prime Minister.

(3)   The President or, in his or her absence, the Prime Minister or other Minister designated for this purpose by the President, shall preside at meetings of the Cabinet.

Article 36   Functions of the Prime Minister

The Prime Minister shall be the leader of Government business in Parliament, shall co-ordinate the work of the Cabinet and shall advise and assist the President in the execution of the functions of Government.

Article 37   Deputy-Ministers

The President may appoint from the members of the National Assembly, including members nominated under Article 46(1)(b) hereof, and the National Council such Deputy-Ministers as he or she may consider expedient, to exercise or perform on behalf of Ministers any of the powers, functions and duties which may have been assigned to such Ministers.

Article 38   **Oath or Affirmation**

Before assuming office, a Minister or Deputy-Minister shall make and subscribe to an oath or solemn affirmation before the President or a person designated by the President for this purpose, in the terms set out in Schedule 2 hereof.

Article 39   **Vote of No Confidence**

The President shall be obliged to terminate the appointment of any member of the Cabinet, if the National Assembly by a majority of all its members resolves that it has no confidence in that member.

Article 40   **Duties and Functions**

The members of the Cabinet shall have the following functions:

(a)   to direct, co-ordinate and supervise the activities of Ministries and Government departments including para-statal enterprises, and to review and advise the President and the National Assembly on the desirability and wisdom of any prevailing subordinate legislation, regulations or orders pertaining to such para-statal enterprises, regard being had to the public interest;

(b)   to initiate bills for submission to the National Assembly;

(c)   to formulate, explain and assess for the National Assembly the budget of the State and its economic development plans and to report to the National Assembly thereon;

(d)   to carry out such other functions as are assigned to them by law or are incidental to such assignment;

(e)   to attend meetings of the National Assembly and to be available for the purposes of any queries and debates pertaining to the legitimacy, wisdom, effectiveness and direction of Government policies;

(f)   to take such steps as are authorised by law to establish such economic organisations, institutions and para-statal enterprises on behalf of the State as are directed or authorised by law;

(g) to formulate, explain and analyse for the members of the National Assembly the goals of Namibian foreign policy and its relations with other States and to report to the National Assembly thereon;

(h) to formulate, explain and analyse for the members of the National Assembly the directions and content of foreign trade policy and to report to the National Assembly thereon;

(i) to assist the President in determining what international agreements are to be concluded, acceded to or succeeded to and to report to the National Assembly thereon;

(j) to advise the President on the state of national defence and the maintenance of law and order and to inform the National Assembly thereon;

(k) to issue notices, instructions and directives to facilitate the implementation and administration of laws administered by the Executive, subject to the terms of this Constitution or any other law;

(l) to remain vigilant and vigorous for the purposes of ensuring that the scourges of apartheid, tribalism and colonialism do not again manifest themselves in any form in a free and independent Namibia and to protect and assist disadvantaged citizens of Namibia who have historically been the victims of these pathologies.

Article 41   Ministerial Accountability

All Ministers shall be accountable individually for the administration of their own Ministries and collectively for the administration of the work of the Cabinet, both to the President and to Parliament.

Article 42   Outside Employment

(1) During their tenure of office as members of the Cabinet, Ministers may not take up any other paid employment, engage in activities inconsistent with their positions as Ministers, or expose themselves to any situation which carries with it the risk of a conflict developing between their interests as Ministers and their private interests.

(2)   No members of the Cabinet shall use their positions as such or use information entrusted to them confidentially as such members of the Cabinet, directly or indirectly to enrich themselves.

Article 43   Secretary to the Cabinet

(1)   There shall be a Secretary to the Cabinet who shall be appointed by the President and who shall perform such functions as may be determined by law and such functions as are from time to time assigned to the Secretary by the President or the Prime Minister. Upon appointment by the President, the Secretary shall be deemed to have been appointed to such office on the reccommendation of the Public Service Commission.

(2)   The Secretary to the Cabinet shall also serve as a depository of the records, minutes and related documents of the Cabinet.

CHAPTER 7

The National Assembly

Article 44   Legislative Power

The legislative power of Namibia shall be vested in the National Assembly with the power to pass laws with the assent of the President as provided in this Constitution subject, where applicable, to the powers and functions of the National Council as set out in this Constitution.

Article 45   Representative Nature

The members of the National Assembly shall be representative of all the people and shall in the performance of their duties be guided by the objectives of this Constitution, by the public interest and by their conscience.

Article 46   Composition

(1)   The composition of the National Assembly shall be as follows:

(a)   seventy-two (72) members to be elected by the registered voters by general, direct and secret ballot. Every Namibian citizen who has the qualifications described in Article 17 hereof shall be entitled to vote in the elections for members of the National Assembly and, subject to Article 47 hereof, shall be eligible for candidature as a member of the National Assembly;

(b)   not more than six (6) persons appointed by the President under Article 32(5)(c) hereof, by virtue of their special expertise, status, skill or experience: provided that such members shall have no vote in the National Assembly, and shall not be taken into account for the purpose of determining any specific majorities that are required under this Constitution or any other law.

(2)   Subject to the principles referred to in Article 49 hereof, the members of the National Assembly referred to in Sub-Article (1)(a) hereof shall be elected in accordance with procedures to be determined by Act of Parliament.

Article 47   Disqualification of Members

(1)   No persons may become members of the National Assembly if they:

(a)   have at any time after Independence been convicted of any offence in Namibia, or outside Namibia if such conduct would have constituted an offence within Namibia, and for which they have been sentenced to death or to imprisonment of more than twelve (12) months without the option of a fine, unless they have received a free pardon or unless such imprisonment has expired at least ten (10) years before the date of their election; or

(b)   have at any time prior to Independence been convicted of an offence, if such conduct would have constituted an offence within Namibia after Independence, and for which they have been sentenced to death or to imprisonment of more than twelve (12) months without the option of a fine, unless they have received a free pardon or unless such imprisonment has expired at least ten (10) years before the date of their election: provided that no person sentenced to death or imprisonment for acts committed in connection with the struggle for the independence of Namibia shall be disqualified under this Sub-Article from being elected as a member of the National Assembly; or

(c)   are unrehabilitated insolvents; or

(d)   are of unsound mind and have been so declared by a competent Court; or

(e)   are remunerated members of the public service of Namibia; or

(f)   are members of the National Council, Regional Councils or Local Authorities.

(2)   For the purposes of Sub-Article (1) hereof:

(a)   no person shall be considered as having been convicted by any Court until any appeal which might have been noted against the conviction or sentence has been determined, or the time for noting an appeal against such conviction has expired;

(b)   the public service shall be deemed to include the defence force, the police force, the prison service, para-statal enterprises, Regional Councils and Local Authorities.

Article 48   Vacation of Seats

(1)   Members of the National Assembly shall vacate their seats:

(a)   if they cease to have the qualifications which rendered them eligible to be members of the National Assembly;

(b)   if the political party which nominated them to sit in the National Assembly informs the Speaker that such members are no longer members of such political party;

(c)   if they resign their seats in writing addressed to the Speaker;

(d)   if they are removed by the National Assembly pursuant to its rules and standing orders permitting or requiring such removal for good and sufficient reasons;

(e)   if they are absent during sittings of the National Assembly for ten (10) consecutive sitting days, without having obtained the special leave of the National Assembly on grounds specified in its rules and standing orders.

(2)   If the seat of a member of the National Assembly is vacated in terms of Sub-Article (1) hereof, the political party which nominated such member to sit in the National Assembly shall be entitled to fill the vacancy by nominating any person on the party's election list compiled for the previous general election, or if there be no such person, by nominating any member of the party.

Article 49   Elections

The election of members in terms of Article 46(1)(a) hereof shall be on party lists and in accordance with the principles of proportional representation as set out in Schedule 4 hereof.

Article 50   Duration

Every National Assembly shall continue for a maximum period of five (5) years, but it may before the expiry of its term be dissolved by the President by Proclamation as provided for in Articles 32(3)(a) and 57(1) hereof.

Article 51   Speaker

(1)   At the first sitting of a newly elected National Assembly, the National Assembly, with the Secretary acting as Chairperson, shall elect a member as Speaker. The National Assembly shall then elect another member as Deputy-Speaker. The Deputy-Speaker shall act as Speaker whenever the Speaker is not available.

(2)   The Speaker or Deputy-Speaker shall cease to hold office if he or she ceases to be a member of the National Assembly. The Speaker or Deputy-Speaker may be removed from office by resolution of the National Assembly, and may resign from office or from the National Assembly in writ-

ing addressed to the Secretary of the National Assembly.

(3)   When the office of Speaker or Deputy-Speaker becomes vacant the National Assembly shall elect a member to fill the vacancy.

(4)   When neither the Speaker nor the Deputy-Speaker is available for duty, the National Assembly, with the Secretary acting as Chairperson, shall elect a member to act as Speaker.

Article 52   Secretary and other Officers

(1)   Subject to the provisions of the laws pertaining to the public service and the directives of the National Assembly, the Speaker shall appoint a person (or designate a person in the public service made available for that purpose), as the Secretary of the National Assembly, who shall perform the functions and duties assigned to such Secretary by this Constitution or by the Speaker.

(2)   Subject to the laws governing the control of public monies, the Secretary shall perform his or her functions and duties under the control of the Speaker.

(3)   The Secretary shall be assisted by officers of the National Assembly who shall be persons in the public service made available for that purpose.

Article 53   Quorum

The presence of at least thirty-seven (37) members of the National Assembly entitled to vote, other than the Speaker or the presiding member, shall be necessary to constitute a meeting of the National Assembly for the exercise of its powers and the performance of its functions.

Article 54   Casting Vote

In the case of an equality of votes in the National Assembly, the Speaker or the Deputy-Speaker or the presiding member shall have and may exercise a casting vote.

Article 55   Oath or Affirmation

Every member of the National Assembly shall make and subscribe to an oath or solemn affirmation before the Chief Justice or a Judge designated by the Chief Justice for this purpose, in the terms set out in Schedule 3 hereof.

Article 56   Assent to Bills

(1)   Every bill passed by Parliament in terms of this Constitution in order to acquire the status of an Act of Parliament shall require the assent of the President to be signified by the signing of the bill and the publication of the Act in the Gazette.

(2)   Where a bill is passed by a majority of two-thirds of all the members of the National Assembly and has been confirmed by the National Council the President shall be obliged to give his or her assent thereto.

(3)   where a bill is passed by a majority of the members of the National Assembly but such majority consists of less than two-thirds of all the members of the National Assembly and has been confirmed by the National Council, but the President declines to assent to such bill, the President shall communicate such dissent to the Speaker.

(4)   If the President has declined to assent to a bill under Sub-Article (3) hereof, the National Assembly may reconsider the bill and, if it so decides, pass the bill in the form in which it was referred back to it, or in an amended form or it may decline to pass the bill. Should the bill then be passed by a majority of the National Assembly it will not require further confirmation by the National Council but, if the majority consists of less than two-thirds of all the members of the National Assembly, the President shall retain his or her power to withhold assent to the bill. If the President elects not to assent to the bill, it shall then lapse.

Article 57   Dissolution

(1)   The National Assembly may be dissolved by the President on the advice of the Cabinet if the Government is unable to govern effectively.

(2)   Should the National Assembly be dissolved a national election for a new National Assembly and a new President shall take place within a period of ninety (90) days from the date of such dissolution.

Article 58   Conduct of Business after Dissolution

Notwithstanding the provisions of Article 57 hereof:

(a)   every person who at the date of its dissolution was a member of the National Assembly shall remain a member of the National Assembly and remain competent to perform the functions of a member until the day immediately preceding the first polling day for the election held in pursuance of such dissolution;

(b)   the President shall have power to summon Parliament for the conduct of business during the period following such dissolution, up to and including the day immediately preceding the first polling day for the election held in pursuance of such dissolution, in the same manner and in all respects as if the dissolution had not occurred.

Article 59   Rules of Procedure, Committees and Standing Orders

(1)   The National Assembly may make such rules of procedure for the conduct of its business and proceedings and may also make such rules for the establishing, functioning and procedures of committees, and formulate such standing orders, as may appear to it to be expedient or necessary.

(2)   The National Assembly shall in its rules of procedure make provision for such disclosure as may be considered to be appropriate in regard to the financial or business affairs of its members.

(3)   For the purposes of exercising its powers and performing its functions any committee of the National Assembly established in terms of Sub-Article (1) hereof shall have the power to subpoena persons to appear before it to give evidence on oath and to produce any documents required by it.

Article 60   Duties, Privileges and Immunities of Members

(1)   The duties of the members of the National Assembly shall include the following:

(a)   all members of the National Assembly shall maintain the dignity and image of the National Assembly both during the sittings of the National Assembly as well as in their acts and activities outside the National Assembly;

(b)   all members of the National Assembly shall regard themselves as servants of the people of Namibia and desist from any conduct by which they seek improperly to enrich themselves or alienate themselves from the people.

(2)   A private members' bill may be introduced in the National Assembly if supported by one-third of all the members of the National Assembly.

(3)   Rules providing for the privileges and immunities of members of the National Assembly shall be made by Act of Parliament and all members shall be entitled to the protection of such privileges and immunities.

Article 61   Public Access to Sittings

(1)   Save as provided in Sub-Article (2) hereof, all meetings of the National Assembly shall be held in public and members of the public shall have access to such meetings.

(2)   Access by members of the public in terms of Sub-Article (1) hereof may be denied if the National Assembly adopts a motion supported by two-thirds of all its members excluding such access to members of the public for specified periods or in respect of specified matters. Such a motion shall only be considered if it is supported by at least one-tenth of all the members of the National Assembly and the debate on such motion shall not be open to members of the public.

Article 62   Sessions

(1)   The National Assembly shall sit:

(a)   at its usual place of sitting determined by the National Assembly, unless the Speaker directs otherwise on the grounds of public interest, security or convenience;

(b) for at least two (2) sessions during each year, to commence and terminate on such dates as the National Assembly from time to time determines;

(c) for such special sessions as directed by Proclamation by the President from time to time.

(2) During such sessions the National Assembly shall sit on such days and during such times of the day or night as the National Assembly by its rules and standing orders may provide.

(3) The day of commencement of any session of the National Assembly may be altered by Proclamation by the President, if the President is requested to do so by the Speaker on grounds of public interest or convenience.

Article 63   Functions and Powers

(1) The National Assembly, as the principal legislative authority in and over Namibia, shall have the power, subject to this Constitution, to make and repeal laws for the peace, order and good government of the country in the best interest of the people of Namibia.

(2) The National Assembly shall further have the power and function, subject to this Constitution:

(a) to approve budgets for the effective government and administration of the country;

(b) to provide for revenue and taxation;

(c) to take such steps as it considers expedient to uphold and defend this Constitution and the laws of Namibia and to advance the objectives of Namibian independence;

(d) to consider and decide whether or not to succeed to such international agreements as may have been entered into prior to Independence by administrations within Namibia in which the majority of the Namibian people have historically not enjoyed democratic representation and participation;

(e)   to agree to the ratification of or accession to international agreements which have been negotiated and signed in terms of Article 32(3)(e) hereof;

(f)   to receive reports on the activities of the Executive, including parastatal enterprises, and from time to time to require any senior official thereof to appear before any of the committees of the National Assembly to account for and explain his or her acts and programmes;

(g)   to initiate, approve or decide to hold a referendum on matters of national concern;

(h)   to debate and to advise the President in regard to any matters which by this Constitution the President is authorised to deal with;

(i)   to remain vigilant and vigorous for the purposes of ensuring that the scourges of apartheid, tribalism and colonialism do not again manifest themselves in any form in a free and independent Namibia and to protect and assist disadvantaged citizens of Namibia who have historically been the victims of these pathologies;

(j)   generally to exercise any other functions and powers assigned to it by this Constitution or any other law and any other functions incidental thereto.

Article 64   Withholding of Presidential Assent

(1)   Subject to the provisions of this Constitution, the President shall be entitled to withhold his or her assent to a bill approved by the National Assembly if in the President's opinion such bill would upon adoption conflict with the provisions of this Constitution.

(2) Should the President withhold assent on the grounds of such opinion, he or she shall so inform the Speaker who shall inform the National Assembly thereof, and the Attorney-General, who may then take appropriate steps to have the matter decided by a competent Court.

(3) Should such Court thereafter conclude that such bill is not in conflict with the provisions of this Constitution, the President shall assent to the said bill if it was passed by the National Assembly by a two-thirds majority of all its members. If the bill was not passed with such majority, the President may withhold his or her assent to the bill, in which event the provisions of Article 56(3) and (4) hereof shall apply.

(4) Should such Court conclude that the disputed bill would be in conflict with any provisions of this Constitution, the said bill shall be deemed to have lapsed and the President shall not be entitled to assent thereto.

Article 65   Signature and Enrolment of Acts

(1) When any bill has become an Act of Parliament as a result of its having been passed by Parliament, signed by the President and published in the Gazette, the Secretary of the National Assembly shall promptly cause two (2) fair copies of such Act in the English language to be enrolled in the office of the Registrar of the Supreme Court and such copies shall be conclusive evidence of the provisions of the Act.

(2) The public shall have the right of access to such copies subject to such regulations as may be prescribed by Parliament to protect the durability of the said copies and the convenience of the Registrar's staff.

Article 66   Customary and Common Law

(1) Both the customary law and the common law of Namibia in force on the date of Independence shall remain valid to the extent to which such customary or common law does not conflict with this Constitution or any other statutory law.

(2) Subject to the terms of this Constitution, any part of such common law or customary law may be repealed or modified by Act of Parliament, and the application thereof may be confined to particular parts of Namibia or to par-

ticular periods.

Article 67   Requisite Majorities

Save as provided in this Constitution, a simple majority of votes cast in the National Assembly shall be sufficient for the passage of any bill or resolution of the National Assembly.

CHAPTER 8

The National Council

Article 68   Establishment

There shall be a National Council which shall have the powers and functions set out in this Constitution.

Article 69   Composition

(1)   The National Council shall consist of two (2) members from each region referred to in Article 102 hereof, to be elected from amongst their members by the Regional Council for such region.

(2)   The elections of members of the National Council shall be conducted according to procedures to be prescribed by Act of Parliament.

Article 70   Term of Office of Members

(1)   Members of the National Council shall hold their seats for six (6) years from the date of their election and shall be eligible for re-election.

(2)   When a seat of a member of the National Council becomes vacant through death, resignation or disqualification, an election for a successor to occupy the vacant seat until the expiry of the predecessor's term of office shall be held, except in the instance where such vacancy arises less than six (6) months before the expiry of the term of the National Council, in which instance such vacancy need not be filled. Such election shall be held in accordance with the procedures prescribed by the Act of Parliament referred to in Article 69(2) hereof.

Article 71   **Oath or Affirmation**

Every member of the National Council shall make and subscribe to an oath or solemn affirmation before the Chief Justice, or a Judge designated by the Chief Justice for this purpose, in the terms set out in Schedule 3 hereof.

Article 72   **Qualifications of Members**

No person shall be qualified to be a member of the National Council if he or she is an elected member of a Local Authority, and unless he or she is qualified under Article 47(1)(a) to (e) hereof to be a member of the National Assembly.

Article 73   **Chairperson and Vice-Chairperson**

The National Council shall, before proceeding to the dispatch of any other business, elect from its members a Chairperson and a Vice-Chairperson. The Chairperson, or in his or her absence the Vice-Chairperson, shall preside over sessions of the National Council. Should neither the Chairperson nor the Vice-Chairperson be present at any session, the National Council shall elect from amongst its members a person to act as Chairperson in their absence during that session.

Article 74   **Powers and Functions**

(1)   The National Council shall have the power to:

(a)   consider in terms of Article 75 hereof all bills passed by the National Assembly;

(b)   investigate and report to the National Assembly on any subordinate legislation, reports and documents which under law must be tabled in the National Assembly and which are referred to it by the National Assembly for advice;

(c)   recommend legislation on matters of regional concern for submission to and consideration by the National Assembly;

(d)   perform any other functions assigned to it by the National Assembly or by an Act of Parliament.

(2)   The National Council shall have the power to establish committees and to adopt its own rules and procedures for the exercise of its powers and the performance of its functions. A committee of the National Council shall be entitled to conduct all such hearings and collect such evidence as it considers necessary for the exercise of the National Council's powers of review and investigations, and for such purposes shall have the powers referred to in Article 59(3) hereof.

(3)   The National Council shall in its rules of procedure make provision for such disclosure as may be considered to be appropriate in regard to the financial or business affairs of its members.

(4)   The duties of the members of the National Council shall include the following:

(a)   all members of the National Council shall maintain the dignity and image of the National Council both during the sittings of the National Council as well as in their acts and activities outside the National Council;

(b)   all members of the National Council shall regard themselves as servants of the people of Namibia and desist from any conduct by which they seek improperly to enrich themselves or alienate themselves from the people.

(5)   Rules providing for the privileges and immunities of members of the National Council shall be made by Act of Parliament and all members shall be entitled to the protection of such privileges and immunities.

Article 75   Review of Legislation

(1)   All bills passed by the National Assembly shall be referred by the Speaker to the National Council.

(2)   The National Council shall consider bills referred to it under Sub-Article (1) hereof and shall submit reports thereon with its recommendations to the

Speaker.

(3)   If in its report to the Speaker the National Council confirms a bill, the Speaker shall refer it to the President to enable the President to deal with it under Articles 56 and 64 hereof.

(4)   (a)   If the National Council in its report to the Speaker recommends that the bill be passed subject to amendments proposed by it, such bill shall be referred by the Speaker back to the National Assembly.

        (b)   If a bill is referred back to the National Assembly under Sub-Article (a) hereof, the National Assembly may reconsider the bill and may make any amendments thereto, whether proposed by the National Council or not. If the bill is again passed by the National Assembly, whether in the form in which it was originally passed, or in an amended form, the bill shall not again be referred to the National Council, but shall be referred by the Speaker to the President to enable it to be dealt with under Articles 56 and 64 hereof.

(5)   (a)   If a majority of two-thirds of all the members of the National Council objects to the principle of a bill, this shall be mentioned in its report to the Speaker. In that event, the report shall also indicate whether or not the National Council proposes that amendments be made to the bill, if the principle of the bill is confirmed by the National Assembly under Sub-Article (b) hereof, and if amendments are proposed, details thereof shall be set out in the report.

        (b)   If the National Council in its report objects to the principle of the bill, the National Assembly shall be required to reconsider the principle. If upon such reconsideration the National Assembly reaffirms the principle of the bill by a majority of two-thirds of all its members, the principle of the bill shall no longer be an issue. If such two-thirds majority is not obtained in the National Assembly, the bill shall lapse.

(6)   (a)   If the National Assembly reaffirms the principle of the bill under Sub-Article 5(b) hereof by a majority of two-thirds of all its mem-

bers, and the report of the National Council proposed that in such event amendments be made to the bill, the National Assembly shall then deal with the amendments proposed by the National Council, and in that event the provisions of Sub-Article 4(b) shall apply *mutatis mutandis*.

(b) If the National Assembly reaffirms the principle of the bill under Sub-Article 5(b) hereof by a majority of two-thirds of all its members, and the report of the National Council did not propose that in such event amendments be made to the bill, the National Council shall be deemed to have confirmed the bill, and the Speaker shall refer the bill to the President to be dealt with under Articles 56 and 64 hereof.

(7) Sub-Articles (5) and (6) hereof shall not apply to bills dealing with the levying of taxes or the appropriation of public monies.

(8) The National Council shall report to the Speaker on all bills dealing with the levying of taxes or appropriations of public monies within thirty (30) days of the date on which such bills were referred to it by the Speaker, and on all other bills within three (3) months of the date of referral by the Speaker, failing which the National Council will be deemed to have confirmed such bills and the Speaker shall then refer them promptly to the President to enable the President to deal with the bills under Articles 56 and 64 hereof.

(9) If the President withholds his or her assent to any bill under Article 56 hereof and the bill is then dealt with in terms of that Article, and is again passed by the National Assembly in the form in which it was originally passed or in an amended form, such bill shall not again be referred to the National Council, but shall be referred by the Speaker directly to the President to enable the bill to be dealt with in terms of Articles 56 and 64 hereof.

Article 76   Quorum

The presence of a majority of the members of the National Council shall be necessary to constitute a meeting of the National Council for the exercise of its powers and the performance of its functions.

Article 77   Voting

Save as is otherwise provided in this Constitution, all questions in the National Council shall be determined by a majority of the votes cast by members present other than the Chairperson, or in his or her absence the Vice-Chairperson or the member presiding at that session, who shall, however, have and may exercise a casting vote in the case of an equality of votes.

CHAPTER 9

The Administration of Justice

Article 78   The Judiciary

(1)   The judicial power shall be vested in the Courts of Namibia, which shall consist of:

   (a)   a Supreme Court of Namibia;

   (b)   a High Court of Namibia;

   (c)   Lower Courts of Namibia.

(2)   The Courts shall be independent and subject only to this Constitution and the law.

(3)   No member of the Cabinet or the Legislature or any other person shall interfere with Judges or judicial officers in the exercise of their judicial functions, and all organs of the State shall accord such assistance as the Courts may require to protect their independence, dignity and effectiveness, subject to the terms of this Constitution or any other law.

(4)   The Supreme Court and the High Court shall have the inherent jurisdiction which vested in the Supreme Court of South-West Africa immediately prior to the date of Independence, including the power to regulate their own procedures and to make court rules for that purpose.

Article 79   The Supreme Court

(1)   The Supreme Court shall consist of a Chief Justice and such additional

Judges as the President, acting on the recommendation of the Judicial Service Commission, may determine.

(2)   The Supreme Court shall be presided over by the Chief Justice and shall hear and adjudicate upon appeals emanating from the High Court, including appeals which involve the interpretation, implementation and upholding of this Constitution and the fundamental rights and freedoms guaranteed thereunder. The Supreme Court shall also deal with matters referred to it for decision by the Attorney-General under this Constituiton, and with such other matters as may be authorised by Act of Parliament.

(3)   Three (3) Judges shall constitute a quorum of the Supreme Court when it hears appeals or deals with matters referred to it by the Attorney-General under this Constitution: provided that provision may be made by Act of Parliament for a lesser quorum in circumstances in which a Judge seized of an appeal dies or becomes unable to act at any time prior to judgment.

(4)   The jurisdiction of the Supreme Court with regard to appeals shall be determined by Act of Parliament.

Article 80   The High Court

(1)   The High Court shall consist of a Judge-President and such additional Judges as the President, acting on the recommendation of the Judicial Service Commission, may determine.

(2)   The High Court shall have original jurisdiction to hear and adjudicate upon all civil disputes and criminal prosecutions, including cases which involve the interpretation, implementation and upholding of this Constitution and the fundamental rights and freedoms guaranteed thereunder. The High Court shall also have jurisdiction to hear and adjudicate upon appeals from Lower Courts.

(3)   The jurisdiction of the High Court with regard to appeals shall be determined by Act of Parliament.

Article 81   Binding Nature of Decisions of the Supreme Court

A decision of the Supreme Court shall be binding on all other Courts of Namibia and all persons in Namibia unless it is reversed by the Supreme Court itself, or is contradicted by an Act of Parliament lawfully enacted.

Article 82   Appointment of Judges

(1)   All appointments of Judges to the Supreme Court and the High Court shall be made by the President on the recommendation of the Judicial Service Commission and upon appointment Judges shall make an oath or affirmation of office in the terms set out in Schedule 1 hereof.

(2)   At the request of the Chief Justice the President may appoint Acting Judges of the Supreme Court to fill casual vacancies in the Court from time to time, or as *ad hoc* appointments to sit in cases involving constitutional issues or the guarantee of fundamental rights and freedoms, if in the opinion of the Chief Justice it is desirable that such persons should be appointed to hear such cases by reason of their special knowledge of or expertise in such matters.

(3)   At the request of the Judge-President, the President may appoint Acting Judges of the High Court from time to time to fill casual vacancies in the Court, or to enable the Court to deal expeditiously with its work.

(4)   All Judges, except Acting Judges, appointed under this Constitution shall hold office until the age of sixty-five (65) but the President shall be entitled to extend the retiring age of any Judge to seventy (70). It shall also be possible by Act of Parliament to make provision for retirement at ages higher than those specified in this Article.

Article 83   Lower Courts

(1)   Lower Courts shall be established by Act of Parliament and shall have the jurisdiction and adopt the procedures prescribed by such Act and regulations made thereunder.

(2)   Lower Courts shall be presided over by Magistrates or other judicial officers appointed in accordance with procedures prescribed by Act of Parliament.

Article 84   Removal of Judges from Office

(1)   A Judge may be removed from office before the expiry of his or her tenure

only by the President acting on the recommendation of the Judicial Service Commission.

(2) Judges may only be removed from office on the ground of mental incapacity or for gross misconduct, and in accordance with the provisions of Sub-Article (3) hereof.

(3) The Judicial Service Commission shall investigate whether or not a Judge should be removed from office on such grounds, and if it decides that the Judge should be removed, it shall inform the President of its recommendation.

(4) If the deliberations of the Judicial Service Commission pursuant to this Article involve the conduct of a member of the Judicial Service Commission, such Judge shall not participate in the deliberations and the President shall appoint another Judge to fill such vacancy.

(5) While investigations are being carried out into the necessity of the removal of a Judge in terms of this Article, the President may, on the recommendation of the Judicial Service Commission and, pending the outcome of such investigations and recommendation, suspend the Judge from office.

Article 85   The Judicial Service Commission

(1) There shall be a Judicial Service Commission consisting of the Chief Justice, a Judge appointed by the President, the Attorney-General and two members of the legal profession nominated in accordance with the provisions of an Act of Parliament by the professional organisation or organisations representing the interests of the legal profession in Namibia.

(2) The Judicial Service Commission shall perform such functions as are prescribed for it by this Constitution or any other law.

(3) The Judicial Service Commission shall be entitled to make such rules and regulations for the purposes of regulating its procedures and functions as are not inconsistent with this Constitution or any other law.

(4) Any casual vacancy in the Judicial Service Commission may be filled by the

Chief Justice or in his or her absence by the Judge appointed by the President.

Article 86   The Attorney-General

There shall be an Attorney-General appointed by the President in accordance with the provisions of Article 32(3)(1)(cc) hereof.

Article 87   Powers and Functions of the Attorney-General

The powers and functions of the Attorney-General shall be:

(a)   to exercise the final responsibility for the office of the Prosecutor-General;

(b)   to be the principal legal adviser to the President and Government;

(c)   to take all action necessary for the protection and upholding of the Constitution;

(d)   to perform all such functions and duties as may be assigned to the Attorney-General by Act of Parliament.

Article 88   The Prosecutor-General

(1)   There shall be a Prosecutor-General appointed by the President on the recommendation of the Judicial Service Commision. No person shall be eligible for appointment as Prosecutor-General unless such person:

(a)   possesses legal qualifications that would entitle him or her to practise in all the Courts of Namibia;

(b)   is, by virtue of his or her experience, conscientiousness and integrity a fit and proper person to be entrusted with the responsibilities of the office of Prosecutor-General.

(2)   The powers and functions of the Prosecutor-General shall be:

(a)   to prosecute, subject to the provisions of this Constitution, in the name of the Republic of Namibia in criminal proceedings;

(b)   to prosecute and defend appeals in criminal proceedings in the High Court and the Supreme Court;

(c)   to perform all functions relating to the exercise of such powers;

(d)   to delegate to other officials, subject to his or her control and direction, authority to conduct criminal proceedings in any Court;

(e)   to perform all such other functions as may be assigned to him or her in terms of any other law.

CHAPTER 10

The Ombudsman

Article 89   Establishment and Independence

(1)   There shall be an Ombudsman, who shall have the powers and functions set out in this Constitution.

(2)   The Ombudsman shall be independent and subject only to this Constitution and the law.

(3)   No member of the Cabinet or the Legislature or any other person shall interfere with the Ombudsman in the exercise of his or her functions and all organs of the State shall accord such assistance as may be needed for the protection of the independence, dignity and effectiveness of the Ombudsman.

(4)   The Ombudsman shall either be a Judge of Namibia, or a person possessing the legal qualifications which would entitle him or her to practise in all the Courts of Namibia.

Article 90   Appointment and Term of Office

(1)   The Ombudsman shall be appointed by Proclamation by the President on

the recommendation of the Judicial Service Commission.

(2)   The Ombudsman shall hold office until the age of sixty-five (65) but the President may extend the retiring age of any Ombudsman to seventy (70).

Article 91   Functions

The functions of the Ombudsman shall be defined and prescribed by an Act of Parliament and shall include the following:

(a)   the duty to investigate complaints concerning alleged or apparent instances of violations of fundamental rights and freedoms, abuse of power, unfair, harsh, insensitive or discourteous treatment of an inhabitant of Namibia by an official in the employ of any organ of Government (whether central or local), manifest injustice, or corruption or conduct by such official which would properly be regarded as unlawful, oppressive or unfair in a democratic society;

(b)   the duty to investigate complaints concerning the functioning of the Public Service Commission, administrative organs of the State, the defence force, the police force and the prison service in so far as such complaints relate to the failure to achieve a balanced structuring of such services or equal access by all to the recruitment of such services or fair administration in relation to such services;

(c)   the duty to investigate complaints concerning the over-utilization of living natural resources, the irrational exploitation of non-renewable resources, the degradation and destruction of ecosystems and failure to protect the beauty and character of Namibia;

(d)   the duty to investigate complaints concerning practices and actions by persons, enterprises and other private institutions where such complaints allege that violations of fundamental rights and freedoms under this Constitution have taken place; ·

(e)   the duty and power to take appropriate action to call for the remedying, correction and reversal of instances specified in the preceding Sub-Articles through such means as are fair, proper and effective, including:

(aa)   negotiation and compromise between the parties concerned;

(bb)   causing the complaint and his or her finding thereon to be reported to the superior of an offending person;

(cc)   referring the matter to the Prosecutor-General;

(dd)   bringing proceedings in a competent Court for an interdict or some other suitable remedy to secure the termination of the offending action or conduct, or the abandonment or alteration of the offending procedures;

(ee)   bringing proceedings to interdict the enforcement of such legislation or regulation by challenging its validity if the offending action or conduct is sought to be justified by subordinate legislation or regulation which is grossly unreasonable or otherwise *ultra vires*;

(ff)   reviewing such laws as were in operation before the date of Independence in order to ascertain whether they violate the letter or the spirit of this Constitution and to make consequential recommendations to the President, the Cabinet or the Attorney-General for appropriate action following thereupon;

(f)   the duty to investigate vigorously all instances of alleged or suspected corruption and the misappropriation of public monies by officials and to take appropriate steps, including reports to the Prosecutor-General and the Auditor-General pursuant thereto;

(g)   the duty to report annually to the National Assembly on the exercise of his or her powers and functions.

Article 92   Powers of Investigation

The powers of the Ombudsman shall be defined by Act of Parliament and shall include the power:

(a)   to issue subpoenas requiring the attendance of any person before the Ombudsman and the production of any document or record relevant to any investigation by the Ombudsman;

(b)   to cause any person contemptuous of any such subpoena to be prosecuted before a competent Court;

(c)   to question any person;

(d)   to require any person to co-operate with the Ombudsman and to disclose truthfully and frankly any information within his or her knowledge relevant to any investigation of the Ombudsman.

Article 93   Meaning of "Official"

For the purposes of this Chapter the word "official" shall, unless the context otherwise indicates, include any elected or appointed official or employee of any organ of the central or local Government, any official of a para-statal enterprise owned or managed, or controlled by the State, or in which the State or the Government has substantial interest, or any officer of the defence force, the police force or the prison service, but shall not include a Judge of the Supreme Court or the High Court or, in so far as a complaint concerns the performance of a judicial function, any other judicial officer.

Article 94   Removal from Office

(1)   The Ombudsman may be removed from office before the expiry of his or her term of office by the President acting on the recommendation of the Judicial Service Commission.

(2)   The Ombudsman may only be removed from office on the ground of mental incapacity or for gross misconduct, and in accordance with the provisions of Sub-Article (3) hereof.

(3)   The Judicial Service Commission shall investigate whether or not the Ombudsman shall be removed from office on the grounds referred to in Sub-Article (2) hereof and, if it decides that the Ombudsman shall be removed, it shall inform the President of its recommendation.

(4)   While investigations are being carried out into the necessity of the removal of the Ombudsman in terms of this Article, the President may, on the recommendation of the Judicial Service Commission and, pending the outcome of such investigations and recommendation, suspend the Ombudsman from

office.

CHAPTER 11

Principles of State Policy

Article 95   **Promotion of the Welfare of the People**

The State shall actively promote and maintain the welfare of the people by adopting, *inter alia*, policies aimed at the following:

(a)   enactment of legislation to ensure equality of opportunity for women, to enable them to participate fully in all spheres of Namibian society; in particular, the Government shall ensure the implementation of the principle of non-discrimination in remuneration of men and women; further, the Government shall seek, through appropriate legislation, to provide maternity and related benefits for women;

(b)   enactment of legislation to ensure that the health and strength of the workers, men and women, and the tender age of children are not abused and that citizens are not forced by economic necessity to enter vocations unsuited to their age and strength;

(c)   active encouragement of the formation of independent trade unions to protect workers' rights and interests, and to promote sound labour relations and fair employment practices;

(d)   membership of the International Labour Organisation (ILO) and, where possible, adherance to and action in accordance with the international Conventions and Recommendations of the ILO;

(e)   ensurance that every citizen has a right to fair and reasonable access to public facilities and services in accordance with the law;

(f)   ensurance that senior citizens are entitled to and do receive a regular pension adequate for the maintenance of a decent standard of living and the enjoyment of social and cultural opportunities;

(g)   enactment of legislation to ensure that the unemployed, the incapacitated, the indigent and the disadvantaged are accorded such social benefits and amenities as are determined by Parliament to be just and affordable with due regard to the resources of the State;

(h)   a legal system seeking to promote justice on the basis of equal opportunity by providing free legal aid in defined cases with due regard to the resources of the State;

(i)   ensurance that workers are paid a living wage adequate for the maintenance of a decent standard of living and the enjoyment of social and cultural opportunities;

(j)   consistent planning to raise and maintain an acceptable level of nutrition and standard of living of the Namibian people and to improve public health;

(k)   encouragement of the mass of the population through education and other activities and through their organisations to influence Government policy by debating its decisions;

(l)   maintenance of ecosystems, essential ecological processes and biological diversity of Namibia and utilization of living natural resources on a sustainable basis for the benefit of all Namibians, both present and future; in particular, the Government shall provide measures against the dumping or recycling of foreign nuclear and toxic waste on Namibian territory.

Article 96   **Foreign Relations**

The State shall endeavour to ensure that in its international relations it:

(a)   adopts and maintains a policy of non-alignment;

(b)   promotes international co-operation, peace and security;

(c)   creates and maintains just and mutually beneficial relations among nations;

(d)   fosters respect for international law and treaty obligations;

(e)   encourages the settlement of international disputes by peaceful means.

Article 97   Asylum

The State shall, where it is reasonable to do so, grant asylum to persons who reasonably fear persecution on the ground of their political beliefs, race, religion or membership of a particular social group.

Article 98   Principles of Economic Order

(1)   The economic order of Namibia shall be based on the principles of a mixed economy with the objective of securing economic growth, prosperity and a life of human dignity for all Namibians.

(2)   The Namibian economy shall be based, *inter alia*, on the following forms of ownership:

   (a)   public;

   (b)   private;

   (c)   joint public-private;

   (d)   co-operative;

   (e)   co-ownership;

   (f)   small-scale family.

Article 99   Foreign Investments

Foreign investments shall be encouraged within Namibia subject to the provisions of an Investment Code to be adopted by Parliament.

Article 100   Sovereign Ownership of Natural Resources

Land, water and natural resources below and above the surface of the land and in the continental shelf and within the territorial waters and the exclusive economic zone of Namibia shall belong to the State if they are not otherwise lawfully owned.

Article 101   Application of the Principles contained in this Chapter

The principles of state policy contained in this Chapter shall not of and by them-selves be legally enforceable by any Court, but shall nevertheless guide the Government in making and applying laws to give effect to the fundamental objec-tives of the said principles. The Courts are entitled to have regard to the said prin-ciples in interpreting any laws based on them.

CHAPTER 12

Regional and Local Government

Article 102   Structures of Regional and Local Government

(1)   For purposes of regional and local government, Namibia shall be divided into regional and local units, which shall consist of such region and Local Authorities as may be determined and defined by Act of Parliament.

(2)   The delineation of the boundaries of the regions and Local Authorities referred to in Sub-Article (1) hereof shall be geographical only, without any reference to the race, colour or ethnic origin of the inhabitants of such areas.

(3)   Every organ of regional and local government shall have a Council as the principal governing body, freely elected in accordance with this Constitution and the Act of Parliament referred to in Sub-Article (1) hereof, with an execu-tive and administration which shall carry out all lawful resolutions and poli-cies of such Council, subject to this Constitution and any other relevant laws.

(4)   For the purposes of this Chapter, a Local Authority shall include all munici-palities, communities, village councils and other organs of local government defined and constituted by Act of Parliament.

(5)   There shall be a Council of Traditional Leaders to be established in terms of an Act of Parliament in order to advise the President on the control and uti-lization of communal land and on all such other matters as may be referred to it by the President for advice.

Article 103 Establishment of Regional Councils

(1) The boundaries of regions shall be determined by a Delimitation Commission in accordance with the principles set out in Article 102 (2) hereof.

(2) The boundaries of regions may be changed from time to time and new regions may be created from time to time, but only in accordance with the recommendations of the Delimitation Commission.

(3) A Regional Council shall be established for every region the boundaries of which have been determined in accordance with Sub-Articles (1) and (2) hereof.

Article 104 The Delimitation Commission

(1) The Delimitation Commission shall consist of a Chairperson who shall be a Judge of the Supreme Court or the High Court, and two other persons to be appointed by the President with the approval of Parliament.

(2) The Delimitation Commission shall discharge its duties in accordance with the provisions of an Act of Parliament and this Constitution, and shall report theron to the President.

Article 105 Composition of Regional Councils

Every Regional Council shall consist of a number of persons determined by the Delimitation Commission for the particular region for which that Regional Council has been established, and who are qualified to be elected to the National Council.

Article 106 Regional Council Elections

(1) Each region shall be divided into constituencies the boundaries of which shall be fixed by the Delimitation Commission in accordance with the provisions of an Act of Parliament and this Constitution: provided that there shall be no fewer than six (6) and no more than twelve (12) constituencies in each region.

(2) Each constituency shall elect one member to the Regional Council for the

region in which it is situated.

(3)   The elections shall be by secret ballot to be conducted in accordance with the provisions of an Act of Parliament, and the candidate receiving the most votes in any constituency shall be the elected member of the Regional Council for that constituency.

(4)   All Regional Council elections for the various regions of Namibia shall be held on the same day.

(5)   The date for Regional Council elections shall be determined by the President by Proclamation in the Gazette.

Article 107   Remuneration of Members of Regional Councils

The remuneration and allowances to be paid to members of Regional Councils shall be determined by Act of Parliament.

Article 108   Powers of Regional Councils

Regional Councils shall have the following powers:

(a)   to elect members to the National Council;

(b)   to exercise within the region for which they have been constituted such executive powers and to perform such duties in connection therewith as may be assigned to them by Act of Parliament and as may be delegated to them by the President;

(c)   to raise revenue, or share in the revenue raised by the central Government within the regions for which they have been established, as may be determined by Act of Parliament;

(d)   to exercise powers, perform any other functions and make such by-laws or regulations as may be determined by Act of Parliament.

Article 109   Management Committees

(1)   Each Regional Council shall elect from amongst its members a Management Committee, which shall be vested with executive powers in accordance with

the provisions of an Act of Parliament.

(2) The Management Committee shall have a Chairperson to be elected by the members of the Regional Council at the time that they elect the Management Committee, and such Chairperson shall preside at meetings of his or her Regional Council.

(3) The Chairperson and the members of the Management Committee shall hold office for three (3) years and shall be eligible for re-election.

Article 110   Administration and Functioning of Regional Councils

The holding and conducting of meetings of Regional Councils, the filling of casual vacancies on Regional Councils and the employment of officials by the Regional Councils, as well as all other matters dealing with or incidental to the administration and functioning of Regional Councils, shall be determined by Act of Parliament.

Article 111   Local Authorities

(1) Local Authorities shall be established in accordance with the provisions of Article 102 hereof.

(2) The boundaries of Local Authorities, the election of Councils to administer the affairs of Local Authorities, the method of electing persons to Local Authority Councils, the methods of raising revenue for Local Authorities, the remuneration of Local Authority Councillors and all other matters dealing with or incidental to the administration and functioning of Local Authorities, shall be determined by Act of Parliament.

(3) Persons shall be qualified to vote in elections for Local Authority Councils if such persons have been resident within the jurisdiction of a Local Authority for not less than one (1) year immediately prior to such election and if such persons are qualified to vote in elections for the National Assembly.

(4) Different provisions may be made by the Act of Parliament referred to in Sub-Article (2) hereof in regard to different types of Local Authorities.

(5) All by-laws or regulations made by Local Authorities pursuant to powers

vested in them by Act of Parliament shall be tabled in the National Assembly and shall cease to be of force if a resolution to that effect is passed by the National Assembly.

CHAPTER 13

The Public Service Commission

Article 112   Establishment

(1)   There shall be established a Public Service Commission which shall have the function of advising the President on the matters referred to in Article 113 hereof and of reporting to the National Assembly thereon.

(2)   The Public Service Commission shall be independent and act impartially.

(3)   The Public Service Commission shall consist of a Chairperson and no fewer than three (3) and no more than six (6) other persons nominated by the President and appointed by the National Assembly by resolution.

(4)   Every member of the Public Service Commission shall be entitled to serve on such Commission for a period of five (5) years unless lawfully removed before the expiry of that period for good and sufficient reasons in terms of this Constitution and procedures to be prescribed by Act of Parliament. Every member of the Public Service Commission shall be eligible for reappointment.

Article 113   Functions

The functions of the Public Service Commission shall be defined by Act of Parliament and shall include the power:

(a)   to advise the President and the Government on:

(aa)   the appointment of suitable persons to specified categories of employment in the public service, with special regard to the balanced structuring thereof;

(bb)   the exercise of adequate disciplinary control over such persons in order to assure the fair administration of personnel policy;

(cc)   the remuneration and the retirement benefits of any such persons;

(dd)   all other matters which by law pertain to the public service;

(b)   to perform all functions assigned to it by Act of Parliament;

(c)   to advise the President on the identity, availability and suitability of persons to be appointed by the President to offices in terms of this Constitution or any other law.

CHAPTER 14

The Security Commission

Article 114   Establishment and Functions

(1)   There shall be a Security Commission which shall have the function of making recommendations to the President on the appointment of the Chief of the Defence Force, the Inspector-General of Police and the Commissioner of Prisons and such other functions as may be assigned to it by Act of Parliament.

(2)   The Security Commission shall consist of the Chairperson of the Public Service Commission, the Chief of the Defence Force, the Inspector-General of Police, the Commissioner of Prisons and two (2) members of the National Assembly, appointed by the President on the recommendation of the National Assembly.

CHAPTER 15

The Police and Defence Forces and The Prison Service

Article 115   Establishment of the Police Force

There shall be established by Act of Parliament a Namibian police force with pre-

scribed powers, duties and procedures in order to secure the internal security of
Namibia and to maintain law and order.

Article 116   The Inspector-General of Police

(1)   There shall be an Inspector-General of Police who shall be appointed by the
President in terms of Article 32 (4)(c)(bb) hereof.

(2)   The Inspector-General of Police shall make provision for a balanced structuring of the police force and shall have the power to make suitable appointments to the police force, to cause charges of indiscipline among members
of the police force to be investigated and prosecuted and to ensure the efficient administration of the police force.

Article 117   Removal of the Inspector-General of Police

The President may remove the Inspector-General of Police from office for good
cause and in the public interest and in accordance with the provisions of any Act of
Parliament which may prescribe procedures considered to be expedient for this
purpose.

Article 118   Establishment of the Defence Force

(1)   There shall be established by Act of Parliament a Namibian Defence Force
with prescribed composition, powers, duties and procedures, in order to
defend the territory and national interests of Namibia.

(2)   The President shall be the Commander-in-Chief of the Defence Force and
shall have all the powers and exercise all the functions necessary for that
purpose.

Article 119   Chief of the Defence Force

(1)   There shall be a Chief of the Defence Force who shall be appointed by the
President in terms of Article 32(4)(c)(aa) hereof.

(2)   The Chief of the Defence Force shall make provision for a balanced structuring of the defence force and shall have the power to make suitable appointments to the defence force, to cause charges of indiscipline among members
of the defence force to be investigated and prosecuted and to ensure the

efficient administration of the defence force.

Article 120   Removal of the Chief of the Defence Force

The President may remove the Chief of the Defence Force from office for good cause and in the public interest and in accordance with the provisions of any Act of Parliament which may prescribe procedures considered to be expedient for this purpose.

Article 121   Establishment of the Prison Service

There shall be established by Act of Parliament a Namibian prison service with prescribed powers, duties and procedures.

Article 122   Commissioner of Prisons

(1)   There shall be a Commissioner of Prisons who shall be appointed by the President in terms of Article 32(4)(c)(cc) hereof.

(2)   The Commissioner of Prisons shall make provision for a balanced structuring of the prison service and shall have the power to make suitable appointments to the prison service, to cause charges of indiscipline among members of the prison service to be investigated and prosecuted and to ensure the efficient administration of the prison service.

Article 123   Removal of the Commissioner of Prisons

The President may remove the Commissioner of Prisons from office for good cause and in the public interest and in accordance with the provisions of any Act of Parliament which may prescribe procedures considered to be expedient for this purpose.

CHAPTER 16

Finance

Article 124   Transfer of Government Assets

The assets mentioned in Schedule 5 hereof shall vest in the Government of

Namibia on the date of Independence.

Article 125   The State Revenue Fund

(1)   The Central Revenue Fund of the mandated territory of South West Africa instituted in terms of Section 3 of the Exchequer and Audit Proclamation, 1979 (Proclamation 85 of 1979) and Section 31(1) of Proclamation R101 of 1985 shall continue as the State Revenue Fund of the Republic of Namibia.

(2)   All income accruing to the central Government shall be deposited in the State Revenue Fund and the authority to dispose thereof shall vest in the Government of Namibia.

(3)   Nothing contained in Sub-Article (2) hereof shall preclude the enactment of any law or the application of any law which provides that:

(a)   the Government shall pay any particular monies accruing to it into a fund designated for a special purpose; or

(b)   any body or institution to which any monies accruing to the State have been paid, may retain such monies or portions thereof for the purpose of defraying the expenses of such body or institution; or

(c)   where necessary, subsidies be allocated to regional and Local Authorities.

(4)   No money shall be withdrawn from the State Revenue Fund except in accordance with an Act of Parliament.

(5)   No body or person other than the Government shall have the power to withdraw monies from the State Revenue Fund.

Article 126   Appropriations

(1)   The Minister in charge of the Department of Finance shall, at least once every year and thereafter at such interim stages as may be necessary, present for the consideration of the National Assembly estimates of revenue, expenditure and income for the prospective financial year.

(2)   The National Assembly shall consider such estimates and pass pursuant thereto such Appropriation Acts as are in its opinion necessary to meet the financial requirements of the State from time to time.

Article 127   The Auditor-General

(1)   There shall be an Auditor-General appointed by the President on the recommendation of the Public Service Commission and with the approval of the National Assembly. The Auditor-General shall hold office for five (5) years unless removed earlier under Sub-Article (4) hereof or unless he or she resigns. The Auditor-General shall be eligible for reappointment.

(2)   The Auditor-General shall audit the State Revenue Fund and shall perform all other functions assigned to him or her by the Government or by Act of Parliament and shall report annually to the National Assembly thereon.

(3)   The Auditor-General shall not be a member of the public service.

(4)   The Auditor-General shall not be removed from office unless a two-thirds majority of all the members of the National Assembly vote for such removal on the ground of mental incapacity or gross misconduct.

CHAPTER 17

Central Bank and National Planning Commission

Article 128   The Central Bank

(1)   There shall be established by Act of Parliament a Central Bank of the Republic of Namibia which shall serve as the State's principal instrument to control the money supply, the currency and the institutions of finance, and to perform all other functions ordinarily performed by a central bank.

(2)   The Governing Board of the Central Bank shall consist of a Governor, a Deputy-Governor and such other members of the Board as shall be prescribed by Act of Parliament, and all members of the Board shall be appoint-

ed by the President in accordance with procedures prescribed by such Act of Parliament.

Article 129　The National Planning Commission

(1) There shall be established in the office of the President a National Planning Commission, whose task shall be to plan the priorities and direction of national development.

(2) There shall be a Director-General of Planning appointed by the President in terms of Article 32(3)(i)(dd) hereof, who shall be the head of the National Planning Commission and the principal adviser to the President in regard to all matters pertaining to economic planning and who shall attend Cabinet meetings at the request of the President.

(3) The membership, powers, functions and personnel of the National Planning Commission shall be regulated by Act of Parliament.

CHAPTER 18

Coming into Force of the Constitution

Article 130　Coming into Force of the Constitution

This Constitution as adopted by the Constituent Assembly shall come into force on the date of Independence.

CHAPTER 19

Amendment of the Constitution

Article 131　Entrenchment of Fundamental Rights and Freedoms

No repeal or amendment of any of the provisions of Chapter 3 hereof, in so far as such repeal or amendment diminishes or detracts from the fundamental rights and freedoms contained and defined in that Chapter, shall be permissible under this Constitution, and no such purported repeal or amendment shall be valid or have any force or effect.

Article 132   Repeal and Amendment of the Constitution

(1)   Any bill seeking to repeal or amend any provision of this Constitution shall indicate the proposed repeals and/or amendments with reference to the specific Articles sought to be repealed and/or amended and shall not deal with any matter other than the proposed repeals or amendments.

(2)   The majorities required in Parliament for the repeal and/or amendment of any of the provisions of this Constitution shall be:

    (a)   two-thirds of all the members of the National Assembly; and

    (b)   two-thirds of all the members of the National Council.

(3)   (a)   Notwithstanding the provisions of Sub-Article (2) hereof, if a bill proposing a repeal and/or amendment of any of the provisions of this Constitution secures a majority of two-thirds of all the members of the National Assembly, but fails to secure a majority of two-thirds of all the members of the National Council, the President may by Proclamation make the bill containing the proposed repeals and/or amendments the subject of a national referendum.

    (b)   The national referendum referred to in Sub-Article (a) hereof shall be conducted in accordance with procedures prescribed for the holding of referenda by Act of Parliament.

    (c)   If upon the holding of such a referendum the bill containing the proposed repeals and/or amendments is approved by a two-thirds majority of all the votes cast in the referendum, the bill shall be deemed to have been passed in accordance with the provisions of this Constitution, and the President shall deal with it in terms of Article 56 hereof.

(4)   No repeal or amendment of this Sub-Article or Sub-Articles (2) or (3) hereof

in so far as it seeks to diminish or detract from the majorities required in Parliament or in a referendum shall be permissible under this Constitution, and no such purported repeal or amendment shall be valid or have any force or effect.

(5) Nothing contained in this Article:

    (a) shall detract in any way from the entrenchment provided for in Article 131 hereof of the fundamental rights and freedoms contained and defined in Chapter 3 hereof;

    (b) shall prevent Parliament from changing its own composition or structures by amending or repealing any of the provisions of this Constitution: provided always that such repeals or amendments are effected in accordance with the provisions of this Constitution.

CHAPTER 20

The Law in Force and Transitional Provisions

Article 133   The First National Assembly

Notwithstanding the provisions of Article 46 hereof, the Constituent Assembly shall be deemed to have been elected under Articles 46 and 49 hereof, and shall constitute the first National Assembly of Namibia, and its term of office and that of the President shall be deemed to have begun from the date of Independence.

Article 134   Election of the First President

(1) Notwithstanding the provisions of Article 28 hereof, the first President of Namibia shall be the person elected to that office by the Constituent Assembly by a simple majority of all its members.

(2) The first President of Namibia shall be deemed to have been elected under Article 28 hereof and upon assuming office shall have all the powers, func-

tions, duties and immunities of a President elected under that Article.

Article 135   Implementation of this Constitution

This Constitution shall be implemented in accordance with the provisions of Schedule 7 hereof.

Article 136   Powers of the National Assembly prior to the Election of a National Council

(1)   Until elections for a National Council have been held:

   (a)   all legislation shall be enacted by the National Assembly as if this Constitution had not made provision for a National Council, and Parliament had consisted exclusively of the National Assembly acting on its own without being subject to the review of the National Council;

   (b)   this Constitution shall be construed as if no functions had been vested by this Constitution in the National Council;

   (c)   any reference in Articles 29, 56, 75 and 132 hereof to the National Council shall be ignored: provided that nothing contained in this Sub-Article shall be construed as limiting in any way the generality of Sub-Articles (a) and (b) hereof.

(2)   Nothing contained in Sub-Article (1) hereof shall detract in any way from the provisions of Chapter 8 or any other provision of this Constitution in so far as they make provision for the establishment of a National Council, elections to the National Council and its functioning after such elections have been held.

Article 137   Elections of the First Regional Councils and the First National Council

(1)   The President shall by Proclamation establish the first Delimitation Commission which shall be constituted in accordance with the provisions of Article 104 (1) hereof, within six (6) months of the date of Independence.

(2)   Such Proclamation shall provide for those matters which are referred to in Articles 102 to 106 hereof, shall not be inconsistent with this Constitution and

shall require the Delimitation Commission to determine boundaries of regions and Local Authorities for the purpose of holding Local Authority and Regional Council elections.

(3)   The Delimitation Commission appointed under such Proclamation shall forthwith commence its work, and shall report to the President within nine (9) months of its appointment: provided that the National Assembly may by resolution and for good cause extend the period within which such report shall be made.

(4)   Upon receipt of the report of the Delimitation Commission the President shall as soon as reasonably possible thereafter establish by Proclamation the boundaries of regions and Local Authorities in accordance with the terms of the report.

(5)   Elections for Local Authorities in terms of Article 111 hereof shall be held on a date to be fixed by the President by Proclamation, which shall be a date within six (6) months of the Proclamation referred to in Sub-Article (4) hereof, or within six (6) months of the date on which the legislation referred to in Article 111 hereof has been enacted, whichever is the later: provided that the National Assembly may by resolution and for good cause extend the period within which such elections shall be held.

(6)   Elections for Regional Councils shall be held on a date to be fixed by the President by Proclamation, which shall be a date within one (1) month of the date of the elections referred to in Sub-Article (5) hereof, or within one (1) month of the date on which the legislation referred to in Article 106 (3) hereof has been enacted, whichever is the later: provided that the National Assembly may by resolution and for good cause extend the period within which such elections shall be held.

(7)   Elections for the first National Council shall be held on a date to be fixed by the President by Proclamation, which shall be a date within one (1) month of the date of the elections referred to in Sub-Article (6) hereof, or within one (1) month of the date on which the legislation referred to in Article 69(2) hereof has been enacted, whichever is the later: provided that the National Assembly may by resolution and for good cause extend the period within which such elections shall be held.

Article 138   Courts and Pending Actions

(1)   The Judge-President and other Judges of the Supreme Court of South-West Africa holding office at the date on which this Constitution is adopted by the Constituent Assembly shall be deemed to have been appointed as the Judge-President and Judges of the High Court of Namibia under Article 82 hereof on the date of Independence, and upon making the oath or affirmation of office in the terms set out in Schedule 1 hereof, shall become the first Judge-President and Judges of the High Court of Namibia: provided that if the Judge-President or any such Judges are sixty-five (65) years of age or older on such date, it shall be deemed that their appointments have been extended until the age of seventy (70) in terms of Article 82(4) hereof.

(2)   (a)   The laws in force immediately prior to the date of Independence governing the jurisdiction of Courts within Namibia, the right of audience before such Courts, the manner in which procedure in such Courts shall be conducted and the power and authority of the Judges, Magistrates and other judicial officers, shall remain in force until repealed or amended by Act of Parliament, and all proceedings pending in such Courts at the date of Independence shall be continued as if such Courts had been duly constituted as Courts of the Republic of Namibia when the proceedings were instituted.

    (b)   Any appeal noted to the Appellate Division of the Supreme Court of South Africa against any judgment or order of the Supreme Court of South-West Africa shall be deemed to have been noted to the Supreme Court of Namibia and shall be prosecuted before such Court as if that judgment or order appealed against had been made by the High Court of Namibia and the appeal had been noted to the Supreme Court of Namibia.

    (c)   All criminal prosecutions initiated in Courts within Namibia prior to the date of Independence shall be continued as if such prosecutions had been initiated after the date of Independence in Courts of the Republic of Namibia.

    (d)   All crimes committed in Namibia prior to the date of Independence which would be crimes according to the law of the Republic of Namibia if it had then existed, shall be deemed to constitute crimes according to the law of the Republic of Namibia, and to be punishable as such in and by the Courts of the Republic of Namibia.

(3) Pending the enactment of the legislation contemplated by Article 79 hereof:

(a) the Supreme Court shall have the same jurisdiction to hear and determine appeals from Courts in Namibia as was previously vested in the Appellate Division of the Supreme Court of South Africa;

(b) the Supreme Court shall have jurisdiction to hear and determine matters referred to it for a decision by the Attorney-General under this Constitution;

(c) all persons having the right of audience before the High Court shall have the right of audience before the Supreme Court;

(d) three (3) Judges shall constitute a quorum of the Supreme Court when it hears appeals or deals with matters under Sub-Articles (a) and (b) hereof: provided that if any such Judge dies or becomes unable to act after the hearing of the appeal or such matter has commenced, but prior to judgment, the law applicable in such circumstances to the death or inability of a Judge of the High Court shall apply *mutatis mutandis*;

(e) until rules of the Supreme Court are made by the Chief Justice for the noting and prosecution of appeals and all matters incidental thereto, the rules which regulated appeals from the Supreme Court of South-West Africa to the Appellate Division of the Supreme Court of South Africa, and were in force immediately prior to the date of Independence, shall apply *mutatis mutandis*.

Article 139   The Judicial Service Commission

(1) Pending the enactment of legislation as contemplated by Article 85 hereof and the appointment of a Judicial Service Commission thereunder, the Judicial Service Commission shall be appointed by the President by

Proclamation and shall consist of the Chief Justice, a Judge appointed by the President, the Attorney-General, an advocate nominated by the Bar Council of Namibia and an attorney nominated by the Council of the Law Society of South-West Africa: provided that until the first Chief Justice has been appointed, the President shall appoint a second Judge to be a member of the Judicial Service Commission who shall hold office thereon until the Chief Justice has been appointed. The Judicial Service Commission shall elect from amongst its members at its first meeting the person to preside at its meetings until the Chief Justice has been appointed. The first task of the Judicial Service Commission shall be to make a recommendation to the President with regard to the appointment of the first Chief Justice.

(2)   Save as aforesaid the provisions of Article 85 hereof shall apply to the functioning of the Judicial Service Commission appointed under Sub-Article (1) hereof, which shall have all the powers vested in the Judicial Service Commission by this Constitution.

Article 140   The Law in Force at the Date of Independence

(1)   Subject to the provisions of this Constitution, all laws which were in force immediately before the date of Independence shall remain in force until repealed or amended by Act of Parliament or until they are declared unconstitutional by a competent Court.

(2)   Any powers vested by such laws in the Government, or in a Minister or other official of the Republic of South Africa shall be deemed to vest in the Government of the Republic of Namibia or in a corresponding Minister or official of the Government of the Republic of Namibia, and all powers, duties and functions which so vested in the Government Service Commission, shall vest in the Public Service Commission referred to in Article 112 hereof.

(3)   Anything done under such laws prior to the date of Independence by the Government, or by a Minister or other official of the Republic of South Africa shall be deemed to have been done by the Government of the Republic of Namibia or by a corresponding Minister or official of the Government of the Republic of Namibia, unless such action is subsequently repudiated by an Act of Parliament, and anything so done by the Government Service

Commission shall be deemed to have been done by the Public Service Commission referred to in Article 112 hereof, unless it is determined otherwise by an Act of Parliament.

(4) Any reference in such laws to the President, the Government, a Minister or other official or institution in the Republic of South Africa shall be deemed to be a reference to the President of Namibia or to a corresponding Minister, official or institution in the Republic of Namibia and any reference to the Government Service Commission or the government service, shall be construed as a reference to the Public Service Commission referred to in Article 112 hereof or the public service of Namibia.

(5) For the purposes of this Article the Government of the Republic of South Africa shall be deemed to include the Administration of the Administrator-General appointed by the Government of South Africa to administer Namibia, and any reference to the Administrator-General in legislation enacted by such Administration shall be deemed to be a reference to the President of Namibia, and any reference to a Minister or official of such Administration shall be deemed to be a reference to a corresponding Minister or official of the Government of the Republic of Namibia.

Article 141   Existing Appointments

(1) Subject to the provisions of this Constitution, any person holding office under any law in force on the date of Independence shall continue to hold such office unless and until he or she resigns or is retired, transferred or removed from office in accordance with law.

(2) Any reference to the Attorney-General in legislation in force immediately prior to the date of Independence shall be deemed to be a reference to the Prosecutor-General, who shall exercise his or her functions in accordance with this Constitution.

Article 142 Appointment of the First Chief of the Defence Force, the First Inspector-General of Police and the First Commissioner of Prisons

The President shall, in consultation with the leaders of all political parties represented in the National Assembly, appoint by Proclamation the first Chief of the Defence Force, the first Inspector-General of Police and the first Commissioner of Prisons.

Article 143 Existing International Agreements

All existing international agreements binding upon Namibia shall remain in force, unless and until the National Assembly acting under Article 63(2)(d) hereof otherwise decides.

CHAPTER 21

Final Provisions

Article 144 International Law

Unless otherwise provided by this Constitution or Act of Parliament, the general rules of public international law and international agreements binding upon Namibia under this Constitution shall form part of the law of Namibia.

Article 145 Saving

(1) Nothing contained in this Constitution shall be construed as imposing upon the Government of Namibia:

(a) any obligations to any other State which would not otherwise have existed under international law;

(b) any obligations to any person arising out of the acts or contracts of prior Administrations which would not otherwise have been recognised by international law as binding upon the Republic of Namibia.

(2)   Nothing contained in this Constitution shall be construed as recognising in any way the validity of the Administration of Namibia by the Government of the Republic of South Africa or by the Administrator-General appointed by the Government of the Republic of South Africa to administer Namibia.

Article 146   Definitions

(1)   Unless the context otherwise indicates, any word or expression in this Constitution shall bear the meaning given to such word or expression in any law which deals with the interpretation of statutes and which was in operation within the territory of Namibia prior to the date of Independence.

(2)   (a)   The word "Parliament" shall mean the National Assembly and, once the first National Council has been elected, shall mean the National Assembly acting, when so required by this Constitution, subject to the review of the National Council.

       (b)   Any reference to the plural shall include the singular and any reference to the singlular shall include the plural.

       (c)   Any reference to the "date of Independence" or "Independence" shall be deemed to be a reference to the day as of which Namibia is declared to be independent by the Constituent Assembly.

       (d)   Any reference to the "Constituent Assembly" shall be deemed to be a reference to the Constituent Assembly elected for Namibia during November 1989 as contemplated by United Nations Security Council Resolution 435 of 1978.

       (e)   Any reference to "Gazette" shall be deemed to be a reference to the Government Gazette of the Republic of Namibia.

Article 147   Repeal of Laws

The laws set out in Schedule 8 hereof are hereby repealed.

Article 148   Short Title

This Constitution shall be called the Namibian Constitution.

SCHEDULE 1

Oath/Affirmation Of Judges

"I,..., do hereby swear/solemnly affirm that as a Judge of the Republic of Namibia I will defend and uphold the Constitution of the Republic of Namibia as the Supreme Law and will fearlessly administer justice to all persons without favour or prejudice and in accordance with the laws of the Republic of Namibia.

(in the case of an oath)
So help me God."

SCHEDULE 2

Oath/Affirmation Of Ministers And Deputy-Ministers

"I,......................................., do hereby swear/solemnly affirm that I will be faithful to the Republic of Namibia, hold my office as Minister/Deputy-Minister with honour and dignity, uphold, protect and defend the Constitution and faithfully obey, execute and administer the laws of the Republic of Namibia, serve the people of Namibia to the best of my ability, not divulge directly or indirectly any matters brought before the Cabinet and entrusted to me under secrecy, and perform the duties of my office and the functions entrusted to me by the President conscientiously and to the best of my ability.

(in the case of an oath)
So help me God."

SCHEDULE 3

Oath/Affirmation Of Members Of The National Assembly And The National Council

"I,..., do hereby swear/solemnly affirm that I will be faithful to the Republic of Namibia and its people and I solemnly promise to uphold and defend the Constitution and laws of the Republic of Namibia to the best of my ability.

(in the case of an oath)
So help me God."

SCHEDULE 4

Election Of Members Of The National Assembly

(1)   For the purpose of filling the seventy-two (72) seats in the National Assembly pursuant to the provisions of Article 46 (1)(a) hereof, the total number of votes cast in a general election for these seats shall be divided by seventy-two (72) and the result shall constitute the quota of votes per seat.

(2)   The total number of votes cast in favour of a registered political party which offers itself for this purpose shall be divided by the quota of votes per seat and the result shall, subject to paragraph (3), constitute the number of seats to which that political party shall be entitled in the National Assembly.

(3)   Where the formula set out in paragraph (2) yields a surplus fraction not absorbed by the number of seats allocated to the political party concerned, such surplus shall compete with other similar surpluses accruing to any other political party or parties participating in the election, and any undistributed seat or seats (in terms of the formula set out in paragraph (2)) shall be awarded to the party or parties concerned in sequence of the

highest surplus.

(4) Subject to the requirements pertaining to the qualification of members of the National Assembly, a political party which qualifies for seats in terms of paragraphs (2) and (3) shall be free to choose in its own discretion which persons to nominate as members of the National Assembly to fill the said seats.

(5) Provision shall be made by Act of Parliament for all parties participating in an election of members of the National Assembly to be represented at all material stages of the election process and to be afforded a reasonable opportunity for scrutinising the counting of the votes cast in such election.

SCHEDULE 5

Property Vesting In The Government Of Namibia

(1) All property of which the ownership or control immediately prior to the date of Independence vested in the Government of the Territory of South West Africa, or in any Representative Authority constituted in terms of the Representative Authorities Proclamation, 1980 (Proclamation AG 8 of 1980), or in the Government of Rehoboth, or in any other body, statutory or otherwise, constituted by or for the benefit of any such Government or Authority immediately prior to the date of Independence, or which was held in trust for or on behalf of the Government of an independent Namibia, shall vest in or be under the control of the Government of Namibia.

(2) For the purpose of this Schedule, "property" shall, without detracting from the generality of that term as generally accepted and understood, mean and include movable and immovable property, whether corporeal or incorporeal and wheresoever situate, and shall include any right or interest therein.

(3) All such immovable property shall be transferred to the Government of Namibia without payment of transfer duty, stamp duty or any other fee or charge, but subject to any existing right, charge, obligation or trust on or

over such property and subject also to the provisions of this Constitution.

(4) The Registrar of Deeds concerned shall upon production to him or her of the title deed to any immovable property mentioned in paragraph (1) endorse such title deed to the effect that the immovable property therein described is vested in the Government of Namibia and shall make the necessary entries in his or her registers, and thereupon the said title deed shall serve and avail for all purposes as proof of the title of the Government of Namibia to the said property.

SCHEDULE 6

The National Flag of The Republic of Namibia

The National Flag of Namibia shall be rectangular in the proportion of three in the length to two in the width, tierced per bend reversed, blue, white and green; the white bend reversed, which shall be one third of the width of the flag, is charged with another of red, one quarter of the width of the flag. In the upper hoist there shall be a gold sun with twelve straight rays, the diameter of which shall be one third of the width of the flag, with its vertical axis one fifth of the distance from the hoist, positioned equidistant from the top edge and from the reversed bend. The rays, which shall each be two fifths of the radius of the sun, issue from the outer edge of a blue ring, which shall be one tenth of the radius of the sun.

SCHEDULE 7

Implementation of This Constitution

1. On the day of Independence, the Secretary-General of the United Nations shall administer to the President, elected in terms of Article 134 hereof, the oath or affirmation prescribed by Article 30 hereof.

2. The President shall appoint the Prime Minister and administer to him or her the oath or affirmation set out in Schedule 2 hereof.

3. The President shall administer to the first Judges of Namibia, appointed under Article 138(1) hereof, the oath or affirmation set out in Schedule 1 hereof.

4. On the day determined by the Constituent Assembly the National Assembly shall first meet, at a time and at a place specified by the Prime Minister.

5. The members of the National Assembly, with the Prime Minister as Chairperson, shall:

    (a) take the oath or affirmation prescribed by Article 55 hereof before the Judge-President or a Judge designated by the Judge-President for this purpose;

    (b) elect the Speaker of the National Assembly.

6. The National Assembly, with the Speaker as Chairperson, shall:

    (a) elect a Deputy-Speaker;

    (b) conduct such business as it deems appropriate;

    (c) adjourn to a date to be determined by the National Assembly.

7 The rules and procedures followed by the Constituent Assembly for the holding of its meetings shall, *mutatis mutandis*, be the rules and procedures to be followed by the National Assembly until such time as the National Assembly has adopted rules of procedure and standing orders under Article 59 hereof.

SCHEDULE 8

Repeal Of Laws

South-West Africa Constitution Act, 1968 (Act No. 39 of 1968)

Rehoboth Self-Government Act, 1976 (Act No. 56 of 1976)

Establishment of Office of Administrator-General for the Territory of South-West Africa Proclamation, 1977 (Proclamation No. 180 of 1977 of the State President)

Empowering of the Administrator-General for the Territory of South-West Africa to make Laws Proclamation, 1977 (Proclamation No. 181 of 1977 of the State President)

Representative Authorities Proclamation, 1980 (Proclamation AG. 8 of 1980)

Representative Authority of the Whites Proclamation, 1980 (Proclamation AG. 12 of 1980)

Representative Authority of the Coloureds Proclamation, 1980 (Proclamation AG. 14 of 1980)

Representative Authority of the Ovambos Proclamation, 1980 (Proclamation AG. 23 of 1980)

Representative Authority of the Kavangos Proclamation, 1980 (Proclamation AG. 26 of 1980)

Representative Authority of the Caprivians Proclamation, 1980 (Proclamation AG. 29 of 1980)

Representative Authority of the Damaras Proclamation, 1980 (Proclamation AG. 32 of 1980)

Representative Authority of the Namas Proclamation, 1980 (Proclamation AG. 35 of 1980)

Representative Authority of the Tswanas Proclamation, 1980 (Proclamation AG. 47 of 1980)

Representative Authority of the Hereros Proclamation, 1980 (Proclamation AG. 50 of 1980)

Representative Authority Powers Transfer Proclamation, 1989 (Proclamation AG. 8 of 1989)

Government of Rehoboth Powers Transfers Proclamation, 1989 (Proclamation AG. 32 of 1989)

<u>Angaben über den Autor:</u>
Axel Harneit-Sievers, geboren 1957 in Bremen, studierte Geschichte und politische Wissenschaft in Hannover. 1990 Abschluß der Promotion zur ökonomischen und politischen Bedeutung afrikanischer Geschäftsleute im kolonialen Nigeria; derzeit Wissenschaftlicher Mitarbeiter am Historischen Seminar der Universität Hannover (Forschungsprojekt "Kriegsfolgen und Kriegsbewältigung in Afrika"). Weitere Veröffentlichung beim Institut für Afrika-Kunde: "SWAPO of Namibia - Geschichte, Programmatik und Politik seit 1959", Hamburg 1985

HAMBURGER BEITRÄGE ZUR AFRIKA-KUNDE

Band 36

PETER MEYNS/DANI WADADA NABUDERE (Eds.)

Democracy and the One-Party State

in Africa

Dieser Sammelband zu einem für die politische Situation vieler afrikanischer Staaten zentralen Thema ist das Ergebnis eines von der "Deutschen Vereinigung für Politische Wissenschaft" (DVPW) und der "African Association of Political Science" (AAPS) erstmals gemeinsam veranstalteten Symposiums. Insgesamt elf afrikanische und drei deutsche Politikwissenschaftler sind in dem Band als Autoren vertreten.

Die Einschätzung des in Afrika weit verbreiteten Einparteisystems und der Zusammenhänge mit grundlegenden Fragen von Demokratie und Menschenrechten ist höchst umstritten. Von einer liberalen europäischen Perspektive wird häufig der Einwand vorgebracht, daß Demokratie in Afrika wegen der anhaltenden Tendenz zu Einparteistrukturen nicht möglich sei; dies wird als Negierung üblicher demokratischer Organisationsformen im Rahmen von Mehrparteisystemen angesehen. Demgegenüber haben afrikanische Politiker und Theoretiker versucht, ein von afrikanischen Realitäten ausgehendes eigenständiges politisches Modell zu entwickeln. Entsprechende Erwartungen und Hoffnungen sind jedoch von den tatsächlichen politischen Entwicklungen der vergangenen drei Jahrzehnte weitgehend enttäuscht worden.

Im Zentrum aller Beiträge des vorliegenden Bandes stehen Fragen nach den spezifischen Gründen für die Herausbildung des Einparteisystems als vorherrschendem politischen Typus in Afrika und nach der Verwirklichung von Zielvorstellungen über demokratische Partizipation und Regierung.

Die generellen Argumente werden in den folgenden Fallstudien zu einzelnen Ländern einer kritischen Überprüfung unterworfen. Dabei werden nicht nur spezifische Einparteisysteme näher analysiert, sondern aus Vergleichsgründen auch Mehrparteisysteme und Militärregime. Näher behandelt werden Äthiopien, Burkina Faso, Ghana, Kenya, Mauritius, Moçambique, Nigeria, Sierra Leone, Tanzania, Uganda, Zambia und Zimbabwe. (XIV, 304 S., ISBN 3-923519-88-5)

INSTITUT FÜR AFRIKA-KUNDE. HAMBURG 1989

HAMBURGER BEITRÄGE ZUR AFRIKA-KUNDE

Band 37

ERNST HILLEBRAND

Sowjetische Theorie - Afrikanische Praxis

Zu den sowjetischen Konzepten einer sozialistischen Agrarpolitik in Afrika

Die Lösung des Agrarproblems in Afrika ist eines der vorrangigsten Ziele der heutigen Entwicklungspolitik. Auch die sowjetische Entwicklungsländerforschung hat die Dringlichkeit dieser Aufgabe im Rahmen einer sozialistisch orientierten Politik in Afrika immer wieder betont. Allerdings ist bis heute im Westen relativ wenig darüber bekannt, wie sich die sowjetischen Wissenschaftler die Lösung der Agrarfrage in Afrika vorgestellt haben. Der Autor der vorliegenden Studie versucht, diese Lücke zu schließen. Geschildert werden neben den allgemeinen entwicklungsstrategischen Vorstellungen der sowjetischen Afrikanistik die konkreten Vorstellungen der sowjetischen Autoren zur sozialistischen Umgestaltung einer teilweise noch vorkapitalistischen Subsistenzlandwirtschaft.

Die agrarpolitischen Vorstellungen der sowjetischen Wissenschaftler haben ihren Widerhall in der Landwirtschaftspolitik der sozialistischen Länder, vor allem Angolas, Moçambiques und Äthiopiens gefunden. Ausgehend von einer detaillierten Schilderung der Agrarpolitik dieser Länder wird untersucht, in welchem Maße sowjetische Vorstellungen die Politik dieser Länder geprägt haben. Ein abschließender Teil ist den Veränderungen in der Entwicklungsländertheorie der Sowjetunion in den letzten Jahren gewidmet. (269 Seiten, ISBN 3-923519-94-X)

INSTITUT FÜR AFRIKA-KUNDE. HAMBURG 1990

ARBEITEN AUS DEM INSTITUT FÜR AFRIKA-KUNDE
Heft 64

CLAUDIUS WENZEL

Die Südafrikapolitik der USA in der Ära Reagan
Konstruktives oder destruktives Engagement?

Südafrika ist in den achtziger Jahren aufgrund der modifizierten, aber nicht abgeschafften Apartheid und der eskalierenden Gewalt unter P.W. Botha immer mehr zu einem "Ausgestoßenen" des internationalen Staatensystems geworden. Wie die westliche Führungsmacht USA auf diese außenpolitische Herausforderung reagiert hat, ob sie einen Beitrag zur Überwindung der Apartheid und der damit verbundenen Destabilisierungspolitik Pretorias im südlichen Afrika geleistet hat, wird in der vorliegenden Studie untersucht.

Ausgangspunkt ist eine Analyse der innenpolitischen Grundlagen U.S.-amerikanischer Außenpolitik (Machtstrukturen, Entscheidungsprozeß, Interessen). Durch die Betrachtung von Reagans "Politik der Stärke", des eingegrenzten außenpolitischen Handlungsspielraumes und des Verhältnisses der Vereinigten Staaten zu Südafrika in historischer Perspektive wird der Rahmen vervollständigt, mit dem die Besonderheiten, Zwänge und Kontinuitäten amerikanischer Außenpolitik in der Reagan-Ära erkennbar und erklärbar sind.

Besondere Beachtung finden im Hauptteil der Arbeit das Konzept des *constructive engagement*, seine Umsetzung in praktische Politik und die Sanktionen des Kongresses, die gegen den Willen der Administration zustande kamen. Ein weiterer Schwerpunkt liegt auf der Regionalpolitik. Die Lösung der Namibia-Frage bei gleichzeitigem Abzug der kubanischen Truppen aus Angola war ein Hauptanliegen der amerikanischen Politik.

Die Untersuchung kommt zu dem Ergebnis, daß die Reagan-Administration mit ihrer assoziativen, Pretoria-freundlichen Politik keinen Beitrag zur Überwindung der Apartheid geleistet hat. Einzig die Sanktionen des Kongresses haben eine vollständige Diskreditierung der amerikanischen Außenpolitik im südlichen Afrika verhindert. Im Vordergrund der Reagan-Politik stand der Kampf gegen "den Kommunismus", nicht gegen die Apartheid. (X + 171 S., ISBN 3-923519-90-7, DM 20,-)

INSTITUT FÜR AFRIKA-KUNDE. HAMBURG 1990

ARBEITEN AUS DEM INSTITUT FÜR AFRIKA-KUNDE

Heft 49

AXEL HARNEIT-SIEVERS

SWAPO of Namibia

Entwicklung, Programmatik und Politik seit 1959

Innerhalb der Auseinandersetzung um die Unabhängigkeit Namibias stellt die "South
West Africa People's Organization of Namibia" (SWAPO) einen der zentralen Akteure
dar. Wesentliches Ziel der vorliegenden Arbeit ist es, historische, politische und programmatische Entwicklungslinien der SWAPO nachzuzeichnen und an einigen Stellen
vertieft zu analysieren. Dabei wird zunächst der Versuch unternommen, bisher weitgehend verstreut vorliegende Informationen zur Geschichte und politischen Entwicklung der SWAPO zu sammeln und in einen einheitlichen Kontext zu bringen; ein
Schwergewicht liegt dabei auf den 1960er Jahren. Sodann wird die Parteikrise von
1975/76 (u.a. anhand unveröffentlichter Dokumente) als Ausgangspunkt einer wichtigen
Reorganisationsphase der SWAPO, die zu organisatorischen wie auch programmatischen Neuerungen von dauerhafter Bedeutung führte, untersucht. Schließlich werden
das SWAPO-Programm - und andere programmatische Äußerungen, die von ihm zum
Teil deutlich abweichen - sowie das tatsächliche Verhalten der Organisation in den
internationalen Verhandlungen um Namibia seit 1978 miteinander konfrontiert, um den
politisch-programmatischen Kern der SWAPO einerseits und potentiell verhandlungs-
fähige Positionen andererseits herauszuarbeiten.

Die Untersuchung kommt zu dem Ergebnis, daß die SWAPO im wesentlichen eine
"nationalistische", d.h. primär auf die Erringung der politischen Unabhängigkeit hin
orientierte Bewegung geblieben ist. Sie scheint aus einer angenommenen sicheren
Machtposition heraus zu Zugeständnissen im Hinblick auf eine Machtteilhabe anderer
politischer Gruppen in einem unabhängigen Namibia bereit zu sein; deutlich ist ebenso
ein großer Pragmatismus in ökonomischen und sozialen Fragen. (III, 195 S., ISBN
3-923519-60-5, DM 28,-)

INSTITUT FÜR AFRIKA-KUNDE. HAMBURG 1985